SHAKESPEARE'S
MIDDLE
TRAGEDIES

SHAKESPEARE'S MIDDLE TRAGEDIES

A Collection of Critical Essays

Edited by
David Young

Prentice Hall, Englewood Cliffs, New Jersey 07632

Library of Congress Cataloging-in-Publication Data

Shakespeare's middle tragedies : a collection of critical essays /
    edited by David Young.
        p.   cm. — (New century views)
    Includes bibliographical references.
    ISBN 0–13–807884–X
    1. Shakespeare, William, 1564–1616—Tragedies.   2. Tragedy.
I. Young, David   (date).   II. Series
PR2983.S449   1993
822.3'3—dc20   92–17043
                                                           CIP

Acquisitions editor: Phil Miller
Editorial assistant: Heidi Moore
Copy editor: Colby Stong
Editorial/production supervision and interior design: Joan Powers
Cover design: Karen Salzbach
Prepress buyer: Herb Klein
Manufacturing buyer: Patrice Fraccio/Robert Anderson

© 1993 by Prentice-Hall, Inc.
A Simon & Schuster Company
Englewood Cliffs, New Jersey 07632

Printed in the United States of America
10 9 8 7 6 5 4 3 2 1

ISBN 0-13-807884-X

Prentice-Hall International (UK) Limited, *London*
Prentice-Hall of Australia Pty. Limited, *Sydney*
Prentice-Hall Canada Inc., *Toronto*
Prentice-Hall Hispanoamericana, S.A., *Mexico*
Prentice-Hall of India Private Limited, *New Delhi*
Prentice-Hall of Japan, Inc., *Tokyo*
Simon & Schuster Asia Pte. Ltd., *Singapore*
Editora Prentice-Hall do Brasil, Ltda., *Rio de Janeiro*

Contents

Introduction   1
  David Young

Part 1.   HAMLET   7

Hamlet and the Shape of Revenge   7
  Mark Rose

Superposed Plays: *Hamlet*   18
  Richard A. Lanham

Man and Wife Is One Flesh: *Hamlet* and the
Confrontation with the Maternal Body   29
  Janet Adelman

Representing Ophelia: Women, Madness, and the
Responsibilities of Feminist Criticism   56
  Elaine Showalter

Viewpoints   70
  Daniel Seltzer, Bert O. States, Richard Fly,
  René Girard

Part 2.   OTHELLO   75

The Joker in the Pack   75
  W. H. Auden

Women and Men in *Othello*   91
  Carol Thomas Neely

Unproper Beds: Race, Adultery, and the Hideous
in *Othello*   117
  Michael Neill

Signs, Speech, and Self   146
    James L. Calderwood

Viewpoints   164
    Susan Snyder, Stephen Greenblatt

Part 3.   *KING LEAR*   169

Action and World in *King Lear*   169
    Maynard Mack

The Avoidance of Love: A Reading of *King Lear*   185
    Stanley Cavell

Lear's Theatre Poetry   198
    Marvin Rosenberg

The Father and the Bride   207
    Lynda E. Boose

"The Base Shall Top Th'Legitimate": The Bedlam Beggar
and the Role of Edgar in *King Lear*   221
    William C. Carroll

Chronology of Important Dates   239

Notes on Contributors   241

Bibliography   244

Introduction

David Young

For nearly three hundred years now, William Shakespeare's middle tragedies—*Hamlet, Othello*, and *King Lear*—have formed a significant part of our history and culture. We have come to consider Shakespeare's artistic accomplishment an ultimate expression of human creative potential, and many believe that these three plays, written in the second half of his career and in the dramatic genre that still commands the most attention, form the very core of his achievement. It is small wonder, then, that the history of their performance, study, and critical interpretation is so rich and complex. Their centrality to Shakespeare and in our cultural heritage has made them crucial, in innumerable ways, and this special status has meant, in turn, that something has been at stake each time they are read, debated, parodied, quoted, and performed. Their standing as cultural icons complicates our response, whereas their expressiveness as works of art calls forth our best efforts in approaching them. But these challenges are more exciting than frustrating; although no reading of, say, *Hamlet*, can feel wholly complete or adequate, be it a production, a book, or a classroom discussion, it is also true that by the same token, *every* reading of that play will be of interest and will reverberate with the cultural meanings and possibilities inherent both in the text itself and in its complex history among us. And so it is with *Othello* and *King Lear.*

When I say "our culture" I do not simply mean the English-speaking world or even western Europe. There is a journal in India wholly devoted to *Hamlet* studies; there is a replica of Shakespeare's Globe Theater in Japan. We may be rightly wary of saying that any work of art is universal, but Shakespeare's best plays seem to come close. The enthusiasm with which the world has embraced these tragedies since their first writing and performance in the early seventeenth century is truly remarkable. Imagine a troop of adult male and boy actors, working under pressure in a society that gave them an equivocal status: they could associate with nobility and at the same time be lumped with criminals and prostitutes. Think of them having to close their theater at times to go out on the road, performing in inn-yards and country houses, because of chronic outbreaks of the plague. Consider that they faced censorship, fickle public taste, political repression, intense rivalry from other theater companies, and the disapproval of the radical religious and social reformers known as Puritans. That such a group, in such conditions, should have given rise to an actor who wrote these plays for the group to perform, in the public playhouse and occasionally at court, can seem incredible. So can the fact that noisy, unruly, and ill-educated audiences, drawn from all walks of life, should have listened with deep appreciation to this complex poetry and followed the intricacies and subtleties of these character relationships and plots. Is it any wonder that we have had fits of disbelief—in Shakespeare's identity and authorship, in the plays' coherence and value, in their fitness to be cultural touchstones—from time to time?

The circumstances of these plays' productions and their original meanings, to their author and his audiences, are not only difficult to explain; they are nearly impossible to recapture. We know a little about acting styles, playhouse dimensions, theatrical conventions and the like, but the live performances, with all their flavor and nuance, their hustle and bustle, their give and take, are gone, as if they had been little more than mist and vapor. Many of our questions, though not of course all of them, could be resolved if timetravel allowed us to visit the contemporary performances of these plays, directed, we assume, by their author, who also played minor roles in them.

The difficulty of knowing exactly what the plays were like originally does not, however, seem to lessen their cultural importance and artistic impact. *Hamlet, Othello,* and *King Lear* remain, to the English-speaking world as well as to the other languages and cultures into which they are regularly translated for study and performance, great works of art by a great writer: difficult to interpret, challenging to produce, fascinating to contemplate.

The twentieth century has witnessed some considerable shifts and adjustments in our understanding of Shakespeare and his canon. We have come to a much fuller appreciation of certain plays and genres that previous centuries tended to undervalue. Thus it is that these tragedies, long considered Shakespeare's crowning achievement, have had to give place a little, to make room for our renewed and enhanced interest in the history plays, the "problem" comedies, and the late romances. The realignment has been salutary for the tragedies. It has meant that they could form new lines of relationship with other parts of Shakespeare's career and canon. It has also meant that they could be taken less for granted, lifted down from their pedestals, dusted off, and interrogated for their actual value. T. S. Eliot, earlier in the century, argued that *Hamlet* was an artistic failure. The idea shocked a lot of people, and its basis has since come to be somewhat discredited, but it had the healthy effect of making people look again at a play that many had been complacently regarding as a flawless masterpiece. A reinvigoration of our reading and interpretation has been a general result of all this fresh consideration of Shakespeare's canon, and if the tragedies still come out on top for most people, it is in a context that takes much better account of Shakespeare's dramatic practice and career as a whole. Just how and why they are "tragic" is one question that we have opened up and begun to wrestle with, taking little or nothing for granted. Several of the essays in this volume find inspiration in aligning a tragedy, or some aspect of it, with comedic practice and convention, and they reflect a trend by which Shakespeare's attitude toward genre is now seen as unfettered, adventurous, and often quite wildly experimental.

I would assert (with appropriate caution and the recognition that my historical position is necessarily relative) that we understand these tragedies more fully and interpret them more accurately than at any time in the past, including Shakespeare's own. We may have a long way to go, and we will obviously never be free from interpretations that distort and productions that feel inadequate, but it is possible to summon up a sense of progress. We have learned, and are still learning, to pay closer attention to the language of Shakespeare's plays, to take better account of the fact that they are performance scripts rather than novels or poems, to guard against imposing our own prejudices and expectations upon them, and to temper methodology and ideology with common sense and historical perspective. It is precisely that historical perspective that should serve to remind us, among other things, that interpreters of Shakespeare who came before us, actors like Garrick, Kean, and Booth, readers like Dr. Johnson, Coleridge, and Bradley, still have much to teach us.

The essays collected in this volume come, almost exclusively, from the fourth quarter of the twentieth century. In doing so they reflect an upheaval in the world of literary studies that is still running its course. Briefly, there has been a shift from text to context: from close, occasionally myopic, attention to the language and organization of the literary work, its wholeness and its self-contained integrity, to a broader consideration of surrounding circumstances—to issues of faith, power, class, gender, and social milieu. This interest in context applies both to then and to now, to the original historical circumstances and to the settings in which interpretation and performance have occurred subsequently, right on up to the present and the self-conscious interpreter. We now tend to pay much more attention to the cultural conditions and considerations that influence and pervade works of literature at the moment of their creation, a renewed historical focus, as well as to the circumstances that affect our own interpretations, a self-questioning that recognizes the force of ideology, cultural relativity, and conscious or unconscious prejudice in the supposedly objective activities of reading and interpretation. Elaine Showalter's essay on Ophelia in this volume is a case in point, touching as it does on the attitudes that shaped the characterization of Ophelia originally, on the subsequent Ophelias represented by performance, illustration, and critical interpretation, and on the current situation of the feminist critic who wishes to address the agenda of feminist concerns while avoiding distortion and special pleading. Michael Neill's essay on *Othello*, ranging widely through the history of the play's performance and commentary to investigate the issue of race, has a similar scope.

Probably none of the commentators represented here has been untouched by the quarter century's shift of emphasis from text to context. Some would no doubt wish to point out that the earlier period of text emphasis has itself been misrepresented for ideological purposes. Before New Historicism, after all, there was Historicism—a good deal of it—and it was by no means complacent or one-sided, a charge that not all of the *new* "isms" and approaches can escape. On the whole, the critical pendulum swing has been healthy, if at times obscured by excessive claims on both sides; and in assembling this collection of essays, I have been heartened to notice how many literary critics have been able to embrace the insights afforded by the newer approaches while maintaining the usefulness and excellence of the older ones. The essayists represented here tend to practice the skills associated with text-intensive study (what tends to be lumped under the rubric of New Criticism) while assimilating new approaches—structural anthropology, psychoanalysis, feminism, cultural materialism—effectively and with exciting results. I am more optimistic about the current level of critical excellence, at least in Shakespeare studies, than I was before I began this task.

The group of *Hamlet* essays will probably strike other readers, as it struck me, with the emphasis on duality that this play seems to call forth, a recognition that the playwright is somehow having nearly everything—style, character, tone, plot—both ways. They also tend to invoke the considerable playfulness of *Hamlet*: its word-play, its habit of questioning itself and teasing its medium, the theater, and its energetic investigation of its own subgenre, revenge tragedy. Not that the play's tragic weight is dismissed or dissipated, but that criticism is perhaps more informed than it used to be, reflecting this quizzical postmodern era, about the paradoxical legerity that accompanies *Hamlet's* weight, a skillful mix of possibilities that involves us deeply without resolving our sense of mystery, a game-playing mood that somehow counterpoises itself to the corrupt world of Denmark and the hero's melancholy.

Writing about *Hamlet* seems to call forth the best from critics, and it has been hard to limit my selection: I could have found comparable essays, given twice the room, to match the insights and fascinations to be found in Mark Rose, Richard A. Lanham, Janet Adelman, and Elaine Showalter, as well as in the necessarily brief excerpts from Bert O. States, Daniel Seltzer, Richard Fly, and René Girard. They will suffice, in any case, to show that our current sense of *Hamlet's* greatness is richly detailed and deeply informed.

The history of *Othello* commentary has been on the whole a discouraging panorama of misperception and distortion. The forces unleashed in this drama by its candor about sex and race, probing our deepest fears and arousing our least conscious prejudices, have been reflected in the confused one-sidedness with which critics have tried to clarify *Othello*, usually by oversimplifying the play and imposing their own forms of prejudice. In light of that, it's a particular pleasure to offer a group of essays that make better sense of the play than I would have thought possible before discovering them. No doubt they partly benefit from the mistakes of their predecessors. I see W. H. Auden as having begun this process, with his clear-sighted, poignant, and occasionally unsettling essay, written in the 1950s and largely neglected by other commentators. The more recent essays by Carol Thomas Neely, James L. Calderwood, and Michael Neill show how a determination to face directly the difficult issues of gender relations and race prejudice, without resort to simplification, has yielded exciting results. The additional excerpts by Susan Snyder and Stephen Greenblatt give glimpses of a sizable body of recent criticism that, if it does not clear up every point of difficulty we have had with *Othello,* marks what seems to me a genuine and heartening new level of insight and honesty in our discourse about it.

King Lear stands, for many, as the Shakespearean tragedy that poses the greatest problems of interpretation: difficult to produce successfully, hard to encompass by means of commentary. Yet *Lear* is also the play by Shakespeare that this century seems most to have embraced as its own, for pondering and questioning, a mirror in which the cruelty and chaos of which we have discovered ourselves capable are most unrelentingly reflected. Its great questions—e.g., "Is man no more than this?" and "Why should a dog, a horse, a rat have life / And thou no breath at all?"—seem to reverberate for us with a special force and a contemporary meaning.

If that means we resonate on what we take to be *Lear's* frequency, it also means we run a particular danger of distorting, sentimentalizing, and parochializing it in terms of our own current preoccupations. Maynard Mack's book-length study, *King Lear in Our Time,* from which I have excerpted here, addresses itself both to the resonances and the dangers in a fashion that has been exemplary to subsequent commentators. Marvin Rosenberg's work on the stage poetry of the play reminds us how much the theatrical dimension must be a part of our consciousness of any playtext. Stanley Cavell, a philosopher who has branched out into literary criticism with notable success, shows us how readily issues of ethics and consciousness can be brought to bear on *Lear.* Lynda E. Boose demonstrates how insights developed by psychoanalysis, cultural anthropology, and feminism can be combined with historical materials to sharpen our sense of the meaning of character and action in Shakespeare's plays; her original essay is more wide-ranging, taking in a number of plays, but it seemed to me so apt on *Lear* that I chose it as representative of what is in fact a considerable body of interesting new work by feminist critics on this challenging text. William C. Carroll's essay on Edgar, finally, uses history and textual analysis to illuminate the play's crucial second plot in memorable fashion.

With *Lear,* as with the other plays, I have reluctantly had to exclude fine materials by other commentators for lack of space. I have used the opportunity of the Bibliography to direct readers to these materials, and I have no doubt overlooked many others, because the material on these three tragedies is so vast.

In choosing these essays I have used no quotas of nation, gender, or critical school. I have simply tried to find pieces that are eminently readable, not least because they maintain a high and exciting level of insight. The criticism that I have discovered has led me to believe that in the final years of the century, the state of Shakespearean criticism is quite reasonably healthy: building on what has gone before, in touch with issues of current concern, informed by a sense of balance that excludes no resources that may prove useful, and rightly wary of excessive reliance on single methodologies that purport to explain everything by appeal to a unitary system. That, at least, is how I see the best work.

I have a number of people to thank for their aid in the making of this anthology. Numerous colleagues and acquaintances—too many to list here— suggested favorite essays, based both on their reading and their teaching experience, suggestions that are reflected in the Bibliography as well as in the selections and viewpoints. Other anthologists—Harold Bloom, Susan Snyder, Janet Adelman, and Robert Heilman—provided useful precedents, mostly positive. I am also grateful to Janet Adelman for her willingness to share substantial portions of her then forthcoming book in page proofs, and to my colleague, Robert Pierce, for looking over the manuscript with his customary good humor and shrewd judgment. My wife, Georgia, and my son, Newell, also offered valuable suggestions and provided steady support and encouragement along the way.

Most of all, however, I owe thanks to my research assistant and former student, Anthony Arnove, who worked side by side with me on this anthology in the summer of 1991: helping to evaluate, select, edit, and adapt these materials, and displaying scholarly skills and critical acumen that would be remarkable in a seasoned scholar, much less a recent undergraduate. He has been Horatio to my Hamlet, or Kent to my Lear, but never, I think, Iago to my Othello.

What Shakespeare will be and mean to us in the next century remains to be discovered; as we close this one out we can claim, I think, that his work continues to provide an interest and an excitement that reward study and invigorate both the theater as a living entity and the culture at large. The planet is better off for having his plays, timely and in some ways, apparently, timeless.

Hamlet and the Shape of Revenge

Mark Rose

Classical and Elizabethan tragedy represent polar opposites in dramatic structure, the one tightly focused with few characters and a sharply defined action, the other loose and sprawling with many characters, multiple locales, and complex plots which may span years of narrative time. And yet all tragedies tend to share certain central concerns. Sophocles' Oedipus fled Corinth to prevent the oracle's prophecy from coming true, but in the process of trying to escape his fate he only succeeded in fulfilling it. Sophocles' play is concerned, we might say, with the degree to which our lives are not in our own control. The words of the player king in *Hamlet* are apposite:

> Our wills and fates do so contrary run
> That our devices still are overthrown;
> Our thoughts are ours, their ends none of our own.
>   (3.2.217–19)

Hamlet, too, is concerned with the limits imposed upon mortal will, with the various restrictions that flesh is heir to; and it is upon this central tragic theme that I wish to dwell, suggesting how Shakespeare employs a characteristically Renaissance self-consciousness to transmute a popular Elizabethan dramatic form, the revenge play, into a tragedy the equal of Sophocles'.

Early in the play Polonius speaks to Ophelia of the "tether" with which Hamlet walks. The image is a useful one to keep in mind, for it suggests both that the prince does have a degree of freedom and that ultimately he is bound. Laertes cautions Ophelia in a similar manner and develops more explicitly the limits on Hamlet's freedom. The prince's "will is not his own," Laertes says,

> For he himself is subject to his birth,
> He may not, as unvalued persons do,
> Carve for himself; for on his choice depends
> The safety and the health of this whole state.
>   (1.3.18–21)

What Laertes means is simply that Hamlet as heir apparent may not be free to marry Ophelia, but he says much more than he realizes. Hamlet is indeed

From *English Literary Renaissance* 1 (1971), 132–43. Reprinted by permission.

subject to his birth, bound by being the dead king's son, and upon his "carving"—his rapier and dagger-work—the safety and health of Denmark do literally depend. Possibly Shakespeare has in mind the imagery of *Julius Caesar* and Brutus's pledge to be a sacrificer rather than a butcher, to carve Caesar as a dish fit for the gods, for, like Brutus, Hamlet is concerned with the manner of his carving. But the word is also Shakespeare's term for sculptor, and perhaps he is thinking of Hamlet as this kind of carver, an artist attempting to shape his revenge and his life according to his own standards. Yet here, too, Hamlet's will is not his own: there is, he discovers, "a divinity that shapes our ends, / Rough-hew them how we will" (5.2.10–11).

From the first scene in which the prince appears, Shakespeare wishes us to perceive clearly that Hamlet is tethered. He contrasts the king's permission to Laertes to return to France with his polite refusal of Hamlet's request to return to Wittenberg. Denmark is in fact a prison for Hamlet, a kind of detention center in which the wary usurper can keep an eye on his disgruntled stepson. Claudius acclaims Hamlet's yielding as "gentle and unforced" and announces that he will celebrate it by firing his cannon to the heavens, but what he has done in fact is to cut ruthlessly the avenue of escape that the prince had sought from a court and a world he now loathes. One other, more desperate avenue still seems open, and as soon as the stage is cleared the prince considers the possibility of this course, suicide, only to remind himself that against this stands another sort of "canon," one fixed by God. Hamlet is tied to Elsinore, bound by his birth; on either side the road of escape is guarded and all that remains to him is his disgust for the world and the feeble wish that somehow his flesh will of itself melt into a puddle.

Hamlet's real prison is of course more a matter of mental than physical space. "Oh God," he exclaims to Rosencrantz and Guildenstern, "I could be bounded in a nutshell and count myself a king of infinite space, were it not that I have bad dreams" (2.2.258–60). The erstwhile friends suppose Hamlet means he is ambitious for the crown, but the bad dream the prince is thinking of, the insubstantial "shadow" as he calls it, is evidently the ghost and its nightmarish revelation. If Claudius has tied him to Elsinore it is of little consequence compared to the way the ghost has bound him to vengeance. Hamlet's master turns out to be even a more formidable figure than the king. Ironically, Laertes' and Polonius's remarks upon what they conceive to be the limits placed upon Hamlet's freedom immediately precede the scene in which the prince at last encounters the ghost and discovers what it means to be subject to one's birth. "Speak," Hamlet says to the ghost, "I am bound to hear," and the ghost in his reply picks up the significant word *bound* and throws it back at the prince: "So art thou to revenge, when thou shalt hear" (1.5.6–7). Hamlet cannot shuffle off his father's spirit any more than he can the mortal coil. The ghost's command is "Remember me," and after his departure Shakespeare dramatizes how from this charge there is no escape. Hamlet rushes about the stage seeking a place to swear his companions to secrecy, but wherever he makes his stand the ghost is there directly—"Hic et ubique," the prince says—its voice crying from the cellarage: "Swear!"

The ghost binds Hamlet to vengeance, but there is another and more subtle way in which the spirit of his father haunts the prince. It is one of the radical ironies of the tragedy that the same nightmarish figure who takes from Hamlet his freedom should also embody the ideal of man noble in reason and infinite in faculties—the ideal of man, in other words, as free. The ghost of King Hamlet, stalking his son dressed in the same armor he wore in heroic combat with Fortinbras of Norway, becomes a peripatetic emblem of human dignity and worth, a memento of the time before the "falling-off" when Hamlet's serpent-uncle had not yet crept into the garden, infesting it with things rank and gross in nature. It is no accident that Hamlet bears the same name as his father: the king represents everything to which the prince aspires. Hamlet, too, has his single-combats, his duels both metaphorical and literal, but the world in which he must strive is not his father's. The memory of those two primal, valiant kings, face to face in a royal combat ratified by law and heraldry, haunts the tragedy, looming behind each pass of the "incensed points" of the modern "mighty opposites," Hamlet and Claudius, and looming also behind the final combat, Hamlet's and Laertes' poisoned play, swaddled in a show of chivalry as "yeasty" as the eloquence of Osric, the waterfly who presides as master of the lists.

Subject to his birth, tethered by Claudius, and bound by the ghost, Hamlet is obsessed with the idea of freedom, with the dignity that resides in being master of oneself. One must not be "passion's slave," a "pipe for Fortune's finger / To sound what stop she please" (3.2.72–74)— nor for that matter a pipe for men to play. The first three acts are largely concerned with the attempts of Claudius and Hamlet to play upon each other, the king principally through Rosencrantz and Guildenstern, Hamlet through "The Mousetrap." It is Hamlet who succeeds, plucking at last the heart of Claudius's mystery, pressing the king to the point where he loses his self-control and rises in a passion, calling for light. "Dids't perceive?" Hamlet asks, and Horatio replies: "I did very well note him" (3.2.293, 296). I should like to see a musical pun in Horatio's word *note*, but perhaps it is farfetched. At any rate, Hamlet's immediate response is to call for music, for the recorders to be brought, as if he thinks to reenact symbolically his triumph over the king. What follows is the "recorder scene" in which Rosencrantz and Guildenstern once again fail with Hamlet precisely where he has succeeded with the king:

> Why, look you now, how unworthy a thing you make of me! You would play upon me; you would seem to know my stops; you would pluck out the heart of my mystery; you would sound me from my lowest note to the top of my compass; and there is much music, excellent voice, in this little organ, yet cannot you make it speak. 'Sblood, do you think I am easier to be played on than a pipe? Call me what instrument you will, though you can fret me, you cannot play upon me.
>
> (3.2.371–80)

Immediately after speaking this, Hamlet turns to Polonius, who has just entered, and leads the old courtier through the game of cloud shapes, making him see the cloud first as a camel, then as a weasel, and finally as a whale. Though Claudius and his instruments cannot play upon him, Hamlet is contemptuously demonstrating that he can make any of them sound what tune he pleases.

Hamlet's disdain for anyone who will allow himself to be made an instrument perhaps suggests his bitter suspicion that he, too, is a kind of pipe. One of the most interesting of the bonds imposed upon Hamlet is presented in theatrical terms. Putting it baldly and exaggerating somewhat for the sake of clarity, one might say that Hamlet discovers that life is a poor play, that he finds himself compelled to play a part in a drama that offends his sense of his own worth. Hamlet is made to sound a tune that is not his own, the whirling and passionate music of the conventional revenger, a stock character familiar to the Elizabethans under a host of names, including Thomas Kyd's Hieronomo, his Hamlet, and Shakespeare's own Titus Andronicus. The role of revenger is thrust upon Hamlet by the ghost, and once again it is profoundly ironic that the figure who represents the dignity of man should be the agent for casting his son in a limited, hackneyed, and debasing role. That Hamlet should be constrained to play a role at all is a restriction of his freedom, but that it should be this particular, vulgar role is especially degrading.

Lest I should seem to be refashioning Shakespeare in the modern image of Pirandello, let me recall at this point that he is a remarkably self-conscious playwright, one who delights in such reflexive devices as the play within the play, the character who is either consciously or unconsciously an actor, or the great set speech on that favorite theme of how all the world is a stage. Of all Shakespeare's plays, perhaps the most reflexive, the most dramatically self-conscious, is *Hamlet*. This is possibly due in part to the circumstance not unprecedented but still rather special that Shakespeare is here reworking a well-known, even perhaps notorious, earlier play, a circumstance which permits him to play off his own tragedy and his own protagonist against his audience's knowledge of Kyd's *Hamlet*. In any case, the self-consciousness of Shakespeare's *Hamlet* is evident. Here the play within the play is not merely a crucial element in the plot but a central figure in the theme. Here Shakespeare actually introduces a troop of professional actors to discuss their art and give us examples of their skill onstage. Here even a figure like Polonius has had some experience on the boards, acting Julius Caesar to a university audience, and nearly every character in the play from the ghost to the king is at some time or other seen metaphorically as an actor. So pervasive is the play's concern with theater that, as many critics have noted, simple terms like *show, act, play,* and *perform* seem drawn toward their specifically theatrical meaning even when they occur in neutral contexts.

If *Hamlet* is Shakespeare's most self-conscious play, the prince is surely his most self-conscious character. An actor of considerable ability himself, he is also a professed student of the drama, a scholar and critic, and a writer able on short notice to produce a speech to be inserted in a play. The prince is familiar with the stock characters of the Elizabethan stage—he lists a string of them when he hears that the players have arrived—and he is familiar, too, with at least two Elizabethan revenge plays (not counting *The Murder of Gonzago*), for at various times he burlesques both *The True Tragedy of Richard III*, that curious mixture of revenge play and chronicle history, and *The Spanish Tragedy*. Moreover, Hamlet habitually conceives of his life as a play, a drama in which he is sometimes actor and sometimes actor and playwright together. We recall immediately that in the third soliloquy ("O, what a rogue and peasant slave am I!") he speaks of having the "motive and the cue for passion" (2.2.571). Only slightly less familiar is his description of how on the voyage to England he devised the plot of sending Rosencrantz and Guildenstern to their deaths with a forged commission:

Being thus benetted round with villains,
Or I could make a prologue to my brains,
They had begun the play. I sat me down,
Devised a new commission, wrote it fair.
(5.2.29–32)

And we remember that in the final scene the dying Hamlet addresses the court—and probably the actual spectators in the Globe as well—as you "that are but mutes or audience to this act" (5.2.336).

Hamlet's first reaction to the ghost is to leap enthusiastically into the familiar role. "Haste me" to know the truth, he cries, that I may "sweep to my revenge" (1.5.29–31). And a few lines later he launches into his vow of vengeance, the furious second soliloquy ("O all you host of heaven!") in which he calls upon heaven, earth, and hell, addresses his heart and his sinews, and pledges to wipe from his brain everything except the commandment of the ghost. It is a tissue of rhetoric passionate and hyperbolical in the true Senecan tradition, a piece of ranting of which Kyd's Hieronomo would be proud. Hamlet's self-consciousness as a revenger is suggested by the speech he requests when the players arrive, the story of Pyrrhus's bloody vengeance for his father's death. What he sees in this story is an image of his own father's fall in the crash of father Priam and, in the grief of Hecuba, the "mobled queen," an image of how Queen Gertrude ought to have behaved after her husband's death. But he also sees in Pyrrhus a horrible reflection of his own role, and, significantly, it is the prince himself who enacts the first dozen lines describing the dismal heraldry of the revenger.

Art for Hamlet is the mirror of nature, designed to provoke self-examination. Very reasonably, then, his interview with the players prompts him in the third soliloquy to consider his own motive and cue for passion, to examine how well he has performed as a revenger. Excepting his stormy vow of vengeance, Hamlet has so far controlled himself rather strictly in his duel with Claudius; he has not, by and large, indulged in much cleaving of the general ear with horrid speech in the normal manner of a revenger, and his contempt for such a manner is implicit in his description of what the common player would do with his cue: amaze the very faculties of eyes and ears and drown the stage with tears. Hamlet's aristocratic taste is for a more subtle species of drama, for plays like the one from which the story of Pyrrhus comes, which he praises to the players for being written with as much "modesty"—by which he means restraint—as cunning. Yet now, with the stock role he is to play brought home to him by the actors, Hamlet falls into the trap of judging himself by the very standards he has rejected and is disturbed by his own silence. Theatrically self-conscious as he is, Hamlet is naturally preoccupied by the relationship between playing and genuine feeling. He touches upon this in his first scene when he speaks to Gertrude of his outward "shapes of grief":

> These indeed seem,
> For they are actions that a man might play,
> But I have that within which passes show;
> These but the trappings and the suits of woe.
> (1.3.83–86)

How is one to distinguish mere shape—in theatrical parlance the word means costume or role as well as form—from the real thing? Or conversely, if the usual shape is lacking, how can one be sure of the substance? After the interview with the players, it is the latter problem which concerns Hamlet, for now he wonders whether his refusal to play the revenger in the usual shape, his reluctance to drown the stage with tears, means simply that he is unpregnant of his cause. As if to prove to himself that this is not so, he winds himself up again to the ranting rhetoric of the revenger, challenging some invisible observer to call him coward, pluck his beard, tweak his nose, and finally hurling at Claudius a passionate stream of epithets:

> Bloody, bawdy villain!
> Remorseless, treacherous, lecherous, kindless villain!
> O vengeance!
> (2.2.591–93)

But this time, at any rate, the role playing is conscious, and a moment later the aristocrat in Hamlet triumphs and he curses himself for a whore, a drab. To rant is cheap and vulgar; moreover, what is presently required is not the player's whorish art but action. And so, with superb irony in his choice of means, Hamlet decides to take his own kind of action:

> I'll have these players
> Play something like the murder of my father
> Before mine uncle.
> (2.2.606–08)

Hamlet's difficulty is aesthetic. His problem is one of form and content, of suiting the action to the word, the word to the action—that is, of finding a satisfactory shape for his revenge. Inevitably he is drawn to the preexisting pattern of the familiar revenge plays: life imitates art. Inevitably, too, his sensibility rebels, refusing to permit him to debase himself into a ranting simpleton. I find no evidence that the idea of revenge, of taking life, is itself abhorrent to Hamlet—he is not after all a modern exponent of nonviolence— rather it is the usual style of the revenger that he disdains. He objects to passionate rhetoric because to him it typifies bestial unreason. The conventional revenger, the Hieronomo or the Titus Andronicus, responds mechanically to circumstances, beating his breast in grief and crying wildly for revenge. Such a man is Fortune's pipe, the puppet of his circumstances, and the prisoner of his own passion. When Hamlet praises the man who is not "passion's slave," he is not merely repeating a humanist commonplace; he is commenting on an immediate problem, asserting a profound objection to the role in which he has been cast. At stake, then, for Hamlet is an aesthetic principle, but it is a moral principle as well: the issue is human dignity. In a play in which earsplitting rhetoric becomes the symbol of the protagonist's burden, it is suitable that "silence" is the final word from his lips as he dies. "The rest," he says, referring to all that must be left unspoken but also to the repose of death, "is silence."

The nature of Hamlet's objection to his role is elaborated in his address to the players—a speech too frequently overlooked in interpretations of this play—which Shakespeare has included because it permits the prince to comment indirectly on his most vital concern, how one ought to play the part of a revenger. Hamlet's demand is for elegance and restraint—in a word, for dignity in playing. Lines are to be spoken "trippingly on the tongue"—that is, with grace—rather than clumsily "mouthed" in the fashion of a town crier. Nor should the player permit himself gross gestures, as sawing the air with his hand; rather he must "use all gently," and even in the very torrent, tempest, and whirlwind of passion—the moment of extremity when the temptation to strut and bellow is greatest— must "acquire and beget a temperance that may give it smoothness" (3.2.7–8). The actor who tears a passion to tatters may win the applause of the groundlings who are only amused by noise, but he is worse than Termagant or Herod, those proverbially noisy stock characters of the old mystery plays which Hamlet disdains as ignorant and vulgar drama. It is interesting that Hamlet mentions Herod and the mythical infidel god Termagant: he means to suggest that undisciplined acting is not merely poor art, an offense against the "modesty of Nature," but an offense to all that a Christian gentleman, a humanist like himself, stands for. "O, there be players," he says a few lines later,

> that I have seen play . . . that neither having th' accent of Christians, nor the gait of Christian, pagan, nor man, have so strutted and bellowed that I have thought

some of Nature's journeymen had made men, and not made them well, they
imitated humanity so abominably.

(3.2.30–37)

To rage and rant is to make oneself into a monster. The crux of the issue is
this: like his father—" 'A was a man, take him for all in all" (1.3.187)—Hamlet
intends to be a man.

The player answers Hamlet's indictment of vulgar acting by assuring him
that his company has improved its style: "I hope we have reformed that
indifferently with us, sir." This complacency irritates Hamlet. "O, reform it
altogether" (3.2.39–40), he snaps in reply. Hamlet's concern is intense and
personal precisely because his own life has taken the shape of a vulgar play, a
crude and commonplace tragedy of revenge. The prince's response—
tantalizingly like Shakespeare's, working over what must have seemed to him
the crude and commonplace material of Kyd's *Hamlet*—is to "reform it
altogether." Since he cannot escape the role, Hamlet intends at least to be a
revenger in a style that offends neither the modesty of nature nor his sense of
human dignity. He intends to exercise discipline. I do not mean to suggest
that Hamlet, like the singing gravedigger, has no feeling for his work. On the
contrary, much of the drama lies in Hamlet's war with himself, his struggle to
reduce his whirlwind passion to smoothness.

Hamlet and *Lear* are the only two of Shakespeare's tragedies with double
plots. The Gloucester plot in *Lear* provides a relatively simple moral exem-
plum of one who stumbled when he saw and lost his eyes in consequence.
This is a commonplace species of Elizabethan moral fable designed to set off
the more complex and ambiguous story of the king. The story of Polonius's
family works analogously in *Hamlet*. Each member of the family is a fairly
ordinary person who serves as a foil to some aspect of Hamlet's extraordinary
cunning and discipline. Polonius imagines himself a regular Machiavel, an
expert at using indirections to find directions out, but compared to Hamlet
he is what the prince calls him, a great baby. Ophelia, unable to control her
grief, lapses into madness and a muddy death, reminding us that it is one of
Hamlet's achievements that he does not go mad but only plays at insanity to
disguise his true strength. And Laertes, of course, goes mad in a different
fashion and becomes the model of the kind of revenger that Hamlet so
disdains.

Hamlet knows he is playing a role, but Laertes is blissfully unselfconscious
about his part. The prince boasts to his mother that his pulse "doth temper-
ately keep time" (3.4.141), but Laertes' brag is of his stereotyped rage: "That
drop of blood that's calm proclaims me bastard" (4.5.117). Laertes—to adapt
Nashe's famous allusion to Kyd's old *Hamlet*—if you entreat him fair in a
frosty morning will shamelessly afford you handfuls of tragical speeches,
ranting in the best manner of English Seneca:

To hell allegiance, vows to the blackest devil,
Conscience and grace to the profoundest pit!

I dare damnation. To this point I stand,
That both the worlds I give to negligence,
Let come what comes, only I'll be revenged
Most thoroughly for my father.

(4.5.131–36)

What comes is not quite the revenge Laertes expects, for the situation is not
so simple as he supposes; rather he finds himself on account of his unthinking
passion an easy instrument for Claudius to play, becoming, in his own word,
the king's "organ." The advice that Polonius gave Laertes might have stood the
young man in good stead if he had followed it: "Give thy thoughts no tongue, /
Nor any unproportioned thought his act" (1.3.59–60). Ironically, Polonius's
words perfectly describe not Laertes' but Hamlet's approach to revenge.
From the very first Hamlet has understood the practical as well as the
aesthetic importance of controlling his rage. "But break my heart, for I must
hold my tongue" (1.2.159), he says at the end of the first soliloquy, and it is
interesting in the light of the play's general association of lack of discipline
with noise, with rant, that even here control is connected with silence.

Shakespeare contrives to have his two revengers, the typical Laertes and
the extraordinary Hamlet, meet at Ophelia's grave, where the prince finds
Laertes true to form tearing a passion to tatters, bellowing to be buried alive
with his sister. Hamlet steps forward and the technical rhetorical terms he
uses, *emphasis* and *phrase*, together with the theatrical simile of making the
stars stand like "wonder-wounded hearers," like an audience, reveal his critical
attitude, his professional interest in the quality of Laertes' performance:

What is he whose grief
Bears such an emphasis, whose phrase of sorrow
Conjures the wand'ring stars, and makes them stand
Like wonder-wounded hearers?

(5.1.256–59)

According to the probably authentic stage direction of the first quarto, Hamlet
at this point leaps into the grave alongside Laertes, suiting outrageous word to
outrageous action by challenging the young man to a contest of noise, of rant.
What will Laertes do to prove his love for Ophelia, weep, tear himself, drink
vinegar, eat a crocodile? Hamlet will match him. Does Laertes mean to
whine, to prate of being buried under a mountain higher than Pelion? Why,
then Hamlet will say he'll be buried too, and let the imaginary mountain be
so high that it touches the sphere of fire and makes Ossa by comparison a
wart. "Nay, an thou'lt mouth," the prince says, using the same word with
which he had earlier described the manner of vulgar actors, "I'll rant as well
as thou" (5.1.285–86).

Hamlet is mocking Laertes' style, but the bitterness of his mockery, the
nastiness of it, derives from his own sincere grief for Ophelia. In a world of
overblown rhetoric, of grotesque elephantine shows, how can a man of taste
and discernment be understood? Moreover, since the usual sound and fury so

often signify nothing, how will a man of genuine feeling be believed? This
burlesque of Laertes is Hamlet's last act of bitter rebellion against the
vulgarity of his world and the role he has been constrained to play in it.
Moreover, it is a reversion to his earlier and fiercer mood, the proud,
contemptuous spirit of the prince before the sea voyage; for, as most critics
observe, the prince who returns from sea is a changed man, resigned,
detached, perhaps "tragically illuminated." Having refused to kill the king
when the time was every way propitious—that is, when he found Claudius
kneeling in empty not genuine prayer—and then, having chosen his own
moment to act only to find that instead of the king he has murdered Polonius,
Hamlet seems to have allowed his sinews to relax. He has let himself be
thrust aboard ship, let himself in effect be cast onto the sea of fortune that is
so common an image in Shakespeare and the Elizabethan poets, an image
recalling that "sea of troubles" against which he had earlier taken arms. When
the opportunity to escape the king's trap arises, Hamlet seizes it, leaping
aboard the pirate ship, but what he is doing now is reacting to circumstances
rather than trying to dominate them wholly. The prince returns to Denmark
at once sad and amused, but, except for the single flash of "towering passion"
at Ophelia's grave, relatively impassive. He has ceased to insist that he must
be above being played upon by any power.

And yet, before Hamlet consents to the duel with Laertes, about which he
has justified misgivings, he plays a scene with that impossible fop, Osric, the
emblem of the empty courtesy of Claudius's court. Just as Hamlet earlier led
Polonius through the game of cloud shapes, so now he toys with Osric, leading
him to proclaim first that the weather is warm, then that it is cold, and finally
warm again. At the penultimate moment, Hamlet is demonstrating that if he
wished he might still play upon the king and his instruments like so many
pipes. Hamlet's mocking Osric, like the scene with Laertes in the grave,
recalls the early proud manner of the prince; nevertheless, Hamlet no longer
seems to be in rebellion, rather than bitter contempt he displays amusement
that at the end he should be forced to share the stage with a waterfly. The
prince's motto is no longer "heart lose not thy nature," but "let be." He has
ceased to struggle for absolute freedom in his role, ceased to insist that he
alone must be the artist who, in all senses of the term, shapes his life. He
understands now that, in Laertes' words, he cannot carve for himself. One can
at best be a collaborator in one's life, for there is always another artist to be
taken into account, "a divinity that shapes our ends, / Rough-hew them how
we will."

The Hamlet who speaks of special providence in the fall of a sparrow is not
perhaps so exciting a figure as the earlier Hamlet heroically refusing to be
manipulated. There is something almost superhuman in the discipline, consciousness, and cunning of the earlier Hamlet: certainly he makes superhuman demands upon himself, insisting that he be in action like an angel, in
apprehension like a god. But Hamlet has discovered that, finally, he is subject

to his birth, that he is neither angel nor god, and, in an ironically different sense, it can now be said of him what he said of his father, " 'A was a man, take him for all." King Hamlet fought his single combat in an unfallen world of law and heraldry; his son must seek to emulate him in a corrupt world of empty chivalry and poisoned foils; and yet, in its way, Hamlet's duel with Laertes is as heroic as his father's with Fortinbras, and in his own manner Hamlet proves himself worthy of the name of soldier.

"Bear Hamlet like a soldier to the stage" (5.2.397) is the command of Fortinbras which concludes the play, a command which not only ratifies Hamlet's heroism by using the term *soldier*, but in its theatrical allusion reminds us that much of his achievement has been in the skill with which he has played his inauspicious role. If all the world is a stage and all the men and women merely players, then the reckoning of quality must be by professional standards. By these standards Hamlet has proven himself a very great actor indeed, for he has taken a vulgar role and reformed it so that it no longer offends the modesty of nature or the dignity of man. Even a man on a tether, to pick up Polonius's image again, has a certain degree of freedom. One may be cast in a vulgar role and still win distinction in the manner the role is played. Or one may be tied to the story line of a crude melodrama and still produce a *Hamlet*.

Superposed Plays: *Hamlet*

Richard A. Lanham

Shakespeare uses a variation on the sonnets strategy in *Hamlet*. He writes
two plays in one. Laertes plays the revenge-tragedy hero straight. He does,
true enough, veer toward self-parody, as when he complains that crying for
Ophelia has interfered with his rants: "I have a speech o' fire, that fain would
blaze / But that this folly drowns it" (4.7.189–90).[1] But he knows his generic
duty and does it. No sooner has his "good old man" (Polonius's role in the
straight, "serious" play) been polished off than he comes screaming with a
rabble army. He delivers predictably and suitably stupid lines like "O thou
vile king, / Give me my father" (4.5.115–16). And the Queen can scarcely
manage a "Calmly, good Laertes" before he begins again: "That drop of blood
that's calm proclaims me bastard, / Cries cuckold to my father, brands the
harlot / Even here between the chaste unsmirchèd brows / Of my true
mother" (4.5.117–20). And just before the King begins to calm him, to the
villainous contentation of both: "How came he dead? I'll not be juggled with. /
To hell allegiance, vows to the blackest devil, / Conscience and grace to the
profoundest pit!" (4.5.130–32). He plays a straight, hard-charging revenge-
hero.

Against him, Ophelia reenacts a delightfully tear-jerking madwoman stage
prop. The King mouths kingly platitudes well enough ("There's such divinity
doth hedge a king . . . " [4.5.123]), comes up with a suitably stagey, two-phase
fail-safe plot, and urges the hero on ("Revenge should have no bounds"). And
the whole comes suitably laced with moralizing guff. So the King plays a
Polonius-of-the-leading-questions: "Laertes, was your father dear to you?"
Laertes, with unusual common sense, returns, "Why ask you this?" And then
the King is off for a dozen Polonian lines on love's alteration by time: "Not that
I think you did not love your father, / But that I know love is begun by time
. . ." 4.7.109–10). Only then can he get back to, as he phrases it, "the quick o'
th' ulcer." And the Queen plays out a careful scene on the brookside where
Ophelia drowned. And wrestling in Ophelia's grave, Hamlet, annoyed at
being upstaged by Laertes, protests, "I'll rant as well as thou." And, as superb

From Richard A. Lanham, *The Motives of Eloquence: Literary Rhetoric in the Renaissance* (New
Haven: Yale University Press, 1976), 129–43. Reprinted by permission of the author.

[1]Ed. Willard Farnham.

18

finale, Laertes, at the fencing match, stands there prating about honor with the poisoned rapier in his hand. The poisoner-poisoned motif releases the Christian forgiveness that forgives us, too, for enjoying all that blood. *Hamlet* offers, then, a story frankly calculated to make the audience as well as the compositor run out of exclamation points.

Hamlet obligingly confesses himself Laertes' foil. "In mine ignorance / Your skill shall, like a star i'th'darkest night, / Stick fiery off indeed" (5.2.244–46). It is the other way about, of course. Laertes foils for Hamlet. Shakespeare is up to his old chiasmatic business, writing a play about the kind of play he is writing. The main play overlaps as well as glossing the play criticized—again, a strategy of superposition. Polonius plays a muddling old proverb-monger, and a connoisseur of language, in the Hamlet play, as well as good old man in the Laertes play. Ophelia, though sentimental from the start, is both more naive and more duplicitous in the Hamlet play; and so with the King and Queen, too, both are more complex figures. Shakespeare endeavors especially to wire the two plots in parallel: two avenging sons and two dead fathers; brother's murder and "this brother's wager"; both Hamlet and Laertes in love with Ophelia; both dishonest before the duel (Hamlet pretending more madness than he displays when he kills Polonius), and so on.

Now there is no doubt about how to read the Laertes play: straight revenge tragedy, to be taken—as I've tried to imply in my summary—without solemnity. We are to enjoy the rants as rants. When we get tears instead of a rant, as with the Laertes instance cited earlier, an apology for our disappointment does not come amiss. We are not to be caught up in Laertes' vigorous feeling any more than in Ophelia's bawdy punning. We savor it. We don't believe the fake King when he maunders on about Divine Right, the divinity that doth hedge a king. We don't "believe" anybody. It is not that kind of play. For explanation, neither the ketchup nor the verbal violence need go further than enjoyment. The more outrageous the stage effects, the more ghastly the brutality, the more grotesque the physical mutilation, the better such a play becomes. Shakespeare had done this kind of thing already and knew what he was about. Such a vehicle packed them in. Just so, when part-sales were falling, would Dickens kill a baby.

The real doubt comes when we ask, "What poetic do we bring to the Hamlet play?" As several of its students have pointed out, it is a wordy play. Eloquence haunts it. Horatio starts the wordiness by supplying a footnote from ancient Rome in the first scene, by improving the occasion with informative reflection. Everybody laughs at Polonius for his moralizing glosses but Hamlet is just as bad. Worse. Gertrude asks him, in the second scene, why he grieves to excess and he gives us a disquisition on seeming and reality in grief. The King follows with *his* bravura piece on grief. Everybody moralizes the pageant. The Hamlet play abounds with triggers for straight revenge-tragedy response. The whole "mystery" of Hamlet's hesitant revenge boils down to wondering why he doesn't go ahead and play his traditional part, complete with the elegant rants we know he can deliver.

The rhetorical attitude is triggered not only by obvious stylistic excess, as we have seen, or by *de trop* moralizing, but by talking about language, by surface reference to surface. This surface reference occurs at every level of the Hamlet play in *Hamlet*, as well as, of course, throughout the Laertes play. Polonius plays a main part here. His tedious prolixity ensures that we notice everyone else's tedious prolixity. And his relish of language, his speech for its own sake, makes us suspect the same appetite in others and in ourselves. The Queen's rejoinder to the marvelous "brevity is the soul of wit" speech in 2.2 could be addressed to almost anybody in the play, including the gravedigger: "More matter, with less art."

Everyone is manipulating everyone else with speechifying and then admitting he has done so. Every grand rhetorical occasion seems no sooner blown than blasted. Polonius offers the famous Gielgud encore about being true to oneself and then sends off Reynaldo to spy and tell fetching lies. The King plays king to angry Laertes then confesses to Gertrude that he has been doing just this. Ophelia is staked out to play innocent maiden so Hamlet can be drawn out and observed. *Hic et ubique*. Is she a stage contrivance or a character? What kind of audience are we to be? Everyone is an actor, Hamlet and his madness most of all. The play is full of minor invitations to attend the surface, the theme of speaking. Even the ghost has to remind himself to be brief—before continuing for thirty-odd lines (1.5). Theatrical gestures are not simply used all the time but described, as in Hamlet's inky cloak and windy suspiration for grief, or the costuming and gesture of the distracted lover, as the innocent Ophelia describes Hamlet's visit:

> My lord, as I was sewing in my closet,
> Lord Hamlet, with his doublet all unbraced,
> No hat upon his head, his stockings fouled,
> Ungartered, and down-gyvèd to his ankle,
> Pale as his shirt, his knees knocking each other,
> And with a look so piteous in purport
> As if he had been loosèd out of hell
> To speak of horrors—he comes before me.
> .   .   .   .
> He took me by the wrist and held me hard.
> Then goes he to the length of all his arm,
> And with his other hand thus o'er his brow
> He falls to such perusal of my face
> As 'a would draw it. Long stayed he so.
> At last, a little shaking of mine arm
> And thrice his head thus waving up and down,
> He raised a sigh so piteous and profound
> As it did seem to shatter all his bulk
> And end his being. That done, he lets me go,
> And with his head over his shoulder turned
> He seemed to find his way without his eyes,

For out o'doors he went without their helps
And to the last bended their light on me.
                    (2.1.77–84, 87–100)

This might have come from an actor's manual. Do we take it as such, respond as professional actors?

The Hamlet play turns in on itself most obviously when the players visit. Dramatic self-consciousness retrogresses a step further as the tragedians of the city talk about themselves doing what they are just now doing in a play depicting them doing just what. . . . The debate is about rightful succession, of course, like both the Laertes and the Hamlet plays. "What, are they children? Who maintains 'em? How are they escoted? Will they pursue the quality no longer than they can sing? Will they not say afterwards, if they should grow themselves to common players (as it is most like, if their means are no better), their writers do them wrong to make them exclaim against their own succession?" (2.2.338–44). Who are the children in the "real" plays? Hamlet had invoked a typical cast a few lines earlier (314 ff.) such as *Hamlet* itself uses and stressed that "he that plays the king shall be welcome." Hamlet will use the play, that is, *as a weapon,* the propaganda side of rhetorical poetic, to complement the Polonius-pleasure side. But before that, there is a rehearsal, for effect, to see whether the players are good enough to play the play within the play. Here, even more clearly than in the Laertes play, we confront the connoisseur's attitude toward language. Polonius supplies a chorus that for once fits: "Fore God, my lord, well spoken, with good accent and good discretion" (2.2.454–55). This to Hamlet, a good actor, as Polonius was in his youth. They proceed in this vein, nibbling the words; "That's good. 'Mobled queen' is good."

The main question pressing is not, How does the feedback work? What relation is there, for example, between rugged Pyrrhus and Hamlet, or Laertes? Or what relation with the King, who also topples a kingdom? And why is Hamlet so keen to reach Hecuba? The main question is, How does all this connoisseurship affect the "serious" part of *Hamlet? Hamlet* is one of the great tragedies. It has generated more comment than any other written document in English literature, one would guess, reverent, serious comment on it as a serious play. Yet finally can we take *any* of its rhetoric seriously? If so, how much and when? The play is full of the usual release mechanisms for the rhetorical poetic. And, at the end, the Laertes play is there as stylistic control, to mock us if we have made the naive response. But what is the sophisticated response?

Hamlet focuses the issue, and the play, the plays, when he finally gets to Hecuba. He who has been so eager for a passionate speech is yet surprised when it comes and when it seizes the player:

O, what a rogue and peasant slave am I!
Is it not monstrous that this player here,

But in a fiction, in a dream of passion,
Could force his soul so to his own conceit
That from her working all his visage wanned,
Tears in his eyes, distraction in his aspect,
A broken voice, and his whole function suiting
With forms to his conceit? And all for nothing,
For Hecuba!
What's Hecuba to him, or he to Hecuba,
That he should weep for her? What would he do
Had he the motive and the cue for passion
That I have?

                                        (2.2.534–46)

Hamlet makes the point that dances before us in every scene. Dramatic, rhetorical motive is stronger than "real," serious motive. Situation prompts feeling in this play, rather than the other way round. Feelings are not real until played. Drama, ceremony, is always needed to authenticate experience. On the battlements Hamlet—with ghostly reinforcement—makes his friends not simply swear but make a big scene of it. Laertes keeps asking for *more ceremonies* for Ophelia's burial and is upset by his father's hugger-mugger interment. Hamlet plays and then breaks off ("Something too much of this") a stoic friendship scene with Horatio in 3.2. The stronger, the more genuine the feeling, the greater the need to display it.

The answer, then, to "What would he do . . . ?" is, presumably, "Kill the King!"? Not at all. "He would drown the stage with tears / And cleave the general ear with horrid speech" (2.2.546–47). He would rant even better. And this Hamlet himself, by way of illustration, goes on to do:

Yet I,
A dull and muddy-mettled rascal, peak
Like John-a-dreams, unpregnant of my cause,
And can say nothing. No, not for a king,
Upon whose property and most dear life
A damned defeat was made. Am I a coward?
Who calls me villain? breaks my pate across?
Plucks off my beard and blows it in my face?
Tweaks me by the nose? gives me the lie i'th'throat
As deep as to the lungs? Who does me this?
Ha, 'swounds, I should take it, for it cannot be
But I am pigeon-livered and lack gall
To make oppression bitter, or ere this
I should ha' fatted all the region kites
With this slave's offal. Bloody, bawdy villain!
Remorseless, treacherous, lecherous, kindless villain!
O, vengeance!

                                        (2.2.551–67)

Hamlet is here having a fine time dining off his own fury, relishing his sublime passion. He gets a bit confused, to be sure: saying nothing is not his problem. If somebody did call him villain or pluck his beard it would be better, for his grievance would then find some dramatic equivalent, would become real enough to act upon. But he enjoys himself thoroughly. He also sees himself clearly, or at least clearly enough to voice our opinion of his behavior: "Why, what an ass am I! This is most brave, / That I, the son of a dear father murdered, / Prompted to my revenge by heaven and hell, / Must like a whore unpack my heart with words" (2.2.568–71).

Hamlet is one of the most appealing characters the mind of man has ever created but he really is a bit of an ass, and not only here but all through the play. He remains incorrigibly dramatic. Do we like him because he speaks to our love of dramatic imposture? Because his solution, once he has seen his own posturing as such, is not immediate action but more playing? "I'll have these players / Play something like the murder of my father / Before mine uncle" (2.2.580–82). Playing is where we will find reality, find the truth. The play works, of course, tells Hamlet again what he already knows, has had a spirit come specially from purgatory to tell him. But that is not the point. Or rather, that is the point insofar as this is a serious play. The rhetorical purpose is to sustain reality until yet another dramatic contrivance—ship, grave scene, duel—can sustain it yet further.

We saw in the sonnets how a passage can invoke opaque attitudes by logical incongruity. Something of the sort happens in the scene after this speech, the "To be or not to be" centerpiece. Plays flourish within plays here, too, of course. The King and Polonius dangle Ophelia as bait and watch. Hamlet sees this. He may even be, as W. A. Bebbington suggested,[2] reading the "To be or not to be" speech from a book, using it, literally, as a stage prop to bemuse the spyers-on, convince them of his now-become-suicidal madness. No one in his right mind will fault the poetry. But it is irrelevant to anything that precedes. It fools Ophelia—no difficult matter—but it should not fool us. The question is whether Hamlet will act directly or through drama? Not at all. Instead, is he going to end it in the river? I put it thus familiarly to penetrate the serious numinosity surrounding this passage. Hamlet anatomizes grievance for all time. But does *he* suffer these grievances? He has a complaint indeed against the King and one against Ophelia. Why not do something about them instead of meditating on suicide? If the book is a stage prop, or the speech a trap for the hidden listeners, of course, the question of relevancy doesn't arise. The speech works beautifully. But we do not usually consider it a rhetorical trick. It is the most serious speech in the canon. But is it? It tells us nothing about Hamlet except what we already know—he is a good actor. Its relevance, in fact, may lurk just here. The real question by this point in the play is exactly this one: *Is* Hamlet or not? Or does he just act? What kind of self does he possess?

2"Soliloquy?," *Times Literary Supplement,* 20 March 1969, p. 289.

The whole play, we know, seeks authenticity, reality behind the arras, things as they are. Hamlet, we are to assume, embodies the only true self, the central self amidst a cast of wicked phonies. The play, seen this way, provided a natural delight for both the Victorians and the existentialists; their sentimentalism about the central self ran the same way. Yet the question really is whether Hamlet is *to be,* to act rather than reenact. Much has been written on the Melancholy-Man-in-the-Renaissance and how his problems apply to Hamlet. Much more has been written on Hamlet's paralysis. Yet, how irrelevant all this commentary is to the real problem, not *what* Hamlet's motive is but *what kind of* motive. Why can't he act? Angels and ministers of grace, he does nothing else. Polonius, Rosencrantz and Guildenstern, Laertes, Claudius, all go to it. But Hamlet never breaks through to "reality." His motives and his behavior remain dramatic from first to last. So, in spite of all those bodies at the end, commentators wonder if *Hamlet* amounts to a tragedy and, if so, what kind. Hamlet lacks the serious, central self tragedy requires. We are compelled to stand back, hold off our identification, and hence to locate the play within rhetorical coordinates, a tragicomedy about the two kinds of self and the two kinds of motive.

We see this theme in that Q_2 scene (4.4) where Fortinbras and his army parade, with seeming irrelevance—at least to many directors, who cut it—across the stage. They parade so that Hamlet can reflect upon them. The theme is motive. The scene begins as a straightforward lesson in the vanity of human wishes. They go, the Captain tells Hamlet, "to gain a little patch of ground / That hath in it no profit but the name" (4.4.18–19). Hamlet seems to get the point, "the question of this straw," the absurd artificiality of human motive, and especially of aristocratic war, war for pleasure, for the pure glory of it. But then out jumps another non sequitur soliloquy:

> How all occasions do inform against me
> And spur my dull revenge! What is a man,
> If his chief good and market of his time
> Be but to sleep and feed? A beast, no more.
> Sure he that made us with such large discourse,
> Looking before and after, gave us not
> That capability and godlike reason
> To fust in us unused. Now, whether it be
> Bestial oblivion, or some craven scruple
> Of thinking too precisely on th' event—
> A thought which, quartered, hath but one part wisdom
> And ever three parts coward—I do not know
> Why yet I live to say, "This thing's to do,"
> Sith I have cause, and will, and strength, and means
> To do't.
>
> (4.4.32–46)

What has reason to do with revenge? His question—why, with all his compelling reasons, doesn't he go on—is again well taken. Shakespeare has carefully given him the realest reasons a revenge hero ever had—father murdered, mother whored, kingdom usurped, his innocent maiden corrupted in her imagination. The answer to Hamlet's question marches about on the stage before him. As usual, he does not fully understand the problem. It is the Player King's tears all over again. Fortinbras's motivation is sublimely artificial, entirely dramatic. Honor. It has no profit in it but the name. Hamlet cannot act because he cannot find a way to dramatize his revenge. Chances he has, but, as when he surprises Claudius praying, they are not dramatic. Claudius is alone. To fall upon him and kill him would not be revenge, as he says, not because Claudius will die shriven but because he will not see it coming, because nobody is watching.

So, when Hamlet continues his soliloquy, he draws a moral precisely opposite to the expected one. Again, logical discontinuity triggers stylistic attitude:

> Examples gross as earth exhort me.
> Witness this army of such mass and charge,
> Led by a delicate and tender prince,
> Whose spirit, with divine ambition puffed,
> Makes mouths at the invisible event,
> Exposing what is mortal and unsure
> To all that fortune, death, and danger dare,
> Even for an eggshell. Rightly to be great
> Is not to stir without great argument,
> But greatly to find quarrel in a straw
> When honor's at the stake. How stand I then,
> That have a father killed, a mother stained,
> Excitements of my reason and my blood,
> And let all sleep, while to my shame I see
> The imminent death of twenty thousand men
> That for a fantasy and trick of fame
> Go to their graves like beds, fight for a plot
> Whereon the numbers cannot try the cause,
> Which is not tomb enough and continent
> To hide the slain? O, from this time forth,
> My thoughts be bloody, or be nothing worth!
>   (4.4.46–66)

He sees but does not see. In some way, Fortinbras represents where he wants to go, what he wants to be, how he wants to behave. But he doesn't see how, nor altogether do we. If ever an allegorical puppet was dragged across a stage it is Fortinbras. Yet he haunts the play. His divine ambition begins the action of the play; he gets that offstage introduction Shakespeare is so fond of; he marches to Norway to make a point about motive; and he marches back at the end, inherits Denmark. Yet he stays cardboard. It is not real motive he represents but martial honor much rather.

Shakespeare sought to give *Hamlet* a pronounced military coloration from first to last. The play begins on guard; the ghost wears armor; Denmark is a most warlike state. Military honor is the accepted motive in a Denmark Fortinbras rightly inherits. Honor will cure what is rotten in Denmark, restore its proper values. Hamlet cannot set the times right because he cannot find in martial honor a full and sufficient motive for human life. Hamlet, says Fortinbras, would have done well had he been king, but we may be permitted to doubt it. He thinks too much. Yet honor and the soldier's life provide the model motive for *Hamlet*. All his working life, Shakespeare was fascinated and perplexed by how deeply the military motive satisfied man. It constituted a sublime secular commitment which, like the religious commitment, gave all away to get all back. Hamlet's selfconsciousness keeps him from it, yes, but even more his search for real purpose. Chivalric war—all war, perhaps—is manufactured purpose. Hamlet can talk about clutching it to his bosom but he cannot do it, for there is nothing *inevitable* about it.

Military honor is finally a role, much like Laertes' role as revenge hero. Both roles are satisfying, both integrate and direct the personality. But once you realize that you are playing the role for just these reasons, using it as a self-serving device, its attraction fades. As its inevitability diminishes, so does its reality. War and revenge both prove finally so rewarding because they provide, by all the killing, the irrefutable reality needed to bolster the role, restore its inevitability. Thus Shakespeare chose them, a revenge plot super-posed on a Fortinbras-honor plot, for his play about motive. They provided a model for the kind of motive men find most satisfying; they combine maxi-mum dramatic satisfaction with the irrefutable reality only bloody death can supply. In the Elizabethan absurdity as in our own, men kill others and themselves because that is the only real thing left to do. It is a rare paradox and Shakespeare builds his play upon it.

But even death is not dependable. We can learn to make sport of it, enjoy it. So the gravedigger puns on his craft. So, too, I suppose, Fortinbras laconically remarks at the end of the play: "Such a sight as this / Becomes the field, but here shows much amiss." Death's reality can vanish too. All our purposes end up, like the skull Hamlet meditates on, a stage prop. It is not accidental that the language which closes the play is theatrical. Hamlet even in death does not escape the dramatic self. When the bodies are "high on a stage . . . placèd to the view" Horatio will "speak to th' yet unknowing world," will authenticate the proceeding with a rhetorical occasion. Hamlet's body, Fortinbras commands, is to be borne "like a soldier to the stage, / For he was likely, had he been put on, / To have proved most royal."

Nor is it accidental that Hamlet kills Polonius. The act is his real attempt at revenge, Polonius his real enemy. Polonius embodies the dramatic self-consciousness which stands between Hamlet and the roles—Avenger and King—he was born to play. But Polonius pervades the whole of Hamlet's world and lurks within Hamlet himself. Only death can free Hamlet. Perhaps this is why he faces it with nonchalance. Much has been said about Hamlet's stoicism, but how unstoical the play really is! Honest feeling demands a dramatic equivalent to make it real just as artifice does. Stoicism demands a preexistent reality, a central self beyond drama, which the play denies. Stoicism is death and indeed, in *Hamlet,* the second follows hard upon the avowal of the first. We have no choice but to play.

And so Hamlet chooses his foil and plays. 1 have been arguing that the play invokes rhetorical coordinates as well as serious ones. It makes sense, if this is so, that it should end with a sublime game and the triumph of chance. Hamlet never solves his problem, nor does chance solve it for him, nor does the play solve it for us. No satisfactory model for motive, no movement from game to sublime, is suggested. Hamlet can finally kill the King because the King thoughtfully supplies a dramatic occasion appropriate to the deed. And Hamlet can kill Laertes because dramatic motive has destroyed naive purpose. And vice versa. But Hamlet cannot get rid of his dramatic self, his dramatic motives. The duel allegorizes the quarrel between kinds of motive which the play has just dramatized. And the duel, like the play, is a zero-sum game. Interest for both sides adds up to zero. The play leaves us, finally, where it leaves Hamlet. We have savored the violence and the gorgeous poetry and been made aware that we do. We have been made to reflect on play as well as purpose. We have not been shown how to move from one to the other. Nor that it *cannot* be done. We are left, like those in the play, dependent on death and chance to show us how to put our two motives, our two selves, together.

Shakespeare as a mature playwright is not supposed to be an opaque stylist. The great unity of his mature tragedies is a style we look through, not at. The gamesman with words fades out with the nondramatic poems and early infatuations like *Love's Labor's Lost. Hamlet* shows, by itself, how wrong this view of Shakespeare's development is. The play depends upon an alternation of opaque and transparent styles for its meaning. The alternation almost *is* the meaning. *Hamlet* is a play about motive, about style, and thus perhaps, of the mature plays, an exception? I don't think so. Where Shakespeare is most sublime he is also most rhetorical and both poetics are likely to be present in force. To illustrate such a thesis would constitute an agreeable task. The lines it would follow are clear enough. They would yield explanation of the double plot more basic than the comic/serious one. They would render the comic/tragic division altogether less important than it now seems.

In play after play the same stylistic strategy illustrates the same juxtaposition of motive, of play and purpose. Richard cannot learn the difference. Hal must. Lear can play the king but he has never *been* a king. *Antony and Cleopatra* juxtaposes not only public and private life but two poetics and two selves. The double plot becomes, over and over, a serious plot-poetic and a play plot-poetic. The fatal innocence of Shakespeare's characters turns out, over and over, to be innocence about the real nature of their motivation. All through the *Henriad* political rhetoric can be *seen* as rhetoric. Egypt is meant to be *seen* as more wordy and more metaphorical than Rome. *Romeo and Juliet* depends on our seeing the Petrarchan rhetoric as such, else we will mistake the kind of play it is, a play where death authenticates game. Lear on the heath, that centerpiece of Shakespearean sublimity, alters his outlines considerably within rhetorical coordinates. Shakespearean tragedy may come to seem, as in *Hamlet*, a juxtaposition of the two motives with a hole in the middle, with no way to connect them. The comedies collapse them. And the problem plays and romances try to make a path between the two, see them in dynamic interchange. The two things that obsessed Shakespeare were style and motive, and his career can be charted coherently from beginning to end in terms of their interrelation. In this he typifies the stylistic strategy of the Renaissance as a whole. The real question of motive lay beyond good and evil. It was the principal task of the self-conscious rhetorical style to point this moral. Human flesh is sullied with self-consciousness, with theatricality, and these will be the ground for whatever authentic morality any of us can muster.

Man and Wife Is One Flesh:
Hamlet and the Confrontation with the
Maternal Body

Janet Adelman

In *Hamlet*, the figure of the mother returns to Shakespeare's dramatic world, and her presence causes the collapse of the fragile compact that had allowed Shakespeare to explore familial and sexual relationships in the histories and romantic comedies without devastating conflict; this collapse is the point of origin of the great tragic period. The son's acting out of the role of the father, his need to make his own identity in relationship to his conception of his father—the stuff of *1 and 2 Henry IV* and *Julius Caesar*—becomes deeply problematic in the presence of the wife/mother: for her presence makes the father's sexual role a disabling crux in the son's relationship with his father. At the same time, the relations between the sexes that had been imagined in the comedies without any serious confrontation with the power of female sexuality suddenly are located in the context of the mother's power to contaminate, with the result that they can never again be imagined in purely holiday terms. Here again, *Hamlet* stands as a kind of watershed, subjecting to maternal presence the relationships previously exempted from that presence.[1]

From the perspective of *Hamlet*, the father-son relationships of the earlier plays begin to look like oedipal dramas from which the chief object of contention has been removed. Both the *Henry IV* plays and *Julius Caesar* manage their sophisticated psychological explorations in effect by denying that women have anything to do with these explorations, ultimately by denying the complications that the mother poses for the father-son relationship. Before *Hamlet*, this relationship tends to be enacted in the political rather than the domestic sphere, and in the absence of women. Insofar as the triangulated conflict characteristic of oedipal material makes its way into these plays, the

From Janet Adelman, *Suffocating Mothers: Fantasies of Maternal Origin in Shakespeare, "Hamlet" to "The Tempest"* (New York: Routledge, Chapman, and Hall, 1992). Reprinted by permission. The original footnotes for this essay have been shortened.

[1]My sense of the shape of Shakespeare's career and of the defensive construction of both the comedies and the histories is deeply indebted to Richard P. Wheeler; see *Shakespeare's Development and the Problem Comedies* (Berkeley: University of California Press, 1981), esp. pp. 46–50, 155–64.

triangle is composed of a son and two fathers, not of a son and his parents; the son's identity is defined by his position between the fathers, not between father and mother. The *Henry IV* plays and *Julius Caesar* both strikingly represent the defining act of the son's manhood as the process of choosing between two fathers; in both, the son attempts to become fully himself by identifying with the *true* father rather than the false, an identification signaled by the son's willingness to carry out the true father's wish that the false father be disowned or killed. But the choice becomes increasingly problematic in these plays. In *1 and 2 Henry IV*, it is a relatively easy matter for Hal to kill off that "father ruffian" Falstaff (*1 Henry IV*, 2.4.254) by exiling him, thus becoming "father" to his brothers (*2 Henry IV*, 5.2.57) and the embodiment of his father's spirit (*2 Henry IV*, 5.2.125); in this cross-generational alliance, he becomes himself in effect by choosing to become his father. Although we may feel that he has diminished himself in his choice, the plays do not finally encourage us to wish other choices on him or to dwell at length on the selfhood he has lost. The choice and its outcome are far more complex in *Julius Caesar*, where becoming oneself by becoming one's ancestral father necessitates killing off—literally, not symbolically—a much more ambiguously powerful father than Falstaff. Brutus is pushed toward conspiracy partly by his desire to live up to the image of his great ancestor and namesake, Junius Brutus, the slayer of tyrants (see, for example, 1.2.158; 1.3.82, 146; 2.1.53, 322). But immediately after Brutus has killed the man whom he himself sees as "the foremost man of all this world" (4.2.22), his enabling ancestral father drops out of the play; reference to him entirely disappears. In place of this father, the figure of Caesar increasingly comes to loom like a paternal ghost over the play, obliterating the memory of the heroic father on whom Brutus had hoped to found his selfhood. This interchange of fathers neatly poses one aspect of Brutus's tragic dilemma: Brutus kills one father apparently to satisfy the wishes of another, only to discover that he has slain the wrong father, that the dead father is not only more powerful but more powerfully his; only in killing Caesar—only as Caesar says "Et tu, Brutus?"—does he come to realize his position as Caesar's son and hence to suffer the disabling guilt that is the consequence of parricide.[2]

The triangulated choice between two fathers that is characteristic of these plays is at the center of *Hamlet*; hence, as in the earlier plays, assuming masculine identity means taking on the qualities of the father's name— becoming a Henry, a Brutus, or a Hamlet—by killing off a false father. Moreover, the whole weight of the play now manifestly creates one father true and the other false. Nonetheless, the choice is immeasurably more difficult for Hamlet than for his predecessors; for despite their manifest differences,

[2]Shakespeare generalizes this guilt by suppressing the rumor that Brutus was Caesar's illegitimate son; *2 Henry VI* testifies to his knowledge of it ("Brutus' bastard hand / Stabbed Julius Caesar," 4.1.137–38). *Hamlet* has often been understood as a reworking of the father-son conflict of the histories and Julius Caesar.

the fathers in *Hamlet* keep threatening to collapse into one another, annihilating in their collapse the son's easy assumption of his father's identity. The initiating cause of this collapse is Hamlet's mother: her failure to serve her son as the repository of his father's ideal image by mourning him appropriately is the symptom of her deeper failure to distinguish properly between his father and his father's brother.[3] Even at the start of the play, before the ghost's crucial revelation, Gertrude's failure to differentiate has put an intolerable strain on Hamlet by making him the only repository of his father's image, the only agent of differentiation in a court that seems all too willing to accept the new king in place of the old. Her failure of memory—registered in her undiscriminating sexuality—in effect defines Hamlet's task in relation to his father as a task of memory: as she forgets, he inherits the burden of differentiating, of idealizing and making static the past; hence the ghost's insistence on remembering (1.5.33, 91) and the degree to which Hamlet registers his failure to avenge his father as a failure of memory (4.4.40). Hamlet had promised the ghost to remember him in effect by becoming him, letting his father's commandment live all alone within his brain; but the intensity of Hamlet's need to idealize in the face of his mother's failure makes his father inaccessible to him as a model, hence disrupts the identification from which he could accomplish his vengeance. As his memory of his father pushes increasingly in the direction of idealization, Hamlet becomes more acutely aware of his own distance from that idealization and hence of his likeness to Claudius,[4] who is defined chiefly by his difference from his father. Difference from the heroic ideal represented in Old Hamlet becomes the defining term common to Claudius and Hamlet: the very act of distinguishing Claudius from his father—"no more like my father / Than I to Hercules" (1.2.152–53)—forces Hamlet into imaginative identification with Claudius. The intensity of Hamlet's need to differentiate between true father and false thus confounds itself, disabling his identification with his father and hence his secure identity as son.

If Gertrude's presence in *Hamlet* undoes the strategy by which father-son relations are protected in the Lancastrian tetralogy and in *Julius Caesar*, it simultaneously undoes the strategy that protects sexual relations in the

---

[3]See René Girard ("Hamlet's Dull Revenge," in *Literary Theory / Renaissance Texts*, ed. Patricia Parker and David Quint [Baltimore, Md.: Johns Hopkins University Press, 1986], pp. 280–302) and especially Joel Fineman ("Fratricide and Cuckoldry: Shakespeare's Doubles," in *Representing Shakespeare*, ed. Murray M. Schwartz and Coppélia Kahn [Baltimore, Md.: Johns Hopkins University Press, 1980], pp. 86–91) for the threat of collapse into No Difference. In Girard's reading, Old Hamlet and Claudius are the enemy twins between whom there is never any difference; Hamlet consequently has to try to make a difference where none exists and then to fire up his dull revenge mimetically when that difference cannot be sustained.

[4]This is the likeness registered stunningly, for example, in Hamlet's "How stand I then, / That have a father kill'd, a mother stain'd" (4.4.56–57), where *have* can indicate either possession or action. This likeness is the staple of most oedipal readings of the play, in which—in Ernest Jones's formulation—Claudius "incorporates the deepest and most buried part of [Hamlet's] own personality" (*Hamlet and Oedipus*, p. 100).

romantic comedies: in *Hamlet*, both kinds of relationship are in effect contaminated by their relocation in the presence of the mother. Maternal absence is as striking in these comedies as in the tetralogy. And if, in the histories, this absence functions to enable the son's assumption of his father's identity, here it functions to protect comic possibility itself by sustaining the illusion that the endlessly appealing girls of the comedies will never become fully sexual women and hence will never lose their androgynous charm: having no mothers, they need not become mothers. Despite the degree to which marriage is the ostentatious goal of Shakespeare's romantic comedies, these plays rarely look forward to the sexual consummation that seals marriage; even *A Midsummer Night's Dream* does so only in the context of a series of magical protections against danger. The comedies tend rather to deflect attention away from female sexuality through a variety of devices: through a comic closure that defers consummation, through the heroine's sometimes unresolved transvestitism or allusion to the male actor who will remain when the play is over and costumes are removed, even through the insistent cuckoldry jokes—jokes that serve both to deflect the imagined sexual act away from the male wooer and to defer it into indefinite future, where, as Lavatch will say in a different mood, "the knaves come to do that for me which I am aweary of" (*All's Well*, 1.3.41). The absence of fully imagined female sexuality is, I think, what enables the holiday tone of these plays; that sexuality is for Shakespeare the stuff of tragedy, not comedy.

The female sexuality largely absent from the comedies invades *Hamlet* in the person of Gertrude, and, once there, it utterly contaminates sexual relationship, disabling holiday. In her presence, Hamlet sees his task as the disruption of marriage itself: "I say we will have no mo marriage," (3.1.149) he says to Ophelia as she becomes contaminated in his eyes, subject to the same "frailty" that names his mother.[5] As he comes to identify himself with his cuckolded father—his "imaginations are as foul / As Vulcan's stithy" (3.2.83–84)—he can think of Ophelia only as a cuckold-maker, like his mother: "if thou wilt needs marry, marry a fool; for wise men know well enough what monsters you make of them" (3.1.139–41). Moreover, Ophelia fuses with Gertrude not only as potential cuckold-maker but also as potential mother:

> Get thee to a nunnery. Why, wouldst thou be a breeder of sinners? I am myself indifferent honest, but yet I could accuse me of such things that it were better my mother had not borne me. (3.1.121–24)

The implicit logic is: why would you be a breeder of sinners like me? In the gap between "breeder of sinners" and "I," Gertrude and Ophelia momentarily collapse into one figure. It is no wonder that there can be no more marriage: Ophelia becomes dangerous to Hamlet insofar as she becomes identified in

---

[5]Ophelia's contamination by association has been a commonplace of *Hamlet* criticism for a long time.

his mind with the contaminating maternal body, the mother who has borne him.

Hamlet thus redefines the son's position between two fathers by relocating it in relation to an indiscriminately sexual maternal body that threatens to annihilate the distinction between the fathers and hence problematizes the son's paternal identification; at the same time, the play conflates the beloved with this betraying mother, undoing the strategies that had enabled marriage in the comedies. The intrusion of the adulterous mother thus disables the solutions of history and comedy as Shakespeare has imagined them; in that sense, her presence initiates tragedy. But how can we understand the mother whose presence has the capacity to undermine the accommodations to which Shakespeare had come? Why should the first mother powerfully present in Shakespeare since the period of his earliest works be portrayed as adulterous? Why should her adulterous presence coincide with the start of Shakespeare's great tragic period?

Given her centrality in the play, it is striking how little we know about Gertrude; even the extent of her involvement in the murder of her first husband is left unclear. We may want to hear her shock at Hamlet's accusation of murder—"Almost as bad, good mother, / As kill a king and marry with his brother" (3.4.28–29)—as evidence of her innocence;[6] but the text permits us to hear it alternatively as shock either at being found out or at Hamlet's rudeness. The ghost accuses her at least indirectly of adultery[7] and incest— Claudius is "that incestuous, that adulterate beast" (1.5.42)—but he neither accuses her of nor exonerates her from the murder. For the ghost, as for Hamlet, her chief crime is her uncontrolled sexuality; that is the object of their moral revulsion, a revulsion as intense as anything directed toward the murderer Claudius. But the Gertrude we see is not quite the Gertrude they see. And when we see her in herself, apart from their characterizations of her, we tend to see a woman more muddled than actively wicked; even her famous sensuality is less apparent than her conflicted solicitude both for her new husband and for her son.[8] She is capable from the beginning of a certain guilty

6Most apparently do: see, for example, Bradley (*Shakespearean Tragedy*, p.136), Wilson (*What Happened in Hamlet?*, pp. 251–53), Bertram Joseph (*Conscience and the King: A Study of Hamlet* [London: Chatto and Windus, 1953], p. 94), and Carolyn Heilbrun ("The Character of Hamlet's Mother").

7Ever since Joseph (*Conscience and the King*, p. 17–18) pointed out that "adulterate" in Shakespeare's time could apply to sexual sin generally, not just to what we moderns narrowly call adultery, critics have cautioned against assuming that Gertrude and Claudius were adulterous in our sense.

8See Smith's fine discussion of the discrepancy between the monstrously sensual Gertrude portrayed by Hamlet, the ghost, and many critics, and the "careful mother and wife" Gertrude appears to be in her brief appearances on stage ("A Heart Cleft in Twain," pp. 194–201); R. A. Foakes notes specifically that Hamlet's attack in 3.4 "proceeds more from his imagination than from anything the audience has seen or heard" ("Character and Speech in 'Hamlet,'" in *Shakespeare Institute Studies: Hamlet*, ed. John Russell Brown and Bernard Harris [New York: Schocken Books, 1963], p. 158).

insight into Hamlet's suffering ("I doubt it is no other but the main, / His father's death and our o'er-hasty marriage" [2.2.56–57]). Insofar as she follows Hamlet's instructions in reporting his madness to Claudius (3.4.189–90; 4.1.7), she seems to enact every son's scenario for the good mother, choosing his interests over her husband's. But she may of course believe that he is mad and think that she is reporting accurately to her husband; certainly her courageous defense of her husband in their next appearance together—where she bodily restrains Laertes, as 4.5.122 specifies—suggests that she has not wholly adopted Hamlet's view of Claudius. Here, as elsewhere, the text leaves crucial aspects of her action and motivation open.[9] Even her death is not quite her own to define. Is it a suicide designed to keep Hamlet from danger by dying in his place?[10] She knows that Claudius has prepared the cup for Hamlet, and she shows unusual determination in disobeying Claudius's command not to drink it ("Gertrude, do not drink. / I will, my lord" [5.2.294–95]). In her last moment, her thoughts seem to be all for Hamlet; she cannot spare Claudius even the attention it would take to blame him ("O my dear Hamlet! / The drink, the drink! I am poison'd" [5.2.315–16]). Muddled, fallible, fully human, she seems ultimately to make the choice that Hamlet would have her make. But even here she does not speak clearly; her character remains relatively closed to us.

The lack of clarity in our impressions of Gertrude contributes, I think, to the sense that the play lacks, in Eliot's famous phrase, an "objective correlative."[11] For the character of Gertrude as we see it becomes for Hamlet—and for *Hamlet*—the ground for fantasies quite incongruent with it; although she is much less purely innocent than Richard III's mother, like that mother she becomes the carrier of a nightmare that is disjunct from her characterization as a specific figure. This disjunction is, I think, the key to her role in the play and hence to her psychic power: her frailty unleashes for Hamlet, and for Shakespeare, fantasies of maternal malevolence, of maternal spoiling, that are compelling exactly as they are out of proportion to the character we know,

---

[9]Bradley (*Shakespearean Tragedy*, p. 137), Joseph (*Conscience and the King*, pp. 96–97), and Putzel ("Queen Gertrude's Crime," p. 43) think that Gertrude repents and gives her allegiance to Hamlet; Eleanor Prosser (*Hamlet and Revenge* [Stanford, Calif.: Stanford University Press, 1967], p. 196), Baldwin Maxwell ("Hamlet's Mother," *Shakespeare Quarterly* 15 [1964]: 242), and Smith ("A Heart Cleft in Twain," p. 205) think that she is unchanged.

[10]Gertrude drinks the cup knowingly in Olivier's *Hamlet.*

[11]T. S. Eliot, "Hamlet," *Selected Essays* (New York: Harcourt Brace, 1932), p. 124. In Eliot's view, the discrepancy between Gertrude and the disgust she arouses in Hamlet is the mark of "some stuff that the writer could not drag to light, contemplate, or manipulate into art" (p. 123) and hence of artistic failure; but, in concluding that Gertrude needs to be insignificant to arouse in Hamlet "the feeling which she is incapable of representing" (p. 125), he inadvertently suggests the aesthetic power of fantasy disengaged from its adequate representation in a single character. For a brilliant analysis of the way in which the feminine stands for the failure of all kinds of representational stability in Eliot's aesthetic, in various psychoanalytic attempts to master the play, and in *Hamlet* itself as the representative of Western tradition, see Jacqueline Rose, "Hamlet—the *Mona Lisa* of Literature," *Critical Quarterly* 28 (1986): 35–49.

exactly as they seem therefore to reiterate infantile fears and desires rather than an adult apprehension of the mother as a separate person.

These fantasies begin to emerge as soon as Hamlet is left alone on stage:

> O that this too too sullied flesh would melt,
> Thaw and resolve itself into a dew,
> Or that the Everlasting had not fix'd
> His canon 'gainst self-slaughter. O God! God!
> How weary, stale, flat, and unprofitable
> Seem to me all the uses of this world!
> Fie on't, ah fie, 'tis an unweeded garden
> That grows to seed; things rank and gross in nature
> Possess it merely. That it should come to this!
> But two months dead . . .
>
> (1.2.129–38)

This soliloquy establishes the initial premises of the play, the psychic conditions that are present even before Hamlet has met with the ghost and has been assigned the insupportable task of vengeance. And what Hamlet tells us in his first words to us is that he feels his own flesh as sullied and wishes to free himself from its contamination by death, that the world has become as stale and unusable to him as his own body, and that he figures all this deadness and staleness and contamination in the image of an unweeded garden gone to seed—figures it, that is, in the familiar language of the fall. And he further tells us that this fall has been caused not by his father's death, as both Claudius and Gertrude seem to assume in their conventional consolations, but by his mother's remarriage,[12] the "this" he cannot specify for fourteen lines, the "this" that looms over the soliloquy, not quite nameable and yet radically present, making his own flesh—"this . . . flesh"—dirty, disrupting his sense of the ongoing possibility of life even as it disrupts his syntax.

Hamlet's soliloquy is in effect his attempt to locate a point of origin for the staleness of the world and his own pull toward death, and he discovers this point of origin in his mother's body. He tells us that the world has been transformed into an unweeded garden, possessed by things rank and gross, because his mother has remarried. And if the enclosed garden—the garden unpossessed—traditionally figures the Virgin Mother, this garden, full of seed, figures his mother's newly contaminated body: its rank weeds localize what Hamlet will later call the "rank corruption" of her sexuality (3.4.150–51), the "weeds" that will grow "ranker" if that sexuality is not curbed (3.4.153–54).[13] In this highly compacted and psychologized version of the fall, death is

---

[12]Critics of all sorts agree that Gertrude's remarriage disturbs Hamlet more profoundly than his father's death.

[13]*Rank* is evocative of sexual disgust in *Hamlet* and elsewhere in Shakespeare: Claudius's offense is "rank" (3.3.36); he and Gertrude live "in the rank sweat of an enseamed bed, / Stew'd in corruption" (3.4.92–93). For other uses of *rank*, see, for example, Desdemona's "will most rank"

the sexualized mother's legacy to her son: maternal sexuality turns the enclosed garden into the fallen world and brings death into that world by making flesh loathsome.[14] If Hamlet's father's death is the first sign of mortality, his mother's remarriage records the desire for death in his own sullied flesh. For in the world seen under the aegis of the unweeded garden, the very corporality of flesh marks its contamination: Hamlet persistently associates Claudius's fleshiness with his bloated sexuality—transforming the generalized "fatness of these pursy times" (3.4.155) into the image of the "bloat king" tempting his mother to bed (3.4.184)—as though in its grossness flesh was always rank, its solidness always sullied.[15]

The opening lines of the soliloquy point, I think, toward a radical confrontation with the sexualized maternal body as the initial premise of tragedy, the fall that brings death into the world: Hamlet in effect rewrites Richard III's sense that he has been spoiled in his mother's womb as the condition of mortality itself. The structure of *Hamlet*—and, I will argue, of the plays that follow from *Hamlet*—is marked by the struggle to escape from this condition, to free the masculine identity of both father and son from its origin in the contaminated maternal body. Hamlet's father's death is devastating to Hamlet—and to Shakespeare—partly, I think, because it returns Hamlet to this body, simultaneously unmaking the basis for the son's differentiation from the mother and the heroic foundation for masculine identity that Shakespeare had achieved in the histories.[16] As in a dream, the plot-conjunction of father's funeral and mother's remarriage expresses this return: it tells us that the idealized father's absence releases the threat of maternal sexuality, in effect subjecting the son to her annihilating power. But the dream-logic of this plot-conjunction is also reversible; if the father's death leads to the mother's sexualized body, the mother's sexualized body, I will argue, leads to the father's death. For the conjunction of funeral and marriage simultaneously expresses two sentences for the son: both "My idealized father's absence leaves me subject to my mother's overwhelming power," and "The discovery of my mother's sexuality kills my idealized father for me, making him

---

(*Othello*, 3.3.236) or Posthumus's description of the woman's part ("lust, and rank thoughts, hers, hers," *Cymbeline*, 2.4.176). Burgundy describes a France "corrupting in it own fertility," in which "the even mead . . . / Wanting the scythe, all uncorrected, rank, / Conceives by idleness" (*Henry V*, 5.2.40, 48–51); in its depiction of a monstrous female fecundity that is out of control, his "rank" is very close to Hamlet's unweeded garden.

[14]Hamlet's sexual disgust and allied hatred of the flesh have been widely recognized; see, for example, Knight (*The Wheel of Fire*, p. 23), Prosser (*Hamlet and Revenge*, p. 175), and especially L. C. Knights ("Prince Hamlet," *Scrutiny* 9 [1940–41]: 151; *An Approach to "Hamlet"* [London: Chatto and Windus, 1960], esp. pp. 50–60). Most trace his recoil from the flesh to his shock at his mother's sensuality: "Is he not . . . her very flesh and blood?" Granville-Barker asks (*Prefaces to Shakespeare*, p. 235).

[15]After giving the reasons for preferring Quarto 1 and 2's "sallied" (= sullied) to Folio's "solid," Jenkins concedes that Shakespeare may have intended a pun (see Arden *Hamlet*, pp. 436–37).

[16]In Bamber's formulation, "What we see in Hamlet is not the Oedipal drama itself but the unraveling of the resolution to the Oedipus complex," (*Comic Women, Tragic Men*, p. 156).

unavailable as the basis for my identity." This fantasy-conjunction thus defines the double task of Hamlet and of Shakespeare in the plays to come: if Hamlet attempts both to remake his mother an enclosed garden in 3.4 and to separate the father he idealizes from the rank place of corruption, Shakespearean tragedy and romance will persistently work toward the de-sexualization of the maternal body and the recreation of a bodiless father, untouched by her contamination.

A small psychological allegory at the beginning of the play—the exchange between Horatio and Marcellus about the ghost's disappearance—suggests what is at stake in this double task. The first danger in *Hamlet* is the father's "extravagant and erring spirit" (1.1.159), wandering in the night, the father who is—Horatio tells us—"like a guilty thing" (1.1.153).[17] As though in a kind of ghostly aubade, this father vanishes at the sound of the cock, who "with his lofty and shrillsounding throat / Awake[s] the god of day" (1.1.156–57). At the approach of the sun-god, the guilty father is banished; and Marcellus's christianizing expansion of this conjunction explicates his banishment:

> It faded on the crowing of the cock.
> Some say that ever 'gainst that season comes
> Wherein our Saviour's birth is celebrated,
> This bird of dawning singeth all night long;
> And then, they say, no spirit dare stir abroad,
> The nights are wholesome, then no planets strike,
> No fairy takes, nor witch hath power to charm,
> So hallow'd and so gracious is that time.
> (1.1.162–69)

Through an incipient pun, Marcellus transforms the god of day into the Son who makes the night wholesome because he is born from the mother's de-sexualized body; and the dangers he protects against are increasingly identified not only with the father's guilty spirit but with the dark female powers of the night. The sequence here—from guilty thing, to sun-god, to the Son whose birth banishes the witch—follows the logic of a purifying fantasy: the female body of the night can be cleansed only as the guilty father gives way to the sun-god, allowing for the emergence of the purified Son.[18]

The exchange between Horatio and Marcellus predicts both Hamlet's confrontation with the night-dangers of the female body and the fantasy-solution to that confrontation: it establishes the Son born of a bodiless father and a purified mother as the only antidote to her power. And it specifically predicts Hamlet's need to remake his father as Hyperion, his attempt to find a

---

[17]The sense that Old Hamlet is somehow guilty has been most vigorously registered through the suspicion that the ghost is up to no good, that he is—as Protestant theology would insist and as Hamlet himself suspects when it is convenient for him to do so—a diabolic agent conducing to damnation.

[18]See Erlich's similar reading of this passage as expressing the wish for a nonsexual birth that can defend against female danger (*Hamlet's Absent Father*, pp. 201–4).

safe basis for his own identity as son in the father he would remake pure. As though in response to this initial encounter with the impure father, the initial strategy of both Hamlet (in the soliloquy) and *Hamlet* is to split the father in two,[19] deflecting his guilt onto Claudius and reconstituting him in the form of the bodiless sun-god:

> That it should come to this!
> But two months dead—nay, not so much, not two—
> So excellent a king, that was to this
> Hyperion to a satyr.
>
>   (1.2.137–40)

The identification of Old Hamlet with Hyperion makes him benignly and divinely distant, separate from ordinary genital sexuality and yet immensely potent, his sexual power analogous to God's power to impregnate the Virgin Mother (often imaged as Spirit descending on the sun's rays) and to such Renaissance mythologizings of this theme as the operation of the sun on Chrysonogee's moist body (*The Faerie Queene*, 3.6.7). Ordinary genital sexuality then becomes the province of Claudius the satyr: below the human, immersed in the body, he becomes everything Hyperion/Old Hamlet is not, and the agent of all ill.

This work of splitting is already implicit in Hamlet's initial image of his mother's body as fallen garden, for that image itself makes a physiologically impossible claim: if Claudius's rank and gross possession now transforms the garden that is the mother's body, then it must not before have been possessed. Insofar as the soliloquy expresses Hamlet's sense of his mother's body as an enclosed garden newly breached, it implies the presence of a formerly unbreached garden; the alternatives that govern Hamlet's imagination of his mother's body are the familiar ones of virgin and whore, closed or open, wholly pure or wholly corrupt. And the insistence that the garden has just been transformed functions to exonerate his father, separating him from his mother's sexualized body: it is the satyr Claudius, not the sun-god father, who has violated the maternal space. Literalized in the plot, the splitting of the father thus evokes the ordinary psychological crisis in which the son discovers the sexuality of his parents, but with the blame handily shifted from father onto another man as unlike father as possible—and yet as like, hence his brother; in effect, the plot itself serves as a cover-up, legitimizing disgust at paternal sexuality without implicating the idealized father. But thus arbitrarily separated, these fathers are always prone to collapse back into one another. The failure to differentiate between Old Hamlet and Claudius is not only Gertrude's: the play frequently insists on their likeness even while positing

---

[19]The place of this dream-technique in the creation of Old Hamlet and Claudius was identified by Jones (*Hamlet and Oedipus*, p. 138) and Maud Bodkin (*Archetypal Patterns in Poetry* [London: Oxford University Press, 1934], pp. 13–14) and has since been widely accepted by psychoanalytic critics.

their absolute difference[20]; for the sexual guilt of the father—his implication in the mother's body—is its premise, its unacknowledged danger. Even Hamlet's attempt to imagine a protective father in the soliloquy returns him to this danger:

> So excellent a king, that was to this
> Hyperion to a satyr, so loving to my mother
> That he might not beteem the winds of heaven
> Visit her face too roughly. Heaven and earth,
> Must I remember? Why, she would hang on him
> As if increase of appetite had grown
> By what it fed on; and yet within a month—
> Let me not think on't . . .
>
> (1.2.139–46)

This image of parental love is so satisfying to Hamlet in part because it seems to enfold his mother safely within his father's protective embrace: by protecting her against the winds of heaven, he simultaneously protects against her, limiting and controlling her dangerous appetite. But as soon as that appetite has been invoked, it destabilizes the image of paternal control, returning Hamlet to the fact of his father's loss: for Gertrude's appetite is always inherently frightening, always potentially out of control; as the image of the unweeded garden itself implied, it has always required a weeder to manage its over-luxuriant growth.[21] The existence of Gertrude's appetite itself threatens the image of the father's godlike control; and in his absence, Gertrude's appetite rages, revealing what had been its potential for voraciousness all along. Having sated herself in a celestial bed, she now preys on garbage (1.5.55–57); and her indifferent voraciousness threatens to undo the gap between then and now, virgin and whore, Hyperion and satyr, on which Hamlet's defensive system depends. Despite the ghost's insistence on the difference, sating oneself in bed and preying on garbage sound suspiciously like the same activity: the imagery of devouring common to both tends to flatten out the distinction. "Could you on this fair mountain leave to feed / And batten on this moor?" Hamlet asks his mother (3.4.66–67), insisting again on a difference that seems largely without substance, inadvertently collapsing the distance between the idealized and the debased versions of Gertrude's appetite and hence between the brothers she feeds on. But in fact the strenuousness of the opposition between them has indicated their resemblance all along: what they have in common is an appetite for Gertrude's appetite; and her appetite can't tell the difference between them.

---

[20]Critics often note that Old Hamlet's crimes seem to be of the same kind as Claudius's.
[21]Elizabeth Abel first called my attention to the implicit presence of a controlling male gardener in Hamlet's image: since she has been a great help to me at virtually every stage of this book, it is a particular pleasure to record this specific debt to her.

The ghost's revelation of Gertrude's adultery is horrifying not only because it reveals that she has not been faithful to him—her rapid remarriage has already done that—but also because it threatens to undo the structure of difference that Hamlet has had to maintain in order to keep his father and Claudius apart. For if Gertrude's appetite for the two men is the same, then Old Hamlet is as fully implicated in her sexuality as Claudius. Hence in part Hamlet's shock when he meets the father he has idealized so heavily: when Old Hamlet appears to his son, not in his mind's idealizing eye (1.2.185) but in the dubious form of the ghost, he reveals not only Claudius's but also his own "foul crimes done in [his] days of nature" (1.5.12). The fathers Hamlet tries so strenuously to keep separated keep threatening to collapse into one another; even when he wants to kill one to avenge the other, he cannot quite tell them apart. In 3.3, on his way to his mother's closet, he comes across Claudius praying, a ready-made opportunity for revenge. But knowing that his father has committed foul crimes, and seeing Claudius praying, Hamlet becomes so unsure that there is an essential difference between them that he worries that God might send the wrong man to heaven. Even as he describes Claudius's murder of his father to himself, he conflates it imagistically with his father's crime: "A took my father grossly, full of bread, / With all his crimes broad blown, as flush as May" (3.3.80–81). Claudius's and Old Hamlet's crimes become equally broad-blown, as the two sinful fathers merge linguistically: the imagery of the rank garden, of over-luxuriant and swollen growth, has passed from Claudius to Old Hamlet, the "blossoms" of whose sin (1.5.76) are now broad-blown and flush. The highly charged word *grossly* registers this failure of differentiation: it hovers indeterminately between the two men, attaching itself first to Claudius (Claudius killed Old Hamlet grossly) and then to Old Hamlet (who died in a gross and unsanctified state); and in its indeterminancy, it associates both Claudius and Old Hamlet with the gross possession of Gertrude's unweeded garden.[22]

Ultimately Hyperion and the satyr refuse to stay separated, so that Hamlet—and *Hamlet*—have to do and redo the distinction over and over again. Whatever Hamlet's original intentions in approaching his mother in 3.4, his most immediate need after the crisis of differentiation in 3.3 is to force her to acknowledge the difference between the two fathers ("Hamlet, thou hast thy father much offended. / Mother, you have my father much offended" [3.4.8–9]). But even as he attempts to force this acknowledgment, he repeats the crisis of differentiation in yet another form. He presents her (and us) with two pictures initially indistinguishable and linguistically collapsed into one another: "Look here upon this picture, and on this, / The counterfeit presentment of two brothers" (3.4.53–54). As he begins the work of distinguishing between them all over again, the sense of counterfeit presentment becomes descriptive not only of the portraits as works of art but of his own portraiture, his own need both to present and to counterfeit these

---

[22]When "grossly" is glossed, editors generally apply it to Old Hamlet's spiritual state.

potentially similar false coins. Once again his father becomes a god, with "Hyperion's curls, the front of Jove himself, / An eye like Mars" (3.4.56–57); and Claudius becomes a "mildew'd ear / Blasting his wholesome brother" (3.4.64–65). But his words undermine the distinction he would reinstate: the most significantly contaminated ear in the play belongs to Old Hamlet.

Finally, the myth of his father as Hyperion cannot be sustained; and its collapse returns both father and son to the contaminated maternal body. No longer divinely inseminating, the sun-god becomes deeply implicated in matter in Hamlet's brutal parody of incarnation:

> *Hamlet:*   If the sun breed maggots in a dead dog, being a good kissing
> carrion—Have you a daughter?
> *Polonius:*   I have, my lord.
> *Hamlet:*   Let her not walk i' th' sun. Conception is a blessing, but as your
> daughter may conceive—friend, look to't.
>
> (2.2.181–86)[23]

Here is male spirit wholly enmeshed in female matter, kissing it, animating it with a vengeance; and—unlike the Son's—this conception is no blessing. If Marcellus's fantasy condenses father and son in a protective dyad, father and son here collapse into one another in their contamination: "Let her not walk i' th' sun," Hamlet warns Polonius; and his bitter pun locates the father-god's contamination in his own flesh. For this conception relocates the son in the dead matter of the unweeded garden: the horrific image of conception as the stirring of maggots in a corpse makes the son himself no more than one of the maggots, simultaneously born from and feeding on death in the maternal body.[24]

In the myth of origins bitterly acknowledged here, the son is wedded to death by his conception, spoiled by his origin in the rank flesh of the maternal body; and there is no idealized father to rescue him from this body. This fantasy of spoiling at the site of origin is, I think, the under-text of the play; it emerges first in muted form as Hamlet waits for the appearance of his ghostly father and meditates on the dram of evil that ruins the noble substance of man. When Hamlet hears the drunken revel of Claudius's court, he first fixes blame on Claudius for the sense of contamination he feels: "They clepe us drunkards, and with swinish phrase / Soil our addition" (1.4.19–20). But as he continues, his bodily language rewrites the source of contamination, increasingly relocating it in the female body. "Indeed, it takes / From our achievements, though perform'd at height, / The pith and marrow of our attribute"

[23]Given my reading of this passage, Warburton's famous emendation of *good* to *god* is nearly irresistible; but I have nonetheless resisted it, staying with the Arden's *good* on the grounds that the word does not, strictly speaking, require emendation.

[24]According to John E. Hankins, Hamlet is quite orthodox here; see his account of the Aristotelian and post-Aristotelian theories that made generation of all kinds dependent on putrifying matter ("Hamlet's 'God Kissing Carrion': A Theory of the Generation of Life," *PMLA* 64 [1949]: 507–16).

(1.4.20–22): through the imagery, the soiling of the male body—its pith and marrow emptied out at the height of performance—is grotesquely equated with intercourse and its aftermath.[25] And this shadowy image of the male body spoiled by the female in intercourse predicts the rest of the speech, where the role of spoiler is taken not by Claudius and his habits but by an unnamed and unspecified female body that corrupts man against his will:

> So, oft it chances in particular men
> That for some vicious mole of nature in them,
> As in their birth, wherein they are not guilty
> (Since nature cannot choose his origin),
>   . . . these men,
> Carrying, I say, the stamp of one defect,
> Being Nature's livery or Fortune's star,
> His virtues else, be they as pure as grace,
> As infinite as man may undergo,
> Shall in the general censure take corruption
> From that particular fault.
>
>   (1.4.23–36, *passim*)

As Hamlet imagines man struggling against his one defect—the mark of his bondage to a feminized Nature or Fortune—the origin he cannot choose increasingly becomes not only the site but the agent of corruption. Even as Hamlet unorthodoxly proclaims man not guilty in his birth, that is, he articulates his own version of original sin: here, as in Richard III's fantasy of himself deformed by Nature in his mother's womb (*3 Henry VI*, 3.2.153–64), man is spoiled in his birth by birth defects not of his own making, and he takes corruption from that particular fault.

Fall/fault/foutre: the complex bilingual pun registers the fantasy that moves under the surface of Hamlet's meditation. For *fault* allusively collapses the female genitals with the act of intercourse that engendered the baby there, and then collapses both with the fall and original sin[26]; through its punning formulations, original sin becomes literally the sin of origin.[27] "Virtue cannot so inoculate our old stock but we shall relish of it" (3.1.117–18): formed and

---

[25]"Marrow" is unusual in Shakespeare; three of its four other occurrences are in a sexual context (see *All's Well*, where Parolles cautions Bertram against "spending his manly marrow" in the arms of his kicky-wicky [2.3.276–77]; see also "Venus and Adonis," l. 142, and *3 Henry VI*, 3.2.125).

[26]See John H. Astington, " 'Fault' in Shakespeare," *Shakespeare Quarterly* 36 (1985): 330–4, for *fault* as a slang term for the female genitals; he does not note its use in this passage. But *fault* could apparently carry the more general suggestion of sexual intercourse as well: as the language lesson in *Henry V* makes clear, French *foutre* was available to corrupt good English words (3.4.47–49), and Shakespeare routinely takes advantage of this potentiality in his use of *fault*.

[27]Critics often portray Hamlet's world as infected by original sin (see, e.g., West, *The Court and the Castle*, p. 28; Levin, *The Question of Hamlet*, p. 58; Robert B. Bennett, "Hamlet and the Burden of Knowledge," *Shakespeare Studies* 15 [1982]: 77–97; Donald V. Stump, "Hamlet, Cain and Abel, and the Pattern of Divine Providence," *Renaissance Papers* 1985 [The Southern Renaissance Conference], pp. 29–30.

deformed in his mother's womb, man takes his corruption from that particular fault. Hamlet is indeed "to the manner born" (1.4.15), as he says at the start of his meditation: "It were better my mother had not borne me," he tells Ophelia (3.1.123–24); but he is "subject to his birth"(1.3.18).[28]

This subjection of male to female is, I think, the buried fantasy of *Hamlet*, the submerged story that it partly conceals and partly reveals; in its shift of contaminating agency from Claudius to the female body as the site of origin, Hamlet's meditation seems to me to be diagnostic of this fantasy. The poisoning of Old Hamlet is ostentatiously modeled on Cain's killing of Abel; Claudius cannot allude to his offense without recalling "the primal eldest curse upon't" (3.3.37). But this version of Cain and Abel turns out in part to be a cover for the even more primal story implicit in the unweeded garden, the prior explanation for the entrance of death into the world: the murder here turns not on the winning of a father's favor but on the body of a woman; and Old Hamlet is poisoned in his orchard-garden (1.5.35; 3.2.255) by the "serpent" who wears his crown (1.5.39).[29] On the surface of the text, that is, the story of Adam and Eve has been displaced, the horrific female body at its center occluded: Eve is conspicuously absent from the Cain-and-Abel version of the fall. But if the plot rewrites the fall as a story of fratricidal rivalry, locating literal agency for the murder in Claudius, a whole network of images and associations replaces his literal agency with Gertrude's, replicating Eve in her by making her both the agent and the locus of death. Beneath the story of fratricidal rivalry is the story of the woman who conduces to death, of the father fallen not through his brother's treachery but through his subjection to this woman; and despite Gertrude's conspicuous absence from the scene in the garden, in this psychologized version of the fall, the vulnerability of the father—and hence of the son—to her poison turns out to be the whole story.[30]

In an astonishing transfer of agency from male to female, malevolent power and blame for the murder tend to pass from Claudius to Gertrude in the deep fantasy of the play.[31] We can see the beginnings of this shift of blame even in the Ghost's initial account of the murder, in which the emotional weight shifts rapidly from his excoriation of Claudius to his much more powerful condemnation of Gertrude's sexuality. And in "The Murder of Gonzago," Hamlet's

[28]Without noting the pun on *fault* or the allusion to original sin, Erlich comes to a similar conclusion about this passage; see his use of it to explicate the "to be or not to be" soliloquy as a meditation on whether or not to be born (*Hamlet's Absent Father*, esp. pp. 182–85).

[29]The allusion to the fall in garden and serpent is commonly recognized (see, e.g., Arthur M. Eastman, "*Hamlet* in the Light of the Shakespearean Canon" in *Perspectives on Hamlet*, ed. William G. Holzberger and Peter B. Waldeck [Lewisburg, Pa.: Bucknell University Press, 1975], p. 53.

[30]Few critics share Flatter's conviction that Gertrude was literally complicit in Old Hamlet's murder (see note 6), but some note the sense of murderous culpability nonetheless associated with her; they attribute it to her (naturalistically conceived) failure to love her husband enough.

[31]The shift of blame from male to female that is the subtext of *Hamlet* is modeled in little by the Player's speech on the death of Priam, where the strumpet Fortune stands in for Pyrrhus at the critical moment of the murder (2.2.488–89).

version of his father's tale, the murderer's role is clearly given less emphasis than the Queen's: Lucianus gets a scant six lines, while her protestations of undying love motivate all the preceding dialogue of the playlet. Moreover, while the actual murderer remains a pasteboard villain, the Queen's protestations locate psychic blame for the murder squarely in her. "None wed the second but who kill'd the first," she tells us (3.2.175). In her formulation, remarriage itself is a form of murder: "A second time I kill my husband dead, / When second husband kisses me in bed" (3.2.179–80). We know that Hamlet has added some dozen or sixteen lines to the play (2.2.535), and although we cannot specify them, these protestations seem written suspiciously from the point of view of the child, whose mother's remarriage often seems like her murder of the image of his father. When Hamlet confronts his mother in her closet immediately after his playlet, he confirms that he at least has shifted agency from Claudius to her: his own killing of Polonius is, he says, "A bloody deed. Almost as bad, good Mother, / As kill a king and marry with his brother" (3.4.28–29). Given the parallel with his killing of Polonius, "as kill a king" first seems to describe Claudius's act; but when the line ends with "brother" rather than "queen" or "wife," the killing attaches itself irrevocably to Gertrude, playing out in miniature the shift of agency from him to her. For Claudius's crime is nearly absent here: in Hamlet's accusation, Claudius becomes the passive victim of Gertrude's sexual will; she becomes the active murderer.

And the play itself is complicit with Hamlet's shift of agency: although the degree of her literal guilt is never specified, in the deep fantasy of the play her sexuality itself becomes akin to murder. The second of the Player Queen's protestations—"A second time I kill my husband dead / When second husband kisses me in bed"—implicitly collapses the two husbands into one and thus makes the equation neatly: when her husband kisses her, she kills him. But this is in fact what one strain in the imagery has been telling us all along. As Lucianus carries the poison onstage in "The Murder of Gonzago," he addresses it in terms that associate it unmistakably with the weeds of that first unweeded garden:

> Thou mixture rank, of midnight weeds collected,
> With Hecate's ban thrice blasted, thrice infected,
> Thy natural magic and dire property
> On wholesome life usurps immediately.
>   (3.2.251–54)

Even as we see him poison the Player-King, the language insists that the poison is not his but hers, its usurpation on wholesome life derivative not from Claudius's political ambitions but from the rank weeds (3.4.153–54) of Gertrude's body. Its "mixture rank" merely condenses and localizes the rank mixture that is sexuality itself[32]:—hence the subterranean logic by which the effects of Claudius's poison on Old Hamlet's body replicate the effects of venereal disease, covering his smooth body with the lazarlike tetter, the "vile and loathsome crust" (1.5.71–72) that was one of the diagnostic signs of syphilis.[33]

In Lucianus's words, the poison that kills Old Hamlet becomes less the distillation of a usurping fratricidal rivalry than the distillation of the horrific female body, the night-witch against whom Marcellus had invoked the protection of the Saviour born from a virgin birth; cursed by Hecate, it is in effect the distillation of midnight itself, the "witching time" when "hell itself breathes out / Contagion to this world" (3.2.379–81). The play here invokes the presence of an unbounded nightmare night-body, breathing out the contagion of her poison; and it gives shape to this horrific night-body through a curious and punning repetition. Horatio tells Hamlet that the ghost first appeared "in the dead waste and middle of the night" (1.2.198); and Hamlet repeats his phrase when he questions Rosencranz and Guildenstern about their relations with the lady Fortune:

Hamlet:	Then you live about her waist, or in the middle of her favors?
Guildenstern:	Faith, her privates we.
Hamlet:	In the secret parts of Fortune? O, most true! She is a strumpet.

(2.2.232–36)

"Waste" and "waist" coalesce in the dangerous middle of this strumpet[34]; and the idealized father turns out to be horribly vulnerable to the poison of her rank midnight weeds. For however mild-mannered Gertrude may be as a literal character, in fantasy she takes on the aspect of this night-body, herself becoming the embodiment of hell and death: the fires in which Hamlet's father is confined, the fires that burn and purge the foul crimes done in his days of nature (1.5.11–13), merely reproduce the fire of the "rebellious hell" that burns in her bones (3.4.82–88).[35] In anticipation of Lear's anatomy— "there's hell, there's darkness, / There's the sulphurous pit" (*King Lear*, 4.6.129–30)—punishment and crime coalesce: death is not only the consequence of sexuality but also its very condition.

---

[32]See Kay Stockholder (*Dream Works: Lovers and Families in Shakespeare's Plays* [Toronto: University of Toronto Press, 1987], pp. 52–53) for a similar formulation.

[33]Skin eruptions of the sort the ghost describes were one of the symptoms of syphilis (see James Cleugh, *Secret Enemy: The Story of a Disease* [London: Thames and Hudson, 1954], pp. 46–50).

[34]See Erlich's similar speculations on this pun (*Hamlet's Absent Father*, pp. 62–63).

[35]The descriptions of hell and of Gertrude's body coalesce in the burning characteristic of venereal disease; see Timon ("Be strong in whore, allure him, burn him up" [4.3.143]) and especially Thersites ("Lechery, lechery, still wars and lechery! . . . A burning devil take them!" [*Troilus*, 5.2.193–95]). For the female genitals as burning hell, see Booth, *Shakespeare's Sonnets*, pp. 499–500.

This anatomy is in its own way perfectly orthodox; it condenses the story of the fall by making female sexuality itself the locus of death:

> Surely her house tendeth to death, & her paths unto the dead. All thei that go unto her, returne not againe, nether take they holde of the waies of life.
>
> For she hathe caused manie to fall downe wounded, and the strong men are all slayne by her. Her house is the waie unto the grave, which goeth downe to the chambers of death.
>
> (*The Geneva Bible*, Proverbs, 2:18–19; 7:26–27)

Every encounter with the "strange woman" of Proverbs—and all women are sexually strangers—is thus a virtual reliving of the fall into mortality. But female sexuality in *Hamlet* is always maternal sexuality: Gertrude's is the only fully sexualized female body in the play, and we experience her sexuality largely through the imagination of her son. In *Hamlet*, that is, Shakespeare re-understands the orthodox associations of woman with death by fusing the sexual with the maternal body, re-imagining the legacy of death consequent upon the fall as the legacy specifically of the sexualized maternal body. And except in the saving case of the Virgin Mother, the maternal body is always already sexual, corrupted by definition. The mother's body brings death into the world because her body itself is death: in the traditional alignment of spirit and matter, the mother gives us the stuff—the female matter—of our bodies and thus our mortality.[36] Birth itself thus immerses the body in death: hence the power of Hamlet's grotesque version of conception as the stirring of maggots in dead matter. Through this fusion of the sexual with the maternal body and the association of both with death, Shakespeare in effect defamiliarizes the trope of the "womb of earth" (1.1.140): death and sexuality are interchangeable in this psychologized version of the fall because both lead back to this maternal body. Hence also Shakespeare's punning equation of death and the maternal body in his reformulation of the Biblical source of danger: in the deep fantasy of the play, the deadly woman of *Proverbs*—"thei that go unto her, returne not againe"—is one with Hamlet's "undiscover'd country, from whose bourn / No traveller returns" (3.1.79–80).[37]

Both death and sexuality return the traveler to the undiscovered country, familiar and yet utterly foreign, of the maternal body itself; and in *Hamlet*, this body is always threatening to swallow up her children, to absorb them back within her bourn, undoing their own boundaries. Death itself is a hell-

---

[36]An incipient pun on matter and *mater* seems to run just below the surface of *Hamlet*, emerging only when Hamlet wittily asks his mother, "Now, mother, what's the matter?" (3.4.7) and perhaps in the "baser matter" of 1.5.104 (Fred Crews long ago electrified a Berkeley colloquium by speculating on this latter possibility after a talk by Avi Erlich.)

[37]Hamlet's famous pun to Ophelia—"Do you think I meant country matters?" (3.2.115)— clarifies the use of "country" here. Erlich first called my attention to this pun in the soliloquy (see *Hamlet's Absent Father*, p. 188; and see the same page, and Booth, *Shakespeare's Sonnets*, p. 526, for the possibility that the *conscience* that makes cowards of us all (3.1.83) similarly puns on the female genitals.

mouth, swallowing Old Hamlet up between its "ponderous and marble jaws" (1.4.50), bringing him and Polonius "not where he eats, but where a is eaten" (4.3.19), where all are subject to "my Lady Worm" (5.1.87); and Gertrude is death's mouth, indiscriminately devouring her husbands "as if increase of appetite had grown / By what it fed on" (1.2.144–45). In this grotesquely oral world, everything is ultimately meat for a single table. Hence I think the slight *frisson* of horror beneath Hamlet's wit as he describes "the funeral bak'd meats" that "Did coldly furnish forth the marriage tables" (1.2.180–81): we are never sure just what it is that is being consumed in the ceremonies of death and sexual union imagined here. And this momentary confusion is diagnostic of the play's fusion of eating and death and sex: in *Hamlet*, the turn toward the woman's body is always felt as the return to the devouring maternal womb, with all the potential not only for incestuous nightmare but for total annihilation implied by that return.

Hence, I think, the logic of the play's alternative name for poison: "union" (5.2.269, 331).[38] For "union" is just another version of Hecate's "mixture rank," the poison that kills Old Hamlet: each is the poisonous epitome of sexual mixture itself and hence of boundary danger, the terrifying adulteration of male by female that does away with the boundaries between them.

Hamlet: Farewell, dear Mother.
Claudius: Thy loving father, Hamlet.
Hamlet: My mother. Father and mother is man and wife, man and wife is one flesh; so my mother.

                                                        (4.3.52–55)

In this fantasy, it does not matter whether Hamlet is thinking of his father or of his incestuous stand-in; all sexuality—licit or illicit—is imagined as an adulterating mixture. And in this rank mixture, the female will always succeed in transforming the male, remaking him in her image, "for the power of beauty will sooner transform honesty from what it is to a bawd than the force of honesty can translate beauty into his likeness" (3.1.111–14). The imagined concourse of male honesty and female beauty ends in the contamination of the male by the female, his translation into a version of her. No wonder Marcellus associates the danger of invasion with the sweaty activity that makes "the night joint-labourer with the day" (1.1.81), obliterating the distinction between the realm of the witch-mother and that of the sungod father; no wonder Hamlet is so intent upon keeping his father's commandment—or perhaps his father himself—all alone within his brain, "unmix'd with baser matter" (1.5.104).[39]

---

[38]The pun associating the poison with marriage and sexual union has been noted at least since Bradley (*Shakespearean Tragedy*, p. 126); Faber sees in Hamlet's forcing Claudius to drink his "union" specifically the playing out of Hamlet's oral aggression ("Hamlet, Sarcasm and Psychoanalysis," p. 89).

[39]See note 36 for the pun on *mater*/matter.

For Hamlet is ultimately subject to the same adulterating mixture; the sexual anxiety registered through the play's two names for poison, like the incestuous marriage at its center, both covers and expresses a more primitive anxiety about the stability and security of individuating boundaries that finds its focus in Hamlet himself. Promiscuous mixture and boundary contamination everywhere infect this play, from its initial worry about invasion to its final heap of poisoned bodies: in a psychic world where boundaries cannot hold, where the self is invaded, its pales and forts broken down, its pith and marrow extracted, where mother-aunts and uncle-fathers (2.2.372) become indistinguishably one flesh, where even camels become weasels become whales (3.2.367–73), identity itself seems on the point of dissolving or being swallowed up. And the overwhelming use of images of oral contamination and oral annihilation to register these threats to the self suggests their origin in the earliest stages of emergent selfhood, when the nascent self is most fully subject to the mother's fantasied power to annihilate or contaminate. Hence, I think, the centrality of Gertrude: for the play localizes its pervasive boundary panic in Hamlet's relationship with his mother, whose contaminated body initially serves him as the metaphor for the fallen world that has sullied him. And the selfhood that Hamlet constructs in response to this threat becomes the crux of the play: withdrawing himself from the sullying maternal body of the world, Hamlet retreats into what he imagines as an inviolable core of selfhood that cannot be known or played upon (1.2.85; 3.2.355–63), constructing an absolute barrier between inner and outer as though there were no possibility of uncontaminating communication between them; unable to risk crossing this boundary in any creative way, through any significant action in the world, he fantasizes crossing it through magical thinking—imagining the revenge that could come "with wings as swift / As meditation" (1.5.29–30) or through the power of his horrid speech (2.2.557)–or he mimes crossing it from within the extraordinary distance of his withdrawal, taking up a variety of roles not to engage the world but to keep it at bay.[40] Hence in part his intense admiration for Horatio, who plays no roles and seems impervious to outer influence, who is "not a pipe for Fortune's finger / To sound what stop she please" (3.2.70–71)[41]; here as elsewhere, Hamlet figures the threat to (masculine) inner integrity as the sexualized female, aligning it with the strumpet Fortune in whose secret parts corrupt men live (2.2.232–36), as though all such threats were derivative from his unreliable mother's body. But there is

---

[40]In this paragraph, as elsewhere, I am drawing on ideas expressed by D. W. Winnicott in a series of essays on the interface between inner and outer in earliest infantile development, especially on the ways in which a developing core of selfhood can meet with a reliable world in a transitional zone that makes creative interaction between inner and outer possible, and on the ways in which this zone can be destroyed.

[41]See Erickson's account of Horatio's defensive function for Hamlet (*Patriarchal Structures*, pp. 66–80); in his account, the imperviousness of Horatio helps Hamlet to ward off the psychic demands of his overwhelming father (pp. 68–69) and allows Hamlet safely to replicate the affectionate bond he cannot have with his mother or Ophelia (pp. 74–78).

no exemption from this body for Hamlet, no pure and unmixed identity for him; like honesty transformed into a bawd, he must eventually see the signs of her rank mixture in himself:

> Why, what an ass am I! This is most brave,
> That I, the son of a dear father murder'd,
> Prompted to my revenge by heaven and hell,
> Must like a whore unpack my heart with words
> And fall a-cursing like a very drab,
> A scullion!
>
> (2.2.578–83)

He himself is subject to his birth: he would imagine himself the unmixed son of an unmixed father, but the whore-mother in him betrays him, returning him to his own mixed origin, his contamination by the sexual female within.[42]

The first mother to reappear in Shakespeare's plays is adulterous, I think, because maternal origin is in itself felt as equivalent to adulterating betrayal of the male, both father and son; *Hamlet* initiates the period of Shakespeare's greatest tragedies because it in effect rewrites the story of Cain and Abel as the story of Adam and Eve, relocating masculine identity in the presence of the adulterating female. This rewriting accounts, I think, for Gertrude's odd position in the play, especially for its failure to specify the degree to which she is complicit in the murder. Less powerful as an independent character than as the site for fantasies larger than she is, she is preeminently mother as other, the intimate unknown figure around whom these fantasies swirl. She is kept ambiguously innocent as a character, but in the deep fantasy that structures the play's imagery, she plays out the role of the missing Eve: her body is the garden in which her husband dies, her sexuality the poisonous weeds that kill him, and poison the world—and the self—for her son. This is the psychological fantasy registered by the simultaneity of funeral and marriage: the reappearance of the mother in *Hamlet* is tantamount to the death of the idealized father because that father is needed as a defense against her rank mixture, her capacity to annihilate or contaminate; as in Marcellus's purifying fantasy, what the idealized father ultimately protects against is the dangerous female powers of the night. The boy-child masters his fear of these powers partly through identification with his father, the paternal presence who has initially helped him to achieve separation from his mother; but if his father fails him—if the father himself seems subject to her—then that protective identification fails. This is exactly the psychological situation at the beginning of *Hamlet*, where Hamlet's father has become unavailable to him, not only through the fact of

---

[42]Critics who use the model of Freud's "Mourning and Melancholia" (see note 12) generally assume that the lost object is Hamlet's father; but Hamlet's discovery of the whore inside himself suggests that the lost, introjected, and then berated object is his mother.

his death but through the complex vulnerability that his death demonstrates. This father cannot protect his son; and his disappearance in effect throws Hamlet into the domain of the engulfing mother, awakening all the fears incident to the primary mother-child bond. Here as in Shakespeare's later plays, the loss of the father turns out in fact to mean the psychic domination of the mother: in the end, it is the specter of his mother, not his uncle-father, who paralyzes his will. The Queen, the Queen's to blame.

This shift of agency and of danger from male to female seems to me characteristic of the fantasy-structure of *Hamlet* and of Shakespeare's imagination in the plays that follow. The ghost's initial injunction sets as the prime business of the play the killing of Claudius; he specifically asks Hamlet to leave his mother alone, beset only by the thorns of conscience (1.5.85–87). But if Gertrude rather than Claudius is to blame, then Hamlet's fundamental task shifts; simple revenge is no longer the issue. Despite his ostensible agenda of revenge, the main psychological task that Hamlet seems to set himself is not to avenge his father's death but to remake his mother [43]: to remake her in the image of the Virgin Mother who could guarantee his father's purity, and his own, repairing the boundaries of his selfhood. Throughout the play, the covert drama of reformation vies for priority with the overt drama of revenge, in fact displacing it both from what we see of Hamlet's consciousness and from center stage of the play: when Hamlet accuses himself of lack of purpose (3.4.107–10), of failing to remember his father's business of revenge (4.4.40), he may in part be right. Even as an avenger, Hamlet seems motivated more by his mother than by his father: when he describes Claudius to Horatio as "he that hath kill'd my king and whor'd my mother" (5.2.64), the second phrase clearly carries more intimate emotional weight than the first. And he manages to achieve his revenge only when he can avenge his mother's death, not his father's: just where we might expect some version of "rest, perturbed spirit" to link his killing of Claudius with his father's initial injunction, we get "Is thy union here? / Follow my mother" (5.2.331–32).

This shift—from avenging the father to saving the mother—accounts in part for certain peculiarities about this play as a revenge play: why, for example, the murderer is given so little attention in the device ostensibly designed to catch his conscience, why the confrontation of Hamlet with Gertrude in the closet scene seems much more central, much more vivid, than any confrontation between Hamlet and Claudius. Once we look at "The

---

[43]In an attempt to preserve Hamlet's nobility, several critics have attributed his behavior in 3.4 to his high-minded and altogether selfless reformist impulses toward his mother (see, for example, Bradley, *Shakespearean Tragedy*, p. 115; Joseph *Conscience and the King*, pp. 95–97; Frye, *The Renaissance "Hamlet"*, pp. 152, 162); but Knights notes that he "seems intent not so much on exposing lust as on indulging an uncontrollable spite against the flesh" ("Prince Hamlet," p. 151). I would add that he shows very few signs of interest in his mother as a real person who might be won to repentance; in my view, she remains almost entirely a fantasy-object for him in this scene.

Murder of Gonzago" for what it is, rather than for what Hamlet tells us it is, it becomes clear that the playlet is in fact designed to catch the conscience of the queen: its challenge is always to her loving posture, its accusation "A second time I kill my husband dead / When second husband kisses me in bed." The confrontation with Gertrude (3.4) follows so naturally from this attempt to catch her conscience that Hamlet's unexpected meeting with Claudius (3.3) feels to us like an interruption of a more fundamental purpose. Indeed, Shakespeare stages 3.3 very much as an interruption: Hamlet comes upon Claudius praying as he is on his way to his mother's closet, worrying about the extent to which he can repudiate the Nero in himself; and we come upon Claudius unexpectedly in the same way. That is: the moment that should be the apex of the revenge plot—the potential confrontation alone of the avenger and his prey—becomes for the audience and for the avenger himself a lapse, an interlude that must be gotten over before the real business can be attended to.[44] It is no wonder that Hamlet cannot kill Claudius here: to do so would be to make of the interlude a permanent interruption of his more fundamental purpose. Not even Hamlet could reasonably expect to manage his mother's moral reclamation immediately after he has killed her husband.

Nor would that avenging death again regain the mother whom Hamlet needs: once his mother has been revealed as the fallen and possessed garden, she can be purified only by being separated from her sexuality. This separation is in fact Hamlet's effort throughout 3.4. In that confrontation, Hamlet first insists that Gertrude acknowledge the difference between Claudius and Old Hamlet, the difference her adultery and remarriage had undermined. But after the initial display of portraits, Hamlet attempts to induce in her revulsion not at her choice of the wrong man but at her sexuality itself, the rebellious hell that mutines in her matron's bones (3.4.82–83), the "rank corruption, mining all within" (3.4.150). Here, as in the play within the play, Hamlet recreates obsessively, voyeuristically, the acts that have corrupted the royal bed, even when he has to subject his logic and syntax to considerable strain to do so:

Queen: What shall I do?
Hamlet: Not this, by no means, that I bid you do;
         Let the bloat King tempt you again to bed,
         Pinch wanton on your cheek, call you his mouse,
         And let him, for a pair of reechy kisses,
         Or paddling in your neck with his damn'd fingers,
         Make you to ravel all this matter out
         That I essentially am not in madness,
         But mad in craft.
                             (3.4.182–90)

[44]As Charney notes, "Hamlet characteristically displaces the expected plot interest from the king . . . to his mother" in the middle of the play; the "crucial prayer scene occurs, as it were, in passing" ("The 'Now Could I Drink Hot Blood' Soliloquy," pp. 82–83).

There has to be an easier way of asking your mother not to reveal that your madness is an act. "Not this, by no means, that I bid you do": Hamlet cannot stop imagining, even commanding, the sexual act that he wants to undo. Moreover, the bloated body of this particular king is not particular to him: it is the sexualized male body, its act any sexual act. The royal bed of Denmark is always already corrupted, already a couch for luxury, as Hamlet's own presence testifies. "Go not to my uncle's bed" (3.4.161), Hamlet tells his mother; but his disgust at the incestuous liaison rationalizes a prior disgust at all sexual concourse, as his attempt to end the specifically incestuous union rationalizes an attempt to remake his mother pure by divorcing her from her sexuality.

Act 3 Scene 4 records Hamlet's attempt to achieve this divorce, to recover the fantasied presence of the a-sexual mother of childhood, the mother who can restore the sense of sanctity to the world her sexuality has spoiled: his first and last word in the scene is "Mother" (3.4.7; 3.4.219). And in his own mind at least, Hamlet does seem to achieve this recovery. He begins the scene by wishing that Gertrude were not his mother ("would it were not so, you are my mother" [3.4.15]); but toward the end, he is able to imagine her as the mother from whom he would beg—and receive—blessing:

> Once more, good night,
> And when you are desirous to be blest,
> I'll blessing beg of you.
>
> (3.4.172–74)

This mother can bless Hamlet only insofar as she herself asks to be blessed by him, signaling her conversion from husband to son and inverting the relation of parent and child; Hamlet is very much in charge even as he imagines asking for maternal blessing. Nonetheless, coming near the end of Hamlet's long scene of rage and disgust, these lines seem to me extraordinarily moving in their evocation of desire for the maternal presence that can restore the sense of the world and the self as blessed.[45] And the blessedness they image is specifically in the relation of world and self: as mother and son mirror each other, each blessing each, Shakespeare images the reopening of the zone of trust that had been foreclosed by the annihilating mother. For the first time, Hamlet imagines something coming to him from outside himself that will neither invade nor contaminate him: the recovery of benign maternal presence for a moment repairs the damage of the fall in him, making safe the boundary-permeability that had been a source of terror. Toward the end of the scene, all those night-terrors are gone: Hamlet's repeated variations on the conventional phrase "good night" mark his progression from rage at his mother's sexuality to repossession of the good mother he had lost. He begins with "Good night. But go not to my uncle's bed. . . . Refrain tonight"

---

[45]Although Barber does not specifically discuss this moment in *Hamlet*, my sense of the importance of the sacred as a psychic category in Shakespeare is greatly indebted to him.

(3.4.161, 167), attempting to separate her from her horrific night-body; but by the end—through his own version of Marcellus's purifying fantasy—he has succeeded in imagining both her and the night wholesome. If he begins by wishing Gertrude were not his mother, he ends with the poignant repeated leave-taking of a child who does not want to let go of the mother who now keeps him safe: "Once more, good night . . . so again, good night. . . . Mother, good night indeed. . . . Good night, Mother" (3.4.172, 179, 215, 219).

In the end, we do not know whether or not Gertrude herself has been morally reclaimed; it is the mark of the play's investment in Hamlet's fantasies that, even here, we are not allowed to see her as a separate person. To the extent that she looks into the heart that Hamlet has "cleft in twain" (3.4.158) and finds the "black and grained spots" (3.4.90) that he sees there, she seems to accept his version of her soiled inner body; in any case, her response allows him to think of his initial Nero-like aggression—speaking daggers though using none (3.2.387)—as moral reclamation. But as usual in this play, she remains relatively opaque, more a screen for Hamlet's fantasies about her than a fully developed character in her own right: whatever individuality she might have had is sacrificed to her status as mother. Nonetheless, though we might wonder just what his evidence is, Hamlet at least believes that she has returned to him as the mother he can call "good lady" (3.4.182). And after 3.4, her remaining actions are ambiguous enough to nourish his fantasy: although there are no obvious signs of separation from Claudius in her exchanges with him, in her last moments she seems to become a wonderfully homey presence for her son, newly available to him as the loving and protective mother of childhood, worrying about his condition, wiping his face as he fights, even perhaps intentionally drinking the poison intended for him.

In the end, whatever her motivation, he seems securely possessed of her as an internal good mother; and this possession gives him a new calm about his place in the world and especially about death, that domain of maternal dread. Trusting her, he can begin to trust in himself and in his own capacity for action; and he can begin to rebuild the masculine identity shattered by her contamination. For his secure internal possession of her idealized image permits the return of his father to him, and in the form that he had always wanted: turning his mother away from Claudius, Hamlet wins her not only for himself but also for his father—for his father conceived as Hyperion, the bodiless godlike figure he had invoked at the beginning of the play. If her sexuality had spoiled this father, her purification brings him back; after 3.4, the guilty father and his ghost disappear, replaced by the distant heavenly father into whom he has been transformed, the one now acting through the sign of the other: "Why, even in that was heaven ordinant. / I had my father's signet in my purse" (5.2.48–49). Unexpectedly finding this sign of the father on his own person, Hamlet in effect registers his repossession of the idealized father within; and, like a good son, Hamlet can finally merge himself with this father, making His will his own. But although we may feel that Hamlet has achieved a new calm and self-possession, the price is high: for the parents lost to him at the beginning of the play can be restored only insofar as they are entirely separated from their sexual bodies. This is a pyrrhic solution to the problems of embodiedness and familial identity; it does not bode well for Shakespeare's representation of sexual union, or of the children born of that union.

In creating for Hamlet a plot in which his mother's sexuality is literally the sign of her betrayal and of her husband's death, Shakespeare recapitulates the material of infantile fantasy, playing it out with a compelling plot logic that allows its expression in a perfectly rationalized, hence justified, way. Given Hamlet's world, anyone would feel as Hamlet does—but Shakespeare has given him this world.[46] And the world Shakespeare gives him sets the stage for the plays that follow[47]: from *Hamlet* on, all sexual relationships will be tinged by the threat of the mother, all masculine identity problematically formed in relationship to her. For despite Hamlet's tenuous recovery of his father's signet ring through the workings of Providence, the stabilizing father lost at the beginning of *Hamlet*—the father who can control female appetite, who can secure pure masculine identity for his son—cannot be brought back from the dead; the ambiguities that attend the bodiless father-Duke of *Measure for Measure* merely serve to make paternal absence visible, underscoring at once the need for his control over the sexuality that boils and bubbles like a witch's cauldron in Vienna and the desperate fictitiousness of that control. The plays that follow *Hamlet* enact and re-enact paternal absence in shadowy and fragmentary form—in the sick king of *All's Well*, in Lear's abdication, in the murder of Duncan, the fatherlessness of Coriolanus, the weakness of Cymbeline; and they thrust the son into the domain of maternal dread inhabited by all the avatars of strumpet fortune—the wicked wives, lovers, daughters, mothers and stepmothers, the witches and engulfing storms—that have the power to shake his manhood (*King Lear*, 1.4.306).

The central elements of the fantasy of maternal power in *Hamlet* will recur in a variety of forms, with first one and then another becoming most prominent; they will sometimes be the psychic property of a single character from whom Shakespeare distances himself, and sometimes find embodiment in the play as a whole in ways that suggest Shakespeare's complicity in them. Despite Shakespeare's sometimes astonishing moments of sympathetic en-

---

[46]See Meredith Skura's account of the ways in which Hamlet's world embodies (and hence justifies) what he feels (*The Literary Use of the Psychoanalytic Process* [New Haven, Conn.: Yale University Press, 1981], p. 47).

[47]See Eastman, "*Hamlet* in the Light of the Shakespearean Canon," for a striking explication of *Hamlet* via its exfoliations in *Othello* and *King Lear*; this essay anticipates my own formulations at several points (see esp. pp. 55–56, on Lear's vagina/hell-mouth, and p. 65, on the "deep desire for spiritual rapprochement" in the blessing of parent and child).

gagement with his female characters, his ability to see the world from their point of view, his women will tend to be like Gertrude, more significant as screens for male fantasy than as independent characters making their own claim to dramatic reality; as they become fused with the mother of infantile need, even their fantasized gestures of independence will be read as the signs of adulterous betrayal. And the women will pay heavily for the fantasies— both of destruction and of cure—invested in them. For their sexual bodies will always be dangerous, the sign of the fall and original sin, the "disease that's in my flesh" (*King Lear*, 2.4.224), "the imposition . . . / Hereditary ours" (*The Winter's Tale*, 1.2.73–74): as they enter into sexuality, the virgins— Cressida, Desdemona, Imogen—will be transformed into whores, their whoredom acted out in the imaginations of their nearest and dearest; and the primary antidote to their power will be the excision of their sexual bodies, the terrible revirginations that Othello performs on Desdemona, and Shakespeare on Cordelia. For the emergence of the annihilating mother in *Hamlet* will call forth a series of strategies for confining or converting her power. Hamlet's desire for the return of the virgin mother who can bless him, undoing the effects of the fall, will be played out in Cordelia's return to Lear, Thaisa's return to Pericles, Hermione's return to Leontes, each of whom must first suffer for her participation in sexuality. And in the absence of these purified figures, parthenogenetic fantasies of exemption from the "woman's part" (*Cymbeline*, 2.4.174) will seem to offer protection against maternal malevolence. Enunciating his desire to "stand / As if a man were author of himself / And knew no other kin" (*Coriolanus*, 5.3.36), Coriolanus speaks for all those who would not be born of woman (*Macbeth*, 4.1.80), undoing the subjection to birth that Hamlet discovered in himself. But the problematic maternal body can never quite be occluded or transformed: made into a monster or a saint, killed off or banished from the stage, it remains at the center of masculine subjectivity, marking its unstable origin. For the contaminated flesh of the maternal body is also home: the home Shakespeare's protagonists long to return to, the home they can never quite escape. . . .

Representing Ophelia: Women, Madness, and the Responsibilities of Feminist Criticism

Elaine Showalter

"As a sort of a come-on, I announced that I would speak today about that piece of bait named Ophelia, and I'll be as good as my word." These are the words which begin the psychoanalytic seminar on *Hamlet* presented in Paris in 1959 by Jacques Lacan. But despite his promising come-on, Lacan was *not* as good as his word. He goes on for some 41 pages to speak about Hamlet, and when he does mention Ophelia, she is merely what Lacan calls "the object Ophelia"—that is, the object of Hamlet's male desire. The etymology of Ophelia, Lacan asserts, is "O-phallus," and her role in the drama can only be to function as the exteriorized figuration of what Lacan predictably and, in view of his own early work with psychotic women, disappointingly suggests is the phallus as transcendental signifier.[1] To play such a part obviously makes Ophelia "essential," as Lacan admits, but only because, in his words, "she is linked forever, for centuries, to the figure of Hamlet."

The bait-and-switch game that Lacan plays with Ophelia is a cynical but not unusual instance of her deployment in psychiatric and critical texts. For most critics of Shakespeare, Ophelia has been an insignificant minor character in the play, touching in her weakness and madness but chiefly interesting, of course, in what she tells us about Hamlet. And while female readers of Shakespeare have often attempted to champion Ophelia, even feminist critics have done so with a certain embarrassment. As Annette Kolodny ruefully admits: "it is after all, an imposition of high order to ask the viewer to attend

From *Shakespeare and the Question of Theory*, ed. Patricia Parker and Geoffrey Hartman. (New York, Methuen, 1985), 77–94. Reprinted by permission. The illustrations that originally accompanied this essay have been omitted.

[1] Jacques Lacan, "Desire and the interpretation of desire in *Hamlet*," in *Literature and Psychoanalysis: The Question of Reading: Otherwise*, ed. Shoshana Felman (Baltimore, 1982), 11, 20, 23. Lacan is also wrong about the etymology of Ophelia, which probably derives from the Greek for "help" or "succour." Charlotte M. Yonge suggested a derivation from "ophis," "serpent." See her *History of Christian Names* (1884, republished Chicago, 1966), 346–7. I am indebted to Walter Jackson Bate for this reference.

to Ophelia's sufferings in a scene where, before, he's always so comfortably kept his eye fixed on Hamlet."[2]

Yet when feminist criticism allows Ophelia to upstage Hamlet, it also brings to the foreground the issues in an ongoing theoretical debate about the cultural links between femininity, female sexuality, insanity, and representation. Though she is neglected in criticism, Ophelia is probably the most frequently illustrated and cited of Shakespeare's heroines. Her visibility as a subject in literature, popular culture, and painting, from Redon who paints her drowning, to Bob Dylan, who places her on Desolation Row, to Cannon Mills, which has named a flowery sheet pattern after her, is in inverse relation to her invisibility in Shakespearean critical texts. Why has she been such a potent and obsessive figure in our cultural mythology? Insofar as Hamlet names Ophelia as "woman" and "frailty," substituting an ideological view of femininity for a personal one, is she indeed representative of Woman, and does her madness stand for the oppression of women in society as well as in tragedy? Furthermore, since Laertes calls Ophelia a "document in madness," does she represent the textual archetype of woman *as* madness or madness *as* woman? And finally, how should feminist criticism represent Ophelia in its own discourse? What is our responsibility towards her as character and as woman?

Feminist critics have offered a variety of responses to these questions. Some have maintained that we should represent Ophelia as a lawyer represents a client, that we should become her Horatia, in this harsh world reporting her and her cause aright to the unsatisfied. Carol Neely, for example, describes advocacy—speaking for Ophelia—as our proper role. "As a feminist critic," she writes, "I must 'tell' Ophelia's story."[3] But what can we mean by Ophelia's story? The story of her life? The story of her betrayal at the hands of her father, brother, lover, court, society? The story of her rejection and marginalization by male critics of Shakespeare? Shakespeare gives us very little information from which to imagine a past for Ophelia. She appears in only five of the play's twenty scenes; the pre-play course of her love story with Hamlet is known only by a few ambiguous flashbacks. Her tragedy is subordinated in the play; unlike Hamlet, she does not struggle with moral choices or alternatives. Thus another feminist critic, Lee Edwards, concludes that it is impossible to reconstruct Ophelia's biography from the text: "We can imagine Hamlet's story without Ophelia, but Ophelia literally has no story without Hamlet."[4]

If we turn from American to French feminist theory, Ophelia might confirm the impossibility of representing the feminine in patriarchal discourse

---

[2]Annette Kolodny, "Dancing through the minefield: some observations on the theory, practice, and politics of feminist literary criticism" (*Feminist Studies*, 6 [1980]),7.

[3]Carol Neely, "Feminist modes of Shakespearean criticism" (*Women's Studies*, 9 [1981]), 11.

[4]Lee Edwards, "The labors of Psyche" (*Critical Inquiry*, 6 [1979]), 36.

as other than madness, incoherence, fluidity, or silence. In French theoretical criticism, the feminine or "Woman" is that which escapes representation in patriarchal language and symbolism; it remains on the side of negativity, absence, and lack. In comparison to Hamlet, Ophelia is certainly a creature of lack. "I think nothing, my lord," she tells him in the Mousetrap scene, and he cruelly twists her words:

> Hamlet: That's a fair thought to lie between maids' legs.
> Ophelia: What is, my lord?
> Hamlet: Nothing.
>
>   (3.2.117–19)

In Elizabethan slang, "nothing" was a term for the female genitalia, as in *Much Ado About Nothing*. To Hamlet, then, "nothing" is what lies between maids' legs, for, in the male visual system of representation and desire, women's sexual organs, in the words of the French psychoanalyst Luce Irigaray, "represent the horror of having nothing to see."[5] When Ophelia is mad, Gertrude says that "Her speech is nothing," mere "unshaped use." Ophelia's speech thus represents the horror of having nothing to say in the public terms defined by the court. Deprived of thought, sexuality, language, Ophelia's story becomes the Story of O—the zero, the empty circle or mystery of feminine difference, the cipher of female sexuality to be deciphered by feminist interpretation.[6]

A third approach would be to read Ophelia's story as the female subtext of the tragedy, the repressed story of Hamlet. In this reading, Ophelia represents the strong emotions that the Elizabethans as well as the Freudians thought womanish and unmanly. When Laertes weeps for his dead sister he says of his tears that "When these are gone, / The woman will be out"—that is to say, that the feminine and shameful part of his nature will be purged. According to David Leverenz, in an important essay called "The Woman in *Hamlet*," Hamlet's disgust at the feminine passivity in himself is translated into violent revulsion against women, and into his brutal behavior towards Ophelia. Ophelia's suicide, Leverenz argues, then becomes "a microcosm of the male world's banishment of the female, because 'woman' represents everything denied by reasonable men."[7]

It is perhaps because Hamlet's emotional vulnerability can so readily be conceptualized as feminine that this is the only heroic male role in Shakespeare which has been regularly acted by women, in a tradition from Sarah

    [5]Luce Irigaray: see *New French Feminisms*, ed. Elaine Marks and Isabelle de Courtivron (New York, 1982), 101. The quotation above, from 3.2., is taken from the Arden Shakespeare, *Hamlet*, ed. Harold Jenkins (London and New York, 1982), 295. All quotations from *Hamlet* are from this text.

    [6]On images of negation and feminine enclosure, see David Wilbern, "Shakespeare's 'nothing'," in *Representing Shakespeare: New Psychoanalytic Essays*, ed. Murray M. Schwartz and Coppélia Kahn (Baltimore, 1981).

    [7]David Leverenz, "The woman in *Hamlet*: an interpersonal view" (*Signs*, 4 [1978]), 303.

Bernhardt to, most recently, Diane Venora, in a production directed by Joseph Papp. Leopold Bloom speculates on this tradition in *Ulysses*, musing on the Hamlet of the actress Mrs Bandman Palmer: "Male impersonator. Perhaps he was a woman? Why Ophelia committed suicide?"[8]

While all of these approaches have much to recommend them, each also presents critical problems. To liberate Ophelia from the text, or to make her its tragic center, is to re-appropriate her for our own ends; to dissolve her into a female symbolism of absence is to endorse our own marginality; to make her Hamlet's anima is to reduce her to a metaphor of male experience. I would like to propose instead that Ophelia *does* have a story of her own that feminist criticism can tell; it is neither her life story, nor her love story, nor Lacan's story, but rather the *history* of her representation. This essay tries to bring together some of the categories of French feminist thought about the "feminine" with the empirical energies of American historical and critical research: to yoke French theory and Yankee knowhow.

Tracing the iconography of Ophelia in English and French painting, photography, psychiatry, and literature, as well as in theatrical production, I will be showing first of all the representational bonds between female insanity and female sexuality. Secondly, I want to demonstrate the two-way transaction between psychiatric theory and cultural representation. As one medical historian has observed, we could provide a manual of female insanity by chronicling the illustrations of Ophelia; this is so because the illustrations of Ophelia have played a major role in the theoretical construction of female insanity.[9] Finally, I want to suggest that the feminist revision of Ophelia comes as much from the actress's freedom as from the critic's interpretation.[10] When Shakespeare's heroines began to be played by women instead of boys, the presence of the female body and female voice, quite apart from details of interpretation, created new meanings and subversive tensions in these roles, and perhaps most importantly with Ophelia. Looking at Ophelia's history on and off the stage, I will point out the contest between male and female representations of Ophelia, cycles of critical repression and feminist reclamation of which contemporary feminist criticism is only the most recent phase. By beginning with these data from cultural history, instead of moving from the grid of literary theory, I hope to conclude with a fuller sense of the responsibilities of feminist criticism, as well as a new perspective on Ophelia.

"Of all the characters in *Hamlet*," Bridget Lyons has pointed out, "Ophelia is most persistently presented in terms of symbolic meanings."[11] Her behavior, her appearance, her gestures, her costume, her props, are freighted with

[8]James Joyce, *Ulysses* (New York, 1961), 76.

[9]Sander L. Gilman, *Seeing the Insane* (New York, 1981), 126.

[10]See Michael Goldman, *The Actor's Freedom: Toward a Theory of Drama* (New York, 1975), for a stimulating discussion of the interpretative interaction between actor and audience.

[11]Bridget Lyons, "The iconography of Ophelia" (*English Literary History*, 44 (1977), 61.

emblematic significance, and for many generations of Shakespearean critics her part in the play has seemed to be primarily iconographic. Ophelia's symbolic meanings, moreover, are specifically feminine. Whereas for Hamlet madness is metaphysical, linked with culture, for Ophelia it is a product of the female body and female nature, perhaps that nature's purest form. On the Elizabethan stage, the conventions of female insanity were sharply defined. Ophella dresses in white, decks herself with "fantastical garlands" of wild flowers, and enters, according to the stage directions of the "Bad" Quarto, "distracted" playing on a lute with her "hair down singing." Her speeches are marked by extravagant metaphors, lyrical free associations, and "explosive sexual imagery."[12] She sings wistful and bawdy ballads, and ends her life by drowning.

All of these conventions carry specific messages about femininity and sexuality. Ophelia's virginal and vacant white is contrasted with Hamlet's scholar's garb, his "suits of solemn black." Her flowers suggest the discordant double images of female sexuality as both innocent blossoming and whorish contamination; she is the "green girl" of pastoral, the virginal "Rose of May" and the sexually explicit madwoman who, in giving away her wild flowers and herbs, is symbolically deflowering herself. The "weedy trophies" and phallic "long purples" which she wears to her death intimate an improper and discordant sexuality that Gertrude's lovely elegy cannot quite obscure.[13] In Elizabethan and Jacobean drama, the stage direction that a woman enters with dishevelled hair indicates that she might either be mad or the victim of a rape; the disordered hair, her offense against decorum, suggests sensuality in each case.[14] The mad Ophelia's bawdy songs and verbal license, while they give her access to "an entirely different range of experience" from what she is allowed as the dutiful daughter, seem to be her one sanctioned form of self-assertion as a woman, quickly followed, as if in retribution, by her death.[15]

Drowning too was associated with the feminine, with female fluidity as opposed to masculine aridity. In his discussion of the "Ophelia complex," the phenomenologist Gaston Bachelard traces the symbolic connections between women, water, and death. Drowning, he suggests, becomes the truly feminine death in the dramas of literature and life, one which is a beautiful immersion and submersion in the female element. Water is the profound and organic symbol of the liquid woman whose eyes are so easily drowned in tears, as her body is the repository of blood, amniotic fluid, and milk. A man

---

[12]See Maurice and Hanna Charney, "The language of Shakespeare's madwomen" (*Signs*, 3 [1977]), 451, 457; and Carroll Camden, "On Ophelia's madness" (*Shakespeare Quarterly* [1964]), 254.

[13]See Margery Garber, *Coming of Age in Shakespeare* (London, 1981), 155–7, and Lyons, op. cit., 65, 70–2.

[14]On dishevelled hair as a signifier of madness or rape, see Charney and Charney, op. cit., 452–3, 457; and Allan Dessen, *Elizabethan Stage Conventions and Modern Interpreters* (Cambridge, 1984), 36–8. Thanks to Allan Dessen for letting me see advance proofs of his book.

[15]Charney and Charney, op. cit., 456.

contemplating this feminine suicide understands it by reaching for what is feminine in himself, like Laertes, by a temporary surrender to his own fluidity—that is, his tears; and he becomes a man again in becoming once more dry—when his tears are stopped.[16]

Clinically speaking, Ophelia's behavior and appearance are characteristic of the malady the Elizabethans would have diagnosed as female love-melancholy, or erotomania. From about 1580, melancholy had become a fashionable disease among young men, especially in London, and Hamlet himself is a prototype of the melancholy hero. Yet the epidemic of melancholy associated with intellectual and imaginative genius "curiously bypassed women." Women's melancholy was seen instead as biological, and emotional in origins.[17]

On the stage, Ophelia's madness was presented as the predictable outcome of erotomania. From 1660, when women first appeared on the public stage, to the beginnings of the eighteenth century, the most celebrated of the actresses who played Ophelia were those whom rumor credited with disappointments in love. The greatest triumph was reserved for Susan Mountfort, a former actress at Lincoln's Inn Fields who had gone mad after her lover's betrayal. One night in 1720 she escaped from her keeper, rushed to the theater, and just as the Ophelia of the evening was to enter for her mad scene, "sprang forward in her place . . . with wild eyes and wavering motion."[18] As a contemporary reported, "she was in truth *Ophelia herself*, to the amazement of the performers as well as of the audience—nature having made this last effort, her vital powers failed her and she died soon after."[19] These theatrical legends reinforced the belief of the age that female madness was a part of female nature, less to be imitated by an actress than demonstrated by a deranged woman in a performance of her emotions.

The subversive or violent possibilities of the mad scene were nearly eliminated, however, on the eighteenth-century stage. Late Augustan stereotypes of female love-melancholy were sentimentalized versions which minimized the force of female sexuality, and made female insanity a pretty stimulant to male sensibility. Actresses such as Mrs Lessingham in 1772, and Mary Bolton in 1811, played Ophelia in this decorous style, relying on the familiar images of the white dress, loose hair, and wild flowers to convey a polite feminine distraction, highly suitable for pictorial reproduction, and appropriate for Samuel Johnson's description of Ophelia as young, beautiful, harmless, and pious. Even Mrs Siddons in 1785 played the mad scene with

[16]Gaston Bachelard, *L'Eau et les rêves* (Paris, 1942), 109–25. See also Brigitte Peucker, "Dröste-Hulshof's Ophelia and the recovery of voice" (*The Journal of English and Germanic Philology* [1983]), 374–91.

[17]Vieda Skultans, *English Madness: Ideas on Insanity 1580–1890* (London, 1977), 79–81. On historical cases of love-melancholy, see Michael MacDonald, *Mystical Bedlam* (Cambridge, 1982).

[18]C. E. L. Wingate, *Shakespeare's Heroines on the Stage* (New York, 1895), 283–4, 288–9.

[19]Charles Hiatt, *Ellen Terry* (London, 1898), 11.

stately and classical dignity. For much of the period, in fact, Augustan objections to the levity and indecency of Ophelia's language and behavior led to censorship of the part. Her lines were frequently cut, and the role was often assigned to a singer instead of an actress, making the mode of representation musical rather than visual or verbal.

But whereas the Augustan response to madness was a denial, the romantic response was an embrace.[20] The figure of the mad woman permeates romantic literature, from the gothic novelists to Wordsworth and Scott in such texts as "The Thorn" and *The Heart of Midlothian*, where she stands for sexual victimization, bereavement, and thrilling emotional extremity. Romantic artists such as Thomas Barker and George Shepheard painted pathetically abandoned Crazy Kates and Crazy Anns, while Henry Fuseli's "Mad Kate" is almost demonically possessed, an orphan of the romantic storm.

In the Shakespearean theater, Ophelia's romantic revival began in France rather than England. When Charles Kemble made his Paris debut as Hamlet with an English troupe in 1827, his Ophelia was a young Irish ingénue named Harriet Smithson. Smithson used "her extensive command of mime to depict in precise gesture the state of Ophelia's confused mind."[21] In the mad scene, she entered in a long black veil, suggesting the standard imagery of female sexual mystery in the gothic novel, with scattered bedlamish wisps of straw in her hair. Spreading the veil on the ground as she sang, she spread flowers upon it in the shape of a cross, as if to make her father's grave, and mimed a burial, a piece of stage business which remained in vogue for the rest of the century.

The French audiences were stunned. Dumas recalled that "it was the first time I saw in the theatre real passions, giving life to men and women of flesh and blood."[22] The 23-year-old Hector Berlioz, who was in the audience on the first night, fell madly in love, and eventually married Harriet Smithson despite his family's frantic opposition. Her image as the mad Ophelia was represented in popular lithographs and exhibited in bookshop and printshop windows. Her costume was imitated by the fashionable, and a coiffure "à la folle," consisting of a "black veil with wisps of straw tastefully interwoven" in the hair, was widely copied by the Parisian beau monde, always on the lookout for something new.[23]

Although Smithson never acted Ophelia on the English stage, her intensely visual performance quickly influenced English productions as well; and indeed the romantic Ophelia—a young girl passionately and visibly driven to picturesque madness—became the dominant international acting style for the next 150 years, from Helena Modjeska in Poland in 1871, to the 18-year-old Jean Simmons in the Laurence Olivier film of 1948.

[20]Max Byrd, *Visits to Bedlam: Madness and Literature in the Eighteenth Century* (Columbia, 1974), xiv.
[21]Peter Raby, *Fair Ophelia: Harriet Smithson Berlioz* (Cambridge, 1982), 63.
[22]Ibid., 68.
[23]Ibid., 72, 75.

Whereas the romantic Hamlet, in Coleridge's famous dictum, thinks too much, has an "overbalance of the contemplative faculty" and an overactive intellect, the romantic Ophelia is a girl who *feels* too much, who drowns in feeling. The romantic critics seem to have felt that the less said about Ophelia the better; the point was to *look* at her. Hazlitt, for one, is speechless before her, calling her "a character almost too exquisitely touching to be dwelt upon."[24] While the Augustans represent Ophelia as music, the romantics transform her into an *objet d'art*, as if to take literally Claudius's lament, "poor Ophelia / Divided from herself and her fair judgment, / Without the which we are pictures."

Smithson's performance is best recaptured in a series of pictures done by Delacroix from 1830 to 1850, which show a strong romantic interest in the relation of female sexuality and insanity.[25] The most innovative and influential of Delacroix's lithographs is *La Mort d'Ophélie* of 1843, the first of three studies. Its sensual languor, with Ophelia half-suspended in the stream as her dress slips from her body, anticipated the fascination with the erotic trance of the hysteric as it would be studied by Jean-Martin Charcot and his students, including Janet and Freud. Delacroix's interest in the drowning Ophelia is also reproduced to the point of obsession in later nineteenth-century painting. The English pre-Raphaelites painted her again and again, choosing the drowning which is only described in the play, and where no actress's image had preceded them or interfered with their imaginative supremacy.

In the Royal Academy show of 1852, Arthur Hughes's entry shows a tiny waif-like creature—a sort of Tinker Bell Ophelia—in a filmy white gown, perched on a tree trunk by the stream. The overall effect is softened, sexless, and hazy, although the straw in her hair resembles a crown of thorns. Hughes's juxtaposition of childlike femininity and Christian martyrdom was overpowered, however, by John Everett Millais's great painting of Ophelia in the same show. While Millais's Ophelia is sensuous siren as well as victim, the artist rather than the subject dominates the scene. The division of space between Ophelia and the natural details Millais had so painstakingly pursued reduces her to one more visual object; and the painting has such a hard surface, strangely flattened perspective, and brilliant light that it seems cruelly indifferent to the woman's death.

These Pre-Raphaelite images were part of a new and intricate traffic between images of women and madness in late nineteenth-century literature, psychiatry, drama, and art. First of all, superintendents of Victorian lunatic asylums were also enthusiasts of Shakespeare, who turned to his dramas for models of mental aberration that could be applied to their clinical practice. The case study of Ophelia was one that seemed particularly useful as an account of hysteria or mental breakdown in adolescence, a period of sexual

---

[24]Quoted in Camden, op. cit., 247.
[25]Raby, op. cit., 182.

instability which the Victorians regarded as risky for women's mental health. As Dr John Charles Bucknill, president of the Medico-Psychological Association, remarked in 1859, "Ophelia is the very type of a class of cases by no means uncommon. Every mental physician of moderately extensive experience must have seen many Ophelias. It is a copy from nature, after the fashion of the pre-Raphaelite school."[26] Dr John Conolly, the celebrated superintendent of the Hanwell Asylum, and founder of the committee to make Stratford a national trust, concurred. In his *Study of Hamlet* in 1863 he noted that even casual visitors to mental institutions could recognize an Ophelia in the wards: "the same young years, the same faded beauty, the same fantastic dress and interrupted song."[27] Medical textbooks illustrated their discussions of female patients with sketches of Ophelia-like maidens.

But Conolly also pointed out that the graceful Ophelias who dominated the Victorian stage were quite unlike the women who had become the majority of the inmate population in Victorian public asylums. "It seems to be supposed," he protested, "that it is an easy task to play the part of a crazy girl, and that it is chiefly composed of singing and prettiness. The habitual courtesy, the partial rudeness of mental disorder, are things to be witnessed. . . . An actress, ambitious of something beyond cold imitation, might find the contemplation of such cases a not unprofitable study."[28]

Yet when Ellen Terry took up Conolly's challenge, and went to an asylum to observe real madwomen, she found them "too *theatrical*" to teach her anything.[29] This was because the iconography of the romantic Ophelia had begun to infiltrate reality, to define a style for mad young women seeking to express and communicate their distress. And where the women themselves did not willingly throw themselves into Ophelia-like postures, asylum superintendents, armed with the new technology of photography, imposed the costume, gesture, props, and expression of Ophelia upon them. In England, the camera was introduced to asylum work in the 1850s by Dr Hugh Welch Diamond, who photographed his female patients at the Surrey Asylum and at Bethlem. Diamond was heavily influenced by literary and visual models in his posing of the female subjects. His pictures of madwomen, posed in prayer, or decked with Ophelia-like garlands, were copied for Victorian consumption as touched-up lithographs in professional journals.[30]

Reality, psychiatry, and representational convention were even more confused in the photographic records of hysteria produced in the 1870s by Jean-

[26]J. C. Bucknill, *The Psychology of Shakespeare* (London, 1859, reprinted New York, 1970), 110. For more extensive discussions of Victorian psychiatry and Ophelia figures, see Elaine Showalter, *The Female Malady: Women, Madness and English Culture* (New York, 1986).

[27]John Conolly, *Study of Hamlet* (London, 1863), 177.

[28]Ibid., 177–8, 180.

[29]Ellen Terry, *The Story of My Life* (London, 1908), 154.

[30]Diamond's photographs are reproduced in Sander L. Gilman, *The Face of Madness: Hugh W. Diamond and the Origin of Psychiatric Photography* (New York, 1976).

Martin Charcot. Charcot was the first clinician to install a fully-equipped photographic atelier in his Paris hospital, La Salpêtrière, to record the performances of his hysterical stars. Charcot's clinic became, as he said, a "living theatre" of female pathology; his women patients were coached in their performances for the camera, and, under hypnosis, were sometimes instructed to play heroines from Shakespeare. Among them, a 15-year-old girl named Augustine was featured in the published volumes called *Iconographies* in every posture of *la grande hystérie*. With her white hospital gown and flowing locks, Augustine frequently resembles the reproductions of Ophelia as icon and actress which had been in wide circulation.[31]

But if the Victorian madwoman looks mutely out from men's pictures, and acts a part men had staged and directed, she is very differently represented in the feminist revision of Ophelia initiated by newly powerful and respectable Victorian actresses, and by women critics of Shakespeare. In their efforts to defend Ophelia, they invent a story for her drawn from their own experiences, grievances, and desires.

Probably the most famous of the Victorian feminist revisions of the Ophelia story was Mary Cowden Clarke's *The Girlhood of Shakespeare's Heroines*, published in 1852. Unlike other Victorian moralizing and didactic studies of the female characters of Shakespeare's plays, Clarke's was specifically addressed to the wrongs of women, and especially to the sexual double standard. In a chapter on Ophelia called "The rose of Elsinore," Clarke tells how the child Ophelia was left behind in the care of a peasant couple when Polonius was called to the court at Paris, and raised in a cottage with a foster-sister and brother, Jutha and Ulf. Jutha is seduced and betrayed by a deceitful knight, and Ophelia discovers the bodies of Jutha and her still-born child, lying "white, rigid, and still" in the deserted parlor of the cottage in the middle of the night. Ulf, a "hairy loutish boy," likes to torture flies, to eat songbirds, and to rip the petals off roses, and he is also very eager to give little Ophelia what he calls a bear-hug. Both repelled and masochistically attracted by Ulf, Ophelia is repeatedly cornered by him as she grows up; once she escapes the hug by hitting him with a branch of wild roses; another time, he sneaks into her bedroom "in his brutish pertinacity to obtain the hug he had promised himself," but just as he bends over her trembling body, Ophelia is saved by the reappearance of her real mother.

A few years later, back at the court, she discovers the hanged body of another friend, who has killed herself after being "victimized and deserted by the same evil seducer." Not surprisingly, Ophelia breaks down with brain fever—a staple mental illness of Victorian fiction—and has prophetic hallucinations of a brook beneath willow trees where something bad will happen to

[31]See Georges Didi-Huberman, *L'Invention de l'hystérie* (Paris, 1982), and Stephen Heath, *The Sexual Fix* (London, 1983), 36.

her. The warnings of Polonius and Laertes have little to add to this history of female sexual trauma.[32]

On the Victorian stage, it was Ellen Terry, daring and unconventional in her own life, who led the way in acting Ophelia in feminist terms as a consistent psychological study in sexual intimidation, a girl terrified of her father, of her lover, and of life itself. Terry's debut as Ophelia in Henry Irving's production in 1878 was a landmark. According to one reviewer, her Ophelia was "the terrible spectacle of a normal girl becoming hopelessly imbecile as the result of overwhelming mental agony. Hers was an insanity without wrath or rage, without exaltation or paroxysms."[33] Her "poetic and intellectual performance" also inspired other actresses to rebel against the conventions of invisibility and negation associated with the part.

Terry was the first to challenge the tradition of Ophelia's dressing in emblematic white. For the French poets, such as Rimbaud, Hugo, Musset, Mallarmé and Laforgue, whiteness was part of Ophelia's essential feminine symbolism; they call her "blanche Ophélia" and compare her to a lily, a cloud, or snow. Yet whiteness also made her a transparency, an absence that took on the colors of Hamlet's moods, and that, for the symbolists like Mallarmé, made her a blank page to be written over or on by the male imagination. Although Irving was able to prevent Terry from wearing black in the mad scene, exclaiming "My God, Madam, there must be only *one* black figure in this play, and that's Hamlet!" (Irving, of course, was playing Hamlet), nonetheless actresses such as Gertrude Eliot, Helen Maude, Nora de Silva, and in Russia Vera Komisarjevskaya, gradually won the right to intensify Ophelia's presence by clothing her in Hamlet's black.[34]

By the turn of the century, there was both a male and a female discourse on Ophelia. A. C. Bradley spoke for the Victorian male tradition when he noted in *Shakespearean Tragedy* (1904) that "a large number of readers feel a kind of personal irritation against Ophelia; they seem unable to forgive her for not having been a heroine."[35] The feminist counterview was represented by actresses in such works as Helena Faucit's study of Shakespeare's female characters, and *The True Ophelia*, written by an anonymous actress in 1914, which protested against the "insipid little creature" of criticism, and advocated a strong and intelligent woman destroyed by the heartlessness of men.[36] In

[32]Mary Cowden Clarke, *The Girlhood of Shakespeare's Heroines* (London, 1852). See also George C. Gross, "Mary Cowden Clarke, *The Girlhood of Shakespeare's Heroines*, and the sex education of Victorian women" (*Victorian Studies*, 16 [1972]), 37–58, and Nina Auerbach, *Woman and the Demon* (Cambridge, Mass., 1983), 210–15.

[33]Hiatt, op. cit., 114. See also Wingate, op. cit., 304–5.

[34]Terry, op. cit., 155–6.

[35]Andrew C. Bradley, *Shakespearean Tragedy* (London, 1904), 160.

[36]Helena Faucit Martin, *On Some of Shakespeare's Female Characters* (Edinburgh and London, 1891), 4, 18; and *The True Ophelia* (New York, 1914), 15.

women's paintings of the *fin de siècle* as well, Ophelia is depicted as an inspiring, even sanctified emblem of righteousness.[37]

While the widely read and influential essays of Mary Cowden Clarke are now mocked as the epitome of naive criticism, these Victorian studies of the girlhood of Shakespeare's heroines are of course as alive and well as psychoanalytic criticism, which has imagined its own prehistories of oedipal conflict and neurotic fixation; and I say this not to mock psychoanalytic criticism, but to suggest that Clarke's musings on Ophelia are a pre-Freudian speculation on the traumatic sources of a female sexual identity. The Freudian interpretation of *Hamlet* concentrated on the hero, but also had much to do with the sexualization of Ophelia. As early as 1900, Freud had traced Hamlet's resolution to an Oedipus complex, and Ernest Jones, his leading British disciple, developed this view, influencing the performances of John Gielgud and Alec Guinness in the 1930s. In his final version of the study, *Hamlet and Oedipus*, published in 1949, Jones argued that "Ophelia should be unmistakably sensual, as she seldom is on stage. She may be 'innocent' and docile, but she is very aware of her body."[38]

In the theater and in criticism, this Freudian edict has produced such extreme readings as that Shakespeare intends us to see Ophelia as a loose woman, and that she has been sleeping with Hamlet. Rebecca West has argued that Ophelia was not "a correct and timid virgin of exquisite sensibilities," a view she attributes to the popularity of the Millais painting; but rather "a disreputable young woman."[39] In his delightful autobiography, Laurence Olivier, who made a special pilgrimage to Ernest Jones when he was preparing his *Hamlet* in the 1930s, recalls that one of his predecessors as actor-manager had said in response to the earnest question, "Did Hamlet sleep with Ophelia?"—"In my company, always."[40]

The most extreme Freudian interpretation reads *Hamlet* as two parallel male and female psychodramas, the counterpointed stories of the incestuous attachments of Hamlet and Ophelia. As Theodor Lidz presents this view, while Hamlet is neurotically attached to his mother, Ophelia has an unresolved oedipal attachment to her father. She has fantasies of a lover who will abduct her from or even kill her father, and when this actually happens, her reason is destroyed by guilt as well as by lingering incestuous feelings. According to Lidz, Ophelia breaks down because she fails in the female developmental task of shifting her sexual attachment from her father "to a man who can bring her fulfillment as a woman."[41] We see the effects of this

[37]Among these paintings are the Ophelias of Henrietta Rae and Mrs F. Littler. Sarah Bernhardt sculpted a bas relief of Ophelia for the Women's Pavilion at the Chicago World's Fair in 1893.

[38]Ernest Jones, *Hamlet and Oedipus* (New York, 1949), 139.

[39]Rebecca West, *The Court and the Castle* (New Haven, 1958), 18.

[40]Laurence Olivier, *Confessions of an Actor* (Harmondsworth, 1982), 102, 152.

[41]Theodor Lidz, *Hamlet's Enemy: Madness and Myth in Hamlet* (New York, 1975), 88, 113.

Freudian Ophelia on stage productions since the 1950s, where directors have hinted at an incestuous link between Ophelia and her father, or more recently, because this staging conflicts with the usual ironic treatment of Polonius, between Ophelia and Laertes. Trevor Nunn's production with Helen Mirren in 1970, for example, made Ophelia and Laertes flirtatious doubles, almost twins in their matching fur-trimmed doublets, playing duets on the lute with Polonius looking on, like Peter, Paul, and Mary. In other productions of the same period, Marianne Faithfull was a haggard Ophelia equally attracted to Hamlet and Laertes, and, in one of the few performances directed by a woman, Yvonne Nicholson sat on Laertes' lap in the advice scene, and played the part with "rough sexual bravado."[42]

Since the 1960s, the Freudian representation of Ophelia has been supplemented by an antipsychiatry that represents Ophelia's madness in more contemporary terms. In contrast to the psychoanalytic representation of Ophelia's sexual unconscious that connected her essential femininity to Freud's essays on female sexuality and hysteria, her madness is now seen in medical and biochemical terms, as schizophrenia. This is so in part because the schizophrenic woman has become the cultural icon of dualistic femininity in the mid-twentieth century as the erotomaniac was in the seventeenth and the hysteric in the nineteenth. It might also be traced to the work of R. D. Laing on female schizophrenia in the 1960s. Laing argued that schizophrenia was an intelligible response to the experience of invalidation within the family network, especially to the conflicting emotional messages and mystifying double binds experienced by daughters. Ophelia, he noted in *The Divided Self*, is an empty space. "In her madness there is no one there. . . . There is no integral selfhood expressed through her actions or utterances. Incomprehensible statements are said by nothing. She has already died. There is now only a vacuum where there was once a person."[43]

Despite his sympathy for Ophelia, Laing's readings silence her, equate her with "nothing," more completely than any since the Augustans; and they have been translated into performances which only make Ophelia a graphic study of mental pathology. The sickest Ophelias on the contemporary stage have been those in the productions of the pathologist-director Jonathan Miller. In 1974 at the Greenwich Theatre his Ophelia sucked her thumb; by 1981, at the Warehouse in London, she was played by an actress much taller and heavier than the Hamlet (perhaps punningly cast as the young actor Anton Lesser). She began the play with a set of nervous tics and tuggings of hair which by the mad scene had become a full set of schizophrenic routines—head banging, twitching, wincing, grimacing, and drooling.[44]

[42]Richard David, *Shakespeare in the Theatre* (Cambridge, 1978), 75. This was the production directed by Buzz Goodbody, a brilliant young feminist radical who killed herself that year. See Colin Chambers, *Other Spaces: New Theatre and the RSC* (London, 1980), especially 63–7.
[43]R. D. Laing, *The Divided Self* (Harmondsworth, 1965), 195n.
[44]David, op. cit., 82–3; thanks to Marianne DeKoven, Rutgers University, for the description of the 1981 Warehouse production.

But since the 1970s too we have had a feminist discourse which has offered a new perspective on Ophelia's madness as protest and rebellion. For many feminist theorists, the madwoman is a heroine, a powerful figure who rebels against the family and the social order; and the hysteric who refuses to speak the language of the patriarchal order, who speaks otherwise, is a sister.[45] In terms of effect on the theater, the most radical application of these ideas was probably realized in Melissa Murray's agitprop play *Ophelia*, written in 1979 for the English women's theater group "Hormone Imbalance." In this blank verse retelling of the Hamlet story, Ophelia becomes a lesbian and runs off with a woman servant to join a guerrilla commune.[46]

While I've always regretted that I missed this production, I can't proclaim that this defiant ideological gesture, however effective politically or theatrically, is all that feminist criticism desires, or all to which it should aspire. When feminist criticism chooses to deal with representation, rather than with women's writing, it must aim for a maximum interdisciplinary contextualism, in which the complexity of attitudes towards the feminine can be analyzed in their fullest cultural and historical frame. The alternation of strong and weak Ophelias on the stage, virginal and seductive Ophelias in art, inadequate or oppressed Ophelias in criticism, tells us how these representations have overflowed the text, and how they have reflected the ideological character of their times, erupting as debates between dominant and feminist views in periods of gender crisis and redefinition. The representation of Ophelia changes independently of theories of the meaning of the play or the Prince, for it depends on attitudes towards women and madness. The decorous and pious Ophelia of the Augustan age and the postmodern schizophrenic heroine who might have stepped from the pages of Laing can be derived from the same figure; they are both contradictory and complementary images of female sexuality in which madness seems to act as the "switching-point, the concept which allows the co-existence of both sides of the representation."[47] There is no "true" Ophelia for whom feminist criticism must unambiguously speak, but perhaps only a Cubist Ophelia of multiple perspectives, more than the sum of all her parts.

But in exposing the ideology of representation, feminist critics have also the responsibility to acknowledge and to examine the boundaries of our own ideological positions as products of our gender and our time. A degree of humility in an age of critical hubris can be our greatest strength, for it is by occupying this position of historical self-consciousness in both feminism and criticism that we maintain our credibility in representing Ophelia, and that, unlike Lacan, when we promise to speak about her, we make good our word.

45See, for example, Hélène Cixous and Catherine Clément, *La Jeune Née* (Paris, 1975).

46For an account of this production, see Micheline Wandor, *Understudies: Theatre and Sexual Politics* (London, 1981), 47.

47I am indebted for this formulation to a critique of my earlier draft of this paper by Carl Friedman, at the Wesleyan Center for the Humanities, April 1984.

Viewpoints

Daniel Seltzer on "The Shape of Hamlet *in the Theater"*[1]

Our experience of Hamlet and his experience of himself—in performance these come to much the same phenomenon—exist in fifteen blocks of activity. Someone else might count them and describe them differently, but I think the differences would not be major ones. In counting these episodes, I omit only a few small sections of dialogue, most of the time merging in any case with more important junctures of action. These fifteen episodes include not only soliloquies and semi-solo speech and activity, but dialogues with other characters that are highly energized.

They are as follows: first, the soliloquy, "O that this too too sullied flesh" and the information about the Ghost that follows it directly; second, the scenes with the Ghost, including the oath of vengeance, surrounded on both sides with dialogue with Horatio and the others; third, the dialogue with Polonius while Hamlet reads his book and satirizes Polonius to his face; fourth, the dialogue with Rosencrantz and Guildenstern, concluding with the apostrophe to man as the "paragon of animals" as well as "the quintessence of dust"; fifth, the quick dialogue with the Players, which is followed by the soliloquy, "O, what a rogue and peasant slave am I!"; sixth, the "To be or not to be" soliloquy; seventh, the so-called Nunnery scene, with its savage verbal assaults upon Ophelia; eighth, the "Advice" to the Players; ninth, the long set-speech of compliment to Horatio, on the subject of reason and moderation; tenth, the dialogue surrounding the actual performance of "The Murder of Gonzago," with Hamlet's responses to its conclusion; eleventh, the speech over the praying Claudius, in which Hamlet decides to put off his revenge until a more damning moment; twelfth, the scene between Hamlet and his mother; thirteenth, the episode in which Hamlet watches Fortinbras's armies and then speaks the soliloquy, "How all occasions do inform against me"; fourteenth, the long scene at Ophelia's grave, first with the Gravediggers and then the confrontation with Laertes; and, finally, the sequence of speeches to Horatio, describing his adventures at sea, then the short conversation with Osric, and the speech discussing the "special providence in the fall of a sparrow." These are the major units of Hamlet's life, with only short and

---

[1]From *Perspectives on Hamlet*, ed. William G. Holzberger and Peter B. Waldeck (Lewisburg, Pa.; Bucknell University Press, 1973), 172–73. Reprinted by permission.

mainly connective dialogues omitted. I think it fascinating that the stage life, which has elicited more imaginative response than any other fictional life in dramatic or nondramatic literature, is set forth for us in essentially only fifteen blocks of stage time, and that, although each is different from the others as well as various within itself, taken as an incremental sequence these blocks build a rhythmic shape that is also the mold of the whole drama.

Bert O. States on "The Word-Pictures in Hamlet"[2]

I imagine the arras through which Hamlet stabs Polonius as a richly figured tapestry of scenes from Renaissance life. Nothing in the text suggests such an idea and I am not urging it on readers or scene designers. I cite it as a private instance of how a fiction teaches one to fill in details which are not there at all and to do so in the style of those which are. This spilling over of a play's "known" or expressed world into what we might call its own blank spaces is one of the most intriguing dimensions of the process of metaphor, and one for which we scarcely have a good critical language. For example, in a slight exchange like "Have you had quiet guard? / Not a mouse stirring." there is, obviously, a very palpable mouse stirring. In that miraculous organ Hamlet calls the mind's eye one sees it scurrying along a dank wall of the imagination and disappearing into such darkness as might shroud a ghost. So the mouse—like the glow worm, the woodcock, the mole, the porpentine, the weasel, the kite, the crab and the serpent—is a creature of some brief influence in the creation of the unique space in which *Hamlet's* story unfolds.

All plays, certainly all Elizabethan plays, create their visual worlds by such suggestive means. But *Hamlet's*, as we all know, is especially luxurious: it hangs in the air more densely, more variously, than other dramatic worlds. For instance, there is very little sense of a thick periphery of "things" in *Macbeth's* metaphysical spaces, though there are rooks and wood choughs enough. Somehow, everything seems critically in thrall to the central deed: even the stones prate of the murderer's whereabouts. *Hamlet's* world, by contrast, opens out far beyond the decayed garden we hear so much about in the criticism. It is a universe made up of an almost encyclopedic procession of persons, animals, objects, processes, and instances from rural, professional, and household affairs, many of them strangely self-contained and portable, all spun out by characters who, even in Shakespeare s immense gallery, have an unusual habit of getting detained in the making of word-pictures. More matter and less art, the Queen reminds Polonius, though Laertes might have said the same to her as she reports his sister's death:

[2]From *The Hudson Review* 26, no. 3 (Autumn 1973), 510–11. Reprinted by permission.

There is a willow grows askant the brook,
That shows his hoar leaves in the glassy stream:
Therewith fantastic garlands did she make
Of crowflowers, nettles, daisies, and long purples,
That liberal shepherds give a grosser name,
But our cold maids do dead men's fingers call them.
There on the pendent boughs her crownet weeds
Clamb'ring to hang, an envious sliver broke,
When down her weedy trophies and herself
Fell in the weeping brook.

Not that this passage is in any sense over-embroidered. On the contrary, it is fine poetry fully and symbolically warranted by the occasion: the perfect exit for Ophelia. What is curious about it, and so much at home in this play, is the way it swerves through these liberal shepherds and cold maids who come trooping in from the country on the stems of long purples which are themselves but garlands on the event. The eye hardly sees Ophelia at all; it sees rather the participation of nature in her drowning. She is, you might say, overwhelmed by scenery.

Richard Fly on "The Ending of Hamlet"[3]

Hamlet may occasionally brood on death and the after-life, may even contemplate suicide, but he cannot be called an "ambassador of death" as G. Wilson Knight and others have claimed.[*] He moves into the final phase of his existence as an agent of life struggling heroically against various forms of ignoble death, and that struggle is not without its victories. He has escaped from the possibility of anonymous death at sea, evaded a summary beheading in a foreign country, and held off the murderous attack of Laertes in the graveyard. And although he knows intuitively that his death is near, there is present in his behavior no enervating acquiescence, no stoic posturing. He dies sword in hand, "benetted round with villainies" (5.2.29), his mind concentrated on his immediate enemies and not turned inward on imagined personal failings or outward on some vague supernatural sanction. He is in these final moments, I believe, the most life-affirming of all Shakespeare's tragic protagonists. Unlike Romeo and Juliet, Brutus, Othello, or Antony and Cleopatra, he is not driven finally to self-slaughter; nor like Titus, the two King Richards, Macbeth, Timon, or Coriolanus does he throw himself suicidally into a self-destructive action. He has been "in continual practice" (line 200) when the fencing challenge comes and he obviously expects to win it. In

[3]From "Accommodating Death: The Ending of *Hamlet*," *Studies in English Literature* 24 (1984), 272–74. Reprinted by permission.
[*]See G. Wilson Knight's chapter, "The Embassy of Death: An Essay on *Hamlet*," in *The Wheel of Fire* (London: Methuen, 1930), 17–46.

fact, he does so well in the duel that Laertes grows discouraged and Claudius pessimistic—an unexpected demoralization which only makes Hamlet more defiant:

> Come for the third, Laertes. You but dally.
> I pray you pass with your best violence;
> I am afeard you make a wanton of me.
> (5.2.286–88)

For a brief moment Hamlet stands in the midst of his enemies, triumphant and seemingly invulnerable. His own unique personality cannot be assimilated into the broader patterns that bring the play to a close. He can glimpse the "divinity" that is shaping his end, the "heaven" that is "ordinant" in human affairs, the "providence" overseeing it all; but that does not diminish his sense of responsibility for his final action. He can observe a cosmic irony working through events to hoist his enemies on their own petards, but that does not lessen the necessity to strike boldly when the arch criminal at last stands exposed before him. He can acknowledge that his life is over, but that too does not relieve him of the need to provide for the "name" that will live behind him and to cast his vote for the new ruler of the state. Such hard-won discriminations must not be lost. A vast shadow of significance seems to envelop these final events, shaking our dispositions with thoughts beyond the reaches of our souls, but that overarching aura of meaning cannot displace the primacy of the specific event, the particular moment, the singular inimitable death. That achievement of differentiation in the face of death is what, I think, makes *Hamlet* our preeminent masterwork of tragedy.

René Girard on "Hamlet's Dull Revenge"[4]

Why should a well-educated young man have second thoughts when it comes to killing a close relative who also happens to be the king of the land and the husband of his own mother? This is some enigma indeed and the problem is not that a satisfactory answer has never been found but that we should expect to find one after our *a priori* exclusion of the one sensible and obvious answer.

Should our enormous critical literature on *Hamlet* fall some day into the hands of people otherwise ignorant of our mores, they could not fail to conclude that our academic tribe must have been a savage breed, indeed. After four centuries of controversies, Hamlet's temporary reluctance to commit murder still looks so outlandish to us that more and more books are being written in an unsuccessful effort to solve that mystery. The only way to

[4]From *Literary Theory / Renaissance Texts*, ed. Patricia Parker and David Quint (Baltimore: Johns Hopkins, 1986), 291. Reprinted by permission.

account for this curious body of literature is to suppose that, back in the twentieth century no more was needed than some ghost to ask for it, and the average professor of literature would massacre his entire household without batting an eyelash.

Part 2
OTHELLO

The Joker in the Pack

W. H. Auden

Reason is God's gift; but so are the passions.
Reason is as guilty as passion.

—J. H. Newman

I

Any consideration of the Tragedy of Othello must be primarily occupied, not with its official hero but with its villain. I cannot think of any other play in which only one character performs personal actions—all the *deeds* are Iago's—and all the others without exception only exhibit behavior. In marrying each other, Othello and Desdemona have performed a deed, but this took place before the play begins. Nor can I think of another play in which the villain is so completely triumphant: everything Iago sets out to do, he accomplishes—(among his goals, I include his self-destruction). Even Cassio, who survives, is maimed for life.

If *Othello* is a tragedy—and one certainly cannot call it a comedy—it is tragic in a peculiar way. In most tragedies the fall of the hero from glory to misery and death is the work, either of the gods, or of his own freely chosen acts, or, more commonly, a mixture of both. But the fall of Othello is the work of another human being; nothing he says or does originates with himself. In consequence we feel pity for him but no respect; our aesthetic respect is reserved for Iago.

Iago is a wicked man. The wicked man, the stage villain, as a subject of serious dramatic interest does not, so far as I know, appear in the drama of Western Europe before the Elizabethans. In the mystery plays, the wicked characters, like Satan or Herod, are treated comically, but the theme of the triumphant villain cannot be treated comically because the suffering he inflicts is real.

A distinction must be made between the villainous character—figures like Don John in *Much Ado*, Richard III, Edmund in *Lear*, Iachimo in *Cymbeline*—and the merely criminal character—figures like Duke Antonio in

From *The Dyer's Hand and Other Essays* (New York: Random House, 1962), 246–72. Reprinted by permission. The original essay has been excerpted for inclusion here.

The Tempest, Angelo in *Measure for Measure,* Macbeth or Claudius in *Hamlet.* The criminal is a person who finds himself in a situation where he is tempted to break the law and succumbs to the temptation: he ought, of course, to have resisted the temptation, but everybody, both on stage and in the audience, must admit that, had they been placed in the same situation, they, too, would have been tempted. The opportunities are exceptional— Prospero, immersed in his books, has left the government of Milan to his brother, Angelo is in a position of absolute authority, Claudius is the Queen's lover, Macbeth is egged on by prophecies and heaven-sent opportunities, but the desire for a dukedom or a crown or a chaste and beautiful girl are desires which all can imagine themselves feeling.

The villain, on the other hand, is shown from the beginning as being a malcontent, a person with a general grudge against life and society. In most cases this is comprehensible because the villain has, in fact, been wronged by Nature or Society: Richard III is a hunchback, Don John and Edmund are bastards. What distinguishes their actions from those of the criminal is that, even when they have something tangible to gain, this is a secondary satisfaction; their primary satisfaction is the infliction of suffering on others, or the exercise of power over others against their will. Richard does not really desire Anne; what he enjoys is successfully wooing a lady whose husband and father-in-law he has killed. Since he has persuaded Gloucester that Edgar is a would-be parricide, Edmund does not need to betray his father to Cornwall and Regan in order to inherit. Don John has nothing personally to gain from ruining the happiness of Claudio and Hero except the pleasure of seeing them unhappy. Iachimo is a doubtful case of villainy. When he and Posthumus make their wager, the latter warns him:

> If she remain unseduced, you not making it appear otherwise, for your ill opinion and th'assault you have made on her chastity you shall answer me with your sword.

To the degree that his motive in deceiving Posthumus is simply physical fear of losing his life in a duel, he is a coward, not a villain; he is only a villain to the degree that his motive is the pleasure of making and seeing the innocent suffer. Coleridge's description of Iago's actions as "motiveless malignancy" applies in some degree to all the Shakespearian villains. The adjective *motiveless* means, firstly, that the tangible gains, if any, are clearly not the principal motive and, secondly, that the motive is not the desire for personal revenge upon another for a personal injury. Iago himself proffers two reasons for wishing to injure Othello and Cassio. He tells Roderigo that, in appointing Cassio to be his lieutenant, Othello has treated him unjustly, in which conversation he talks like the conventional Elizabethan malcontent. In his soliloquies with himself, he refers to his suspicion that both Othello and Cassio have made him a cuckold, and here he talks like the conventional jealous husband who desires revenge. But there are, I believe, insuperable objections to taking these reasons, as some critics have done, at their face value. If one of Iago's goals is to supplant Cassio in the lieutenancy, one can only say that his plot fails for, when Cassio is cashiered, Othello does not appoint Iago in his place. It is true that, in Act 3, Scene 3, when they swear blood-brotherhood in revenge, Othello concludes with the words

. . . now thou are my lieutenant

to which Iago replies:

I am your own for ever

but the use of the word *lieutenant* in this context refers, surely, not to a public military rank, but to a private and illegal delegation of authority—the job delegated to Iago is the secret murder of Cassio, and Iago's reply, which is a mocking echo of an earlier line of Othello's, refers to a relation which can never become public. The ambiguity of the word is confirmed by its use in the first line of the scene which immediately follows. Desdemona says

Do you know, sirrah, where the Lieutenant Cassio lies?

(One should beware of attaching too much significance to Elizabethan typography, but it is worth noting that Othello's lieutenant is in lower case and Desdomona's in upper). As for Iago's jealousy, one cannot believe that a seriously jealous man could behave towards his wife as Iago behaves towards Emilia, for the wife of a jealous husband is the first person to suffer. Not only is the relation of Iago and Emilia, as we see it on stage, without emotional tension, but also Emilia openly refers to a rumor of her infidelity as something already disposed of.

> Some such squire it was
> That turned your wit, the seamy side without
> And made you to suspect me with the Moor.

At one point Iago states that, in order to revenge himself on Othello, he will not rest till he is even with him, wife for wife, but, in the play, no attempt at Desdemona's seduction is made. Iago does not make an assault on her virtue himself, he does not encourage Cassio to make one, and he even prevents Roderigo from getting anywhere near her.

Finally, one who seriously desires personal revenge desires to reveal himself. The revenger's greatest satisfaction is to be able to tell his victim to his face—"You thought you were all-powerful and untouchable and could injure me with impunity. Now you see that you were wrong. Perhaps you have forgotten what you did; let me have the pleasure of reminding you."

When at the end of the play, Othello asks Iago in bewilderment why he has thus ensnared his soul and body, if his real motive were revenge for having been cuckolded or unjustly denied promotion, he could have said so, instead of refusing to explain.

In Act 2, Scene 1, occur seven lines which, taken in isolation, seem to make Iago a seriously jealous man.

> Now I do love her too,
> Not out of absolute lust (though peradventure
> I stand accountant for as great a sin)
> But partly led to diet my revenge
> For that I do suspect the lusty Moor
> Hath leaped into my seat; the thought whereof
> Doth like a poisonous mineral gnaw my vitals.

But if spoken by an actor with serious passion, these lines are completely at variance with the rest of the play, including Iago's other lines on the same subject.

> And it is thought abroad, that twixt my sheets
> He's done my office: I know not if't be true
> Yet I, for mere suspicion in that kind,
> Will do, as if for surety.

It is not inconceivable, given the speed at which he wrote, that, at some point in the composition of Othello, Shakespeare considered making Iago seriously jealous and, like his prototype in Cinthio, a would-be seducer of Desdemona, and that, when he arrived at his final conception of Iago, he overlooked the incompatibility of the *poisonous mineral* and the *wife-for-wife* passages with the rest.

In trying to understand Iago's character one should begin, I believe, by asking why Shakespeare should have gone to the trouble of inventing Roderigo, a character who has no prototype in Cinthio. From a stage director's point of view, Roderigo is a headache. In the first act we learn that Brabantio had forbidden him the house, from which we must conclude that Desdemona had met him and disliked him as much as her father. In the second act, in order that the audience shall know that he has come to Cyprus, Roderigo has to arrive on the same ship as Desdemona, yet she shows no embarrassment in his presence. Indeed, she and everybody else, except Iago, seem unaware of his existence, for Iago is the only person who ever speaks a word to him. Presumably, he has some official position in the army, but we are never told what it is. His entrances and exits are those of a puppet: whenever Iago has company, he obligingly disappears, and whenever Iago is alone and wishes to speak to him, he comes in again immediately.

Moreover, so far as Iago's plot is concerned, there is nothing Roderigo does which Iago could not do better without him. He could easily have found another means, like an anonymous letter, of informing Brabantio of Desdemona's elopement and, for picking a quarrel with a drunken Cassio, he has, on his own admission, other means handy.

Three lads of Cyprus, noble swelling spirits
That hold their honour in a wary distance,
The very elements of this warlike isle
Have I to-night flustered with flowing cups.

Since Othello has expressly ordered him to kill Cassio, Iago could have murdered him without fear of legal investigation. Instead, he not only chooses as an accomplice a man whom he is cheating and whose suspicions he has constantly to allay, but also a man who is plainly inefficient as a murderer and also holds incriminating evidence against him.

A man who is seriously bent on revenge does not take unnecessary risks nor confide in anyone whom he cannot trust or do without. Emilia is not, as in Cinthio, Iago's willing accomplice, so that, in asking her to steal the handkerchief, Iago is running a risk, but it is a risk he has to take. By involving Roderigo in his plot, he makes discovery and his own ruin almost certain. It is a law of drama that, by the final curtain, all secrets, guilty or innocent, shall have been revealed so that all, on both sides of the footlights, know who did or did not do what, but usually the guilty are exposed either because, like Edmund, they repent and confess or because of events which they could not reasonably have foreseen. Don John could not have foreseen that Dogberry and Verges would overhear Borachio's conversation, nor Iachimo that Pisanio would disobey Posthumus' order to kill Imogen, nor King Claudius the intervention of a ghost.

Had he wished, Shakespeare could easily have contrived a similar kind of exposure for Iago. Instead, by giving Roderigo the role he does, he makes Iago as a plotter someone devoid of ordinary worldly common sense.

One of Shakespeare's intentions was, I believe, to indicate that Iago desires self-destruction as much as he desires the destruction of others but, before elaborating on this, let us consider Iago's treatment of Roderigo, against whom he has no grievance—it is he who is injuring Roderigo—as a clue to his treatment of Othello and Cassio.

When we first see Iago and Roderigo together, the situation is like that in a Ben Jonson comedy—a clever rascal is gulling a rich fool who deserves to be gulled because his desire is no more moral than that of the more intelligent avowed rogue who cheats him out of his money. Were the play a comedy, Roderigo would finally realize that he had been cheated but would not dare appeal to the law because, if the whole truth were made public, he would cut a ridiculous or shameful figure. But, as the play proceeds, it becomes clear that Iago is not simply after Roderigo's money, a rational motive, but that his main game is Roderigo's moral corruption, which is irrational because Roderigo has given him no cause to desire his moral ruin. When the play opens, Roderigo is shown as a spoiled weakling, but no worse. It may be foolish of him to hope to win Desdemona's affection by gifts and to employ a go-between, but his conduct is not in itself immoral. Nor is he, like Cloten in

Cymbeline, a brute who regards women as mere objects of lust. He is genuinely shocked as well as disappointed when he learns of Desdemona's marriage, but continues to admire her as a woman full of most blessed condition. Left to himself, he would have had a good bawl, and given her up. But Iago will not let him alone. By insisting that Desdemona is seducible and that his real rival is not Othello but Cassio, he brings Roderigo to entertain the idea, originally foreign to him, of becoming a seducer and of helping Iago to ruin Cassio. Iago had the pleasure of making a timid conventional man become aggressive and criminal. Cassio beats up Roderigo. Again, at this point, had he been left to himself, he would have gone no further, but Iago will not let him alone until he consents to murder Cassio, a deed which is contrary to his nature, for he is not only timid but also incapable of passionate hatred.

> I have no great devotion to the deed:
> And yet he has given me satisfying reasons.
> 'Tis but a man gone.

Why should Iago want to do this to Roderigo? To me, the clue to this and to all Iago's conduct is to be found in Emilia's comment when she picks up the handkerchief.

> My wayward husband hath a hundred times
> Wooed me to steal it. . .
>   what he'll do with it
> Heaven knows, not I,
> I nothing but to please his fantasy.

As his wife, Emilia must know Iago better than anybody else does. She does not know, any more than the others, that he is malevolent, but she does know that her husband is addicted to practical jokes. What Shakespeare gives us in Iago is a portrait of a practical joker of a peculiarly appalling kind, and perhaps the best way of approaching the play is by a general consideration of the Practical Joker.

II

Social relations, as distinct from the brotherhood of a community, are only possible if there is a common social agreement as to which actions or words are to be regarded as serious means to a rational end and which are to be regarded as play, as ends in themselves. In our culture, for example, a policeman must be able to distinguish between a murderous street fight and a boxing match, or a listener between a radio play in which war is declared and a radio news-broadcast announcing a declaration of war.

Social life also presupposes that we may believe what we are told unless we have reason to suppose, either that our informant has a serious motive for deceiving us, or that he is mad and incapable himself of distinguishing between truth and falsehood. If a stranger tries to sell me shares in a gold mine, I shall be a fool if I do not check up on his statements before parting with my money, and if another tells me that he has talked with little men who came out of a flying saucer, I shall assume that he is crazy. But if I ask a stranger the way to the station, I shall assume that his answer is truthful to the best of his knowledge, because I cannot imagine what motive he could have for misdirecting me.

Practical jokes are a demonstration that the distinction between seriousness and play is not a law of nature but a social convention which can be broken, and that a man does not always require a serious motive for deceiving another.

Two men, dressed as city employees, block off a busy street and start digging it up. The traffic cop, motorists and pedestrians assume that this familiar scene has a practical explanation—a water main or an electric cable is being repaired—and make no attempt to use the street. In fact, however, the two diggers are private citizens in disguise who have no business there.

All practical jokes are anti-social acts, but this does not necessarily mean that all practical jokes are immoral. A moral practical joke exposes some flaw in society which is a hindrance to a real community or brotherhood. That it should be possible for two private individuals to dig up a street without being stopped is a just criticism of the impersonal life of a large city where most people are strangers to each other, not brothers; in a village where all the inhabitants know each other personally, the deception would be impossible.

A real community, as distinct from social life, is only possible between persons whose idea of themselves and others is real, not fantastic. There is, therefore, another class of practical jokes which is aimed at particular individuals with the reformatory intent of de-intoxicating them from their illusions. This kind of joke is one of the stock devices of comedy. The deceptions practiced on Falstaff by Mistress Page, Mistress Ford and Dame Quickly, or by Octavian on Baron Ochs are possible because these two gentlemen have a fantastic idea of themselves as lady-charmers; the result of the jokes played upon them is that they are brought to a state of self-knowledge and this brings mutual forgiveness and true brotherhood. Similarly, the mock deaths of Hero and of Hermione are ways of bringing home to Claudio and to Leontes how badly they have behaved and of testing the genuineness of their repentance.

All practical jokes, friendly, harmless or malevolent, involve deception, but not all deceptions are practical jokes. The two men digging up the street, for example, might have been two burglars who wished to recover some swag which they knew to be buried there. But, in that case, having found what they were looking for, they would have departed quietly and never been heard of again, whereas, if they are practical jokers, they must reveal afterwards what they have done or the joke will be lost. The practical joker must not only deceive but also, when he has succeeded, unmask and reveal the truth to his victims. The satisfaction of the practical joker is the look of astonishment on the faces of others when they learn that all the time they were convinced that they were thinking and acting on their own initiative, they were actually the puppets of another's will. Thus, though his jokes may be harmless in themselves and extremely funny, there is something slightly sinister about every practical joker, for they betray him as someone who likes to play God behind the scenes. Unlike the ordinary ambitious man who strives for a dominant position in public and enjoys giving orders and seeing others obey them, the practical joker desires to make others obey him without being aware of his existence until the moment of his theophany when he says: "Behold the God whose puppets you have been and behold, he does not look like a god but is a human being just like yourselves." The success of a practical joker depends upon his accurate estimate of the weaknesses of others, their ignorances, their social reflexes, their unquestioned presuppositions, their obsessive desires, and even the most harmless practical joke is an expression of the joker's contempt for those he deceives.

But, in most cases, behind the joker's contempt for others lies something else, a feeling of self-insufficiency, of a self lacking in authentic feelings and desires of its own. The normal human being may have a fantastic notion of himself, but he believes in it; he thinks he knows who he is and what he wants so that he demands recognition by others of the value he puts upon himself and must inform others of what he desires if they are to satisfy them.

But the self of the practical joker is unrelated to his joke. He manipulates others but, when he finally reveals his identity, his victims learn nothing about his nature, only something about their own; they know how it was possible for them to be deceived but not why he chose to deceive them. The only answer that any practical joker can give to the question: "Why did you do this?" is Iago's: "Demand me nothing. What you know, you know."

In fooling others, it cannot be said that the practical joker satisfies any concrete desire of his nature; he has only demonstrated the weaknesses of others and all he can now do, once he has revealed his existence, is to bow and retire from the stage. He is only related to others, that is, so long as they are unaware of his existence; once they are made aware of it, he cannot fool them again, and the relation is broken off.

The practical joker despises his victims, but at the same time he envies them because their desires, however childish and mistaken, are real to them, whereas he has no desire which he can call his own. His goal, to make game of others, makes his existence absolutely dependent upon theirs; when he is alone, he is a nullity. Iago's self-description, *I am not what I am*, is correct and the negation of the Divine *I am that I am*. If the word motive is given its normal meaning of a positive purpose of the self like sex, money, glory, etc., then the practical joker is without motive. Yet the professional practical joker is certainly driven, like a gambler, to his activity, but the drive is negative, a fear of lacking a concrete self, of being nobody. In any practical joker to whom playing such jokes is a passion, there is always an element of malice, a projection of his self-hatred onto others, and in the ultimate case of the absolute practical joker, this is projected onto all created things. . . .

Since the ultimate goal of Iago is nothingness, he must not only destroy others, but himself as well. Once Othello and Desdemona are dead his "occupation's gone."

To convey this to an audience demands of the actor who plays the role the most violent contrast in the way he acts when Iago is with others and the way he acts when he is left alone. With others, he must display every virtuoso trick of dramatic technique for which great actors are praised, perfect control of movement, gesture, expression, diction, melody and timing, and the ability to play every kind of role, for there are as many "honest" Iagos as there are characters with whom he speaks, a Roderigo Iago, a Cassio Iago, an Othello Iago, a Desdemona Iago, etc. When he is alone, on the other hand, the actor must display every technical fault for which bad actors are criticized. He must deprive himself of all stage presence, and he must deliver the lines of his soliloquies in such a way that he makes nonsense of them. His voice must lack expression, his delivery must be atrocious, he must pause where the verse calls for no pauses, accentuate unimportant words, etc.

III

If Iago is so alienated from nature and society that he has no relation to time and place—he could turn up anywhere at any time—his victims are citizens of Shakespeare's Venice. To be of dramatic interest, a character must to some degree be at odds with the society of which he is a member, but his estrangement is normally an estrangement from a specific social situation.

Shakespeare's Venice is a mercantile society, the purpose of which is not military glory but the acquisition of wealth. However, human nature being what it is, like any other society, it has enemies, trade rivals, pirates, etc., against whom it must defend itself, if necessary by force. Since a mercantile society regards warfare as a disagreeable, but unfortunately sometimes unavoidable, activity and not, like a feudal aristocracy, as a form of play, it replaces the old feudal levy by a paid professional army, nonpolitical employees of the State, to whom fighting is their specialized job.

In a professional army, a soldier's military rank is not determined by his social status as a civilian, but by his military efficiency. Unlike the feudal knight who has a civilian home from which he is absent from time to time but to which, between campaigns, he regularly returns, the home of the professional soldier is an army camp and he must go wherever the State sends him. Othello's account of his life as a soldier, passed in exotic landscapes and climates, would have struck Hotspur as unnatural, unchivalrous, and no fun.

A professional army has its own experiences and its own code of values which are different from those of civilians. In *Othello*, we are shown two societies, that of the city of Venice proper and that of the Venetian army. The only character who, because he is equally estranged from both, can simulate being equally at home in both, is Iago. With army folk he can play the blunt soldier, but in his first scene with Desdemona upon their arrival in Cyprus, he speaks like a character out of *Love's Labour's Lost*. Cassio's comment

Madam, you may relish him more in the soldier than the scholar

is provoked by envy. Iago has excelled him in the euphuistic flirtatious style of conversation which he considers his forte. Roderigo does not feel at home, either with civilians or with soldiers. He lacks the charm which makes a man a success with the ladies, and the physical courage and heartiness which make a man popular in an army mess. The sympathetic aspect of his character, until Iago destroys it, is a certain humility; he knows that he is a person of no consequence. But for Iago, he would have remained a sort of Bertie Wooster, and one suspects that the notion that Desdemona's heart might be softened by expensive presents was not his own but suggested to him by Iago.

In deceiving Roderigo, Iago has to overcome his consciousness of his inadequacy, to persuade him that he could be what he knows he is not, charming, brave, successful. Consequently, to Roderigo and, I think, to Roderigo only, Iago tells direct lies. The lie may be on a point of fact, as when he tells Roderigo that Othello and Desdemona are not returning to Venice but going to Mauritania, or a lie about the future, for it is obvious that, even if Desdemona is seducible, Roderigo will never be the man. I am inclined to think that the story Iago tells Roderigo about his disappointment over the lieutenancy is a deliberate fabrication. One notices, for example, that he contradicts himself. At first he claims that Othello had appointed Cassio in spite of the request of three great ones of the city who had recommended Iago, but then a few lines later, he says

Preferment goes by letter and affection,
Not by the old gradation where each second
Stood heir to the first.

In deceiving Cassio and Othello, on the other hand, Iago has to deal with characters who consciously think well of themselves but are unconsciously insecure. With them, therefore, his tactics are different; what he says to them is always possibly true. . . .

In Cinthio nothing is said about the Moor's color or religion, but Shakespeare has made Othello a black Negro who has been baptized.

No doubt there are differences between color prejudice in the twentieth century and color prejudice in the seventeenth and probably few of Shakespeare's audience had ever seen a Negro, but the slave trade was already flourishing and the Elizabethans were certainly no innocents to whom a Negro was simply a comic exotic. Lines like

> . . . an old black ram
> is tupping your white ewe. . .
> The gross clasps of a lascivious Moor. . .
> What delight shall she have to look on the devil

are evidence that the paranoid fantasies of the white man in which the Negro appears as someone who is at one and the same time less capable of self-control and more sexually potent than himself, fantasies with which, alas, we are only too familiar, already were rampant in Shakespeare's time.

The Venice of both *The Merchant of Venice* and *Othello* is a cosmopolitan society in which there are two kinds of social bond between its members, the bond of economic interest and the bond of personal friendship, which may coincide, run parallel with each other or conflict, and both plays are concerned with an extreme case of conflict.

Venice needs financiers to provide capital and it needs the best general it can hire to defend it; it so happens that the most skillful financier it can find is a Jew and the best general a Negro, neither of whom the majority are willing to accept as a brother.

Though both are regarded as outsiders by the Venetian community, Othello's relation to it differs from Shylock's. In the first place, Shylock rejects the Gentile community as firmly as the Gentile community rejects him; he is just as angry when he hears that Jessica has married Lorenzo as Brabantio is about Desdemona's elopement with Othello. In the second place, while the profession of usurer, however socially useful, is regarded as ignoble, the military profession, even though the goal of a mercantile society is not military glory, is still highly admired and, in addition, for the sedentary civilians who govern the city, it has a romantic exotic glamour which it cannot have in a feudal society in which fighting is a familiar shared experience.

Thus no Venetian would dream of spitting on Othello and, so long as there is no question of his marrying into the family, Brabantio is delighted to entertain the famous general and listen to his stories of military life. In the army, Othello is accustomed to being obeyed and treated with the respect due to his rank and, on his rare visits to the city, he is treated by the white aristocracy as someone important and interesting. Outwardly, nobody treats him as an outsider as they treat Shylock. Consequently, it is easy for him to persuade himself that he is accepted as a brother and when Desdemona accepts him as a husband, he seems to have proof of this.

It is painful to hear him say

> But that I love the gentle Desdemona
> I would not my unhoused free condition
> Put into circumscription or confine
> For the sea's worth

for the condition of the outsider is always unhoused and free. He does not or will not recognize that Brabantio's view of the match

If such actions may have passage free,
Bond-slaves and pagans shall our statesmen be

is shared by all his fellow senators, and the arrival of news about the Turkish
fleet prevents their saying so because their need of Othello's military skill is
too urgent for them to risk offending him. . . . But for his occupation, he
would be treated as a black barbarian.

The overcredulous, overgood-natured character which, as Iago tells us,
Othello had always displayed is a telltale symptom. He had *had* to be
overcredulous in order to compensate for his repressed suspicions. Both in his
happiness at the beginning of the play and in his cosmic despair later, Othello
reminds one more of Timon of Athens than of Leontes.

Since what really matters to Othello is that Desdemona should love him as
the person he really is, Iago has only to get him to suspect that she does not,
to release the repressed fears and resentments of a lifetime, and the question
of what she has done or not done is irrelevant.

Iago treats Othello as an analyst treats a patient except that, of course, his
intention is to kill not to cure. Everything he says is designed to bring to
Othello's consciousness what he has already guessed is there. Accordingly, he
has no need to tell lies. Even his speech, "I lay with Cassio lately," can be a
truthful account of something which actually happened: from what we know of
Cassio, he might very well have such a dream as Iago reports. Even when he
has worked Othello up to a degree of passion where he would risk nothing by
telling a direct lie, his answer is equivocal and its interpretation is left to
Othello.

Othello: What hath he said?
Iago: Faith that he did—I know not what he did.
Othello: But what?
Iago: Lie—
Othello: With her?
Iago: With her, on her, what you will.

Nobody can offer Leontes absolute proof that his jealousy is baseless; similarly, as Iago is careful to point out, Othello can have no proof that Desdemona really is the person she seems to be.

Iago makes his first decisive impression when, speaking as a Venetian with
firsthand knowledge of civilian life, he draws attention to Desdemona's
hoodwinking of her father.

Iago: I would not have your free and noble nature
             Out of self-bounty be abused, look to't:
             I know our country disposition well:
             In Venice they do let God see the pranks
             They dare not show their husbands: their best conscience
             Is not to leave undone but keep unknown.
Othello: Dost thou say so?

Iago:	She did deceive her father, marrying you:
	And when she seemed to shake and fear your looks,
	She loved them most.
Othello:	And so she did.
Iago:	Why, go to then.
	She that so young could give out such a seeming
	To seal her father's eyes up, close as oak.
	He thought 'twas witchcraft.

And a few lines later, he refers directly to the color difference.

Not to affect many proposed matches,
Of her own clime, complexion and degree,
Whereto we see in all things nature tends,
Foh! one may smell in such a will most rank,
Foul disproportion, thoughts unnatural.
But pardon me: I do not in position
Distinctly speak of her, though I may fear
Her will, recoiling to her better judgment
May fall to match you with her country-forms,
And happily repent.

Once Othello allows himself to suspect that Desdemona may not be the person she seems, she cannot allay the suspicion by speaking the truth but she can appear to confirm it by telling a lie. Hence the catastrophic effect when she denies having lost the handkerchief.

If Othello cannot trust her, then he can trust nobody and nothing, and precisely what she has done is not important. In the scene where he pretends that the Castle is a brothel of which Emilia is the Madam, he accuses Desdemona, not of adultery with Cassio, but of nameless orgies.

Desdemona:	Alas, what ignorant sin have I committed?
Othello:	Was this fair paper, this most goodly book
	Made to write whore on. What committed?
	Committed. O thou public commoner,
	I should make very forges of my cheeks
	That would to cinders burn up modestly
	Did I but speak thy deeds.

And, as Mr. Eliot has pointed out, in his farewell speech his thoughts are not on Desdemona at all but upon his relation to Venice, and he ends by identifying himself with another outsider, the Moslem Turk who beat a Venetian and traduced the state.

Everybody must pity Desdemona, but I cannot bring myself to like her. Her determination to marry Othello—it was she who virtually did the proposing—seems the romantic crush of a silly schoolgirl rather than a mature affection; it is Othello's adventures, so unlike the civilian life she knows, which captivate her rather than Othello as a person. He may not have

practiced witchcraft, but, in fact, she is spellbound. And despite all Brabantio's prejudices, her deception of her own father makes an unpleasant impression: Shakespeare does not allow us to forget that the shock of the marriage
kills him.

Then, she seems more aware than is agreeable of the honor she has done
Othello by becoming his wife. When Iago tells Cassio that "our General's wife
is now the General" and, soon afterwards, soliloquizes

> His soul is so infettered to her love
> That she may make, unmake, do what she list
> Even as her appetite shall play the god
> With his weak function

he is, no doubt, exaggerating, but there is much truth in what he says. Before
Cassio speaks to her, she has already discussed him with her husband and
learned that he is to be reinstated as soon as is opportune. A sensible wife
would have told Cassio this and left matters alone. In continuing to badger
Othello, she betrays a desire to prove to herself and to Cassio that she can
make her husband do as she pleases.

Her lie about the handkerchief is, in itself, a trivial fib but, had she really
regarded her husband as her equal, she might have admitted the loss. As it is,
she is frightened because she is suddenly confronted with a man whose
sensibility and superstitions are alien to her.

Though her relation with Cassio is perfectly innocent, one cannot but share
Iago's doubts as to the durability of the marriage. It is worth noting that, in
the willow-song scene with Emilia, she speaks with admiration of Ludovico
and then turns to the topic of adultery. Of course, she discusses this in general
terms and is shocked by Emilia's attitude, but she does discuss the subject
and she does listen to what Emilia has to say about husbands and wives. It is
as if she had suddenly realized that she had made a *mésalliance* and that the
sort of man she ought to have married was someone of her own class and color
like Ludovico. Given a few more years of Othello and of Emilia's influence
and she might well, one feels, have taken a lover.

IV

And so one comes back to where one started, to Iago, the sole agent in the
play. A play, as Shakespeare said, is a mirror held up to nature. This particular
mirror bears the date 1604, but, when we look into it, the face that confronts
us is our own in the middle of the twentieth century. We hear Iago say the
same words and see him do the same things as an Elizabethan audience heard
and saw, but what they mean to us cannot be exactly the same. To his first
audience and even, maybe, to his creator, Iago appeared to be just another
Machiavellian villain who might exist in real life but with whom one would

never dream of identifying oneself. To us, I think, he is a much more alarming figure; we cannot hiss at him when he appears as we can hiss at the villain in a Western movie because none of us can honestly say that he does not understand how such a wicked person can exist. For is not Iago, the practical joker, a parabolic figure for the autonomous pursuit of scientific knowledge through experiment which we all, whether we are scientists or not, take for granted as natural and right?

As Nietzsche said, experimental science is the last flower of asceticism. The investigator must discard all his feelings, hopes and fears as a human person and reduce himself to a disembodied observer of events upon which he passes no value judgment. Iago is an ascetic. "Love" he says, "is merely a lust of the blood, and a permission of the will."

The knowledge sought by science is only one kind of knowledge. Another kind is that implied by the Biblical phrase, "Then Adam knew Eve, his wife," and it is this kind I still mean when I say, "I know John Smith very well." I cannot know in this sense without being known in return. If I know John Smith well, he must also know me well.

But, in the scientific sense of knowledge, I can only know that which does not and cannot know me. Feeling unwell, I go to my doctor who examines me, and says "You have Asian flu," and gives me an injection. The Asian virus is as unaware of my doctor's existence as his victims are of a practical joker.

Further, to-know in the scientific sense means, ultimately, to-have-power-over. To the degree that human beings are authentic persons, unique and self-creating, they cannot be scientifically known. But human beings are not pure persons like angels; they are also biological organisms, almost identical in their functioning, and, to a greater or lesser degree, they are neurotic, that is to say, less free than they imagine because of fears and desires of which they have no personal knowledge but could and ought to have. Hence, it is always possible to reduce human beings to the status of things which are completely scientifically knowable and completely controllable.

This can be done by direct action on their bodies with drugs, lobotomies, deprivation of sleep, etc. The difficulty about this method is that your victims will know that you are trying to enslave them and, since nobody wishes to be a slave, they will object, so that it can only be practiced upon minorities like prisoners and lunatics who are physically incapable of resisting.

The other method is to play on the fears and desires of which you are aware and they are not until they enslave themselves. In this case, concealment of your real intention is not only possible but essential for, if people know they are being played upon, they will not believe what you say or do what you suggest. An advertisement based on snob appeal, for example, can only succeed with people who are unaware that they are snobs and that their snobbish feelings are being appealed to and to whom, therefore, your adver-tisement seems as honest as Iago seems to Othello.

Iago's treatment of Othello conforms to Bacon's definition of scientific enquiry as putting Nature to the Question. If a member of the audience were to interrupt the play and ask him: "What are you doing?" could not Iago answer with a boyish giggle, "Nothing. I'm only trying to find out what Othello is really like"? And we must admit that his experiment is highly successful. By the end of the play he does know the scientific truth about the object to which he has reduced Othello. That is what makes his parting shot, "What you know, you know," so terrifying for, by then, Othello has become a thing, incapable of knowing anything.

And why shouldn't Iago do this? After all, he has certainly acquired knowledge. What makes it impossible for us to condemn him self-righteously is that, in our culture, we have all accepted the notion that the right to know is absolute and unlimited. The gossip column is one side of the medal; the cobalt bomb the other. We are quite prepared to admit that, while food and sex are good in themselves, an uncontrolled pursuit of either is not, but it is difficult for us to believe that intellectual curiosity is a desire like any other, and to realize that correct knowledge and truth are not identical. To apply a categorical imperative to knowing, so that, instead of asking, "What can I know?" we ask, "What, at this moment, am I meant to know?"—to entertain the possibility that the only knowledge which can be true for us is the knowledge we can live up to—that seems to all of us crazy and almost immoral. But, in that case, who are we to say to Iago—"No, you mustn't."

Women and Men in *Othello*

Carol Thomas Neely

What should such a fool
Do with so good a woman?

Relations between love, sexuality, and marriage are under scrutiny in *Othello*, as in the comedies, problem plays, and *Hamlet*. In more extreme form than in the problem plays, we see here the idealization and degradation of sexuality, the disintegration of male authority and the loss of female power, the isolation of men and women, and the association of sexual consummation with death. The festive comedies conclude with the anticipation of fertile marriage beds. The problem comedies achieve their resolutions with the help of midpoint bedtricks. The marriage bed is at the very heart of the tragedy of *Othello*; offstage but dramatically the center of attention in the first scene and again in the first scene of the second act, it is literally and symbolically at the center of the last scene and is explicitly hidden from sight at the conclusion. Whether the marriage is consummated, when it is consummated, and what the significance of this consummation is for Othello and Desdemona have all been an important source of debate about the play. Throughout its critical history, *Othello*, like the other problem plays, has generated passionate and radically conflicting responses—responses that are invariably tied to the critics' emotional responses to the characters and to the gender relations in the play. Othello, Iago, and Desdemona have been loved and loathed, defended and attacked, judged and exonerated by critics just as they are by characters within the play.

"Almost damned in a fair wife" is Leslie Fiedler's alternate title for his chapter on *Othello* in *The Stranger in Shakespeare*. In it he asserts of the women in the play: "Three out of four, then, [are] weak, or treacherous, or both."[1] Thus he seconds Iago's misogyny and broadens the attack on what

From *Broken Nuptials in Shakespeare's Plays* (New Haven: Yale University Press, 1985), 105–35. Reprinted by permission of the author. The original footnotes to this essay have been shortened.

[1]Leslie Fiedler, *The Stranger in Shakespeare* (New York: Stein and Day, 1972), p. 169. The three he refers to are Emilia, Bianca, and Barbary. His description of Desdemona after her marriage as "a passive, whimpering Griselda" (p. 142) suggests that his statistics might more accurately be put at four out of four.

Leavis has called "The sentimentalist's *Othello*," the traditional view of the play held by Coleridge, Bradley, Granville-Barker, Knight, Bayley, Gardner, and many others.[2] These "Othello critics," as I shall call them, accept Othello at his own high estimate. They are enamored of his "heroic music," affirm his love, and, like him, are overwhelmed by Iago's diabolism, to which they devote much of their analysis.[3] Like Othello, they do not always argue rationally or rigorously for their views and so are vulnerable to attacks on their romanticism or sentimentality. Reacting against these traditionalists, "Iago critics" (Eliot, Empson, Kirschbaum, Rossiter, and Mason, as well as Fiedler and Leavis)[4] take their cues from Iago. Like him, they are attracted to Othello, unmoved by his rhetoric, and eager to "set down the pegs that make this music."[5] They attack Othello at his most vulnerable point, his love. They support their case by quoting Iago's estimates of Othello; they emphasize Iago's realism and "honesty"[6] while priding themselves on their own. Their realism or cynicism gives them, with Iago, an apparent invulnerability. But, like "Othello critics," they share the bias and blindness of the character whose perspective they adopt. Most damagingly, both groups of critics, like both Othello and Iago, badly misunderstand and misrepresent the women in the play.

Iago critics implicitly demean Desdemona, for if Othello's character and love are called into question, then her love for him loses its justification and validity. Explicitly they have little to say about her. Othello critics idealize her along with the hero, but, like him, they have a tendency to see her as an object. The source of her sainthood seems a passivity verging on catatonia: "Desdemona is helplessly passive. She can do nothing whatever. She cannot retaliate even in speech; no, not even in silent feeling. . . . She is helpless

[2] F. R. Leavis, "Diabolic Intellect and the Noble Hero or the Sentimentalist's *Othello*," in *The Common Pursuit* (London: Chatto & Windus, 1952), pp. 136–59; *Coleridge's Shakespearean Criticism*, ed. Thomas M. Raysor (Cambridge, Mass.: Harvard University Press, 1930), 1: 121–25; A. C. Bradley, *Shakespearean Tragedy*, 2d ed. (London: Macmillan, 1964), pp. 175–242; H. Granville-Barker, *Prefaces to Shakespeare* (London: B. T. Batsford, 1958), 2: 3–149; G. Wilson Knight, *The Wheel of Fire* (1930: rpt. London: Oxford University Press, 1946), pp. 107–31; John Bayley, *The Characters of Love* (New York: Basic Books, 1960), pp. 125–201; Helen Gardner, "The Noble Moor," *Proceedings of the British Academy* 41 (1955): 189–205.

[3] On Othello's music, see especially Knight, *Wheel of Fire*, pp. 107–18, and Bayley, *Characters of Love*, pp. 150–59. On Iago, see especially Bradley, *Shakespearean Tragedy*, pp. 207–37, and Knight, pp. 125–26.

[4] T. S. Eliot, "Shakespeare and the Stoicism of Seneca," *Selected Essays* (New York: Harcourt Brace, 1950), pp. 110–11; A. P. Rossiter, *Angel with Horns* (New York: Theatre Arts, 1961), pp. 189–208; H. A. Mason, *Shakespeare's Tragedies of Love* (New York: Barnes & Noble, 1970), pp. 59–161; William Empson, "Honest in *Othello*," in *The Structure of Complex Words* (London: Chatto & Windus, 1951), pp. 218–49; Leo Kirschbaum, "The Modern Othello," *ELH* 11 (1944): 283–96.

[5] *Othello*, Arden Shakespeare, ed. M. R. Ridley (Cambridge, Mass.: Harvard University Press, 1958), 2.1.200. All *Othello* quotations are from this edition, for I find persuasive Ridley's arguments for using the 1622 Quarto rather than the First Folio as his copy text.

[6] For such quotations, see Fiedler, *Stranger in Shakespeare*, p. 158, and Mason, *Shakespeare's Tragedies of Love*, pp. 75–76. On Iago's honesty, see Empson, "Honest in *Othello*," and Mason, p. 75.

because her nature is infinitely sweet and her love absolute. . . . Desdemona's suffering is like that of the most loving of dumb creatures tortured without cause by the being he adores."[7] Iago critics, finding the same trait, condemn Desdemona for it. "But the damage to her symbolic value is greater when we see her passively *leaving everything to Heaven*. She ought in a sense to have *embodied* Heaven, given us a human equivalent that would 'make sense' of Heaven. For this task she had the wrong sort of purity."[8] When Desdemona is credited with activity, she is condemned for that, too; she is accused of being domineering, of using witchcraft, of rebelliousness, disobedience, wantonness.[9] Although discussion of her has frequently been an afterthought to the analysis of the men, recently she has been the focus of a number of studies.[10] Both Othello and Iago critics tend to see good versus evil as the play's central theme, Othello versus Iago as the play's central conflict, and hence, the major tragedies as its most important context.

A third group of "Iago-Othello critics," including Kenneth Burke, Arthur Kirsch, Stephen Greenblatt, Stanley Cavell, Edward Snow, and Richard Wheeler, elide the divisions between the first two groups and view the play from a perspective more like my own.[11] They see Othello and Iago as closely identified with each other; they are "two parts of a single motive—related not as the halves of a sphere, but each implicit in the other."[12] They find the source of the tragedy in Iago-Othello's anxieties regarding women, sexuality, and marriage—anxieties that are universal and generated by underlying social or psychological paradigms. Like Iago-Othello, these critics find the tragedy inevitable and locate its "cause" in an impersonal, implacable agency outside of the protagonists: for Burke, this "cause" is the "disequilibrium of monoga-

[7]Bradley, *Shakespearean Tragedy*, p. 179. See also Granville-Barker, *Prefaces*, p. 124; Knight, *Wheel of Fire*, pp. 119–20.

[8]Mason, *Shakespeare's Tragedies of Love*, p. 147. See also Fiedler, *Stranger in Shakespeare*, passim.

[9]Robert Dickes, "Desdemona: An Innocent Victim?" *American Imago* 27 (1970): 279–97; Fiedler, *Stranger in Shakespeare*, pp. 141–42; Richard Flatter, *The Moor of Venice* (London: William Heinemann, 1950), pp. 72–74; G. Bonnard, "Are Othello and Desdemona Innocent or Guilty?" *English Studies* 30 (1949): 175–84; Jan Kott, *Shakespeare Our Contemporary* (with three new essays), trans. Boleslaw Taborski (Garden City, N.Y.: Doubleday/Anchor, 1966), pp. 118–19.

[10]Neglect of her is apparent even in R. B. Heilman's *Magic in the Web* (Lexington: University of Kentucky Press, 1956) and in Marvin Rosenberg's *The Masks of Othello* (Berkeley: University of California Press, 1961), books that seek for Desdemona a middle ground between passivity and aggressiveness and that frequently illuminate the details of the play.

[11]Kenneth Burke, "*Othello*: An Essay to Illustrate a Method," *Hudson Review* 4 (1951–52): 165–203; Arthur Kirsch, *Shakespeare and the Experience of Love* (Cambridge: Cambridge University Press, 1981), pp. 10–39; Stephen Greenblatt, *Renaissance Self-Fashioning from More to Shakespeare* (Chicago: University of Chicago Press, 1980), pp. 232–54; Stanley Cavell, *The Claim of Reason: Wittgenstein, Scepticisin, Morality, and Tragedy* (Oxford: Clarendon Press, 1979), pp. 481–96; Edward Snow, "Sexual Anxiety and the Male Order of Things in *Othello*," *English Literary Renaissance* 10 (1980): 384–412; Richard P. Wheeler, " 'And my loud crying still': The Sonnets, *The Merchant of Venice*, and *Othello*," in *Shakespeare's Rough Magic: Renaissance Essays for C. L. Barber*, ed. Peter Erickson and Coppélia Kahn (Newark: University of Delaware Press, 1985).

[12]Burke, "*Othello*," p. 196.

mistic love" (p. 168); for Kirsch, it is "the polarization of erotic love," with its psychological and theological roots; for Greenblatt, it is ambivalent Christian views of marital sexuality as chaste and adulterous; for Snow, it is "the male order of things," the patriarchal society that represses male sexuality and suppresses female sexuality at the behest of the superego; for Cavell, it is universal (male) fears of impotence and deflowering, and of mortality; for Wheeler, it is the conflict among male autonomy, female sexuality, and nurturing femininity. These critics do not ignore or sanctify Desdemona; nor do they condemn her explicitly. All emphasize her active, loving, passionate sensuality and extol her worth. An effect of their focus is, however, that she, more than Iago, becomes the cause of Othello's destruction; it is her relaxed, frank, sexuality and the passionate response it arouses in Othello which generate the tragedy.[13] These critics show how Desdemona's virtues catalyze Othello's sexual anxieties, but they fail to emphasize enough that she has the potential to provide a cure for them.

With this third group of critics, I argue that the play's central theme is love—specifically marital love—that its central conflict is between the men and the women, and that contexts as illuminating as the tragedies are its source, Cinthio's *Gli Hecatommithi* and Shakespeare's preceding comedies.[14] Within *Othello* it is Emilia who most explicitly speaks to this theme, recognizes this central conflict, and inherits from the heroines of comedy the role of potential mediator of it. She is dramatically and symbolically the play's fulcrum. It is as an Emilia critic, then, that I should like to approach the play, hoping to perceive it with something akin to her clear-sighted passion.

Gli Hecatommithi could have provided *Othello* with its theme and organizing principle as well as with its plot. The battle of the sexes in marriage is its central motif and dominates the frame, subject matter, and arrangement of the tales. In the introduction the company debates whether harmony can be achieved in marriage. Ponzio denies this, supporting his view with platitudes

---

[13]See, for example, Cavell, "we need to ask not so much how Iago gained his power as how Desdemona lost hers" (486); Greenblatt, "Desdemona performs no such acts of defiance, but her erotic submission, conjoined with Iago's murderous cunning, far more effectively, if unintentionally, subverts her husband's carefully fashioned identity" (244); and Snow, "The tragedy of the play, then, is the inability of Desdemona to escape or triumph over restraints and Oedipal prohibitions that domesticate woman to the conventional male order of things" (407). By downplaying the power of Iago or subsuming him as a part of Othello, these critics underestimate, I think, the role the fantasy of cuckoldry plays in Othello's destruction. It is this fantasy which calls out and makes deadly whatever anxieties Othello feels about Desdemona's sexuality, and the fantasy is not, I would argue, inevitable.

[14]I do not mean to suggest that critics have not noted that love is a theme in the play. This theme is at the center of John Bayley's study of *Othello* in *The Characters of Love*. Helen Gardner emphasizes the play's concern with the union of romantic love and marriage in "The Noble Moor," as well as in her useful survey of criticism, " 'Othello': A Retrospect, 1900–67," in *Shakespeare Survey* 21 (1968): 1–11. Rosalie Colie, in *"Othello* and the Problematics of Love," in *Shakespeare's Living Art* (Princeton, N.J.: Princeton University Press, 1974), pp. 148–67, brilliantly sees *Othello* as an "unmetaphoring" and a reanimation of the conventions of Renaissance love lyrics.

that Iago would relish: "Better bury a woman than marry her"; "For there to be peace between husband and wife, the husband must be deaf and the wife blind." Fabio, the group's leader, asserts instead that "the only rational love is that which has marriage as its goal, and that this is the quiet of true and wise lovers, coupled together, cooling their amorous flames with sage discourse and in legitimate union."[15] *Othello* similarly presents marriage as either potentially strife-ridden or harmonious. In *Gli Hecatommithi* the debate continues in the tales, and in the Third Decade it is intensified by the inflammatory subject matter—the infidelity of husbands and wives. The seventh tale, the source of *Othello*, is a rebuttal of the sixth, in which a husband discovers his wife's infidelity and, as the company judges, "most prudently" *(prudentissimamente)* arranges to have her "accidentally" drowned. In the eighth tale, a contrast to the two preceding it, harmony supersedes warfare. A wife forgives her unfaithful husband and wins him back, behaving with a "prudence" *(la prudenza)* exactly opposite to the behavior of the husbands in tales six and seven. *Othello* similarly rings changes on the theme of male and female in a series of parallel and contrasting couples—Desdemona/Othello, Emilia/Iago, Bianca/Cassio—along with fantasy couples—Roderigo/Desdemona, Cassio/Desdemona, Othello/Emilia. Throughout the tales of the Third Decade it is most often the men who intensify the conflicts, practicing infidelity or taking revenge on wives they suspect of infidelity; the wives, even when wronged, often succeed in mending the relationships. The men in *Othello* similarly seek revenge; the women similarly seek to secure harmonious relationships but fail to do so.

Their predecessors in this task are the heroines of Shakespearean comedy, to which *Othello* shows pervasive and profound resemblances.[16] Though it is almost always assumed that *Othello* is dominated by a tightly meshed plot, the play seems, like many of the comedies, loosely plotted, held together by theme. The conflicts introduced in the first act between Desdemona and her father and between Venetians and Turks evaporate before they are under way exactly as do those between Hermia and Egeus in *Midsummer Night's Dream* and between Duke Frederick and Duke Senior in *As You Like It*. As in the comedies, these early plot developments are presented in a flat, compressed

[15]The translation is Geoffrey Bullough's, in *Narrative and Dramatic Sources of Shakespeare* (London: Routledge & Kegan Paul, 1973), 7:239. Subsequent Italian quotations are from M. Giovanbattista Giraldi Cintio, *De Gli Hecatommithi* (Vinegia: G. Scotto, 1566), vol. 1. Translations are my own.

[16]The play's resemblances to comedy have often been noted. Barbara Heliodora C. De Mendonça, in " 'Othello': A Tragedy Built on a Comic Structure," *Shakespeare Survey* 21 (1968): 31–38, and Richard Zacha, "Iago and the *Commedia dell'arte*," *Arlington Quarterly* 2 (Autumn 1969): 98–116, discuss the play's similarities of subject, plot, and character with the *commedia dell'arte*. Mason, *Tragedies of Love*, pp. 73–97, and Fiedler, *Stranger in Shakespeare*, pp. 43–55, show how the first act or the first two acts form a Shakespearean comedy in miniature. Susan Snyder, *The Comic Matrix of Shakespeare's Tragedies* (Princeton, N.J.: Princeton University Press, 1979), pp. 70–90, explores how *Othello* releases conflicts that are latent in Shakespeare's comic treatment of love.

way; they seem almost an excuse to get the characters to the woods or to Cyprus where the play's real conflicts emerge. Iago plots the remainder of the play; but his scheme is slight, repetitive, and flawed. It has been found lacking in both motive (like Rosalind's plot in *As You Like It*) and goal (like Don John's plot in *Much Ado About Nothing*), and although the play's increasing intensity is undeniable, there is little actual plot development between the end of the first phase of the temptation scene (3.3.275) and the attempt on Cassio's life in Act 5. Iago's destruction of Othello, like Rosalind's education of Orlando, is not merely linear. Both are continually starting over; they are repeated variations on opposite themes: Iago works to induce fantasy and Rosalind to dispel it. Neither entirely succeeds. Iago's plot, like those of the comedies, rests on coincidence and absurdity. The handkerchief is like the givens of the comedies—the fairy juice, the caskets, the disguises, the identical twins; it is trivial and ridiculous but, as I shall show, symbolically all-important. The play proceeds as much by a clash of attitudes, viewpoints, and sexes as by plot developments.

Structure, too, imitates that of the pastoral comedies in its movement from an urban center to an isolated retreat, with resultant intensity, freedom, breakdown, and interaction among disparate characters.[17] Though Othello refers to Cyprus as a "town of war," once the threats of Turks and the storm have lifted, it is instead Venus's isle, a place for celebration—relaxation, drinking, eating (dinner arrangements are a frequent topic of conversation here as in Arden), flirting, sleeping, lovemaking. In the comedies, the potential corruption of these activities is suggested in witty banter, songs, comic simile and metaphor; in *Othello*, this corruption becomes literal.

The play is a terrifying completion of the comedies. In them, realism and romanticism, lust and desire, heterosexual and homosexual bonds, male and female power are held in precarious balance. The men's idealism, misogyny, foolishness, and anxiety are mocked, transformed, and dispelled—"laugh[ed] to scorn" (*AYL*, 4.2.19)—by disguises and mock deaths, by parodied or aborted nuptials, by delayed or deceitful consummations. The women, through their "high and plenteous wit and invention" (4.1.185), transform the men from foolish lovers into—we trust—sensible husbands, and at the end submit to their control. Although "The cuckoo then, on every tree, / Mocks married men," (*LLL*, 5.2.896–97), the mockery grounds love without seriously threatening it. The comedies' relaxed incorporation of marital sexuality is evident in their endings, which look forward to fruitful, harmonious marital consummation—in the fairy-blessed beds of the *Midsummer Night's Dream* couples; the rewon beds of Bassanio and Portia, Gratiano and Nerissa in *Merchant of Venice*; the "well-deserved bed" of Silvius and the rest in *As You Like It*. But in *Othello*, the marriage has taken place before the play begins, and its consummation may already be under way, imaged by Iago as a theft, a violent attack. In the play, women's wit is constrained, their power over men

---

[17]See Alvin Kernan, Introduction to *Othello* in *The Complete Signet Classic Shakespeare*, and Fiedler, *Stranger in Shakespeare*.

is lost, and the men are transformed downward—"to be now and now a sensible man, by and by a fool, and presently a beast" (2.3.296–97). The men's profound anxieties and murderous fantasies cannot be restrained by the women's affection, wit, and shrewishness. The play ends as it began, in a world of men—political, loveless, undomesticated.[18]

The men in *Othello* extend and darken the anxieties of the comedy heroes. They are, in Emilia's words, "murderous coxcombs" (5.2.234). Three out of the five attempt murder; five out of the five are foolish and vain. Roderigo, most obviously a coxcomb, shows in exaggerated fashion the dangerous combination of romanticism and misogyny and the dissociation of love and sex that all the men share. He is a parody of the conventional Petrarchan lover: love is a "torment," death a "physician" (1.3.308–09), Desdemona "full of most blest condition" (2.1.247), and consummation of their relationship securely impossible. Yet he easily accepts Desdemona's supposed adultery and the necessity of Cassio's murder; his casual cynicism comes to outdo Iago's: " 'Tis but a man gone" (5.1.10). The other men have similarly divided and possessive views of women. Brabantio shifts abruptly from protective affection for the chaste Desdemona—"of spirit/ So still and quiet, that her motion/ Blush'd at her self" (1.3.94–96)—to physical revulsion from the assertive sexuality revealed by her elopement—"I had rather to adopt a child than get it" (1.3.191). Cassio's divided view is more conventionally accommodated. He idealizes the "divine Desdemona," flirting courteously and cautiously with her and rejecting Iago's insinuations about her sexuality; this side of women is left to Bianca, who is a "monkey" and a "fitchew" and is used and degraded for it. Othello's conflict regarding women is more profound, and the other men's solutions are not open to him. Because of his marriage and his integrity, he cannot, like Roderigo, assert Desdemona's chastity and corruptibility simultaneously; like Cassio, direct his divided emotions toward different objects; or, like Brabantio, disown the problem.

Othello's shifts from the idealization of women to their degradation are "extravagant and wheeling" (1.1.136). Iago is the catalyst, but Othello makes his task easy. At the play's start, Othello's idealistic love, like that of the comedy heroes, needs some realistic grounding in the facts of sex. For Othello, sex is secondary and potentially either frivolous or debilitating and in conflict with his soldier's duty:

> no, when light-wing'd toys,
> And feather'd Cupid, foils with wanton dullness
> My speculative and active instruments,
> That my disports corrupt and taint my business,
> Let housewives make a skillet of my helm,
> And all indign and base adversities
> Make head against my reputation!
> (1.3.268–74)

18Fiedler, *Stranger in Shakespeare*, p. 194.

Marriage and consummation naturally pose a threat to this idealistic love. Othello's greeting on Cyprus suggests his preference for a perpetually unconsummated courtship:

> If it were now to die,
> 'Twere now to be most happy, for I fear
> My soul hath her content so absolute,
> That not another comfort, like to this
> Succeeds in unknown fate.
>
>   (2.1.189–93)

In response Desdemona asserts instead quotidian joys:

> The heavens forbid
> But that our loves and comforts should increase,
> Even as our days do grow.

Perhaps she, like Rosalind or Viola or the ladies in *Love's Labor's Lost*, might have tempered Othello's idealism, his need for absolute, unchanging love. Instead, it is nudged by Iago into its antithesis—contempt for women, disgust at sexuality, terror of cuckoldry, the preference for literal death over metaphorical "death." The acceptance of cuckoldry and sexuality found in the comedies—"as horns are odious, they are necessary" (*AYL*, 3.3.49–50)—is impossible for Othello. Instead he turns Petrarchan imagery against Desdemona—"O thou black weed, why art so lovely fair?" (4.2.69)—praising and damning her simultaneously. His conflicts are resolved, his needs to idealize and degrade her to maintain their love intact are momentarily reconciled only when he kills her, performing a sacrifice which is also a murder.[19]

Iago, though primarily the manipulator of these conflicts in the other men, is also the victim of his own. His cynical generalizations are, like those of Jaques, the parody and inverse of the romantics' claims; they are self-conscious, defensive, self-aggrandizing, and divorced from reality: "My muse labours/ And thus she is deliver'd" (2.1.127–28). Like the other men, he accepts generalizations—especially generalizations about women—as true, provided they are "apt and of great credit" (2.1.282), "probable, and palpable to thinking" (1.2.76). Like the others, he is careful not to contaminate his fantasies about women with facts. Roderigo does not court Desdemona in person, Othello does not immediately confront Desdemona and Cassio with his suspicions, and Iago never tries to ascertain whether or not Emilia is unfaithful.

In fact—like Don John and Parolles—he has little contact with the women in the play. He is at ease in Act 2 engaging Desdemona in witty banter, but he is subdued and almost speechless in Act 4 when confronted with her misery

---

[19]See Winifred M. T. Nowottny's excellent discussion of the way in which the murder reconciles Othello's conflicts, "Justice and Love in *Othello*," *University of Toronto Quarterly* 21 (1951–52): esp. 340–44.

and fidelity. Treating Emilia with casual contempt throughout, he is astounded by her exposure of him in the last scene. Like Brabantio, Iago assumes that "consequence" will "approve" his "dream" (2.3.58) and ignores evidence to the contrary.

Even protected as it is from reality, Iago's cynicism/misogyny has cracks just as Othello's idealism does. He has a grudging admiration for and envy of Desdemona's "blest condition," Othello's "constant, noble loving, nature" (2.1.289), and Cassio's "daily beauty" (5.1.19). He aspires to Cassio's job and Othello's "content" and tries to identify with their love for Desdemona—"now I do love her too" (2.1.286), although this love is immediately subsumed under notions of lust and revenge. The tension between his theoretical misogyny and his awareness of Desdemona's particular virtue drives him to resolve the conflicts, to turn that virtue "into pitch" (2.3.351), just as his verses extravagantly praise the deserving woman the better to be able to diminish her.[20] Othello's conflict has the opposite issue; he murders Desdemona to redeem her from degradation.

The women in *Othello* are not murderous, nor are they foolishly idealistic or anxiously cynical, as the men are. From the start they, like the comedy heroines, combine realism with romance, mockery with affection. Bianca comically reflects the qualities of the women as Roderigo does those of the men. The play associates her with the other two women by means of the overheard conversation about her which Othello takes to be about Desdemona and by means of her irate and essentially just response to Emilia's attack: "I am no strumpet, but of life as honest / As you, that thus abuse me" (5.1.120–21). At this point, Iago tries to fabricate evidence against her, just as Othello, in the scene immediately following, fabricates a case against Desdemona. Bianca's active, open-eyed enduring affection is similar to that of the other women. She neither romanticizes love nor degrades sex. She sees Cassio's callousness but accepts it wryly—" 'Tis very good, I must be circumstanc'd" (3.4.199). She mocks him to his face but not behind his back, as he does her. Her active pursuit of Cassio is in contrast to his indifference, to Roderigo's passivity, and to Othello's naiveté. Even when jealous, she continues to feel affection for Cassio, accusing him openly and demanding that he come to dinner on her terms. The play's humanization of her, much like, for example, that of the bourgeois characters at the end of *Love's Labor's Lost,* underlines the folly of the male characters (and critics) who see her as merely a whore.[21]

---

[20]Jane Adamson, *Othello as Tragedy.: Some Problems of Judgment and Feeling* (Cambridge: Cambridge University Press, 1980), has a fine analysis of Iago's self-defensive strategies, his "lust for imperviousness."

[21]Timothy Murray, in "*Othello,* An Index and Obscure Prologue to Foul Generic Thoughts," an unpublished paper circulated to the seminar on Gender and Genre in Shakespeare at the Second International Shakespeare Congress, Stratford-upon-Avon, August 1981, vigorously, if a bit improbably, argues for Bianca as the play's hero and thus establishes himself as a Bianca critic.

Emilia articulates the balanced view that Bianca embodies—"and though we have some grace, / Yet have we some revenge" (4.3.92–93). She, like other Shakespearean shrews, especially Beatrice and Paulina, combines sharp-tongued honesty with warm affection. Her views are midway between Desdemona's and Bianca's and between those of the women and those of the men. She rejects the identification with Bianca yet sympathizes with female promiscuity. She corrects Desdemona's occasional naiveté but defends her chastity. Although she comprehends male jealousy and espouses sexual equality, she seems remarkably free from jealousy herself. She wittily sees cuckoldry and marital affection as compatible: "Who would not make her husband a cuckold, to make him a monarch?" (4.3.74–75). She understands, but tolerates, male fancy; the dangers of such tolerance become evident in this play as they never do in the comedies.

Desdemona's and Emilia's contrasting viewpoints in the willow scene have led critics to think of them as opposites, but both are strong, realistic, and compliant.[22] When we first see them together, they encourage and participate in Iago's misogynist banter but reject his stereotypes. Desdemona here defends Emilia from Iago's insults just as Emilia will ultimately defend Desdemona from Othello's calumny. While Desdemona is no shrew (though she might be said to approach one in the matter of Cassio's reinstatement), her love is everywhere tempered by realism and wit like that of the comedy heroines. During courtship she hides, as they did, behind a sort of disguise, in this case not male dress, but a mask of docility and indifference which conceals her passion from both her father and Othello. Like Iago's docile and deserving woman she is one that could "think, and ne'er disclose her mind, / See suitors following, and not look behind" (2.1.156–57). Eventually, though, she takes the lead in the courtship as the heroines do; she finds an excuse to be alone with Othello, mocks him by speaking of him "dispraisingly" (3.3.73), and traps him into a proposal using indirection not unlike Rosalind's with Orlando.

After marriage, as during courtship, Desdemona's love tempers romance with realism, obedience with self-assertion. She is indifferent to Cassio's elaborate compliments (2.1.87 ff.). She rejects Othello's desire to stop time, instead emphasizing love's growth.[23] Her healthy, casual acceptance of sexuality is evident in her banter with Iago and with the clown, in her affirmation that she "did love the Moor, to live with him" (1.3.248), and in her refusal to

[22]Adamson discusses in detail parallels and contrasts between Emilia and Desdemona (and Bianca) in chapter 7 and emphasizes Emilia's "range of attitudes and feelings," which encompasses those of Desdemona and Iago (245–46).

[23]Rosalind, likewise, educates Orlando in the necessities of time, and Bianca stresses its importance to Cassio. She, like Rosalind, is more anxious about time than Desdemona, who is assured of future meetings with Othello. Compare Bianca's "What, keep a week away? seven days and nights?" and "I pray you bring me on the way a little, / And say, if I should see you soon at night" (3.4.171, 195–96) with Desdemona's "Why then to-morrow night, or Tuesday morn, / Or Tuesday noon, or night, or Wednesday morn" (3.3.61–62).

postpone consummation of "the rites for which I love him" (1.3.257). She will not allow herself to be idealized; nor will she romanticize Othello. She had spoken "dispraisingly" of him during courtship, and she mocks him gently after marriage:

> Tell me, Othello: I wonder in my soul,
> What you could ask me, that I should deny?
> Or stand so mammering on?
>
> Shall I deny you? no, farewell, my lord.
> (3.3.69–71, 87)

She reminds herself, in an emphatically short line:

>   nay, we must think
> Men are not gods;
> Nor of them look for such observances
> As fits the bridal.
> (3.4.145–48)

Her concise statement about her love reveals its balance and health:

> I saw Othello's visage in his mind,
> And to his honours, and his valiant parts
> Did I my soul and fortunes consecrate.
> (1.3.252–54)

She loves Othello for his body and mind, for his reputation and actions; she consecrates herself to him spiritually and practically.

Desdemona's spirit, clarity, and realism do not desert her entirely in the latter half of the play as many critics and performances imply. Her inability to defend herself is partly the result of Othello's refusal to voice his suspicions directly. When he does so in the brothel scene, she persistently questions him to discover exactly what he is accusing her of and defends herself as "stoutly" (3.1.45) as she had earlier defended Cassio:

> If to preserve this vessel for my lord
> From any hated foul unlawful touch,
> Be not to be a strumpet, I am none.
> (4.2.85–87)

Her naiveté and docility in the willow scene are partly a result of her confusion and fear, but perhaps also partly a protective facade behind which she waits, as she did during courtship, while determining the most appropriate and fruitful reaction to Othello's rage. The conversation and the song with its alternate last verses explore alternate responses to male perfidy— acceptance "*Let nobody blame him, his scorn I approve*"—or retaliation "*If I court moe women, you'll couch with moe men*" (4.3.51–56). Emilia supports retaliation—"The ills we do, their ills instruct us so" (103)—though, like Bianca, she practices acceptance. Desdemona's final couplet suggests that she is groping for a third response, one that is midway between "grace" and "revenge," one that would be more active than acceptance yet more loving than retaliation:

> God me such usage send,
> Not to pick bad from bad, but by bad mend!
> (4.3.104–05)

The lines are a reply to Emilia and a transformation of an earlier couplet of Iago's: ". . . fairness and wit / The one's for use, the other using it" (2.1.129–30). Desdemona will put fairness and wit to *use* in a sense that includes and goes beyond the sexual one, acknowledging and using "bad" to heal it. Her earlier command to have the wedding sheets put on her bed seems one expression of this positive usage. Just before her death, as earlier in the handkerchief and brothel scenes, Desdemona strives to "mend" Othello's debased view of her, transforming the "sins" he accuses her of into "loves I bear to you"; a testimony to her pure, active, humble, fertile affections. But Othello recorrupts them: "And for that thou diest" (5.2.40–41).[24]

The men's sense of identity and worth is dependent not only on their relations with women but on their bonds with other men who guarantee their honor and reputation. Vanity, rivalry, and dependence characterize the relations among all the men in the play. Jaques's portrait of the soldier aptly sums up traits which they share: "Full of strange oaths and bearded like the pard, / jealous in honor, sudden and quick in quarrel, / Seeking the bubble reputation / Even in the cannon's mouth" (2.7.149–52), traits which are those of coxcombs but grow murderous here. Cassio, of course, explicitly voices the men's concern with "the bubble reputation" and reveals how central their position and image are to their sense of identity: "I ha' lost my reputation! I ha' lost the immortal part, sir, of myself, and what remains is bestial" (2.3.255). This identity is highly vulnerable because the men view reputation as detachable, external; it is a matter of rank or title, something to be conferred—or removed—by other men.[25] Hence Iago continues to care about the rank of lieutenant in spite of his continuing intimacy with Othello. Cassio equally relishes his title; "The lieutenant is to be saved before the ancient," he boasts (2.3.103). Othello must fire Cassio for appearances' sake and because Montano "is of great fame in Cyprus" (3.1.46). Othello's dependence on others' "rich opinion" (2.3.286) creates conflict in his love; "feather'd Cupid"

---

[24]Kirsch, p. 32, Greenblatt, p. 251, and Snow, p. 389 (see n. 11) all analyze this passage as conveying "the ultimate horror of the play" (Kirsch, p. 32)—namely, Othello's association of Desdemona's sexuality and his own with guilt and shame and contamination.

[25]David L. Jeffrey and Patrick Grant suggest, in "Reputation in *Othello*," *Shakespeare Studies* 6 (1970): 197–208, that Othello corrupts the ideal of reputation, desiring "bad fame" rather than "good fame," secular rather than heavenly glory. It seems difficult to determine whether the characters are to be viewed as debasing the ideal or whether it is the ideal itself which Shakespeare is questioning.

potentially threatens "reputation" in the first act, and later he finds the scorn due the cuckold almost as difficult to bear as the loss of Desdemona.

Although they are neither "bearded like a pard" nor "full of strange oaths," the men in this play, in their vanity, desire the swaggering manliness which such characteristics conjure up. Iago successfully plays on the others' nervousness about this "manliness," driving them to acts of "malicious bravery" (1.1.100). He jovially calls them "man" while questioning their manhood or urging new proofs of it. He goads Cassio into "manly" drunkenness and good fellowship—"What, man, 'tis a night of revels, the gallants desire it" (2.3.39). He urges Othello, "Good sir, be a man" (4.1.65). He flatters Roderigo's manly pride: "if thou hast that within thee indeed, which I have greater reason to believe now than ever, I mean purpose, courage, and valour, this night show it" (4.2.213–16). His suggestive battle cries to Roderigo imply a connection that all the men assume between sexual and martial prowess: "Wear thy good rapier bare, and put it home. . . . fix most firm thy resolution" (5.1.2, 5); perhaps the gull's melodramatic attack on Cassio is "satisfying" even beyond Iago's "reasons," compensating him for his lack of sexual success. Inversely, cuckoldry is seen by Othello as invalidating his military glories; only the murder of Desdemona and his own suicide restore his pride in his "occupation."

Since the reputation and manliness which the men covet is achieved in competition with others, all the men are "jealous in honor, sudden and quick in quarrel." Iago's success derives largely from his ability to manipulate male rivalries, verifying his friendship with each man by shared contempt toward another. In this way, he feeds the men's need for self-esteem, insures their bond with him, and exacerbates their potential rivalries with each other.[26] He enrages Brabantio by claiming that his friend has "robbed" his daughter. He gulls Roderigo by demeaning Othello and urging that they have common cause against him: "my cause is hearted, thine has no less reason, let us be communicative in our revenge against him: if thou canst cuckold him, thou doest thyself a pleasure, and me a sport" (1.3.366–69). He almost offhandedly belittles Othello to Cassio, Cassio to Montano, Othello to Lodovico. His entrapment of Othello begins by insinuating not Desdemona's unfaithfulness but Othello's cuckoldry, his loss of "good name." This cuckoldry triply threatens Othello: with the loss of Desdemona's love; with the supremacy of Cassio, his lieutenant, over him; and with the loss of his reputation and the scorn of other men.[27]

---

[26]Similarly, in *Julius Caesar*, male bonds are established largely through alliances against mutual enemies. The conspirators are linked by their desire to destroy Caesar; Antony's love for Caesar finds its fullest expression when he defends his honor against those who murdered him, and the triumvirate is precariously held together by their desire to avenge Caesar's murder.

[27]Coppélia Kahn, *Man's Estate: Masculine Identity in Shakespeare* (Berkeley: University of California Press, 1981), pp. 140–46, discusses the nature and function of cuckoldry in the play.

Iago offers to compensate for these losses with his own love—to replace Othello's other bonds with their friendship. Iago's attack is set up when Othello demands that Iago prove his love by complying with his general's wishes (he has just been threatened by Desdemona's seeming to put similar pressure on him): "If thou dost love me, / Show me thy thought" (3.3.119–20). It concludes with Othello's attempt to replace his love for Desdemona with a vow of vengeance and a (coerced) bond with Iago, through which it seems he can restore his heroism and control by regaining the love and dependence he fears he has lost:

Iago: Witness, you ever-burning lights above,
             You elements that clip us round about,
             Witness that here Iago doth give up
             The excellency of his wit, hand, heart,
             To wrong'd Othello's service: let him command,
             And to obey him shall be in me remorse,
             What bloody work so ever.
Othello:
             I greet thy love;
             Not with vain thanks, but with acceptance bounteous.
                                                         (3.3.470–78)

Iago's feigned love gives him power which Desdemona's genuine love cannot counteract; he destroys his superior by destroying Othello's belief in his own superiority and the bonds which confirm that superiority. Nowhere is his power and its roots in Othello's fear of inferiority to other men more ruthlessly and painfully demonstrated than when Iago engineers Othello's eavesdropping of his and Cassio's mockery of Bianca; here, Othello's wounded vanity, obsessive jealousy, and competitive concern for reputation and manliness coalesce in his terse asides with their sexual-martial double entendres:

Do you triumph, Roman, do you triumph?
So, so, so, so; laugh that wins.
Ha' you scor'd me? Well.
I see that nose of yours, but not that dog I shall throw 't to.
                                            (4.1.118,122,126,140)[28]

Iago likewise gains power by imposing on the play, through his bawdy, an image of heterosexuality which, like male bonds, is seen as competitive and violent. Sexuality here is not merely represented as an act of male assertion, as in *Much Ado*, or as painful debilitation, as in *All's Well*, but as a violent, bestial overpowering of the woman by the man which degrades both: "an old black ram / Is tupping your white ewe," "you'll have your daughter cover'd with a Barbary horse," "he hath boarded a land carrack"; Desdemona is in the

---

[28]Editors have been unclear about the precise implications of *Roman* and *triumph* but the latter perhaps contains a sexual innuendo.

"gross clasps of a lascivious Moor" (1.1.88–89; 110–11; 2.2.50; 1.1.126). This vision of sexuality comes to replace the tender, hallowed passion of Desdemona for Othello, her desire to participate in "the rites for which I love him" (1.3.257), as Othello imagines that Cassio "lie[s] with her, lie[s] on her" (4.1.38), "pluck[s] up kisses by the roots" (3.3.429). The inevitable culmination of this fantasy occurs when Othello clasps, covers, and stifles Desdemona— Down, strumpet. . . . Nay and you strive . . ." (5.2.80,82), silencing her "even in the bed she hath contaminated" (4.1.203)—and then kills himself.[29]

Although the men's aggression destroys the women, their attempts at heroic violence against each other do not completely succeed. Othello vows to kill Cassio but never does, and Roderigo's murder attempt on Cassio fails. It takes Cassio and Iago together to kill poor Roderigo, and Othello cannot kill Iago. The cowardice, clumsiness, and insecurity that belie male pretensions to valor are manifested comically—as in the *Twelfth Night* duel or in the gulling of Parolles—in the hesitation of Lodovico and Gratiano to answer Roderigo's and Cassio's cries for help: "Two or three groans; it is a heavy night, / These may be counterfeits, let's think't unsafe / To come into the cry without more help" (5.1.42–45). Even after Iago's entrance, they still hang back, ascertaining his identity (5.1.51) but ignoring his cry (thus allowing him to murder Roderigo), introducing themselves (5.1.67), discovering Cassio's identity (5.1.70), and finally coming to his side after Bianca, who has just entered (5.1.75). They still offer no assistance but only perfunctory sympathy and an anticlimactic explanation: "I am sorry to find you thus, I have been to seek you" (5.1.81).

Male friendship, like male courage, is in this play sadly deteriorated from the Renaissance ideal. In romance and comedy, the world of male friendship in which the work opens (see, for example, the *Arcadia, Two Gentlemen of Verona, The Merchant of Venice, Love's Labor's Lost*) is disrupted and transcended by romantic love. In the problem comedies, male friendship is already corrupted as friends exploit and betray each other. As *Othello* begins, romantic love already dominates, but friendship is reasserted in perverted form. Iago's hypocritical friendship for all of the men, which aims to gratify his own will and gain power over them, is the model for male friendship in the play. Brabantio's "love" for Othello evaporates when his friend marries his daughter. Roderigo intends to use Iago though he is worse used by him. Othello has no hestitation in cashiering Cassio and ordering his death. The men's vanity and rivalry, their preoccupation with rank and reputation, and their cowardice render them as incapable of friendship as they are of love.

The women, in contrast, are indifferent to reputation and partially free of

[29]Madelon Gohlke, " 'I wooed thee with my sword': Shakespeare's Tragic Paradigms," in *The Woman's Part: Feminist Criticism of Shakespeare,* ed. Carolyn Ruth Swift Lenz, Gayle Greene, and Carol Thomas Neely (Urbana: University of Illinois Press, 1980), discusses the way in which men who make themselves vulnerable to women must destroy those women to regain their control and relieve their own sense of powerlessness (see especially pp. 155–56).

vanity, jealousy, and competitiveness. Desdemona's willingness "to incur a general mock" is evident in her elopement and her defense of it, and in her request to go to Cyprus. Emilia braves scorn to defend her mistress, "Let heaven, and men, and devils, let 'em all, / All, all cry shame against me, yet I'll speak" (5.222–23). If Cassio's description of Bianca corresponds at all to fact, she too ignores reputation, comically, to pursue him—"she haunts me in every place . . . she falls thus about my neck; . . . so hangs, and lolls, and weeps upon me" (4.1.131–36)—and we see her brave the confusion of the night and the ugliness of Iago's insinuations to come to Cassio's side when he is wounded. Bianca's jealousy is also in contrast to the men's; instead of corroding within, it is quickly vented and dissipates, leaving her affection for Cassio essentially unchanged. Furthermore, she makes no effort to discover her rival, to obtain "proof," or to get revenge. Likewise Emilia, though expert at noting and analyzing jealousy, seems untouched by it herself. Even her argument for the single standard is good-natured; it contains little hatred of men and no personal animosity toward Iago.

Desdemona is neither jealous nor envious nor suspicious. She is not suspicious or possessive about Othello's job, his intimacy with Iago, or his "love" for Cassio, but supports all three. She seems entirely lacking in the sense of class, race, rank, and hierarchy that concerns the men and is shared by Emilia, who refuses to be identified with Bianca. She treats her father, the Duke, Othello, Cassio, Iago, Emilia, even the clown, with precisely the same combination of politeness, generosity, openness, and firmness. Emilia's and Desdemona's lack of competitiveness, jealousy, and class consciousness facilitates their growing intimacy, which culminates in the willow scene. The scene, sandwiched between two exchanges of Iago and Roderigo, sharply contrasts the genuine intimacy of the women with the hypocritical friendship of the men, while underlining the women's isolation and powerlessness.[30] Emilia's concern for Desdemona is real, and her advice well meant, whereas Iago's concern for Roderigo is feigned, his advice deadly—"whether he kill Cassio, / Or Cassio him, or each do kill the other, / Every way makes my game" (5.1.12–14). Roderigo accepts Iago's "satisfying reasons," finding them sufficient to justify murder; Desdemona rejects Emilia's reasonable justification of wives' adultery without rejecting the concern that prompts her to offer it. In the willow scene sympathy stretches from Emilia and Desdemona to include Barbary and the protagonist of the song—all victims of male perfidy; in the Roderigo/Iago scenes, enmity reaches Cassio. In this play romantic love is destroyed by the semblance of male friendship, which itself soon disintegrates. Meanwhile, friendship between women is established and dominates the play's final scene. Othello chooses Iago's friendship over Desdemona's love temporarily and unwittingly; Emilia's choice of Desdemona over Iago is

---

[30]Carole McKewin, "Counsels of Gall and Grace: Intimate Conversations between Women in Shakespeare's Plays," in Lenz et al., *The Woman's Part*, pp. 128–29.

voluntary and final. Though the stakes here are higher, the friendship of Desdemona and Emilia is reminiscent of the generous, witty female friendship in the comedies, where women share their friends' hardships (Rosalind and Celia), vigorously defend their honor (Beatrice and Hero), support their stratagems (Portia and Nerissa), and sympathize with and aid even their rivals (Julia and Sylvia, Viola and Olivia, Helen and Diana, Mariana and Isabella). But in *Othello*, without the aid of disguise, bedtricks, or mock deaths, the women cannot protect each other from male animosity.

Because of the men's vanity, competitiveness, and concern for honor and reputation, when they do act, they try to exonerate themselves, persistently placing blame for their actions outside themselves. Even Cassio, while abusing himself for his drunkenness, comes to personify that drunkenness as a "devil," something which invades him. Roderigo blames Iago for his failure to prosper: "Iago hurt [me]. Iago set [me] on" (5.2.329–30). Iago, at the last, instead of boasting about the execution of his grand design (as, for example, Satan does in *Paradise Lost*), tries to shift responsibility for it elsewhere—to Bianca, to Emilia, and finally, even after the facts are known, to Othello: "I told him what I thought, and told no more / Than what he found himself was apt and true" (5.2.177–78). Othello's longing for passivity and his denial of responsibility are intertwined throughout the play. He both sees himself as passive and desires passivity. His narrative history before the senate, the basis for our original impression of the heroic Othello, describes, when closely examined, what he has suffered rather than what he has done; he speaks of "moving accidents by flood and field; / Of hair-breadth scapes 'i th' imminent deadly breach; / Of being taken by the insolent foe; / And sold to slavery, and my redemption hence" (1.3.135–38), and of his subsequent enslavement by Desdemona, whom he entertained with similar tales, for example, "of some distressed stroke / That my youth suffer'd" (1.3.157–58). Pity is indeed the appropriate response to his tale. His farewell to arms is, curiously, a farewell to "content," to "the tranquil mind" (3.3.354), and to the instruments of war; it is they who are seen as active and heroic, not himself. His vow of revenge, likening him to the "compulsive course" of the "Pontic sea," reveals the longing for external control and validation which underlies the heroic stance. In a parallel passage after his error is revealed, he again wants to be swept along by a current: "Blow me about in winds, roast me in sulphur, / Wash me in steep-down gulfs of liquid fire!" (5.2.280–81), to be consumed by hell-fire rather than by desire. Two of his significant actions in the play—the cashiering of Cassio and the murder of Desdemona—are, in a sense, "compulsive," achieved, as he himself notes, only when passion "Assays to lead the way" (2.3.198), and he feels out of control or seeks a false sense of being under the control of an impersonal "cause." Even at his suicide, when he *is* in control, he sees himself as "you" rather than "I," object rather than actor, as "being wrought, / Perplex'd in the extreme . . . one whose subdued eyes, . . . Drops tears as fast as the Arabian trees / Their medicinal gum" (5.2.246–51). In the anecdote that accompanies his suicide, Othello is actor and acted upon, hero and victim, and his action is again violent and enraged. But it is also premeditated—and gives him, at last, the command over himself he has not achieved throughout.

Desdemona's self-recriminations must be seen in the light of Othello's evasions. Critics have found them puzzling, excessive, intolerable, even neurotic[31]; perhaps they are all of these. But her unwarranted self-accusations—"beshrew me much, Emilia, / I was (unhandsome warrior as I am) / Arraigning his unkindness with my soul; / But now I find I had suborn'd the witness, / And he's indited falsely" (3.4.148–52)—and her false assumption of responsibility for her death—"Nobody, I myself, farewell" (5.2.125) provide the sharpest possible contrast to the men's excuses. Her last request, "Commend me to my kind lord," not only conveys her forgiveness but is one final active effort to restore their mutual love. She is not, however, a willing victim and does not sacrifice herself to Othello, although she does not attribute guilt to him either. She defends her innocence and pleads for her life; but he murders her anyway.

Desdemona's cryptic lines after she is apparently dead give to her actual death some of the functions and the feel of Shakespearean mock deaths. Like the women who stage them, she defends her innocence—"A guiltless death I die" (5.2.123)—assumes responsibility for the death, and seeks to transform Othello into a "kind lord." When the audience finds that the woman it has thought dead remains alive, the poignant, momentary impression that this may be a mock death intensifies the horror of the scene. Desdemona's refusal to blame and hurt Othello is at the heart of her loving virtue. Hero, Helen, and Hermione likewise do not blame their detractors directly. But this virtue coalesces in dangerous ways with Othello's need to blame and hurt her.

From the beginning, Desdemona has viewed love as risk and challenge. She has violently uprooted herself from her father's protection and the conventional expectations of Venetian society, whereas Othello has put himself into "circumscription and confine" for her. She has initiated while Othello has responded. She is neither the "rose" or "chrysolite" of Petrarchan convention seen by Othello nor the saint extolled by critics. She sets the stage for her wooing by an extraordinarily active listening, which Othello naturally notices and describes; she would "with a greedy ear / Devour up my discourse" (1.3.149–50). She engenders his love by her own: "She lov'd me for the dangers I had pass'd, / And I lov'd her that she did pity them" (168–69); she proposes and elopes. She is the one who challenges her father directly, who

[31]Dickes, "Desdemona, an Innocent Victim?" and Stephen Reid, "Desdemona's Guilt," *American Imago* 27 (1970): 279–97; 245–62. Adamson offers a sympathetic discussion of the defensive aspects of Desdemona's passivity, as she does of the men's, (pp. 235–58; see n. 20 above). Gayle Greene, " 'This that you call love' " Sexual and Social Tragedy in *Othello,*" *Journal of Women's Studies in Literature* 1 (1979): 16–32, sees this passivity as grounded in a social ideal of femininity; both see Desdemona as more consistently passive than I do.

determines to go to Cyprus. She moves after marriage to bring the lovers'
idiom down to earth, using all of her "plenteous wit and invention" at their
reunion and in the discussion of Cassio. All the characters in the play make
mention of her energizing power. Cassio, hyperbolically, attributes to her the
ability to influence recalcitrant nature:

> Tempests themselves, high seas, and howling winds,
> The gutter'd rocks, and congregated sands,
> Traitors ensteep'd, to clog the guiltless keel,
> As having sense of beauty, do omit
> Their common natures, letting go safely by
> The divine Desdemona.
>
> (2.1.68–73)

Othello is awed by her power to move man and beast—"She might lie by an
emperor's side, and command him tasks. . . . O, she will sing the savageness
out of a bear" (4.1.180–81, 184–85)—testifying, late in the play, to his
ineradicable love for her. Iago, in soliloquy, attributes to her unlimited power
over Othello—"she may make, unmake, do what she list" (2.3.337). And
Desdemona herself, vowing support for Cassio, reveals her sense of her own
persistence and controlling force:

> If I do vow a friendship, I'll perform it
> To the last article.
>
> (3.1.21–22)

But Desdemona's energy, assertiveness, and power are made possible by
Othello's loving response to her, just as his subduing of himself to her, his
"garner[ing] up" (4.2.58) of his heart is engendered by her love for him. Each
has "thrive[d]" (1.3.25) in the apparent security of their mutual love, but their
joyous subduing of themselves to each other leaves them vulnerable. With
that certainty lost, with their responses to each other mistrusted, Othello is
plunged into chaos and Desdemona into helplessness. In this crisis, he seeks
to be "unhoused" again, and she refuses to acknowledge the loss of her new
home: "Commend me to my kind lord" (5.2.126).

All of the women, in spite of their affection, good sense, and energy, fail to
transform or to be reconciled with the men. The sexes, so sharply differenti-
ated in the play, badly misunderstand each other.[32] The men, as we have seen,
persistently misconceive the women; the women fatally overestimate the
men. Each sex, trapped in its own values and attitudes, misjudges the other.
Iago acts on the hypothesis that women, on the one hand, share his concern
with reputation and propriety ("Be wise, and get you home" [5.2.224], he
orders Emilia) and, on the other, enact his salacious fantasies. Othello as-

---

[32]Although Greene's discussion, which appeared after the original publication of mine, takes
quite a different view of the women and the play, she likewise pinpoints this mutual misunder-
standing as the source of the tragedy.

sumes, with Iago's prompting, that just as he is the stereotypical soldier, foreigner, older husband, so Desdemona will be the stereotypical mistress, Venetian, young bride. He responds to Iago's claim to knowledge about Desdemona—"knowing what I am, I know what she shall be"—with comic enthusiasm: "O thou art wise, 'tis certain" (4.1.73–74). Likewise the women attribute their own qualities to the men. Desdemona projects her lack of jealousy onto Othello. Emilia attributes to Iago her own capacity for empathy: "I know it grieves my husband, / As if the case were his" (3.3.3–4). Even Bianca, because she does not view herself as a whore in her relationship with Cassio, is surprised that he should treat her as one. Hence, although the women recognize the foolishness of the men's fancies, they are all too tolerant of them. Emilia steals the handkerchief for the sake of Iago's "fantasy" (3.3.303) and thus assures the success of his plot. Desdemona's salutation to Othello in Act 3 is lamentably prophetic—"Be it as your fancies teach you, / What e'er you be, I am obedient" (3.3.88–90). He leaves her to be instructed in her whoredom.

The lost handkerchief becomes the emblem of the women's power and its loss. Both Othello's original description of the handkerchief and its part in the plot reveal that it is a symbol of women's loving, civilizing, sexual power. It has passed from female sibyl to female "charmer" to Othello's mother to Desdemona. Othello is merely a necessary intermediary between his mother and his wife—"She dying, gave it me, / And bid me, when my fate would have me wive, / To give it her" (3.4.61–63). Its creator, the sibyl, who "In her prophetic fury sew'd the work," and its next owner, the Egyptian charmer who "could almost read / The thoughts of people," reveal the source of its power in women's passionate intuitive knowledge. This knowledge, it seems, enables them to use and control sexuality. The middle ground that women find between lust and abstinence (as the men in the play cannot do) is suggested in the description of the process by which the handkerchief is made. The worms that did "breed" the silk, emblems of death, sexuality, and procreation, are "hallow'd." The thread they spin vitally and naturally from themselves is artificially improved, dyed in "mummy" which is "conserve[d] from maiden's hearts." The handkerchief then represents marital chastity—sexuality transformed by loving fidelity. Its function is to chasten and control men's love and desire:

> she told her, while she kept it
> 'Twould make her amiable, and subdue my father
> Entirely to her love; but if she lost it,
> Or made a gift of it, my father's eye
> Should hold her loathly, and his spirits should hunt
> After new fancies.
>
> (3.4.56–61)

It represents women's ability to moderate men's erratic (and erotic) "fancies," to "subdue" their promiscuity (assumed to be the norm under the double standard outlined by Emilia), and perhaps, by extension, their vanity, romanticism, jealousy, and rage as well. The handkerchief is the symbol of Desdemona's loving power over Othello:

> Excellent wretch, perdition catch my soul,
> But I do love, thee, and when I love thee not,
> Chaos is come again.
>
> (3.3.91–93)

The handkerchief is lost, literally and symbolically, not because of the failure of Desdemona's love, but because of Othello's loss of faith in that love. Once lost, the female power it symbolizes is degraded and constrained, and comedy gives way to tragedy.

After the handkerchief's original loss, all of the characters, men and women alike, misuse its power and misinterpret its symbolism, marking the disruption of all the love relationships in the play. The abuse begins when Othello pushes it aside, rejecting Desdemona's loving attempt to heal the pain on his forehead, and Emilia picks it up to give it to Iago, thereby making herself subservient to him and placing her loyalty to her husband above affection for Desdemona. Her silence about its whereabouts confirms her choice. Shakespeare's alteration of his source—removing Iago from an active role in the theft of the handkerchief and dramatizing its loss in these particular circumstances—emphasizes the handkerchief's symbolism and the active role played by Desdemona and Emilia in the misunderstandings that follow from its loss. In Iago's hands, its function is reversed; it is used to confirm his power over Emilia and Othello and to induce in Othello loathing for Desdemona. Iago's first mention of it incites Othello to reject love and embrace vengeance (3.3.441–86). Now the hero, under Iago's tutelage, proceeds to reinterpret the handkerchief as *his* love token—a pledge of his love and possession of Desdemona and of her sexual fidelity—"She is protectress of her honour too, / May she give that?" (4.1.14–15). Hence its loss provides "proof" of his suspicions. The reinterpretation continues in his altered description of its history in the last act. As he uses it to support his "cause" against Desdemona, it becomes "the recognizance and pledge of love / Which *I* first gave her . . . an antique token / *My father* gave my mother" (5.2.215–18; italics mine). It is now a symbol of the male control and love which Desdemona has betrayed; hence she must be punished—"Yet she must die, else she'll betray more men" (5.2.6).[33]

Desdemona, too, alters her view of the handkerchief. Instinctively using it to cure Othello's pain, she almost succeeds. She "loves" the handkerchief (3.3.297) and recognizes the danger of its loss. But when pressed by Othello, she rejects its significance—"Then would to God that I had never seen it!" (3.4.75). Her rejection reflects the failure of her power. In Desdemona's earlier discussion of Cassio she was in control; now her persistence is foolish

---

[33]Critics also willfully reinterpret—and misinterpret—the handkerchief.

and provokes Othello's rage. Even in the early part of this scene, Desdemona deftly parries and "mends" Othello's ugly insinuations, turning his implied sexual vices into passionate virtues:

Othello: . . . this hand is moist, my lady.
Desdemona: It yet has felt no age, nor known no sorrow.
. . . .
Othello: For here's a young and sweating devil here,
                     That commonly rebels: 'tis a good hand,
                     A frank one.
Desdemona: You may indeed say so,
                     For 'twas that hand that gave away my heart.
                                                          (3.4.32–41)

But after the tale of the handkerchief she loses the initiative. She tries to regain it by—just barely—lying, and by changing the subject. But the attempt to calm and heal Othello fails. Her lie, like Ophelia's similarly well-intentioned lie to Hamlet, is generated by her love but signals the loss of her maiden's power and innocence; it confirms—Othello believes—his notions about female depravity, as Ophelia's lie confirms Hamlet's similar views. Both women, rejected by their lovers, do not regain the initiative in the relationship.

The handkerchief next creates conflict in the Iago/Emilia and Cassio/Bianca relationships. Both men use it, as Othello has done, to consolidate their power over women. When Emilia regrets its theft, Iago snatches it from her and dismisses her, "Be not you known on 't" (3.3.324). Cassio similarly gives orders to Bianca regarding it and dismisses her (3.4.185–89). She, though jealous, agrees to copy the work; her willingness to be "circumstanc'd" (200) is a flaw which all the women share. Later, however, she returns the handkerchief in a scene parallel and in contrast to that when the handkerchief was lost. Bianca, like Othello, is jealous. She flings down the handkerchief as he pushed it aside, and it lies on the stage ignored by the couple, who go off to a possible reconciliation. But Bianca's refusal to be used by the handkerchief or by Cassio leads to a truce and a supper engagement, whereas Othello's refusal to be healed by it opens the breach in his relationship with Desdemona that culminates in her murder.

Eventually the handkerchief's original function is reestablished; it becomes the vehicle through which civilizing control is returned to the women. The reference to it by Othello in the last scene enlightens Emilia; it ends Iago's domination of her, engenders her accusations of Othello and Iago, and enables her to prove Desdemona's faithful "amiable" love. Othello is once again "subdue[d]" to this love. Emilia, stealing the handkerchief, is catalyst for the play's crisis; revealing its theft, she is catalyst for the play's denouement.

Her reiteration of "husband" and "mistress" in the last scene emphasizes the play's central division and the "divided duty" of Emilia. When Iago's villainy is made known, she shifts her allegiance unhesitatingly. Instead of tolerating both Iago's "fancy" and Desdemona's virtue, she denounces the one and affirms the other. She questions Iago's manliness: "Disprove this villain, if thou be'st a man: / He said thou told'st him that his wife was false, / I know thou didst not, thou art not such a villain" (5.2.173–75). Then she rejects the wifely virtues of silence, obedience, and prudence that are demanded of her, "unhousing" herself:

> I will not charm my tongue, I am bound to speak:
> . . . .
> 'Tis proper I obey him, but not now:
> Perchance, Iago, I will ne'er go home.
>   (5.2.185,197–98)

Her epithet just before she is stabbed appropriately refers to all the men in the play: Iago, to whose taunts it is a response; Othello, who responds to it; and Cassio, Roderigo, and Brabantio as well:

> O murderous coxcomb! what should such a fool
> Do with so good a woman?
>   (5.2.234–35)

Emilia, another "good woman," dies without self-justifications or calls for revenge; instead she testifies to Desdemona's innocence and love just as her mistress had done at her own death. Her request to be laid by her mistress, her reiteration of the willow song, and her own attempts to "by bad mend" complete her identification with Desdemona.

Emilia's story has utterly destroyed Iago's bond with Othello and foiled his attempt to "make up [his] will," (1.3.393), to complete himself by compensating for his own misshapenness through the stories that allow him to shape others.[34] He and his fantasies are repudiated by Roderigo, by Othello, and by Emilia. Her refusal of obedience destroys Iago's plot and refutes his philosophy, which requires that she act in her own self-interest. Iago's final, Othello-like attempt to deny his wife's betrayal is to call her "villainous whore" and stab her, thus validating her confession and her epitaph for him. But this act, like all of the other events of the night, "fordoes" Iago instead of "mak[ing]" him (5.1.128). He has not eradicated Othello's love for Desdemona or turned her virtue into pitch. The deaths of Roderigo, Desdemona, Emilia, and Othello destroy the power over others which is the source of his self-engendering and identity. His final silence—"Demand me nothing, what you know, you know, / From this time forth I never will speak word" (5.2.304–05)—is, for him, the equivalent of suicide.[35] Iago's silence, his impervious-

---

[34]Cf. *OED, make* (96c), where "to make up" is "to supply (deficiencies); to make complete," and (a) "To fill up what is wanting to," and *to be made up* is "to be completed in former growth," and other Shakespearean uses of "scarce made up" to mean not completely formed or completely human, as in Richard III's reference to himself as "Cheated of feature by dissembling Nature, / Deformed, unfinished, sent before my time / Into this breathing world scarce half made up" (1.1.19–21), and Belarius's contemptuous reference to Cloten's inadequacy in *Cymbeline,* "Being scarce made up, / I mean to man, he had not apprehension / Of roaring terrors" (4.2.109–11).

[35]*Fordo* means "to put [a living being] out of existence" (*OED,* 1), "to kill, to ruin, to undo or bring to nought" (*OED* 1. 2. 3. 4. 5.); Shakespeare uses it with reference to suicide, as in *Hamlet,*

ness, his unmade-upness, his refusal to suffer, all mitigate his scapegoat function throughout the last scene, emphasizing instead his role as catalyst to Othello's tragedy. It is Othello's speech, his pain, his recreation of a self to which we attend.

While the division between Iago and Emilia is absolute after he kills her, some connections between Othello and Desdemona are reestablished in the last act. Desdemona, as we have seen, continues to affirm their relationship up to the moment of her death, and Othello in the last scene does move away from the men and toward the women. Othello, like Desdemona and Emilia, dies in pain testifying to love, whereas Iago lives, silent; Othello, like the women, stays to acknowledge at least partial responsibility for his actions, while Iago flees, accepting none. But Othello cannot abandon his masculine identity by asserting a new one: "That's he that was Othello; here I am" (5.2.285). Instead of applying Emilia's accusation to himself, he stabs Iago; the two men are one in their desire to place guilt elsewhere and eliminate its bearer. With Iago's exit, Othello turns his attention, characteristically, to his honor and a suicide weapon. Emilia's death, though it reenacts Desdemona's, is a mere parenthesis in his search, scarcely noticed by him. Although male bombast is virtually silenced at the end of this play, as it is in the comedies— Iago will "never more speak word" (5.2.305) and the terseness and precision of Roderigo's dying epithet for Iago ("O inhuman dog") are equaled in Cassio's epitaph for the dead Othello ("For he was great of heart")—Othello's rhetoric continues unchecked.[36] Throughout the scene, he persists in seeing himself and Desdemona as ill-fated, "unlucky," as victims of Iago who has "ensnar'd" (5.2.303) him. Desdemona is still imagined as the remote, passive, perfect object of romantic love. She is "cold, cold" as her "chastity" (5.2.276–77), associated with "monumental alabaster" (5.2.5), with an "entire and perfect chrysolite" (5.2.146), and with a "pearl" (5.2.348). In his last speeches, his own brand of Iago's "motive-hunting," he strives to reconstitute his heroic reputation. He leaves the play exactly as he had entered it, affirming his services to the state (cf. 1.2.17), confessing, asking for justice and judgment (cf. 1.3.122–25), telling stories about his past, and putting his "unhoused free condition" into its ultimate "confine" for love of Desdemona. His suicide both punishes himself as an Iago-like "dog" and reasserts his identity as a decisive, just commander and a passionate lover of Desdemona: "I kiss'd thee ere I kill'd thee, no way but this, / Killing myself, to die upon a kiss" (1.3.359–60). His love remains idealistic, anxious, self-justifying—consummated "no way" but in death.

Indeed, most of the characters remain where they started—or return

---

5.1.221, and *Lear*, 5.3.25 and 29. Iago, characteristically, places the agent of his fordoing outside of himself. Stephen Greenblatt illuminates how Iago fashions and destroys himself through his improvisational narratives: "The only termination possible in his case is not revelation but silence" (p. 238).

[36]See Adamson, *Othello as Tragedy*, pp. 283–99, for an acute analysis of the ways in which Othello's rhetoric in the last scene protects him from guilt and pain.

there. Here there is not even the tentative movement beyond folly that we find in the comedy heroes. Roderigo was upbraiding Iago in the play's first lines and is still doing so in the letter that is his last communication. Cassio has again received a promotion and is again caught up in events he does not comprehend. Brabantio, had he lived, likely would have responded to Desdemona's death exactly as he did to her elopement: "This sight would make him do a desperate turn" (1.3.208). Iago, like Jaques, Malvolio, and Shylock, the villains of the comedies, is opaque and static. His cryptic last words, "What you know, you know," (1.3.304) reveal no more about him than did his overexplanatory soliloquies. Desdemona, just before her death, challenges Othello as she had challenged her father and defends herself with the same straightforward precision she used before the senate:

And have you mercy too! I never did
Offend you in my life, . . . never lov'd Cassio,
But with such general warranty of heaven,
As I might love: I never gave him token.
(1.3.59–62)

Bianca comes forth to seek Cassio at her last appearance as at her first; both times she frankly declares her affection and is brusquely dismissed. Emilia's function and attitudes do change, however, though her character perhaps does not. She moves from tolerating men's fancies to exploding them and from prudent acceptance to courageous repudiation. She ceases to function as reconciler of the views of the men and the women, and the separation between them widens.

The play's ending is tragic; but it is also cankered comedy. The final speech effects a disengagement even greater than that which is usual at the end of the tragedies. Avoiding mention of the love of Othello and Desdemona and direct reference to Othello's murder and suicide, it focuses on the "state matters" (3.4.153) which the lovers themselves earlier sought refuge in and on the punishment of Iago, who does, at this point, become a scapegoat. Lodovico asks us to see the tragedy as Iago's "work," to look forward with relish to his torture, and to avert our gaze from the bed and its significance. But the restoration of military order provides little satisfaction here. The speech does not look back over the events of the play, creating a sense of completion and exhaustion as in *Romeo and Juliet* and *King Lear;* it does not look forward to a new beginning, however equivocally, as do *Hamlet* and *Macbeth.* The conflict between the men and the women has not been eliminated or resolved. The men have been unable to turn the women's virtue into pitch, but the women have been unable to mend male fantasies. The comic resolution of male with female, idealism with realism, love with sex, the individual with society is aborted. The play concludes, not with symmetrical pairings off and a movement toward marriage beds, but with one final triangle: Emilia, Desdemona, and Othello dead on wedding sheets. We are made to look with Iago, ominously a survivor, at the "tragic lodging of this bed"; *lodging* here, with its resonance from other Shakespearean uses, concludes the play on a note of arrested growth, devastated fertility.[37] "The object poisons sight"; it signifies destruction without catharsis, release without resolution.[38] The pain and division of the ending are unmitigated, and the clarification it offers is intolerable. "Let it be hid" is our inevitable response.

---

[37]See *Richard II*, 3.3.161; *II Henry VI*, 3.2.176; and *Macbeth*, 4.1.55, where *lodging* is used to describe the destruction of young corn on the brink of maturity (as it still is today in central Illinois). Ridley cites these parallels in his detailed and informative note on the word in the Arden edition (p. 197), demonstrating that Quarto's *lodging* is richer in meaning than Folio's more familiar *loading*.

[38]Edward Snow argues, in a more thoroughgoing way than I would wish to, that "Repression pervades the entire world of *Othello*," that in it there is "neither transcendence nor catharsis" (pp. 384–85).

Unproper Beds: Race, Adultery, and the Hideous in *Othello*

Michael Neill

There is a glass of ink wherein you see
How to make ready black-faced tragedy.

—George Chapman, Bussy D'Ambois, 4.2.89–90

I

The ending of *Othello* is perhaps the most shocking in Shakespearean tragedy. "I am glad that I have ended my revisal of this dreadful scene," wrote Dr. Johnson; "it is not to be endured."[1] His disturbed response is one that the play conspicuously courts: indeed Johnson does no more than paraphrase the reaction of the scandalized Venetians, whose sense of the unendurable nature of what is before them produces the most violently abrupted of all Shakespearean endings. Though its catastrophe is marked by a conventional welter of stabbing and slaughter, *Othello* is conspicuously shorn of the funeral dignities that usually serve to put a form of order upon such spectacles of ruin: in the absence of any witness sympathetic enough to tell the hero's story, the disgraced Othello has to speak what amounts to his own funeral oration—and it is one whose lofty rhetoric is arrested in mid-line by the "bloody period" of his own suicide (5.2.353). "All that's spoke is marred," observes Gratiano, but no memorializing tributes ensue. Even Cassio's "he was great of heart" (5.2.357) may amount to nothing more than a faint plea in mitigation for one whose heart was swollen to bursting with intolerable emotion[2]; and in place of the reassuring processional exeunt announced by the usual command to take up the tragic bodies, we get only Lodovico's curt order to close up the scene

From *Shakespeare Quarterly* 40, no. 4 (Winter 1989), 383–412. Reprinted by permission. The illustrations that originally accompanied this essay have been omitted.

[1]Quoted in James R. Siemon, " 'Nay, that's not next': *Othello*, 5.2. in performance, 1760–1900," *Shakespeare Quarterly*, 37 (1986), 38–51, esp. p. 39.

[2]See Balz Engler, "Othello's Great Heart," *English Studies*, 68 (1987), 129–36. All *Othello* quotations are from the New Penguin edition, ed. Kenneth Muir (Harmondsworth: Penguin Books, 1968). All other Shakespeare quotations are from *The Riverside Shakespeare*, ed. G. Blakemore Evans (Boston: Houghton Mifflin, 1974).

of butchery: "The object poisons sight: / Let it be hid" (5.2.360–61).[3] The
tableau on the bed announces a kind of plague, one that taints the sight as the
deadly effluvia of pestilence poison the nostrils.

The congruence between Dr. Johnson's desperately averted gaze and
Lodovico's fear of contamination is striking; but it is only Johnson's agitated
frankness that makes it seem exceptional. It makes articulate the anxiety
evident almost everywhere in the play's history—a sense of scandal that
informs the textual strategies of editors and theatrical producers as much as it
does the disturbed reactions of audiences and critics. Contemplating the
"unutterable agony" of the conclusion, the Variorum editor, Furness, came to
wish that the tragedy had never been written[4]; and his choice of the word
"unutterable" is a telling one, for this ending, as its stern gestures of erasure
demonstrate, has everything to do with what cannot be uttered and must not
be seen.

The sensational effect of the scene upon its earliest audiences is apparent
from the imitations it spawned[5] and from the mesmerized gaze of Henry
Jackson, who left the first surviving account of *Othello* in performance. He
saw *Othello* acted by the King's Men at Oxford in 1610 and wrote how

> the celebrated Desdemona, *slain in our presence by her husband*, although she
> pleaded her case very effectively throughout, yet moved us more after she was
> dead, when, *lying in her bed*, she entreated the pity of the spectators by her very
> countenance.[6]

More than any other scene, it was this show of a wife murdered by her
husband that gripped Jackson's imagination; but even more disturbing than
the killing itself seems to have been the sight of the dead woman "lying in her
bed"—a phrase that echoes Emilia's outrage: "My mistress here lies murdered in her bed" (5.2.184). For Jackson, the *place* seems to matter almost as
much as the fact of wife-murder—just as it did to the nineteenth-century
Desdemona, Fanny Kemble, when she confessed to "feel[ing] horribly at the
idea of being murdered *in my bed*."[7]

---

[3]The exceptional nature of this ending is also noted by Helen Gardner, "The Noble Moor," in
Anne Ridler, ed., *Shakespeare Criticism 1935–1960* (Oxford: Oxford Univ. Press, 1963), pp. 348–
70, esp. p. 366.

[4]The Variorum *Othello*, ed. H. H. Furness (Philadelphia: J. B. Lippincott, 1886), p. 300;
quoted in Siemon, p. 39.

[5]Sensationalized bedchamber scenes that seem indebted to *Othello* include Lussurioso's
murderous irruption into his father's bedchamber in *The Revenger's Tragedy* (c. 1606), Evadne's
heavily eroticized murder of the king in *The Maid's Tragedy* (c. 1610), and the climactic bedroom
scene that forms part of Ford's extensive reworking of *Othello* in *Love's Sacrifice* (c. 1632).
Shakespeare himself appears to play on recollections of his own coup de theatre in the bedroom
scene of *Cymbeline* (c. 1609); and it is treated to a parodic reversal in Fletcher's *Monsieur Thomas*
(c. 1615), where the humiliation of the comic protagonist is accomplished by means of "A *bed
discovered with a* [female] *black More in it*" (5.5.2, s.d.), provoking his Emilia-like cry, "Rore
againe, devill, rore againe" (5.5.41).

[6]Quoted in Julie Hankey, ed., *Othello*, Plays in Performance Series (Bristol: Bristol Classical
Press, 1987), p. 18, italics added.

[7]Quoted in Hankey, p. 315, italics added.

The same anxious fascination is reflected in the first attempts to represent the play pictorially: it was the spectacle of the violated marriage bed that Nicholas Rowe selected to epitomize the tragedy in the engraving for his 1709 edition; and his choice was followed by the actors David Garrick and Sarah Siddons, wanting memorials of their own performances.[8] In the great period of Shakespeare illustration from the 1780s to the 1920s, the bedchamber scene was overwhelmingly preferred by publishers and artists, whose images combined to grant it the same representative significance as the graveyard in *Hamlet* or the monument in *Antony and Cleopatra*—as if announcing in this display of death-in-marriage a gestic account of the play's key meanings. . . .[9] Both graveyard and monument, however, in their different ways help to clothe the tragic ending in traditional forms of rhetoric and ceremony that mitigate its terrors, shackling death within a frame of decorum. What makes the ending of *Othello* so unaccountably disturbing and so threatening to its spectators is precisely the brutal violation of decorum that is registered in the quasi-pornographic explicitness of the graphic tradition. The illustrators' voyeuristic manipulation of the parted curtains and their invariable focus upon the unconscious invitation of Desdemona's gracefully exposed body serve to foreground not merely the perverse eroticism of the scene but its aspect of forbidden disclosure.

Even more striking is the fact that these images were often designed to draw readers into texts whose bowdlerizing maneuvers aimed, as far as possible, to conceal everything that their frontispieces offer to reveal. While they could scarcely contrive to remove the scandalous property itself, late eighteenth and nineteenth-century editors sought to restrict the curiosity that the final scene gratifies and to obscure its most threatening meanings by progressively excising from the text every explicit reference to the bed.[10]

Predictably enough, an even more anxious censorship operated in the

[8]See Norman Sanders, ed., *Othello*, New Cambridge edition, (Cambridge: Cambridge Univ. Press, 1984), p. 48.

[9]The art file at the Folger Shakespeare Library, for example, contains 109 illustrations of individual scenes in the play, no fewer than 40 of which show Act 5, Scene 2: the bed is invariably the center of attention and often occupies the entire space. For further discussion, see Paul H. D. Kaplan, "The Earliest Images of Othello," *SQ*, 39 (1988), 171–86.

[10]The process of cutting can be traced in Hankey. Already by 1773 Bell's edition had removed the exchange between Iago and Othello at 4.1.3–8 about Desdemona's being "naked with her friend in bed"; while in 1829 Cumberland's acting edition found it necessary to take out Desdemona's instructions to Emilia, "Lay on my bed my wedding sheets" (4.2.104). Macready followed the Cumberland text in finding any reference to the physical reality of the wedding night as indelicate as the word "whore" itself. Thus at 2.3.26 his Iago could no more be allowed to wish "happiness to their sheets!" than to envisage that happiness in "he hath not yet made wanton the night with her" (2.3.15–16). Predictably, most versions from Bell onwards cut the more lurid details of Iago's fantasy of lying with Cassio and its strange sexual displacements (3.3.418–23); more surprisingly, not one Desdemona from Macready's time until the early part of this century was permitted to greet Othello in the murder scene with "Will you come to bed, my lord?" (5.2.24). Even her promise to Cassio that Othello's "bed shall seem a school" (3.3.24) was thought too strong meat for eighteenth-century Dublin and for English audiences after John Philip Kemble's production of 1785.

theatre itself, where, however, its consequences were much more difficult to predict. In the most striking of many effacements, it became the practice for nineteenth-century Othellos to screen the murder from the audience by closing the curtains upon the bed. This move was ostensibly consistent with a general attempt at de-sensationalizing the tragedy, an attempt whose most obvious manifestation was the restrained "Oriental" Moor developed by Macready and others.[11] But the actual effect of the practice was apparently quite opposite, raising to a sometimes unbearable intensity the audience's scandalized fascination with the now-invisible scene. Years later Westland Marston could still recall the "thrilling" sensation as Macready thrust "his dark despairing face, through the curtains," its "contrast with the drapery" producing "a marvellous piece of colour"[12]; and so shocking was this moment, according to John Forster, that in his presence a woman "hysterically fainted" at it.[13]

The reasons for so extreme a reaction can be glimpsed in the offended tone of the Melbourne *Argus* critic, attacking an 1855 production that had flouted this well-established convention: "[The] consummation," he indignantly insisted, "should take place behind the curtain and out of sight."[14] The revealing word "consummation," when set beside the "hysterical" reaction to Macready's "marvellous piece of colour,"[15] suggests that the bed was so intensely identified with the anxieties about race and sex stirred up by the play that it needed, as far as possible, to be removed from the public gaze. Yet the effect of such erasure was only to give freer play to the fantasy it was designed to check, so that the violent chiaroscuro of Macready's blackened face thrust between the virgin-white curtains was experienced as a shocking sado-erotic climax. It was, of course, a stage picture that significantly repeated an off-stage action twice imagined in the first half of the play, when Othello, first in Venice (1.2) and then in Cyprus (2.3), is unceremoniously roused from his nuptial bed. The unconscious repetition must have had the effect of underlining the perverse eroticism of the murder just at the point where the parting of the bed-curtains and the display of Desdemona's corpse was about to grant final satisfaction to the audience's terrible curiosity about the absent scene that dominates so much of the play's action.

    [11]For an account of the Orientalizing process that culminated in Beerbohm Tree's confident pronouncement that "Othello was an Oriental, not a negro: a stately Arab of the best caste," see Hankey, pp. 65–67, esp. p. 67.

    [12]Westland Marston, *Our Recent Actors*, quoted in Hankey, pp. 64, 317.

    [13]William Archer and Robert Lowe, eds., *Dramatic Essays by John Forster and George Henry Lewes*, quoted in Hankey, p. 64.

    [14]Quoted in Hankey, p. 317. This critic's reaction was echoed in the murmurs of dissatisfaction with which the audience greeted Rossi's 1881 London performance, when the Italian actor strangled his Desdemona in full view of the audience (see Siemon, p. 47).

    [15]To some observers Macready's restrained, gentlemanly, and dignified Moor seemed "almost English" (Hankey, p. 66), but the startling color contrast of this scene seems to have acted as a disturbing reminder of Othello's blackness and therefore (to the Victorian mind) of his savage sexuality.

For all their ostentatious pudency, then, the Victorian attempts at contain-
ing the danger of the play's ending reveal a reading unsettlingly consistent
with the most sensational recent productions, like Bernard Miles's 1971
Mermaid *Othello* or Ronald Eyre's at the National in 1979, with their
extraordinary emphasis on the significance and visibility of a bed.[16] It is a
reading in which the stage direction opening 5.2, "*Enter . . . Desdemona in
her bed*," announces ocular proof of all that the audience have most desired
and feared to look upon, exposing to cruel light the obscure erotic fantasies
that the play both explores and disturbingly excites in its audience. Forster's
story of the woman who fainted at the sight of Macready's "dark despairing
face" records a moment when (despite more than half a century of bleaching,
"civilizing," and bowdlerizing) a subterranean image erupted to confirm the
deep fears of racial/sexual otherness on which the play trades—fears that are
made quite embarrassingly explicit in the feverish self-betrayals of a
nineteenth-century Russian literary lady reacting to Ira Aldridge's performance of the part. In her account the play exhibits nothing less than the
symbolic rape of the European "spirit" by the "savage, wild flesh" of black
otherness:

> A full-blooded Negro, incarnating the profoundest creations of Shakespearean art,
> giving *flesh and blood* for the aesthetic judgment of educated European
> society. . . . How much nearer can one get to truth, to the very source of the
> highest aesthetic satisfaction? But *what is truth. . . ?* As the spirit is not the body,
> so the truth of art is not this profoundly raw flesh which we can take hold of, and
> call by name and, if you please, feel, pinch with our unbelieving, all-feeling
> hand. . . . Not the Moscow Maly Theatre, but the African jungle should have been
> filled and resounded with . . . the cries of this black, powerful, howling flesh. But
> by the very fact that that flesh is so powerful—that it is genuinely black, so
> naturally *un-white* does it howl—that savage flesh did its fleshly work. It murdered
> and crushed the spirit. . . . one's spirit cannot accept it—and in place of the
> highest enjoyment, this blatant flesh introduced into art, this *natural* black
> Othello, pardon me, causes only . . . revulsion.[17]

It is as if in Macready's coup the strange mixture of thrilled agitation, horror,
and shame voiced here became focused with an unbearable intensity upon the

---

16Both directors introduced the bed early, making it into the centerpiece of the brothel scene;
and Miles, whose production notoriously highlighted the sexual suggestiveness of the murder
with a naked Desdemona, emphasized the perverse excitements of the earlier scene by leaving
Iago and Roderigo at the end "to argue amongst the discarded bedclothes and around the bed
itself. . . . [while Roderigo handled] the sheets in rapture." Eyre transposed this piece of stage
business to his Othello at the beginning of the scene: Donald Sinden was directed to pull the
sheets from Desdemona's laundry basket, throw them about the stage, and then at the line "This
is a subtle whore" (1. 20) press the soiled linen to his face—"sniffing [at it] like a hound,"
according to one reviewer. See Hankey, pp. 291, 281.

17N. S. Sokhanskaya ("N. Kokhanovskaya") in a letter to the Slavophile newspaper *Dyen*
(1863), quoted in Herbert Marshall and Mildred Stock, *Ira Aldridge: The Negro Tragedian*
(London: Rockliff 1958), pp. 265–66. See also Siemon, p. 45, for English reactions to the scene
"that [mimic] the language and strategies of pornography."

occupation of the bed, where the transgression of racial boundaries was displayed as an offence punishable by death.

II

The racial fear and revulsion lurking beneath the ambiguous excitements of the theatrical and pictorial traditions is made crudely explicit in an early nineteenth-century caricature, apparently of Ira Aldridge's Othello, published as Number 9 in the series *Tregear's Black Jokes*. The caricaturist sublimates his anxiety at the scene's sexual threat through the burlesque device of transforming Desdemona into an obese black woman, her snoring mouth grotesquely agape. The racialism paraded here for the amusement of early nineteenth-century Londoners is rarely so openly exhibited, but it has tainted even the most respectable *Othello* criticism until well into the present century. A sense of racial scandal is a consistent thread in commentary on the play from Rymer's notorious effusions against the indecorum of a "Blacka-moor" hero,[18] to Coleridge's assertion that Othello was never intended to be black and F. R. Leavis's triumphant demonstration that Othello was never intended for a hero.[19] It is as apparent in A. C. Bradley's nervously footnoted anxiety about how "the aversion of our blood" might respond to the sight of a black Othello[20] as it is in Charles Lamb's frank discovery of "something extremely revolting in the courtship and wedded caresses of Othello and Desdemona."[21] "To imagine is one thing," Bradley protests, "and to see is another," making painfully explicit his reaction against what Edward Snow describes as the play's insistence upon "bringing to consciousness things known in the flesh but 'too hideous to be shown.' "[22] For the neo-Freudian Snow, however, these forbidden things are the male psyche's repressed fears of female otherness, which the accident of Othello's race "merely forces him to live out with psychotic intensity."[23] It is clear, however, that for Bradley it was precisely Othello's blackness that made the play's sexual preoccupations so upsetting.

---

[18]Thomas Rymer, *A Short View of Tragedy* (1693), quoted in Brian Vickers, ed., *Shakespeare: The Critical Heritage*, 6 vols. (London and Boston: Routledge & Kegan Paul, 1974), Vol. 2, 27.

[19]F. R. Leavis, "Diabolic Intellect and the Noble Hero," in *The Common Pursuit* (London: Chatto and Windus, 1952), pp. 136–59. For acute analyses of the racial assumptions underlying Leavis's approach, see Hankey, pp. 109–16, and Martin Orkin, "Othello and the 'plain face' of Racism," *SQ*, 38 (1987), 166–88, esp pp. 183–86, now incorporated in his *Shakespeare Against Apartheid* (Craighall, South Africa: Ad Donker, 1987). Both show how much Leavis's interpretation contributed to Olivier's version of the tragedy.

[20]*Shakespearean Tragedy* (1904; rpt. New York. St. Martin's Press, 1985), p. 165 n.

[21]Quoled in Hankey, pp. 65–66.

[22]"Sexual Anxiety and the Male Order of Things in *Othello*," *English Literary Renaissance*, 10 (1980), 384–412, esp. p. 387.

[23]p. 400.

For Coleridge the idea of a black hero was unacceptable because blackness was equivalent to savagery and the notion of savage heroism an intolerable oxymoron. His application of critical skin-lightener began a tradition of sterile and seemingly endless debate about the exact degree and significance of Othello's racial difference, on which critics dissipated their energies until well into the present century—M. R. Ridley's still-current Arden edition (1958), with its ludicrous attempt to substitute "contour" for "colour" as the principle of discrimination, being only the most disgraceful recent example.[24] Since Coleridge, arguments about race in *Othello* have almost invariably been entangled, more or less explicitly, with arguments about culture in which gradations of color stand for gradations of "barbarity," "animality," and "primitive emotion." If the dominant nineteenth-century tradition sought to domesticate the play by removing the embarrassment of savagery, the most common twentieth-century strategy has been to anthropologize it as the study of an assimilated savage who relapses into primitivism under stress. This was essentially Leavis's solution, and one can still hear it echoed in the New Cambridge editor's admiration for the weird mimicry of Laurence Olivier's "West African"/"West Indian" Othello,[25] which he describes as a "virtuoso . . . portrait of a *primitive* man, at odds with the sophisticated society into which he has forced himself, *relapsing into barbarism* as a result of hideous misjudgement."[26]

At the other extreme stand revisionist readings like Martin Orkin's, which have sought to rehabilitate the tragedy by co-opting it to the anti-racist cause, insisting that "in its rejection of human pigmentation as a means of identifying worth, the play, as it always has done, continues to oppose racism."[27] Orkin's is an admirably motivated attempt to expose the racialist ideology underlying various critical and theatrical interpretations of the tragedy, but Shakespeare

---

[24]See M. R. Ridley, ed., *Othello*, Arden edition (London: Methuen, 1958), p. li.

[25]The geographical referent of Olivier's mimicry significantly varies in different accounts of the production: Hankey, for example, refers to his "extraordinary transformation into a black African" (p. 111); Sanders praises "his careful imitation of West Indian gait and gesture" (p. 47); while Richard David speaks of "Olivier's . . . 'modern' negro, out of Harlem rather than Barbary" (*Shakespeare in the Theatre* [Cambridge: Cambridge Univ. Press, 1978], p. 46). The embarrassing conclusion must be that Olivier's much-praised fidelity to detail was simply fidelity to a generalized stereotype of "blackness."

[26]Norman Sanders, p. 47, italics added. Sanders almost exactly paraphrases Laurence Lerner's account of the way in which "the primitive breaks out again in Othello," which Orkin uses to exemplify the way in which even liberal South African critics of the play find themselves reacting to it in terms of the paradigms of apartheid (pp. 184–85). Olivier himself declared that Othello "is a savage man," adding hurriedly, "not on account of his colour; I don't mean that" (Hankey, p. 109); but it is a little difficult to know quite what else he could have meant—especially in the light of reviewers' reactions to his mimicry of negritude, which concluded "that Othello's brutality was either of the jungle and essentially his own, or that, as one of Nature's innocents, he had taken the infection from a trivial and mean white society" (p. 111). Whatever the case, the choice is simply between noble and ignoble savagery. For a good account of the ideas behind the Olivier production and critical reactions to it, see Hankey, pp. 109–13.

[27]p. 188.

would surely have been puzzled to understand the claim that his play
"opposes racism," cast as it is in a language peculiar to the politics of our own
century.[28] It would no more have been possible for Shakespeare to "oppose
racism" in 1604, one might argue, than for Marlowe to "oppose anti-semitism"
in 1590: the argument simply could not be constituted in those terms. Julie
Hankey, indeed, contemplating the pitfalls presented by Shakespeare's treatment of racial matters, concludes that his construction of racial difference is
virtually beyond recovery, having become after four hundred years hopelessly
obscured by a "patina of apparent topicality."[29] Hankey's position has at least
the merit of historicist scruple but seems in the end evasive, not unlike those
liberal critiques that rob the play of its danger by treating Othello's color
simply as a convenient badge of his estrangement from Venetian society[30]—in
effect a distraction to be cleared out of the way in order to expose the real
core of the drama, its tragedy of jealousy.[31] But the history that Hankey
herself traces is a testimony to the stubborn fact that *Othello* is a play full of
racial feeling—perhaps the first work in English to explore the roots of such
feeling; and it can hardly be accidental that it belongs to the very period in
English history in which something we can now identify as a racialist ideology
was beginning to evolve under the pressures of nascent imperialism.[32] In this
context it is all the more curious, as Hankey notices, that Henry Jackson in
1610 seemed utterly to ignore this aspect of the tragedy, presenting it simply
as a drama of wife-murder whose culprit is described in the most neutral
language as "her husband." We cannot now tell whether Jackson was blind to
the racial dimension of the action, or thought it of no interest or merely too
obvious to require mention. But I want to argue that his attention to the bed
suggests a way round the dilemma posed by this odd silence: to explain why
the bed should have caught his eye is to begin to understand theatrical

[28]The word "racism" itself dates from only 1936, and "racialism" from 1907 (*OED*).

[29]p. 15.

[30]Here I include my own essay "Changing Places in *Othello*," *Shakespeare Survey*, 37 (1984),
115–31; I ought to have noticed more clearly the way in which racial identity is constructed as
one of the most fiercely contested "places" in the play.

[31]Honorable exceptions include Eldred Jones, *Othello's Countrymen: The African in English
Renaissance Drama* (London: Oxford Univ. Press, 1965): G. K. Hunter's celebrated lecture on
"Othello and Colour Prejudice," *Proceedings of the British Academy*, 53 (1967), 139–57; Doris
Adler, "The Rhetoric of *Black* and *White* in *Othello*," *SQ*, 25 (1974), 248–57; G. M. Matthews,
"*Othello* and the Dignity of Man," in Arnold Kettle. ed., *Shakespeare in a Changing World*
(London: Lawrence & Wishart, 1964), pp. 123–45; and Karen Newman. " 'And wash the Ethiop
white': femininity and the monstrous in *Othello*," in Jean E. Howard and Marion F. O'Connor,
eds., *Shakespeare Reproduced: The text in history and ideology* (New York and London:
Methuen, 1987), pp. 141–62.

[32]For more recent theoretical accounts of the evolution of a discourse of "Englishness" and
"otherness" as an enabling adjunct of colonial conquest, see Stephen Greenblatt, *Renaissance
Self-Fashioning: From More to Shakespeare* (Chicago and London: Univ. of Chicago Press, 1980).
pp. 179–92; David Cairns and Shaun Richards, *Writing Ireland: colonialism, nationalism and
culture* (Manchester: Manchester Univ. Press, 1988), chap. 1, "What ish my Nation?" pp. 1–21;
and Anne Laurence, "The Cradle to the Grave: English Observation of Irish Social Customs in
the Seventeenth Century," *The Seventeenth Century*, 3 (1988), 63–84.

strategies for thinking about racial otherness that are specific to the work's own cultural context. If Jackson elected to say nothing about these matters, it may have been because there was for him no real way of voicing them, in that they were still in some deep sense *unutterable*. But they were there on the bed for all to see.

What is displayed on the bed is something, in Othello's own profoundly resonant phrase, "too hideous to be shown" (3.3.107). The wordplay here (unusually, in this drama of treacherously conflicting meanings) amounts to a kind of desperate iteration: what is *hideous* is what should be kept *hidden*, out of sight.[33] "Hideous" in this sense is virtually an Anglo-Saxon equivalent for the Latinate "obscene"—referring to that which is profoundly improper, not merely indecent but tainted (in the original sense) or unclean; and that which should also, according to Shakespeare's own folk-etymology, be kept unseen, *off-stage*, hidden.[34] The play begins with Iago's evocation of just such an obscenity; it ends by seeking to return it to its proper darkness, closing the curtains that Iago first metaphorically plucked aside. In his frequently perceptive study of *Othello*, Edward Snow, observing that the play's "final gesture is on the side of repression," goes on to stress how necessarily that gesture is directed at the bed: "it is not just any object that is to be hidden but the 'tragic lodging' of the wedding-bed—the place of sexuality itself."[35] But Snow's own strategy expressly requires that he himself suppress the anxiety that attaches to the bed as the site of racial transgression—the anxiety on which depends so much of the play's continuing power to disturb.

III

One of the terrifying things about *Othello* is that its racial poisons seem so casually concocted, as if racism were just something that Iago, drawing in his improvisational way on a gallimaufry of quite unsystematic prejudices and superstitions, made up as he went along. The characteristic pleasure he takes in his own felicitous invention only makes the effect more shocking. Iago lets horrible things loose and delights in watching them run; and the play seems to share that narcissistic fascination—or perhaps, better, Iago is the voice of its own fascinated self-regard. The play thinks abomination into being and then taunts the audience with the knowledge that it can never be *un*thought: "What you know, you know." It is a technique that works close to the unstable ground of consciousness itself; for it would be almost as difficult to say

33 The wordplay, which may well reflect a folk-etymology, occurs elsewhere in Shakespeare: see, for example, *Twelfth Night*, 4.2.31 ("hideous darkness"), and *King John*, 5.4.22.

34 The proper derivation is from *caenum* = dirt; but the imagery of Carlisle's speech in *Richard II* clearly seems to imply the folk-etymology from *scaenum* = stage: "*show* so heinous, black, obscene a deed" (4.2. 122); see also *Love's Labor's Lost*, 1.1.235–39.

35 p. 385.

whether its racial anxieties are ones that the play discovers or implants in an audience as to say whether jealousy is something that Iago discovers or implants in Othello. Yet discovery, in the most literal theatrical sense, is what the last scene cruelly insists on. Like no other drama, *Othello* establishes an equivalency between psychological event (what happens "inside") and offstage action (what happens "within"); thus it can flourish its disclosure of the horror on the bed like a psychoanalytic revelation.

The power of the offstage scene over the audience's prying imagination is immediately suggested by the irritable speculation of Thomas Rymer, the play's first systematic critic. Rymer spends several pages of his critique exposing what he regards as ludicrous inconsistencies between what the play tells the audience and what verisimilitude requires them to believe about the occupation of "the Matrimonial Bed." The time scheme, he insists, permits Othello and his bride to sleep together only once, on the first night in Cyprus, but "*once* will not do the Poets business: the *Audience* must suppose a great many bouts, to make the plot operate. They must deny their senses, to reconcile it to common sense."[36]

Rymer's method is taken to extraordinary extremes in a recent article by T.G.A. Nelson and Charles Haines, who set out to demonstrate, with a mass of circumstantial detail, that the marriage of Othello and Desdemona was never consummated at all. In this previously unsuspected embarrassment is to be found an explanation for the extreme suggestibility of the hero, and thus the hidden spring of the entire tragic action.[37] Their essay is remarkable not for the ingenuity of its finally unsustainable argument about the sequential "facts" of a plot whose time-scheme is so notoriously undependable, but for what it unconsciously reveals about the effect of *Othello* upon its audiences. Their entire procedure mirrors with disturbing fidelity the habit of obsessive speculation about concealed offstage action, into which the play entraps the viewer as it entraps its characters. Nelson and Haines become victims, like the hero himself, of the scopophile economy of this tragedy and prey to its voyeuristic excitements.

Recently, Norman Nathan has attempted a point-by-point rebuttal of Nelson and Haines, the ironic effect of which is to entrap him in the very speculation he wishes to cut short. "If a lack of consummation is so important to this play, why isn't the audience so informed?" he somewhat testily enquires.[38] An answer might be—to make them ask the question. *Othello* persistently goads its audience into speculation about what is happening behind the scenes. This preoccupation with offstage action is unique in

[36]Rymer, quoted in Vickers, Vol. 2, p. 43.

[37]T.G.A. Nelson and Charles Haines, "Othello's Unconsummated Marriage," *Essays in Criticism*, 33 (1983), 1–18. Their arguments were partially anticipated in a little-noticed article by Pierre Janton, "Othello's Weak Function," *Cahiers Élisabéthains*, 7 (1975), 43–50, and are paralleled in William Whallon, *Inconsistencies* (Cambridge: D. S. Brewer; Totowa, N.J.: Biblio, 1983). I regard my own willingness to take these arguments seriously ("Changing Places in *Othello*," p. 116, n. 1) as further evidence for the point I am making.

[38]"Othello's Marriage is Consummated," *Cahiers Élisabéthains*, 34 (1988), 79–82, esp. p. 81.

Shakespeare. Elsewhere, whenever offstage action is of any importance, it is almost always carefully described, usually by an eyewitness whose account is not open to question, so that nothing of critical importance is left to the audience's imagination. But in *Othello* the real imaginative focus of the action is always the hidden marriage-bed, an inalienably private location, shielded, until the very last scene, from every gaze.[39] This disquietingly absent presence creates the margin within which Iago can operate as a uniquely deceitful version of the *nuntius*, whose vivid imaginary descriptions taint the vision of the audience even as they colonize the minds of Brabantio and Othello:

> *Iago:* Even now, now, very now, an old black ram
> Is tupping your white ewe. . . .
>
> you'll have your daughter covered with a Barbary horse. . . . your
> daughter and the Moor are now making the beast with two backs.
> (1.1.89–90, 111–116)

It is important that this fantasy, in which all the participants in this scene (Iago, Roderigo, and Brabantio) participate, should have the characteristic anonymity of pornography—it trades only in perverted erotic stereotypes ("fair daughter" and "lascivious Moor" [1.1.123, 127]). Since the audience is exposed to these obscenities before it is allowed to encounter either Othello or Desdemona in person, they serve to plant the suggestion, which perseveres like an itch throughout the action, that the attractive public face of this marriage is only the mask for something unspeakably adulterate. The scenes that follow contrive to keep alive the ugly curiosity that Iago has aroused, even while the action concentrates on Othello's public magnificence, on Desdemona's courageous resistance to patriarchal authority, and upon idealized affirmations of the love between them.

Act 1, Scene 2 opens with the entry of Othello and Iago *"with torches,"* the torches serving as a reminder of the hero's sudden arousal from his marriage bed, so that Iago's probing "are you fast married?" (1.1.11) is implicitly a question about consummation. With Iago's bawdy innuendo to Cassio, "he tonight hath boarded a land carack" (1.1.50), it continues the fitful illumination of that offstage scene. This lurid vision of the bed, kindled again in Brabantio's jealous outrage, may contaminate even the idealizing language of Othello—the high rhetoric that contrasts "My thrice-driven bed of down" with "the flinty and steel couch of war" (1.1.228–29); and it invites a prying

---

39This aspect of the play is recognized by Stanley Cavell in *Disowning Knowledge In Six Plays of Shakespeare* (Cambridge; Cambridge Univ. Press, 1987): "My guiding hypothesis about the structure of the play is that the thing *denied our sight* throughout the opening scene—the thing, the scene, that Iago takes Othello back to again and again, retouching it for Othello's enchafed imagination—is what we are shown in the final scene, the scene of murder" (p. 132). See also James L. Calderwood, *The Properties of Othello* (Amherst: Univ. of Massachusetts Press, 1989), p. 125.

curiosity about the "rites" of love acknowledged in Desdemona's touching erotic frankness[40]:

> if I be left behind
> A moth of peace, and he go to the war,
> The rites for which I love him are bereft me. . . .
>   (1.3.252–54)

But it is not until the soliloquy after Roderigo's exit that Iago's diseased preoccupation with Othello's bed begins to reveal a fascination deeper and more brooding than mere strategem requires:

> I hate the Moor,
> And it is thought abroad that *'twixt my sheets*
> He's done my office.
>   (1.3.380–82, italics added)

The office between the sheets is Iago's characteristically debased version of Desdemona's "rites for which I love him"; with its reduction of lovemaking to the right and duty of a patriarchal place-holder, it equates adultery with Cassio's usurpation of Iago's place as Othello's "officer," seeing in both a kind of illicit substitution or counterfeiting for which the deceits of his own "double knavery" are merely a just requital.

Retrospectively regarded, Act 1, built as it is around the boisterous and threatening disruption of a wedding night, has something of the character of one of those satiric rituals (rough musics, charivari, and skimmingtons) by which society expressed its disapprobation of transgressive marriages and adulterous liaisons.[41] And the storm that ensues, with its ominous division of the bride and groom, might be read as confirming its threats, mimicking the erotic violence always latent in the dangerous translations of a wedding night and liable to be released by any unsanctioned match. The happy reunion in Cyprus, however, makes it seem as if a particularly testing rite of passage has been successfully negotiated, a suggestion supported by the elated sensuality of the language in which Cassio imagines it—

---

[40]Nelson and Haines, for example, use her lines as prime evidence for the non-consummation of the marriage on its first night (p. 13).

[41]Among the grounds cited for such exhibitions of popular censure were "a great disparity in age between bride and groom . . . or the fact that the husband was regarded as a 'stranger'. . . . Charivaris thus stigmatized marriages in which bride and groom . . . failed to maintain a 'proper distance'"; see Daniel Fabre, "Families: Privacy versus Custom" in Philippe Ariès and Georges Duby, gen. eds., *A History of Private Life*, trans. Arthur Goldhammer, 3 vols. (Cambridge, Mass., and London: Harvard Univ. Press [Belknap Press], 1987, Vol. 3 (*Passions of the Renaissance*), 533. For English forms of the charivari, see David Underdown, *Revel, Riot and Rebellion: Popular Politics and Culture in England 1603–1660* (Oxford: Clarendon Press, 1985), pp. 99–103. The grotesque animal imagery of Iago's speeches outside Brabantio's house echoes the horned masks and animal heads of the wild procession paraded at the offender's windows (see Underdown, p. 101).

Great Jove, Othello guard,
And swell his sail with thine own powerful breath,
That he may bless this bay with his tall ship,
Make love's quick pants in Desdemona's arms . . .
(2.1.77–80)

—and seemingly confirmed in Othello's joyous eroticization of his triumphant arrival:

If after every tempest come such calms,
May the winds blow till they have wakened death,
And let the labouring bark climb hills of seas,
Olympus-high, and duck again as low
As hell's from heaven. If it were now to die,
'Twere now to be most happy. . . .
(2.1.179–84)

But the exhilarated poetry of the scene is undercut by the sardonic presence of Iago, who greets his general's arrival with a typically reductive pun ("The Moor! I know his *trumpet*" [2.1.174, italics added]) and who remains after the general exeunt to focus attention on the hidden scene of marital celebration:

When the blood is made dull with the act of sport, there should be, again to inflame it and give satiety a fresh appetite, loveliness in favour, sympathy in years, manners and beauties: all which the Moor is defective in. Now for want of these required conveniences, her delicate tenderness will find itself abused, begin to heave the gorge, disrelish and abhor the Moor. Very nature will instruct her in it and compel her to some second choice. . . . Lechery, by this hand. . . . When these mutualities so marshal the way, hard at hand comes the master and main exercise, th'incorporate conclusion.
(2.1.220–28, 249, 252–54)

With its concentration on the imputed grotesquerie of racial mésalliance, this speech is almost an exact repetition of Iago's first scene with Roderigo, and like that scene it ends with a soliloquy, with Iago brooding on the adulterous violation of his own sheets: "I do suspect the lusty Moor / Hath leapt into my seat. . . . I fear Cassio with my night-cap too" (2.1.286–87, 298).

Thus when Act 2, Scene 3 opens with Othello and his bride preparing once again for bed—

Come, my dear love,
The purchase made, the fruits are to ensue:
That profit's yet to come 'tween me and you
(2.1.8–10)

—the suggestion of a new beginning is already bitterly ironized. Their departure is at once the occasion for Iago's prurient commentary:

He hath not yet made wanton the night with her; and she is sport for Jove. . . . And, I'll warrant her, full of game. . . . What an eye she has! Methinks it sounds a

parley to provocation. . . . And when she speaks, is it not an alarum to love? . . .
Well, happiness to their sheets!

                                                                                    (2.1.15–26)

In terms of Iago's unfolding plot, this is largely superfluous. More important is its dramatic function—together with the carefully offhand suggestion of
racial outrage in the "black Othello" (2.1.29)—in concentrating the audience's
imagination once again upon the erotic act in the bedroom. In this way the
speech helps to prepare us for the interruption of the second bedding by the
rough music of a "dreadful bell," the "black sanctus" that accompanies the
second of Iago's charivari-like improvisations, with its weird travesty of nuptial
disharmonies ("Friends all but now . . . like bride and groom / Devesting
them for bed: and then . . . tilting one at others' breasts / In opposition
bloody" [2.1.173–78]).[42]

Up to this point in the play, Iago's operation has been principally aimed at
converting the absent/present bed into a locus of imagined adultery by
producing Othello's abduction of Desdemona as an act of racial adulteration,
violating the natural laws of kind; in this way the marriage is systematically
confused with Othello's and Cassio's supposed adulterous couplings with
Emilia and with the vindictive counter-adultery that Iago briefly contemplates
with Desdemona. More generally it is projected as being of a piece with the
usurpation of "natural" rights in Cassio's appropriation of the lieutenancy owed
to Iago. The audience can become deeply implicated in this network of
interlocking prejudices and suspicions just because it is Iago's habit to work by
implication and association; feelings and attitudes that would hardly survive
inspection in the light of reason are enabled to persist precisely because they
work away in this subterranean fashion. The accomplishment of his plan,
though it means bringing "this monstrous birth to the world's light" (substantially from Act 3, Scene 3, onwards), never fully allows the audience to escape
this entanglement. To the extent that it takes the form of a sinister parody of
the ingenious symmetries of revenge tragedy (the biter bit or the adulterer
cuckolded), his plot allows us a certain ironic distance, a space in which the
villain is subject to our judgment; but to the extent that it actually continues
the process of realizing Iago's fantasies of sexual adulteration, culminating in
the hideous ocular proof of the final scene, it traps us in a guilty involvement.

In the temptation scene (3.3) the "secrets" that Othello sees himself
patiently excavating from Iago's mind are already horribly present to the
audience—not just because we are party to the villain's plotting but because
these ugly conceits in some sense echo the secret and unscrutinized imagin-
ings he has planted inside our heads. As the monster at the heart of the
psychic labyrinth is brought to light, the confession of Iago's hidden thoughts
gradually slides into the revelation of Desdemona's hidden deeds—

---

[42]For a full discussion of the charivari-like aspects of this scene, see Nelson and Haines, pp. 5–
7.

In Venice they do let God see the pranks
They dare not show their husbands.
                    (3.3.200–201)

From that hint of invisible vice, the tempter edges, with his technique of elaborate *occupatio* rhetorically exhibiting what he repeatedly insists can never be shown, into the scopophile excitements of erotic encounters evoked in increasingly lurid visual detail. The tupping ram of Act 1, Scene 1, makes its reappearance in another promiscuously mixed gallery of copulating beasts[43]:

Would you, the supervisor, grossly gape on?
Behold her topped? . . .
It were a tedious difficulty, I think,
To bring them to that prospect. Damn them then
If ever mortal eyes do see them bolster
More than their own! . . .
It is impossible you should see this,
Were they as prime as goats, as hot as monkeys,
As salt as wolves in pride, and fools as gross
As ignorance made drunk.
                    (3.3.392 ff.)

The still merely verbal but powerfully suggestive metonym "bolster" gives way to the ruthlessly detailed night-piece in which Iago claims to have become an unwilling partner in Cassio's dream of fornication. Once again nothing is shown—the love act is merely a sleeping fantasy, "Desdemona" is only "Iago." Yet this doubly fictive scene of adultery is made to seem doubly adulterate by the homoerotic displacement of the kisses that grow upon Iago's lips—kisses that themselves disturbingly mirror the one real adultery of the play, the seduction of Othello in which Iago is at this very moment engaged.[44] The revelation is given an extra stamp of authenticity by being presented as Cassio's unwitting self-betrayal in a moment of compulsive secrecy: "Sweet Desdemona, / Let us be wary, let us hide our loves" (3.3.416–17). Iago's invention seems to part the curtains to display not merely the hidden scene but hidden thoughts themselves.

It is not, however, until the second temptation scene (4. 1) that Iago is ready to move to a direct evocation of Desdemona's adultery; and here, for the first time, the bed itself comes into full imaginative view, providing the climax of the brutally brief passage of stichomythia on which the scene opens:

Iago: Will you think so?
Othello: Think so, Iago?

---

[43]"Topped" here is simply a variant of "tupped," a verbal form deriving from the dialectal "tup" = ram (*OED*).

[44]I have analyzed the adulterous character of the temptation scene in "Changing Places in *Othello*."

Iago: What!
        To kiss in private?
Othello: An unauthorized kiss.
Iago: Or to be naked with her friend *in bed*
        An hour or more, not meaning any harm?
Othello: *Naked in bed,* Iago, and not mean harm?
                                    (4.1.1–5, italics added)

In the peculiarly concrete vividness with which those two naked bodies on the
bed are made to flash out of the darkness of uncertainty onto the screen of
Othello's fantasy, this becomes a moment of rhetorical discovery—a counterpart to the physical discovery of 5.2. It is what—together with the trium-
phantly reintroduced detail of the handkerchief, that visible sign of
Desdemona's hidden self[45]—provokes the crisis of the scene:

Othello: Lie with her? Lie on her? . . . Lie with her! Zounds,
        that's fulsome! Handkerchief—confession—
        handkerchief!

                                    (4.1.35–37)

Imaginatively linked to the stained sheets of the wedding bed, as Lynda
Boose and Edward Snow have shown,[46] and connected with the exposure of
secrets by its former owner's magical ability "almost [to] read / The thoughts
of people" (3.4.57–58), the handkerchief stands for "an essence that's not
seen" (4.1.16). As it renders the invisible visible and the private public, it
proves the natural unnatural and property itself "unproper": "There's millions
now alive / That nightly lie in those unproper beds / Which they dare swear
peculiar" (4.1.67–69). Thus it confirms the grotesque propriety of the fate that
Iago, relishing his fictive symmetries, decrees for Desdemona: "And did you
see the handkerchief? . . . Do it not with poison; strangle her in her bed,
even the bed she hath contaminated" (4.1.172, 206–7).

From this point on, as Othello moves towards his murderous final exposure
of those "villainous secrets" for which Emilia is "a closet lock and key"
(4.2.21), the bed becomes more and more explicitly the "place" upon which
the action is centered. Above all it provides the emotional focus of Desdemona's two scenes before the murder, where (as though in unconscious
collusion with Othello's fantasies) she perfects her tableau of murderous
consummation. Its hidden program is supplied by the fashion, increasingly

[45]For the handkerchief as "the public surrogate of secrecy," see Kenneth Burke's suggestive
"*Othello*: An Essay to Illustrate a Method" in Susan Snyder, ed., *Othello: Critical Essays* (New
York and London: Garland, 1988), pp. 127–68, esp. p. 160.

[46]See Snow (cited above, n. 22) and Lynda E. Boose, "Othello's Handkerchief: 'The Recognizance and Pledge of Love,'" *English Literary Renaissance*, 5 (1975), 360–74. See also Nelson and
Haines, pp. 8–10. Peter Stallybrass ("Patriarchal Territories: The Body Enclosed" in Snyder,
Othello, pp. 251–74, esp. pp. 254, 269) identifies the handkerchief as a social symbol connected
to the policing and purification of bodily orifices. Some useful historical perspectives on its
significance are suggested by Karen Newman (cited in n. 31, above), pp. 155–56.

popular among aristocratic women in the early seventeenth century, for having one's corpse wound in the sheets from the wedding night[47]:

>   Prithee tonight
> Lay on my bed my wedding sheets, remember,
> And call thy husband hither.
>   (4.2.103–5)

Desdemona:	He hath commanded me to go to bed,
	And bade me to dismiss you. . . .
	Give me my nightly wearing, and adieu.
	We must not now displease him. . . .
Emilia:	I have laid those sheets, you bade me, on the bed. . . .
Desdemona:	If I do die before thee, prithee shroud me
	In one of those same sheets.
	(4.3.12–24)

There is something oddly somnambulant about Desdemona's preparation for her death, as there is about Othello's conduct of the murder. It emerges particularly through the repetition compulsion associated with the wedding sheets, equating sheets and shroud, marriage-bed and death-bed, that mirrors the murderous repetition of Othello's vow: "Thy bed, lust-stained, shall with lust's blood be spotted" (5.1.36). The suggestion of automatism can work as it does only because of the remorselessly cumulative effect of the play's gestures towards the absent presence of the bed. The scope of the action appears to narrow progressively, closing ineluctably through these later scenes upon the final disclosure: "*Enter Othello, [with a light,] and Desdemona in her bed.*"[48] The appearance of the bed from within the curtained alcove at the rear of the stage envisaged in the Folio direction signals a moment of quite literal *discovery*, when the hidden object of the play's imaginative obsession at last stands revealed. The torch plays its part in this symbology of revelation. Like the torches that accompany Othello's first entrance from the marriage-chamber in 1.2, it recalls the emblematic brands of Hymen. In common with so many of the play's images of light and dark, however, its traditional significance is inverted, or at least radically confused; for the bringing to light of the hidden scene of Othello's fantasy corresponds to the simultaneous and deliberate occlusion of his reason: "It is the cause, it is the cause, my soul: / Let me not name it to you." To name his motive would be to render it liable to scrutiny, but Othello cannot bear the thought of what he then might see: "put

---

[47] See Clare Gittings, *Death, Burial and the Individual in Early Modern England* (London and Sydney: Croom Helm, 1984), pp. 111–12.

[48] I give the stage direction in its Folio form, with the necessary addition (in square brackets) of Q1's torch. It is not clear whether the bed is merely to be displayed inside the discovery space or to be thrust forward onto the main stage. Economy of design favors the former alternative, theatrical effectiveness the latter, which is supported by Richard Hosley in "The Staging of Desdemona's Bed," *SQ*, 14 (1963), 57–65. Hosley further suggests that Lodovico's final order may have been a signal for the bed to be "drawn in" again, making his gesture of effacement even more absolute.

out the light" (5.2.1–2, 7). The scene is rhetorically framed by gestures of repression ("Let me not name it to you," "Let it be hid"), as the tableau at its center is physically framed by the curtains that finally close upon it.

It would be laboring the point to demonstrate in detail the centrality of the bed in the play's denouement. The pattern of alternating revelations and concealments in the final scene is enacted through and largely organized around the opening and closing of those bed-curtains which, like theatrical inverted commas, figure so conspicuously in representations of the final scene (5.2.1, 105, 121, 361). In the murder on the bed, with its shocking literalization of Desdemona's conceit of wedding-sheets-as-shroud ("thou art on thy death-bed" [5.2.52]), the nuptial consummation that the play has kept as remorselessly in view as tormentingly out of sight achieves its perverse (adulterate) performance. It is on the bed, moreover, that Othello (in the quarto stage direction) throws himself, as though in a symbolic reassertion of the husband's place, when he first begins to glimpse the depths of Iago's treachery (5.2.197). His place is symbolically usurped in Emilia's request to "lay me by my mistress' side" (5.2.235), and its loss is cruelly brought home in the despair of "Where should Othello go?" (5.2.269). He can reclaim it finally only through a suicide that symmetrically repeats Desdemona's eroticized murder:

> I kissed thee, ere I killed thee: no way but this,
> Killing myself, to die upon a kiss.
>
> (5.2.354–55)

The action of the play has rescued Othello and Desdemona from the calculated anonymity of Iago's pornographic fantasies, only for the ending to strip them of their identities once more: for most of the final scene, Othello is once again named only as "the Moor," and it is as if killing Desdemona had annihilated his sense of self to the point where he must repudiate even his own name ("That's he that was Othello: here I am" [5.2.281]). Lodovico's speech reduces the corpses to the condition of a single nameless "object"— "the tragic loading of this bed" (5.2.359), "it"—something scarcely removed from the obscene impersonality of the image in which they were first displayed, "the beast with two backs" (1.1.117–18).[49] Like a man rubbing a dog's nose in its own excrement, Lodovico, as the voice of Venetian authority, forces Iago (and the audience with him) to look on what his fantasy has made ("This is thy work" [5.2.360]). But Iago's gaze is one that confirms the abolition of the lovers' humanity, and it thereby helps to license Lodovico's revulsion: "let it be hid." In that gesture of concealment, we may discern the official equivalent of Iago's retreat into obdurate silence: "Demand me nothing. What you know, you know: / From this time forth I never will speak

---

[49]The relation between names and identity in the play is sensitively analyzed by Calderwood, pp. 40–45, 50–52.

word" (5.2.300–301). Iago will no more utter his "cause" than Othello can nominate his; what they choose not to speak, we might say, Lodovico elects not to see.

IV

In so far as Lodovico voices the reaction of the audience, he articulates a scandal that is as much generic as it is social. It was precisely their sense of the play's ostentatious violation of the laws of kind that led Victorian producers to mutilate its ending. From the late eighteenth century it became usual to finish the play on the heroic note of Othello's suicide speech, tactfully removing the Venetians' choric expressions of outrage and dismay, as if recognizing how intolerably Lodovico's "Let it be hid" serves to focus attention on what it insists must not be attended to. By diverting the audience's gaze from this radical impropriety, the cut was meant to restore a semblance of tragic decorum to the catastrophe.[50] Other cuts sought to disguise as far as possible the erotic suggestiveness of the scene: in particular Othello's "To die upon a kiss" was almost invariably removed so as to ensure that at the curtain Desdemona's body would remain in chaste isolation upon a bed "unviolated by Othello's own bleeding corpse."[51] In this way the significance of the bed might be restricted to the proper monumental symbolism so solemnly emphasized in Fechter's mid-century production, where it was made to appear "as portentous as a catafalque prepared for a great funeral pomp."[52]

Of course Shakespeare's ending does play on such iconic suggestions but much more ambiguously. When Othello's imagination transforms the sleeping Desdemona to "monumental alabaster" (5.2.5), his figure draws theatrical power from the resemblance between Elizabethan tester tombs and the beds of state on which they were modelled.[53] But his vain rhetorical effort to clothe the violence of murder in the stony proprieties of ritual is thoroughly subverted by other conventional meanings that reveal the bed as a site of forbidden mixture, a place of literary as well as social and racial adulteration.

---

[50]For a suggestive discussion of ideas of propriety and property in the play, see Calderwood, pp. 9–15.

[51]Siemon, p. 50.

[52]Henry Morley, The *Journal of a London Playgoer*, quoted in Hankey, p. 307. Fechter was the first to remove the bed from its traditional central position to the side of the stage, where he placed it with its back to the audience. If this was intended to diminish the threat of the scene, it apparently had the reverse effect, as Sir Theodore Martin complained, "bringing it so far forward that every detail is thrust painfully on our senses" (quoted in Siemon, p. 40).

[53]The sense of this connection clearly persisted into the Restoration theatre: Rowe's illustration for *Antony and Cleopatra* (1709) shows the dead Cleopatra in her monument lying on what is evidently a bed, but in a posture recalling tomb-sculpture. It was not for nothing that the marriage-bed became a favorite model for so many Elizabethan and Jacobean dynastic tombs, where the figures of man and wife, frequently surrounded on the base of the tomb by their numerous offspring, signify the power of biological continuance, the authority of lineage.

If the first act of *Othello*, as Susan Snyder has shown, is structured as a miniature romantic comedy,[54] then the last act returns to comic convention in the form of cruel travesty. For the tragedy ends as it began with a bedding—the first clandestine and offstage, the second appallingly public; one callously interrupted, the other murderously consummated. A bedding, after all, is the desired end of every romantic plot; and Desdemona's "Will you come to bed, my lord" (5.2.24) sounds as a poignant echo of the erotic invitations which close up comedies like *A Midsummer Night's Dream*: "Lovers to bed" (5.1.364). But where comic decorum kept the bed itself offstage, consigning love's consummation to the illimitable end beyond the stage-ending, the bed in *Othello* is shamelessly displayed as the site of a blood-wedding which improperly appropriates the rites of comedy to a tragic conclusion.

The result, from the point of view of seventeenth-century orthodoxy, is a generic monster. Indeed, just such a sense of the monstrosity of the play, its promiscuous yoking of the comic with the tragic, lay at the heart of Rymer's objections to it. Jealousy and cuckoldry, after all, like the misalliance of age and youth,[55] were themes proper to comedy; and the triviality of the handkerchief plot epitomized for Rymer the generic disproportion that must result from transposing them into a tragic design. The words "monster" and "monstrous" punctuate his attempts to catalogue the oxymoronic mixtures of this "Bloody Farce," a play he thought would have been better entitled "the *Tragedy of the Handkerchief.*"[56] Iago himself, as the inventor of this "burlesk" plot, was the very spirit of the play's monstrosity: "The *Ordinary* of *Newgate* never had like Monster to pass under his examination."[57] Much of the force of Rymer's invective stems from the way in which he was able to insinuate a direct connection between what he sensed as the generic monstrosity of the tragedy and the social and moral deformity he discovered in its action: the rhetorical energy that charges his use of "monster" and "monstrous" derives from their electric potency in the language of the play itself. It is clear, moreover, that for Rymer ideas of literary and biological kind were inseparable, so that the indecorum of the design was consequential upon the impro-

---

54The *Comic Matrix of Shakespeare's Tragedies* (Princeton: Princeton Univ. Press, 1979), pp. 70–74. See also Cavell, p. 132.

55The misalliance of youth and age in the play is treated by Janet Stavropoulos, "Love and Age in *Othello*," *Shakespeare Studies*, XIX (1987), 125–41.

56Rymer, quoted in Vickers, pp. 54, 51. Jonson seems to anticipate Rymer's mockery in the jealousy plot of *Volpone* (1606) when Corvino denounces his wife: "to seek and entertain a parley / With a known knave, before a multitude! You were an actor with your handkerchief" (2.3.38–40). In a paper exploring the relations between *Othello* and the myth of Hercules, "Othello *Furens*," delivered at the Folger Shakespeare Library on February 17, 1989, Robert S. Miola has suggested that the handkerchief is a version of the robe of Nessus; such ludicrous shrinkages are characteristic of comic jealousy plots—as, for example, in the transformation of Pinchwife's heroic sword to a penknife in Wycherley's *The Country Wife*. Certain objects become grotesquely enlarged to the jealous imagination or absurdly diminished in the eyes of the audience—it is on such disproportion that the comedy of jealousy depends.

57Rymer, quoted in Vickers, p. 47.

priety of choosing a hero whose racially defined inferiority must render him incapable of the lofty world of tragedy. "Never in the World had any Pagan Poet his Brains turn'd at this Monstrous rate," declared Rymer; and he went on to cite Iago's "Foul disproportion, thoughts unnatural" as a kind of motto for the play: "The Poet here is certainly in the right, and by consequence the foundation of the Play must be concluded to be Monstrous. . . ."[58]

Rymer's appropriation of Iago's language is scarcely coincidental. Indeed it is possible to feel an uncanny resemblance between the scornful excitement with which Rymer prosecutes the unsuspected deformities of Shakespeare's design and Iago's bitter pleasure in exposing the "civil monsters" lurking beneath the ordered surface of the Venetian state. It is as if the same odd ventriloquy which bespeaks the ensign's colonization of the hero's mind were at work in the critic. It may be heard again in Coleridge's objection to the play's racial theme: "it would be something *monstrous* to conceive this beautiful Venetian girl falling in love with a veritable negro. It would argue a *disproportionateness*, a want of balance in Desdemona."[59] Even G. K. Hunter, in what remains one of the best essays on race in *Othello*, echoes this revealing language when he insists that "we feel the *disproportion* and the difficulty of Othello's social life and of his marriage (as a social act)."[60] For all Hunter's disconcerting honesty about the play's way of implicating the audience in the prejudice it explores, there is a disturbance here that the nervous parenthesis, "as a social act," seems half to acknowledge. The qualification admits, without satisfactorily neutralizing, his echo of Iago—for whom, after all, concepts of the social (or the "natural") serve exactly as useful devices for tagging sexual/racial transgression.

"Foul disproportion, thoughts unnatural" (3.3.231) is only Iago's way of describing the feelings of strangeness and wonder in which Othello discerns the seeds of Desdemona's passion for him: "She swore, in faith 'twas strange, 'twas passing strange, / 'Twas pitiful, 'twas wondrous pitiful" (1.3. 159–60). Like *Romeo and Juliet*, the play knows from the beginning that such a sense of miraculous otherness, though it may be intensified by the transgression of social boundaries, is part of the ground of all sexual desire; what Iago enables the play to discover is that this is also the cause of desire's frantic instability. That is why the fountain from which Othello's current runs can become the very source out of which his jealousy flows.[61] Much of the play's power to disturb comes from its remorseless insistence upon the intimacy of jealousy and desire, its demonstration that jealousy is itself an extreme and corrupted (adulterate) form of sexual excitement—an incestuously self-begotten monster of appetite, born only to feed upon itself, a creature of disproportionate desire

[58]Rymer, quoted in Vickers, pp. 37, 42.

[59]T. M. Raysor, ed., *Shakespearean Criticism*, 2 vols. (London: J. M. Dent, 1960), Vol. 1, 42, italics added.

[60]"Othello and Colour Prejudice," p. 163, my italics.

[61]For an account of the social basis of these contradictions, see Stallybrass, pp. 265–67.

whose very existence constitutes its own (natural) punishment. The more Othello is made to feel his marriage is a violation of natural boundaries, the more estranged he and Desdemona become; the more estranged they become, the more he desires her. Only murder, it seems, with its violent rapture of possession, can break such a spiral; but it does so at the cost of seeming to demonstrate the truth of all that Iago has implied about the natural consequences of transgressive desire.

Iago's clinching demonstration of Desdemona's strangeness makes her a denizen of Lady Wouldbe's notorious metropolis of prostitution, the city that Otway in *Venice Preserved* was to type "the whore of the Adriatic"[62]: In Venice they do let God see the pranks / They dare not show their husbands." It produces in Othello a terrible kind of arousal, which finds its expression in the pornographic emotional violence of the brothel scene—"I took you for that cunning whore of Venice / That married with Othello" (4.2.88–89)— where it is as if Othello were compelled to make real the fantasy that possessed him in the course of Iago's temptation: "I had been happy if the general camp, / Pioners and all, had tasted her sweet body" (3.3.342–43). It is an arousal which his imagination can satisfy only in the complex fantasy of a revenge that will be at once an act of mimetic purgation (blood for blood, a blot for a blot), a symbolic reassertion of his sexual rights (the spotted sheets as a parodic sign of nuptial consummation), and an ocular demonstration of Desdemona's guilt (the blood-stain upon the white linen as the visible sign of hidden pollution): "Thy bed, lust-stained, shall with lust's blood be spotted" (5.1.36).[63] In this lurid metonymy for murder, Othello's mind locks onto the bed as the inevitable setting of the fatal end to which his whole being, as in some somnambulist nightmare, is now directed; and it is an ending that, through the long-deferred disclosure of the scene of sexual anxiety, can indeed seem to have been inscribed upon Othello's story from the very beginning.

In order fully to understand the potency of this theatrical image, it is necessary to see how it forms the nexus of a whole set of ideas about adultery upon which Othello's tragedy depends—culturally embedded notions of adulteration and pollution that are closely related to the ideas of disproportion and monstrosity exploited by Iago. The fact that they are linked by a web of association that operates at a largely subliminal level—or perhaps, more precisely, at the level of ideology—makes them especially difficult to disentangle and resistant to rational analysis,[64] and that is an essential aspect of the

[62]For the opposite view of Venice, described by the traveler Thomas Coryat in *Coryat's Crudities* as "that most glorious, renowned and Virgin Citie of Venice," see Stallybrass, p. 265.

[63]A curious sidelight is cast on nineteenth-century attempts to contain the scandal of the play's ending by the habit of having Othello finish off Desdemona with his dagger on "I would not have thee linger in thy pain"—a piece of stage business which must have heightened the sado-erotic suggestiveness of the scene (see Siemon, pp. 46–47).

[64]Kenneth Burke beautifully observes the power of inarticulate suggestion in the play: ". . . there is whispering. There is something vaguely feared and hated. In itself it is hard to locate, being woven into the very nature of 'consciousness'; but by the artifice of Iago it is made local.

play's way of entrapping the audience in its own obsessions. It is above all for "disproportion"—a word for the radical kinds of indecorum that the play at once celebrates and abhors—that the bed, not only in Iago's mind but in that of the audience he so mesmerizes, comes to stand.

V

Contemplating the final spectacle of the play, G. M. Matthews produces an unwitting paradox: "All that Iago's poison has achieved is an object that 'poisons sight': a bed on which a black man and a white girl, although they are dead, are embracing. Human dignity, the play says, is indivisible."[65] But if what the bed displays is indeed such an icon of humanist transcendence, then this ending is nearer to those of romantic comedy—or to that of *Romeo and Juliet*—than most people's experience of it would suggest: why should such an assertion of human dignity "poison sight"? Part of the answer lies in the fact that Matthews, in his desire for humane reassurance, has falsified the body count. To be fair, it is quite usual to imagine two bodies stretched out side by side under a canopy—and this is how it is commonly played. But if Emilia's "lay me by my mistress' side" (5.2.235) is (as it surely must be) a dramatized stage direction, there should be three.[66] The tableau of death will then recall a familiar tomb arrangement in which the figure of a man lies accompanied by two women, his first and second wives; and read in this fashion, the bed can look like a mocking reminder of the very suspicions that Iago voiced about Othello and Emilia early in the play—a memorialization of adultery. It would be absurd to suggest that this is how Lodovico or anyone else on the stage consciously sees it; but, for reasons that I hope to make clear, I think the covert suggestion of something adulterous in this alliance of corpses, combined with the powerful imagery of erotic death surrounding it, helps to account for the peculiar intensity of Lodovico's sense of scandal. The scandal is exacerbated by the fact that one of the bodies is black.

Jealousy can work as it does in this tragedy partly because of its complex entanglement with the sense that Iago so carefully nurtures in Othello of his own marriage as an adulterous transgression—an improper mixture from which Desdemona's unnatural counterfeiting naturally follows. "[I]t is the dark essence of Iago's whole enterprise," writes Stephen Greenblatt, ". . . to play upon Othello's buried perception of his own sexual relations with Desdemona as adulterous."[67] Despite his teasing glance at the play's moral rhetoric

The tinge of malice vaguely diffused through the texture of events and relationships can here be condensed into a single principle, a devil, giving the audience as it were flesh to sink their claw-thoughts in" (p. 131).

[65]"*Othello* and the Dignity of Man," p. 145.

[66]Significantly, eighteenth- and nineteenth-century promptbooks reveal that Emilia's request was invariably denied.

[67]p. 233.

of color ("dark essence"), Greenblatt is really concerned only with notions of specifically sexual transgression according to which " 'An adulterer is he who is too ardent a lover of his wife.' "[68] But this perception can be extended to another aspect of the relationship in which the ideas of adultery and disproportionate desire are specifically linked to the question of race.

In the seventeenth century adultery was conceived (as the history of the two words reminds us) to be quite literally a kind of *adulteration*—the pollution or corruption of the divinely ordained bond of marriage, and thus in the profoundest sense a violation of the natural order of things.[69] Its unnaturalness was traditionally expressed in the monstrous qualities attributed to its illicit offspring, the anomalous creatures stigmatized as bastards.[70] A bastard, as the moral deformity of characters like Spurio, Edmund, and Thersites and the physical freakishness of Volpone's illegitimate offspring equally suggest, is of his very nature a kind of monster—monstrous because he represents the offspring of an unnatural union, one that violates what are proposed as among the most essential of all boundaries.[71]

It is Iago's special triumph to expose Othello's color as the apparent sign of just such monstrous impropriety. He can do this partly by playing on the same fears of racial and religious otherness that had led medieval theologians to define marriage with Jews, Mahometans, or pagans as "interpretative adultery."[72] More generally, any mixture of racial "kinds" seems to have been

[68]Greenblatt, p. 248, quoting St. Jerome. Compare Tamyra's prevarication with her amorous husband (whom she is busy cuckolding with Bussy) in Chapman's *Bussy D'Ambois*: "your holy friar says / All couplings in the day that touch the bed / Adulterous are, even in the married" (3.1.91–93).

[69]In addition to their usual technical sense, "adulterous" and "adulterate" came at about this time to carry the meaning "corrupted by base intermixture"; while by extension "adulterate" also came, like "bastard," to mean "spurious" and "counterfeit" (*OED*, adulterate, *ppl. a.* 2; adulterous, 3; bastard, *sb.* and *a*, 4. See also adulterate, *v.* 3; adulterine, 3). Thus Ford's Penthea, who imagines her forced marriage to Bassanes as a species of adultery, finds her blood "seasoned by the forfeit / Of noble shame with *mixtures of pollution*" (*The Broken Heart*, 4.2.149–50, italics added).

[70]So, by one of those strange linguistic contradictions that expose cultural double-think, an illegitimate son could be at once "spurious" and "unnatural" and a "natural son." When the bastard, Spurio, in a play that performs innumerable variations on the theme of the counterfeit and the natural, declares that "Adultery is my nature" (*The Revenger's Tragedy*, 1.3.177), he is simultaneously quibbling on the idea of himself as a "natural son" and elaborating a vicious paradox, according to which—by virtue of his adulterate birth (*natura*)—he is naturally unnatural, essentially counterfeit, and purely adulterous. A very similar series of quibbling associations underlies the counterfeiting Edmund's paean to the tutelary of bastards in *King Lear*: "Thou, Nature, art my goddess" (1.2.1 ff.).

[71]When Ford's Hippolita curses her betrayer, Soranzo, for what she regards as his adulterous marriage to Annabella, she envisages adultery's monstrous offspring as constituting its own punishment—"mayst thou live / To father bastards, may her womb bring forth / Monsters" (*'Tis Pity She's a Whore*, 4.1.99–101)—a curse that seems likely to be fulfilled when Soranzo discovers the existence of the "gallimaufry" (heterogeneous mixture) that is already "stuffed in [his bride's] corrupted bastard-bearing womb" (4.3.13–14).

[72]*OED*, adultery, 1b. It scarcely matters that Othello's contempt for the "circumcised dog" he killed in Aleppo shows that he sees himself as a Christian, since "Moor" was a virtual synonym for Muslim or pagan; and it is as a "pagan" that Brabantio identifies him (1.2.119).

popularly thought of as in some sense adulterous—a prejudice that survives in the use of such expressions as "bastard race" to denote the "unnatural" offspring of miscegenation.[73] More specifically, Iago is able to capitalize upon suggestions that cloud the exotic obscurity of Othello's origins in the world of Plinian monsters, "the Anthropophagi, and men whose heads / Do grow beneath their shoulders" (1.3.143–44); even the green-eyed monster that he conjures from beneath the general's "civil" veneer serves to mark Othello's resemblance to yet another Plinian race, the Horned Men (Gegetones or Cornuti).[74] In the Elizabethan popular imagination, of course, the association of African races with the monsters supposed to inhabit their continent made it easy for blackness to be imagined as a symptom of the monstrous[75]—not least because the color itself could be derived from an adulterous history. According to a widely circulated explanation for the existence of black peoples (available in both Leo Africanus and Hakluyt), blackness was originally visited upon the offspring of Noah's son Cham as a punishment for adulterate disobedience of his father.[76]

In such a context the elopement of Othello and Desdemona, in defiance of her father's wishes, might resemble a repetition of the ancestral crime, confirmation of the adulterous history written upon the Moor's face.[77] Thus if

[73]In seventeenth-century English the word "bastard" was habitually applied to all products of generic mixture: thus mongrel dogs, mules, and leopards (supposedly half-lion and half-panther) were all, impartially, bastard creatures; and this is the sense that Perdita employs when she dismisses streaked gillyvors as "Nature's bastards" (*The Winter's Tale*, 4.4.83). In Jonson's *Volpone* the bastard nature of Volpone's "true . . . family" is redoubled by their having been "begot on . . . Gypsies, and Jews, and black-moors" (1.1.506–7). Jonson's location of this adulterate mingle-mangle in Venice may even suggest some general anxiety about the vulnerability of racial boundaries in a city so conspicuously on the European margin—one apparent also in *The Merchant of Venice*.

[74]John Block Friedman, *The Monstrous Races in Medieval Art and Thought* (Cambridge Mass.: Harvard Univ. Press, 1981), pp. 16–17. Calderwood notes the resonance of Othello's lodging at the Saggitary—or Centaur (1.3. 1 15)—stressing the monster's ancient significance as a symbol of lust, barbarism, and (through the Centaurs' assault on Lapith women) the violation of kind (Calderwood, *The Properties of Othello*, pp. 22–25, 36).

[75]See Newman, "Femininity and the monstrous in *Othello*," pp. 145–53: Elliot H. Tokson, *The Popular Image of the Black Man in English Drama. 1550–1688* (Boston: G. K. Hall, 1982), pp. 80–81; Friedman, pp. 101–2; and Calderwood, *The Properties of* Othello, p. 7.

[76]Flouting his father's taboo upon copulation in the Ark, Cham, in the hope of producing an heir to all the dominions of the earth, "used company with his wife . . . for the which wicked and detestable fact, as an example for contempt of Almightie God, and disobedience of parents, God would a sonne should bee borne whose name was Chus, who not onely it selfe, but all his posteritie after him should bee so blacke and lothsome, that it might remaine a spectacle of disobedience to all the worlde. And of this blacke and cursed Chus came all these blacke Moores which are in Africa" (George Best, "Experiences and reasons of the Sphere. . . ," in Richard Hakluyt, *The Principal Navigations, Voyages, Traffiques & Discoveries of the English Nation*, 12 vols. (1598–1600: rpt. Glasgow: J. MacLehose, 1903–5). Vol. VII, 264.

[77]The association of blackness with adultery is also encouraged by a well-known passage in Jeremiah, where the indelible blackness of the Moor's skin is analogized to the ingrained (but hidden) vices of the Jews: "Can the blacke More change his skin? or the leopard his spottes. . . . I have sene thine adulteries, & thy neyings, filthines of thy whoredome" (Jeremiah, 13:23–27, Geneva version). In the context of *Othello*, the passage's rhetorical emphasis on discovery is suggestive, as is the Geneva version's marginal note, "Thy cloke of hypocrasie shal be pulled of

he sees Desdemona as the fair page defaced by the adulterate slander of whoredom, Othello feels this defacement, at a deeper and more painful level, to be a taint contracted from him: "Her name that was as fresh / As Dian's visage is now begrimed and black / As mine own face" (3.3.383–85). Tragedy, in Chapman's metaphor, is always "black-fac'd"; but Othello's dark countenance is like an inscription of his tragic destiny for more reasons than the traditional metaphoric associations of blackness with evil and death. Iago's genius is to articulate the loosely assorted prejudices and superstitions that make it so and to fashion from them the monster of racial animus and revulsion that devours everything of value in the play. Iago's trick is to make this piece of counterfeiting appear like a revelation, drawing into the light of day the hidden truths of his society. It is Iago who teaches Roderigo, Brabantio, and at last Othello himself to recognize in the union of Moor and Venetian an act of generic adulteration—something conceived, in Brabantio's words, "in spite of nature" (1.3.96): "For nature so preposterously to err, / Being not deficient, blind, or lame of sense, / Sans witchcraft could not" (1.3.62–64). Even more graphically, Iago locates their marriage in that zoo of adulterate couplings whose bastard issue (imaginatively at least) are the recurrent "monsters" of the play's imagery: "you'll have your daughter covered with a Barbary horse; you'll have your nephews neigh to you, you'll have coursers for cousins, and jennets for germans" (1.1.111–14). Wickedly affecting to misunderstand Othello's anxiety about how Desdemona might betray her own faithful disposition ("And yet how nature erring from itself—"), Iago goes on to plant the same notion in his victim's mind:

Ay, there's the point: as, to be bold with you,
Not to affect many proposèd matches
Of her own clime, complexion, and degree,
Whereto we see in all things *nature* tends,
Foh! One may smell in such a will most rank,
Foul *disproportion, thoughts unnatural.*
(3.3.226–31, italics added)

If at one moment Iago can make infidelity appear as the inevitable expression of Desdemona's Venetian nature, as the denizen of an unnatural city of prostituted adulterers, at another he can make it seem as though it were actually Desdemona's marriage that constituted the adulterous lapse, from which a liaison with one of her own kind would amount to the exercise of "her better judgement" (3.3.234)—a penitent reversion to her proper nature. The contradictions, as is always the way with an emotion like jealousy, are not self-canceling but mutually reinforcing.

and thy shame sene." A second marginal note observes that the prophet "compareth idolaters to horses inflamed after mares," a comparison that may be echoed in Iago's obscene vision of Othello as "a barbary horse" (1.1.112). I am grateful to my colleague Dr. Kenneth Larsen for drawing this passage to my attention.

In this way the relentless pressure of Iago's insinuation appears to reveal a particularly heinous assault on the natural order of things. Not only in its obvious challenge to patriarchal authority and in the subversion of gender roles implicit in its assertion of female desire,[78] but in its flagrant transgression of the alleged boundaries of kind itself, the love of Desdemona and Othello can be presented as a radical assault on the whole system of differences from which the Jacobean world was constructed.[79] The shocking iconic power of the bed in the play has everything to do with its being the site of that assault.

In early modern culture the marriage bed had a peculiar topographic and symbolic significance. It was a space at once more private and more public than for us. More private because (with the exception of the study or cabinet) it was virtually the *only* place of privacy available to the denizens of sixteenth- and early seventeenth-century households[80]; more public because as the domain of the most crucial of domestic offices—perpetuation of the lineage— it was the site of important public rituals of birth, wedding, and death. In the great houses of France, this double public/private function was even symbol- ized by the existence of two beds: an "official bed, majestic but unoccupied," located in the *chambre de parement,* and a private bed screened from view in the more intimate domain of the bedchamber proper.[81] Everywhere the same double role was acknowledged in the division of the bridal ritual between the public bringing to bed of bride and groom by a crowd of relatives and friends, and the private rite of consummation which ensued after the formal drawing of the bed curtains.[82] Part of the scandal of *Othello* arises from its structural reversal of this solemn division: the offstage elopement in Act 1 turning the public section of the bridal into a furtive and private thing; the parted curtains of Act 5 exposing the private scene of the bed to a shockingly public gaze. The scene exposed, moreover, is one that confirms with exaggerated horror the always ambiguous nature of that "peninsula of privacy": "the bed heightened private pleasure. . . . But the bed could also be a symbol of guilt, a shadowy place [or a place of subterfuge], a scene of crime; the truth of what went on here could never be revealed."[83] The principal cause of these anxieties, and

[78]See Newman, passim; and Greenblatt, pp. 239–54.

[79]Whether or not one accepts Foucault's notion of the sixteenth century as the site of a major cultural shift in which a "pre-classical *episteme*" based on the recognition of similarity was replaced by a "classical *episteme*" based on the recognition of difference, it seems clear that the definition of racial "difference" or otherness was an important adjunct to the development of national consciousness in the period of early colonial expansion. See the work by Cairns and Richards, Laurence, and Greenblatt (cited above, n. 32).

[80]See Danielle Régnier-Bohler, "Imagining the Self" in Ariès and Duby (cited above, n. 41), Vol. 2 (*Revelations of The Medieval World*), 311–93, esp. pp. 327–30.

[81]See Dominique Barthélemy and Philippe Contamine, "The Use of Private Space" in Ariès and Duby, Vol. 2, 395–505, esp. p. 500.

[82]See Lawrence Stone, *The Family, Sex and Marriage in England 1500–1800* (New York: Harper and Row, 1977), p. 334; and Georges Duby and Philippe Braunstein, "The Emergence of the Individual," in Ariès and Duby, Vol. 2, 507–630, esp. p. 589.

[83]Règnier-Bohler, p. 329.

hence of the fiercely defended privacy of the marriage bed, lay in the fact that it was a place of licensed sexual and social metamorphosis, where the boundaries of self and other, of family allegiance and of gender, were miraculously abolished as man and wife became "one flesh."[84] Because it was a space that permitted a highly specialized naturalization of what would otherwise constitute a wholly "unnatural" collapsing of differences, it must itself be protected by taboos of the most intense character. In the cruel system of paradoxy created by this play's ideas of race and adultery, Othello as both stranger and husband can be *both* the violator of these taboos and the seeming victim of their violation—adulterer and cuckold—as he is both black and "fair," Christian general and erring barbarian, insider and outsider, the author of a "monstrous act" and Desdemona's "kind lord."[85] As the most intimate site of these contradictions, it was inevitable that the bed should become the imaginative center of the play—the focus of Iago's corrupt fantasy, of Othello's tormented speculation, and always of the audience's intensely voyeuristic compulsions.

At the beginning of the play, the monstrousness of Desdemona's passion is marked for Brabantio by its being fixed upon an object "naturally" unbearable to sight: "To fall in love with what she feared to look on! / . . . Against all rules of nature" (1.3.98—101). At the end she has become, for Lodovico, part of the "object [that] poisons sight." The bed now is the visible sign of *what has been improperly revealed* and must now be hidden from view again—the unnamed horror that Othello fatally glimpsed in the dark cave of Iago's imagination; "some monster in his thought / Too hideous to be shown" (3.3.106-7); it is the token of everything that must not be seen and cannot be spoken ("Let me not name it to you, you chaste stars" [5.2.2]), everything that the second nature of culture seeks to efface or disguise as "unnatural"—all that should be banished to outer (or consigned to inner) darkness; a figure for unlicensed desire itself. That banishment of what must not be contemplated is what is embodied in Lodovico's gesture of stern erasure. But, as Othello's quibble upon the Latin root of the word suggests, a *monster* is also what, by virtue of its very hideousness, demands to be *shown*. What makes the tragedy of *Othello* so shocking and painful is that it engages its audience in a conspiracy to lay naked the scene of forbidden desire, only to confirm that the penalty for such exposure is death and oblivion; in so doing, the play takes us into territory we

---

[84]The archaic spells that form part of the convention of epithalamia and wedding masques testify to a continuing sense (albeit overlaid with a show of sophisticated playfulness) of the marriage bed as a dangerously liminal space in the marital rite of passage.

[85]Othello is made up of such paradoxical mixtures—at once the governing representative of rational order and the embodiment of ungovernable passion, cruel and merciful, general and "enfettered" subordinate, "honourable murderer"—he is an entire anomaly. See Newman, p. 153: "Othello is both hero and outsider because he embodies not only the norms of male power and privilege . . . but also the threatening power of the alien: Othello is a monster in the Renaissance sense of the word, a deformed creature like the hermaphrodites and other strange spectacles which so fascinated the early modern period."

recognize but would rather not see. It doesn't "oppose racism," but (much more disturbingly) illuminates the process by which such visceral superstitions were implanted in the very body of the culture that formed us. The object that "poisons sight" is nothing less than a mirror for the obscene desires and fears that *Othello* arouses in its audiences[86]—monsters that the play at once invents and naturalizes, declaring them unproper, even as it implies that they were always "naturally" there.

If the ending of this tragedy is unendurable, it is because it first tempts us with the redemptive vision of Desdemona's sacrificial self-abnegation and then insists, with all the power of its swelling rhetorical music, upon the hero's magnificence as he dismantles himself for death—only to capitulate to Iago's poisoned vision at the very moment when it has seemed poised to reaffirm the transcendent claims of their love—the claims of kind and kindness figured in the union between a black man and a white woman and the bed on which it was made.

---

[86]For discussion of the "satisfaction" that the final scene grants an audience, see Calderwood, pp. 125–26.

Signs, Speech, and Self

James L. Calderwood

1. Signs and Ensigns

Earlier I suggested that Othello solves his semiotic dilemma—how to manifest his perfect soul publicly when its most apparent outward sign is his devilishly black skin and moorish looks—by acquiring marital property, by projecting his virtues outward into Venice through the refracting prism of Desdemona's beauty. But marital property is merely one of several modes of expression in this play, and in the present chapter I want to explore more fully how Othello's self seeks signs of various sorts in which to publicize its identity.

As Desdemona's case indicates, the most natural or at least most apparent sign of inner meaning is the body. The lovely Desdemona is a perfect example of Pietro Bembo's neoplatonic contention in *The Book of the Courtier* that the body is on the whole an accurate index of inner virtue and that beauty in particular is a circle whose center is goodness.[1] Shakespeare, however, entertains neoplatonism only when it suits him. Lacking the courtier's implicit faith in signs, he founds his play on the rupture between outward signifiers and inward signifieds, between the Moor's evil-seeming black face and his "perfect soul," between his ancient's honest-seeming white exterior and the ulcerous evil that breeds around his heart. The body is a capricious sign; it may or may not tell the truth. But what else can you rely on? Except in the case of angels, souls do not converse with other souls directly; and most sublunar creatures lack Falstaff's instinctive ability to discern the true Prince even through buckram ("By the Lord, I knew ye as well as he that made ye!"). As Bembo himself says:

> For, finding itself deep in an earthly prison, and deprived of spiritual contemplation in exercising its office of governing the body, the soul of itself cannot clearly perceive the truth; wherefore, in order to have knowledge, it is obliged to turn to the senses as to its source of knowledge; and so it believes them and bows before

From James L. Calderwood, *The Properties of Othello* (Amherst: The University of Massachusetts Press, 1989), 53–57, copyright © 1989 by the University of Massachusetts Press.

[1]Baldesar Castiglione, *The Book of the Courtier*, trans. Charles S. Singleton (Garden City, N.Y.: Anchor Books, 1959), pp. 336–48, esp. pp. 342–47. Bembo acknowledges that there are cases in which the beautiful are also wicked but holds that in such cases wickedness has perverted the natural goodness of beauty.

them and lets itself be guided by them, especially when [as in the young and passionate] they have so much vigor that they almost force it; and, being fallacious, they fill it with errors and false opinions.[2]

As the bodily senses are the avenue to knowing others, so, reversely, one's own body is the avenue to being known. Misrepresented by his body, however, Othello is obliged to take as the sign of his soul another body, Desdemona's. For a military man, it is like choosing a champion and staking the entire battle on single combat outside one's citadel. The analogy has a certain appropriateness here inasmuch as the semiotics of the self has a military dimension to it. Iago points it out. In Act 1, Scene 1 he tells Roderigo that with the Cypriot wars afoot he must go seek out the General:

> Though I do hate him as I do hell-pains,
> Yet, for necessity of present life,
> I must show out a flag and sign of love,
> Which is indeed but sign.
>
> (1.1.156)

Iago's interest in flag-waving here follows from his mention of the wars and derives from the fact that he is Othello's ancient, or ensign. In Elizabethan armies, "the ensign had no command or administrative function. His job was simply to carry the colors (in the middle of his band in a set battle, at the head of his band during a charge or assault) and to conduct himself in such a way as to bring honor to his person."[3] As Othello's flag-carrying ensign, then, Iago literally holds Othello's identity—or at any rate the sign of Othello's identity—in his own hands.[4] How appropriate, therefore, that he remain the Moor's ancient at the beginning of the play instead of graduating to lieutenant. For *lieutenant*, in its French sense of "in lieu of," is obviously more suitable to the Cassio whom Othello suspects of wearing his nightcap and who ultimately takes his place as commander of Cyprus.[5]

He who threads his identity into a flag, and entrusts that flag to an ensign like Iago, is in grave danger of coming apart at the seams. Externalizing one's inner meanings is hazardous even in the best of cases, even when one's flag is Desdemona. For she too is Othello's ensign in Venice, the beautiful white flag that parades the virtues and value of the Moor. To make the parallel with Iago more exact, Desdemona is not only Othello's flag but his flag-bearer as well. In this role she carries onto the sexual battlefield the handkerchief in whose

[2]Ibid., pp. 338–39.

[3]Henry J. Webb, *Elizabethan Military Science: The Books and Practice* (Madison, Milwaukee, and London: University of Wisconsin Press, 1965), p. 84.

[4]Mark Rose brings this point to my attention in private correspondence, adding, "Nancy Vickers mentioned the role of the ensign as a flag-bearer in a paper at the Shakespeare Association meeting last year [1986], but whether she made the more general point about sign and identity I don't recall." Professor Vickers's paper is as yet unpublished, as far as I can tell.

[5]Michael Neill emphasizes the French meaning of *lieutenant* and the various ways in which Cassio qualifies for the title, most notably of course because he is presumed to act in lieu of Othello with Desdemona—see his "Changing Places in *Othello*," pp. 120–21.

magic web his identity as husband is so closely woven. When she lets that flag fall—the ultimate sin for an ensign—it passes into the keeping of Bianca, is captured as it were by that mortal enemy of all virtuous wives, the whore. At crucial points like this in *Othello,* signs take on literal significance. With the flag that betokens a chaste marriage in the possession of Bianca, Desdemona's and Othello's identities are both forfeited. In Othello's embittered imagination, she becomes a strumpet, he a purchaser of her sexual favors, and their bedroom a brothel.

We never see Iago carrying Othello's flag into battle. Instead of a sign he bears the sign of a sign—the title of ensign or ancient. Thus Desdemona's loss of the handkerchief cannot be paralleled by Iago's loss of a real battle flag. Iago loses merely the sign of a sign, his title, which he does not really lose but willingly surrenders in return for another: "Now art thou my lieutenant" . . . "I am your own forever."

Iago's passage from ancient to lieutenant is a passage from sign to substitute; now he no longer signifies the Moor's identity but assumes it, functioning "in lieu of" the general. Othello's outward signifier fuses with his inward signified as he makes Iago his own, and of course as Iago makes Othello *his* own. If Iago as ancient had seemed an arbitrary sign of the general's identity, with a stress on difference, he now becomes a natural sign, with a stress on resemblance. Their "marriage" is a form of semiotic bonding that has overtones of demonic possession. Signs have thus taken a grotesquely proper revenge on Othello, insofar as his nobly natural impulse has been to assume that signifiers and signifieds *are* indissoluble, that words and meanings are wedded to one another in the most literal of senses.

2. The Narrative Subject

If the ensign may become the general whose sign he is, and if signifiers may become their signifieds, then surely the style may be the man. Our bodies tell us and others who we are—our bodies and especially what our bodies do and how they do it, their physical style. Who can mistake Magic Johnson's headlong orchestration of a three-on-two fast break, Itzhak Perlman's agonizings at the violin, or Ronald Reagan's smiling, waving, miming regretful deafness to reporters' questions as he makes for Air Force One? But of course the most distinctive thing our bodies do is speak. And if speech is incorrigibly common by virtue of the repeatability of words, voices and verbal styles are blessedly uncommon. Voice prints will identify us as readily as fingerprints, and Othello's style of speech rings distinctively familiar in everyone's ear.[6]

6If there is anything barbaric about the Moor, it is not his language. (The word *barbarian,* as Herodotus says, derives from the fact that to the Greeks the speech of outsiders sounded like *bar-bar-bar.*) For analyses stressing language in *Othello* see Matthew N. Proser, *The Heroic Image in*

Othello descants the Othello music, those arias of splendid sonority that rise and fall like the stormy waters off Cyprus and sometimes flow as inexorably as the Pontic Sea.[7] In his mouth, casual greetings take on the character of sacred vows, and even when he confesses himself rough with words he does so in the accents of Demosthenes[8]:

> Rude am I in my speech,
> And little blessed with the soft phrase of peace;
> For since these arms of mine had seven years' pith,
> Till now some nine moons wasted, they have used
> Their dearest action in the tented field;
> And little of this great world can I speak
> More than pertains to feats of broil and battle,
> And therefore little shall I grace my cause
> In speaking for myself.
>
> (1.3.83)

By Act 4, however, we will find ourselves saying "That's he that was Othello. Here he is":

> Lie with her? Lie on her? We say lie on her, when they belie her. Lie with her! 'Zounds, that's fulsome.—Handkerchief—confessions—handkerchief!—To confess, and be hanged for his labor—first, to be hanged, and then to confess.—I tremble at it. Nature would not invest herself in such shadowing passion without some instruction. It is not words that shakes me thus. Pish! Noses, ears, and lips.—Is it possible?—Confess—handkerchief!—O devil!

These are the first lines of prose Othello utters—surely, one would think, a significant moment. To see just how significant, however, requires a context. Let us return to his verse self and better times.

In the opening act, Othello is in command of speech, and at first his speeches are mostly commands: "Holla, stand there!" . . . "Keep up your

---

Five Shakespearean Tragedies (Princeton: Princeton University Press, 1965), pp. 92–135; Terence Hawkes, *Shakespeare's Talking Animals* (London: Edward Arnold, 1973), pp. 132–42; Lawrence Danson, *Tragic Alphabet* (New Haven: Yale University Press, 1974), pp. 97–121; Madelon Gohlke, " 'All that is spoke is marred': Language and Consciousness in *Othello*," *Women's Studies* 9 (1982): 157–76; and Harold E. Toliver's chapter on the play in *Transported Language in Shakespeare and Milton* (University Park and London: Pennsylvania State University Press, 1988).

[7]"The Othello Music" is the title of G. Wilson Knight's chapter on the play in his *The Wheel of Fire* (1930; New York: Meridian Books, 1957). Of course Iago puts a different light on Othello's rhetoric when he speaks of it as "bombast circumstance / Horribly stuffed with epithets of war" (1.1.14).

[8]All of Shakespeare's presumably crude speakers speak well in the cause of inarticulacy. Still, Othello contrasts with, say, Coriolanus, who not only proclaims his indifference to fine words but also truculently avoids occasions where they are to be used either about him or by him. Othello has a naive trust in the honesty of words that Coriolanus would scorn. Terence Hawkes makes a useful distinction between the plain spoken "language of men" which characterizes Othello early in the play and the duplicitous language of "manliness" which he is taught by Iago (*Shakespeare's Talking Animals*, pp. 132–42).

bright swords." . . . "Hold your hands" (1.2). He is so sure of himself that he is willing to obey Brabantio and proceed to the Senate, where amid the nervous scurryings of rumor his speech stands out in its calm confidence, most notably when he assumes the role of narrator in response to the Duke's invitation "Say it, Othello" (1.2.129). Since Othello's self-exonerating speeches here are central to his concept of self, let us consider them and him in terms of narrative and monologue.

In effect Othello says "She willingly came with me." But in his mouth nothing is ever that simple. "She willingly came" is transformed into an extended account of his oblique courtship of Desdemona, which consisted of his saying, as heroic lovers often do, "Here I am, Othello. Let me tell you the meaning of that name, and you will love me." Of all Shakespeare's characters, Othello testifies most thoroughly to the fact that everyone is a biography, a life-story constantly being written and revised, told and retold. As the neurologist Oliver Sacks observes, "Biologically, physiologically, we are not so different from each other; historically, as narratives—we are each of us unique."[9] This is more than usually true of the Moor because as a "wheeling stranger / Of here and everywhere" he cannot rely, as Venetians can, on the unity of residential place to lend coherence to his life—what Kenneth Burke would call a "scene-agent ratio" (you *are* by virtue of where you are).[10] Instead he must continually reestablish his sense of self narratively. Thus not only is he telling himself at this moment before the Senate, but the subject of his telling is further tellings. His story about his courtship of Desdemona is recursively suspended to admit in evidence the stories of which that courtship consisted.[11] For a moment we seem on the edge of an *Arabian Nights* infinite recursion whereby Shakespeare's dramatic story yields to Othello's senatorial story, which yields to his courtship stories of cannibals and Anthropophagi, which might perhaps yield to . . . But fortunately do not.

This narrative in which the narrator is in several senses the "subject" gives us a divided perspective on Othello. In the first place, as story-telling subject or seemingly autonomous self, he is present and in command of the scene, exercising such dominion over shifters as to transform *I* into his own proper name, while everyone else is distanced and subordinated to the status of *he* or *she*. All words and meanings come under his monopoly; the capitalist of self is also the capitalist of speech who puts words profitably to work to earn

---

[9]Oliver Sacks, *The Man Who Mistook His Wife for a Hat* (New York: Harper and Row, 1987), p. 111. See also in this respect Stephen J. Greenblatt's article on narrative self-fashioning in *Othello*: "Improvisation and Power" in *Literature and Society*, ed. Edward W. Said (Baltimore and London: Johns Hopkins University Press, 1980), pp. 57–99, esp. p. 73.

[10]Kenneth Burke, *A Grammar of Motives and A Rhetoric of Motives* (Cleveland and New York: World Publishing Company, 1962), pp. 7–9.

[11]For a perceptive analysis of *Othello* based on the rhetorical and juridical implications of "dilation" and "delation," in which the meanings of accusation, amplification, and delay combine, see Patricia Parker's "Shakespeare and Rhetoric: 'dilation' and 'delation' in *Othello*," in Parker and Hartman, *Shakespeare and the Question of Theory*, pp. 54–74.

Desdemona's love and the Senate's approval.[12] He imposes his image of himself on others through sheer force of continuity, his meanings rolling rhetorically forth in sentences of such sustained syntactic complexity that he might be writing instead of speaking, since he is no more subject to interruption than the author of a treatise.

In these respects, as storyteller in the Senate, Othello aggrandizes himself as subject. Moreover, because of the recursiveness of his story, because he is a voice telling about himself telling about himself, his possession of the *I* is reaffirmed within his own story. Normally, that is, the *I* that speaks and the *I* that is spoken, although they tend to merge in the imagination, are demonstrably discrete, the former being the speaking subject, the latter the grammatical subject.[13] In fact the grammatical "subject" has an element of the accusative about it, inasmuch as it is not merely the doer of verbal deeds within each sentence but the done-unto, the object of the speaking subject's speech. Othello, however, fends off this accusative element, keeping it at one further remove by mirroring and embedding the speaking subject in the grammatical one. The *I* who is spoken about is also a speaker telling stories to Desdemona. It's not until we get to the *I* who stands for the adventurous hero, instead of for the speaking voice, that Othello takes on an accusative aspect—appropriately, for instance, in his brief mention of having been "taken by the insolent foe" and sold to slavery, an embarrassing occasion in which his being physically enslaved is analogous to his enthrallment to the words of his own speech.

Thus the act of telling about himself subtly subverts Othello's domination of speech and, through speech, his domination of the Senate and of Desdemona and Brabantio earlier. After all, his life is being recast in verbal forms. He says that he ran through his biography for Brabantio "even from my boyish days / To the very moment that he bade me tell it" (1.3.134) and that at Desdemona's request he later dilated on "all [his] pilgrimage" (1.3.155). But the story of his life does not stop there; even now before the Senate a further episode is being appended, "Othello's Courtship of Desdemona." Normally the speaking subject is enormously in excess of the grammatical subject; we *are* far more than we can say. But so great is the stress on Othello's representations of himself that the events of his life seem lived just one Shandy-like step ahead of the words that seize and digest them into story.

This near-fusion of Othello and his life story entails a special vulnerability.

---

[12]This is a point of some relevance to Shakespeare as well. Who could be more conscious than he of the fact that the words you command define your identity? Out of his poetic words materialized not only theatrical performances but such self-defining properties as New Place, the cottage on the south side of Chapel Lane, 107 acres of arable land in Old Stratford, a lucrative lease of tithes of corn, grain, and hay, and of course a coat of arms and rights to the title of "Master."

[13]Calling these two subjects the "speaking" and the "grammatical" is a desperate attempt to evade "the subject of the enunciation" and "the subject of the enunciating," as they are called in linguistics.

His identity is as riskily entrusted to narrative signs here as it is to the flag and handkerchief borne by his two ensigns, Iago and Desdemona. Add to this the fact that Othello's distinctive *style*, which from one perspective is inseparably specific to him, from another perspective marks his speech as rhetorically fashioned and hence separable from him, and we see that what seems most natural to him is also most alien from him. Thus if the structure of his self is so exclusively constituted by the structure of his speech, then to destroy Othello you need merely put his language on the rack. Bastinado his diction, twist his syntax. Make him say "Lie with her? Lie on her? We say lie on her, when they belie her. Lie with her! 'Zounds, that's fulsome.— Handkerchief—confessions—handkerchief!" and his body is at your mercy.

Thus Othello is at double risk. His identity, which ought by rights to exceed his speech, is dangerously confined and entrusted to it. Even at its moment of greatest power before the Senate, his speech unavoidably splits him into a speaking and a spoken *I*—perhaps the first suggestion we have of the fission of self that will later cause Desdemona to say "My lord is not my lord" (3.4.125).[14]

3. *Signs and De-Signs*

In light of the fact that Brabantio, Desdemona, and now the Senate have succumbed to his eloquence, it is little wonder Othello puts his faith in words. Like Harry Hotspur, another romantic warrior, he is a platonic idealist for whom abstractions have a worshipful reality. Hotspur's favorite abstraction is *honor*, Othello's is *honest*.[15] For him *honest* is a transcendental signifier that stabilizes discourse; he believes not only in the word *honest* but in the honesty of words. Although he speaks the language of high romance,[16] he naively assumes that even the most ethereal of words are bonded to their

---

[14]This view of the self as composing speech and being composed by it strikes a balance between the contemporary arguments about our using or being used by language and by other impersonal systems operating on and through us. Marxist critics in particular—reacting to their suspicion that the concept of capitalistic private ownership underlies the extreme romantic and bourgeois individualism that extols "originality" and the authority of the author—have so stressed intertextuality, contextuality, and the "production" of text that writing is in danger of becoming not only an intransitive activity but an inhuman one as well. It goes without saying that language speaks through authors (and through plowmen and auto mechanics) and that authors can be regarded as points of convergence for diverse ideological, social, and economic formations. But although language ought to have, it did not speak with the same vocabulary, style, and eloquence through Barnaby Googe as it did through Shakespeare; and the ideological, social, and economical forces in Stratford that converged on Gilbert as well as on William Shakespeare perhaps ought to have but did not produce a jointly written *Hamlet* and *King Lear*.

[15]For the full range of the meanings of *honest* in *Othello*, see William Empson's chapter in his *The Structure of Complex Words* (Norfolk, Conn., 1951).

[16]Mark Rose discusses *Othello* as a recapitulation and subversion of Shakespeare's earlier representations of chivalry in the history plays (and of Elizabethan England's efforts to "turn reality into a romance"); see "Othello's Occupation," pp. 293–311.

meanings and those meanings bonded in turn to what they represent. Call Iago honest and he *is* honest. Which means that honest Iago has only to pin the word *dishonest* securely on Desdemona to guarantee her death.

Iago is honest enough to say "The Moor is of a free and open nature, / That thinks men honest that but seem to be so" (1.3.400). The Moor's logocentrism extends to his judgment of people. For him, a person is like a sign in which signifier and signified are paired by nature; what you see is what you get. Iago's blunt straightforward manner and Desdemona's beauty are reliable indices of honesty and virtue. Even the naive Desdemona is more subtly Venetian in this respect than Othello: she saw the Moor's visage in his mind, disregarding the black signifiers without—although on the other hand she is like him in taking his stories about himself at face value.

Not that Othello is content with signifiers. He trustingly accepts *seems* for *so*, but it is the *so*, the signified within, that he seeks. Thus when Iago's vaguenesses begin to stir in his imagination, his first reaction is to brush aside words and get to the unmediated thing itself: "If thou dost love me," he demands of Iago, "Show me thy thought" (3.3.120). Still, even here he has not dispensed with mediation entirely; Iago's hidden thought must somehow be "shown," even in words:

I prithee speak to me as to thy thinkings,
As thou dost ruminate, and give thy worst of thoughts
The worst of words.

(3.3.136)

The following fifty or so lines play increasingly passionate variations on this theme, building up to Othello's angry "By heaven, I'll know thy thoughts!" (3.3.166). By this time mediation disappears; he would understand Iago's mind not as mortal men are obliged to do, by reason and discourse, but as angels (and perhaps devils) do, by instinct or intuition.

Unfortunately Iago refuses to speak, and Othello lacks clairvoyance. Honesty grows suspect; it is not what it is. If Iago is honest and speaks out, then Cassio and Desdemona will surely prove dishonest; whereas as long as he is dishonestly secretive, they remain honest in name, whatever they may be in fact. No wonder Othello says "What dost thou mean?" What Iago means, he says, is that he is something of an idealist himself, claiming in Cassio-like terms that "who steals my purse steals trash" but "he that filches from me my good name" steals true value (3.3.160–65). Therefore he will not speak his thoughts.

What is Othello to make of this? Honest Iago is unforthcomingly dishonest, yet for noble reasons that make him seem more deeply honest than if he had spoken straight out. With Iago's honesty apparently growing in proportion to his dishonesty, no wonder Othello is puzzled and frustrated.

By this time Iago's insinuations have set Othello adrift on a sea of deconstructive signifiers in accordance with the sign theory Iago proclaimed earlier to Roderigo: "I must show out a flag and sign of love, / Which is indeed but sign" (1.1.158). Iago's style is to run up flags and signs that can be switched at a moment's notice. In fact his signs are really "designs" in a double sense, a kind of deconstructive scheming, inasmuch as they "de-sign" or divest signs of meaning in order to fulfill his villainous designs. The sign for him is a one-sided coin, signifier up; its signified, the thought that could make the coin's face value good (or in this case bad), is nowhere to be found. Iago's worst words can express no worst thoughts, for the simple reason that he has no worst thoughts; he knows perfectly well that Desdemona and Cassio are above suspicion. Unanchored either to referents or to signifieds, his insinuations float free, deferring meaning indefinitely and obliging Othello to drift on an endless current of suggestion.

4. Ocular Proof and Body Language

If Othello cannot gain access to Iago's conclusive thoughts by way of words, how then? The answer is simple and familiar; the epistemology of the West rests on it: merely look. "To be once in doubt," Othello says, "is once to be resolved," and the way to be resolved, as the empiricists especially argued, is to follow the optic nerve:

> I'll see before I doubt; when I doubt, prove;
> And on the proof, there is no more but this—
> Away at once with love or jealousy.
>   (3.3.196)

This is more famously expressed later when he collars Iago and demands "Villain, be sure thou prove my love a whore! Be sure of it. Give me the ocular proof" (3.3.364), after which, just to be sure there is no mistake, he adds,

> Make me to see it, or at the least so prove it
> That the probation bear no hinge nor loop
> To hang a doubt on; or woe upon thy life!
>   (3.3.369)

Clearly the eye's the thing wherein he'll catch the conscience of the quean. To break free of slippery signifers like *honesty* and gain access to the unmediated truth, he will dismiss words altogether and take the incomparably honest eye to friend.

Iago seizes on the idea with enthusiasm. First he ocularizes his language, painting lascivious images of Cassio and Desdemona in the fiction of the dreaming Cassio (3.3.415–30). When Othello begins to rage, Iago both taunts him by complaining "Yet we see nothing done"—as though the game were too easily won—"She may be honest yet" (3.3.436). Then he leads Othello, still with no more than a noose of words, to the terrible speech quoted earlier in which he falls from verse into prose:

> Lie with her? Lie on her? We say lie on her, when they belie her. Lie with her!
> 'Zounds, that's fulsome.—Handkerchief—confessions—handkerchief!—To confess,
> and be hanged for his labor—first, to be hanged, and then to confess.—I tremble
> at it. Nature would not invest herself in such shadowing passion without some
> instruction. It is not words that shakes me thus. Pish! Noses, ears, and lips.—Is it
> possible?—Confess—handkerchief!—O devil!

If Othello simply fell from verse to prose here it would be startling enough, but in fact he plunges right on through prose to a series of incoherent cries and babblings at the edge of the sublinguistic. In view of his earlier sublimations of language, his logocentric concern for signifieds, it is ironic that his discourse should be reduced to a random play of signifiers alone. Now he is caught up in the low material stuff that words are made on, the carnal body of sounds stripped of sense.

Thus Shakespeare draws a painful parallel between Othello's (non) language and his (non) love. In the Senate Scene earlier, recoiling almost in disgust from the notion that he might want to take Desdemona to Cyprus for sexual reasons, Othello purified his wife Lady Macbeth-like, by unsexing her there, and then. If we say as so many critics have, either in praise or complaint, that Othello's love is idealistic and lacks body, then in this scene that metaphor unmetaphors itself. Desdemona becomes not a body to bed but a soul to enfranchise ("to be free and bounteous to her mind" [1.3.268]), a Petrarchan divinity inviting allegorization as the antithesis to Iago's diabolism, which is characterized by a misogynistic obsession with the repellancies of the body. That antithesis moves toward a degrading synthesis, however, when Othello becomes convinced of Desdemona's villainy. Then he too sees evil in her body, particularly in the hand into which his kerchief was entrusted; "This hand," he observes, "is moist, my lady" (3.4.36), adding a gloss on moistness:

> This argues fruitfulness and liberal heart.
> Hot, hot, and moist. This hand of yours requires
> A sequester from liberty, fasting and prayer,
> Much castigation, exercise devout;
> For here's a young and sweating devil here
> That commonly rebels. 'Tis a good hand,
> And a frank one.

'Tis a good hand, not morally but semiotically, a synecdochic sign that frankly announces the presence of a young and sweating devil. That Othello the reborn Christian regards the body as devilish we might have suspected from his puritanical rejection of sexual pleasure in the Senate Scene, but now the demonic equation emerges clearly, forecasting the necessity of exorcism.

Before that, however, we see Desdemona's divinity and Othello's style collapse together. In his disjointed speech, he is assaulted by images of her as a body to be lain with or on, and then finally as no more than a repellant concatenation of physical parts—"Noses, ears, and lips."[17] Everything descends not merely to body here but rather, as in a *sparagmos,* to a torn and dismembered body. Noses, ears, and lips are to the intact physique as Othello's fragmented utterance is to authentic syntax—indeed as Othello's own trembling and shaking limbs at this moment are to his fine physical presence in earlier scenes. What issues from Othello is not romantic verse or even plain prose but something not quite speech, a verbal epilepsy—a regression from language in its abstract and symbolic role as the instrument of godlike reason to language as the almost preverbal Artaud-like noises expelled by a creature in pain.[18]

When Othello falls into his epilepsy one further parallel ensues, for his seizure consists of an obliteration of consciousness and a consequent deterioration of reflective man to that state which Hamlet called bestial oblivion. The idealistic Othello to whom the bodily and material are a source of corruption—to whom love must be ethereally chaste or else, the only imaginable alternative, "a cistern for foul toads to knot and gender in!" (4.2.61)—is now reduced to nothing but body, a lump of quivering matter. And if the body is the Devil's empire, as Luther maintained, and Iago is at least a demi-devil, then Othello and Desdemona are now most perilously abandoned within His Satanic Majesty's dominion.[19]

5. The Storied Self

Othello clearly can go no further in this verbal direction. Despite his sinking cry "It is not words that shakes me thus," it is still precisely words that shakes him thus. It is past time to shift to ocular proofs, for the eye is incorruptibly honest. Iago obliges by staging the play-within, at last bringing forth for inspection his secret thoughts, not in slippery phrases and vague insinuations but open and palpable as a pageant. Now at last Othello is satisfied. There in full and damning sight are the smiling Cassio, the beckoning Iago, the embraces, then Cassio's whore, and finally the handkerchief itself (4.1.105–68). In keeping with his own prescription for revenge, he has seen, doubted, proved, and there is no more but this: "How shall I murder him, Iago?" (4.1.169).

---

[17]Peter Stallybrass makes an excellent case for the metaphoric significance of these particular bodily parts in terms of "the body geography of the Renaissance" in his "Patriarchal Territories," pp. 138–39.

[18]The nearest analog to this moment in *Othello* is Lear's howling entrance with Cordelia's dead body, which can be regarded as part of a pattern of linguistic uncreation (as I have done in "Creation Uncreation in *King Lear*," *Shakespeare Quarterly* 37, no. 1 [Spring 1986]: 616–36).

[19]Luther's scatological notions of the Devil are discussed by Norman O. Brown, *Life Against Death*, pp. 177–304.

However, what Iago knows and Othello does not is that ocular proofs are no more transcendental and unmediated than verbal ones:

As [Cassio] shall smile, Othello shall go mad;
And his unbookish jealousy must conster
Poor Cassio's smiles, gestures, and light behavior
Quite in the wrong.

(4.1.101)

Here Iago rather brilliantly translates the visual into the verbal to demonstrate that the observing eye is not all that different from the reading eye (or the hearing ear). Iago employs space as a blank sheet on which he writes his lubricous meanings with the stylus of Cassio's smiles, gestures, and light behavior. And Othello, convinced that he is simply registering the naked phenomenological truth, reads what Iago has written, and misconsters all. No surprises there. Othello is, after all, an unbookish barbarian; the subtleties of mediation undo him quite. Thus he stands apart, entering his crude glosses in the margins of Iago's fleeting text—"Now he denies it faintly, and laughs it out. . . . Do you triumph, Roman? . . . By heaven, that should be my handkerchief!" Even afterwards when Iago remarks upon the handkerchief and he is obliged to ask "Was that mine?" he still believes he has been recording the unmediated truth. And because he does, he chooses to regard Desdemona herself as a fair paper and goodly book in which Cassio has written the word *whore* (4.2.71).

These bookish metaphors call to mind the role played by printing in the development of Western capitalism.

> [Book publishing] was one of the first industries that required a capital investment to procure the means of production. It was also one of the first enterprises in which speculation played a prominent role. Publishing involved the marketing of a mass-manufactured product. It was a highly competitive field, where price was dictated by the laws of supply and demand.[20]

More important, Marshall McLuhan claims that the book as "portable commodity" created the price system: "For until commodities are uniform and repeatable the price of an article is subject to haggle and adjustment."[21] Thus we might argue that the introduction of book metaphors in *Othello*, and especially that in which Desdemona is represented as a book written in by the "pens" of other men, suggests the reduction of the unique and privately owned Desdemona to a repeatable commodity, as portable and purchasable a piece of goods as a book. The commonness of the book parallels the commonness of the money for which Roderigo trades his land and whores market their favors.

In any event, interpreting Iago's stagy inscriptions drives the unlearned

[20]Robert K. Logan, *The Alphabetic Effect* (New York: William Morrow and Co., 1986), p. 217.
[21]McLuhan, *The Gutenberg Galaxy* (Toronto: University of Toronto Press, 1962), p. 164.

Othello mad, as Iago predicted. Not mad like Lear: it is a measure of his delusion that we must put his "madness" within quotation marks, as we do Desdemona's "dishonesty." Whereas Lear, casting aside his protective cultural clothing, is battered into honest madness by the true immediacy of the storm, Othello is driven "mad" by the pseudo-storms of Iago's mediated stagings.[22] Still, the storm within Othello is real enough to overwhelm the sense he struggles to retain. Out of the whirlwind of his passion Desdemona hears words that are both demeaning and demeaned, signifers that no longer signify:

> Upon my knees, what doth your speech import?
> I understand a fury in your words,
> But not the words.

> (4.2.31)

After this he curses her in the presence of Lodovico, strikes her, and banishes her from his presence.

Following his epileptic speech, Othello's syntax improves, but his meanings still twitch furiously until Act 4, Scene 3 and Emilia's ominous comment to Desdemona, "How goes it now? He looks gentler than he did" (4.3.11). The calm, if not gentleness, of his manner reoccurs in the Murder Scene, which recapitulates in small the larger fall of Othello's speech throughout the play. Diapasons of his former style and stately rhythms reappear as he enters now intoning "It is the cause." As self-assured as he was at his first entrance, he addresses himself to a respiritualized Desdemona whose soul, heaven forfend, he would not kill. Indeed he is even willing to take auricular confession. But when she remains simply a loving woman instead of a contrite fallen nun, Othello's style falters and then fails him altogether. "Alas," Desdemona cries, "why gnaw you so your nether lip? / Some bloody passion shakes your very frame"—just as it did during his seizure. His words grow increasingly abusive as his frustration mounts, until at last he seizes on murder as a kind of manual correlative to ocular proof—a transcendental signified meant to terminate the play of speech: "But while I say one prayer!" . . . "It is too late."

The last phase of Othello's story is another story, beginning "Soft you; a word or two before you go." In his early stories about himself, he was subsumed by narrative, simultaneously telling and being told. So it is again at the end. He hushes other speakers to convert them into an audience of his own speech. Once again he becomes the speaking *I*—but also the subject to be spoken of, not only by himself but by his audience. He must speak to them because it is they who will speak of him: "Speak of me as I am." And then, typically, he tells their story for them—

---

[22]In this respect Othello more resembles Gloucester than Lear—the blind Gloucester deceived by Edgar at Dover "Cliffs," although he is cast into furious despair, not rescued from it.

>   Then must you speak
> Of one that loved not wisely but too well;
> Of one not easily jealous, but, being wrought,
> Perplex'd in the extreme; of one whose hand,
> Like the base Indian, threw a pearl away
> Richer than all his tribe; of one whose subdued eyes,
> Albeit unused to the melting mood,
> Drops tears as fast as the Arabian trees
> Their medicinable gum. Set you down this;
> And say besides, that in Aleppo once,
> Where a malignant and a turban'd Turk
> Beat a Venetian and traduc'd the state,
> I took by th' throat the circumcised dog,
> And smote him, thus.

Just as he told his life story up to the moment Brabantio asked him to tell it, and continued it up to the moment the Duke said "Say it, Othello," so now he resumes the tale, bringing his life up to date and providing us with a brief chronicle of the play itself. If his life has always been lived just a breath ahead of his stories about himself, now life and story terminally coincide at the moment of death: "O bloody period!" Lodovico exclaims as the dagger makes its fatal point. When Gratho adds "All that is spoke is marred," his words suggest not merely that Othello's suicide casts a foul light on his fine words but that his bloody period has blotted the fair written page of his self. Inasmuch as he is both the speaker and "all that is spoke," his assimilation to story is complete.

6. Monologue/Dialogue

Othello's narrative monopoly on language in the first act and his subsequent loss of that monopoly during his verbal exchanges with Iago suggest that Mikhail Bakhtin's views about monologue and dialogue may provide a means of making helpful distinctions between the two.[23] Taking that perspective, let us see how the play looks.

As noted earlier, Othello's speech bears some similarities to writing. For instance when he speaks in monologue he commands language as a writer does when he writes. The high formality of his opening lines—"Most potent, grave, and reverend signiors, / My very noble and approved good masters"—

---

[23]See Mikhail Bakhtin, especially *Speech Genres and Other Essays*, trans. Vern McGee (Austin: University of Texas Press, 1986), and *Bakhtin: Essays and Dialogues on His Work*, ed. Gary Saul Morson (Chicago and London: University of Chicago Press, 1986). Actually in Bakhtin's view there is no such thing as monologue, since all utterance answers and is answerable, but I use the term for convenience.

reserves a solemn and sizable space for his holding forth. The assurance that he will proceed without interruption allows him amplitude of utterance. He can afford the large phrase and sustained period, the rhythms of repetition, the crafting of parallels, subordinations, parentheses, antitheses, and the lingering evocations of detail that help unfold his rhetorical plot from that opening apostrophe to the formal closure of "This only is the witchcraft I have used."

All of this unhurried stylizing of speech has a greater affinity to writing than to utterance. This affinity appears also in Othello's near total investment of meaning in words alone. When he tells his story, nothing is assumed, everything is said. Once under way, his words roll on autonomously, indifferent to their immediate nonverbal context, each sentence responding to the thrust of the one before it and preparing the way for the one following it. Like most forms of public address, Othello's speech is designed not to further dialogue but to suspend it. As a performance, the proper response to it is applause, which is just what it gets: "I think this tale would win my daughter too."

In Act 3, however, Othello finds himself in Iago's dialogistic territory, a place of disjunctive utterances and echoings, of eyebrows raised and fingers laid along the nose, of musings meant to be overheard and silences loud with implication. Meaning resides now in the unspoken aspects of the scene or immediate context even more than it does in words. With Iago, the unsaid always says more than the said. The thrust of speech comes not syntactically from within as in monologue, where phrases and sentences build on their predecessors, but responsively from without, each utterance answering one before it and preparing for one to follow, a reply that invites a reply, as when Iago repeats Othello's words in the form of a question—"Honest, my lord?" "Think, my lord?" The extent to which meaning arises from the scene—this speaker, this audience, this shared subject, this known past and anticipated future—is suggested by Iago's sly employment of deictics and demonstratives. "Ha! I like not *that*," he begins (3.3.35); or "scan *this thing* no farther; leave *it* to time" (3.3.252) and "I see, sir, that you are eaten up with passion. / I do repent me that I put *it* to you" (3.3.396). Such terms, meaningless in themselves, imply a shared understanding and a community of interest: we two, here and now, faced with this difficulty, knowing what we know.

The irony lies in the fact that Iago is inviting Othello out of his fortress of monologue into a social scene where he must share his *I*, honor the verbal rights of others, and cultivate a negative capability. Such projections and outgoings should have been implicit in his love for Desdemona, but of course we have seen how much Othello's love went forth only in search of his own reflection and how constitutionally opposed to dialogue his famous style is. Monologue makes its own meaning, and Othello's verbal idealism lodges all meaning in words.[24] Obliged to attend to meanings situated, or in Iago's slick

24As Bakhtin says, arguing against Saussure's *langue*: "Can the expressive aspect of speech be

practice seemingly situated, outside language, in silence, in undivulged thought, in pitch and accent and smiles and nods and handkerchiefs, and perhaps most of all in such "common knowledge" as the sly sexual maneuvers of Venetian ladies (3.3.207–10), Othello breaks down.

But after all what should we have expected? The Moor is a stranger. He is not privy to the world shared by Venetians: the social order, habits, standards, expectations, all that stands behind the simplest remark one person makes to another, guaranteeing that what is meant by the one is at least roughly what is understood by the other. He always speaks from a place outside or at the borders of this cultural scene. Perfectly natural, then, that he should situate as much meaning as possible in words, and especially in his own words. To grasp meanings lying outside and around and behind words he is dependent on those in the know. And of course Iago is always in the know. Othello's cry "By heaven, I'll know thy thought" stands beside his bemused comment "Dost thou say so?" (3.3.211) as testimony to a desire that can never be wholly satisfied by the stranger, the knowledge that is simply known, the understanding that is understood, all that is given to Venetians because of experiences shared while Othello was engineering hairbreadth escapes off in antres vast and deserts idle.

In light of these considerations, the Murder Scene is a mockery of dialogue. Othello enters in the old vein, intoning his music, fashioning a lyric poem about the finalities of death; and although what follows has the appearance of dialogue, especially in the stichomythic exchanges, everything Othello says is designed to impose his own exclusive interpretation on the occasion and to prevent further speech. Cassio's "mouth is stopped" (3.3.74), and so should Desdemona's be: "Peace, and be still!" (3.3.48). Desdemona is cast in the role of questioner, inviting response, and Othello as answerer, having the final word. Even when she prays, it is he who utters "Amen," setting the conventional verbal seal on her words:

Desdemona:	Then heaven
	Have mercy on me!
Othello:	Amen, with all my heart!
Desdemona:	Then Lord have mercy on me!
Othello:	I say, amen.

regarded as a phenomenon of *language* as a system? Can one speak of the expressive aspect of language units, i.e., words and sentences? The answer to these questions must be a categorical 'no.' . . . The word *darling*—which is affectionate both in the meaning of its root and its suffix—is in itself, as a language unit, just as neutral as the word *distance*" (*Speech Genres and Other Essays*, p. 60; excerpted in *Bakhtin: Essays and Dialogues on His Work*, p. 96). More succinctly: "If an individual word is pronounced with expressive intonation it is no longer a word, but a complete utterance expressed by one word" (p. 62). In other words, I take it, you can define a word in a dictionary and indicate its grammatical functions, but you cannot assign it a suprasegmental phoneme that represents its prosodic meaning—you cannot say how it is to be uttered. Only on a given occasion, spoken with a certain duration, pitch, and intensity, will *darling* escape its lexical abstractness and express affection, contempt, surprise, passion, or the emptiness of the formulaic Hollywood greeting.

Amen puts a period to prayer as a period puts an end to a sentence; and inasmuch as we hear Desdemona repeatedly beginning lines that Othello concludes—as in the examples just cited—he is literally the periodic end-stop of dialogistic verse. This is increasingly the case as the scene moves on—

Desdemona:	Let [Cassio] confess a truth.
Othello:	He hath confessed.
Desdemona:	What, my lord?
Othello:	That he hath used thee.
Desdemona:	How? Unlawfully?
Othello:	Ay.

—until it reaches its unhappy climax when Othello puts a terminal end-stop to her speech:

Desdemona:	But half an hour!
Othello:	Being done, there is no pause.
Desdemona:	But while I say one prayer.
Othello:	It is too late.
	Smothers her.

Othello may stop Cassio's mouth and then Desdemona's, but human affairs are incorrigibly dialogistic; there is always an Emilia at the door crying "My lord, my lord! What ho! My lord, my lord!" and demanding that the world outside be allowed to speak its disruptive piece. What the world says is that Othello is a murdering fool. And Othello—what does he say?

That is, after all this playing-off of monologue against dialogue, how should we understand Othello's last speech? Has he profited stylistically from his experience? Perhaps. The speech is a monologue of sorts, an attempt to redefine himself and bring to a final close, a bloody period, both his words and his life. Yet it is also open-ended, not merely acknowledging but relying on the subsequent speech of others ("Then must you speak"), and as it were open-beginninged in that it issues from prior speech ("Soft you") and comments on what has gone before ("these unlucky deeds"). Moreover, as that definite description suggests—perhaps with a gesture in the direction of Desdemona—it takes its source in the immediate context and is grounded in common knowledge ("I have done the state some service, and they know it. / No more of that"). Finally its most significant meaning derives not from words alone, as in the Senate Scene, but from an act that can be known for certain only if you are there to see it, since it is represented verbally by nothing more enlightening than "thus." To be sure, the deed emerges from the words "I took by the throat the circumcised dog, / And smote him, thus," but without the stage direction *Stabs himself* an actor or director reading the script might momentarily assume that Othello is supposed to seize and stab Iago, or even Lodovico or Gratiano.

Perhaps the merger of monologue and dialogue in the speech does justice to Othello's insistence on asserting his distinctive status as tragic hero, which allows him to say the last word himself ("O bloody period!"), while at the same time registering his chastened awareness that he is about to become merely words in the mouths of other men, a phrasal link in an endless chain of utterance.

Viewpoints

Susan Snyder on "Othello's Alien Status"*

Othello's disintegration of self is the dark side of comedy's rejection of singleness, its insistence on completing oneself with another. But Shakespeare goes deeper in his exploration of comic assumptions by showing that the desired merging of self and other is in any case impossible. The more or less schematized pairings-off of the comedies combine necessary opposition (male/female) with sympathies in age, background, and temperament. It is enough in comedy to suggest compatibility by outward signs and look no farther than the formal union. But in *Othello* Shakespeare has taken pains in several ways to emphasize the separateness of his lovers.

Cinthio's Moor in the source tale is handsome, apparently fairly young, and a longtime Venetian resident. Apart from sex, his only real difference from Desdemona is one of color, and Cinthio does not dwell on it much. Shakespeare dwells on it a great deal. Black-white oppositions weave themselves continually into the verbal fabric of *Othello*. Indeed, the blackness of Cinthio's hero may have been one of the story's main attractions for Shakespeare. Certainly he altered other details of the story to reinforce this paradigmatic separation into black and white, to increase Othello's alienness and widen the gulf between his experience and Desdemona's. Shakespeare's Moor is a stranger to Venice and to civil life in general; his entire career, except for the brief period in which he courted Desdemona, has been spent in camp and on the battlefield (1.3.83–87). Even Othello's speech reminds us constantly, if subtly, of his apartness. It is hardly rude, as he claims to the Venetian Senate, but it is certainly different from theirs. His idiom naturally invokes Anthropophagi and Pontic seas, roots itself in the exotic rather than the everyday social life that is familiar to the others but not to him. He knows as little of Venetian ways as Desdemona knows of "antres vast and deserts idle," and he is given no time to learn. While Cinthio's Moor and his bride live for some time in Venice after their marriage, Othello and Desdemona must go at once to Cyprus—and not even in the same ship. No wonder that, when Iago generalizes about the habits of his countrywomen ("In Venice they do let God see the pranks / They dare not show their husbands"), Othello can only respond helplessly, "Dost thou say so?" (3.3.206–9). Shakespeare has deprived him of

* From Synder, Susan, *The Comic Matrix of Shakespeare's Tragedies* (Princeton, N.J.: Princeton University Press, 1979), 31–32. Copyright © 1979 by Princeton University Press. Reprinted by permission of Princeton University Press.

any common ground with Desdemona on which he can stand to fight back—not only to facilitate Iago's deception, but to heighten the tragic paradox of human love, individuals dependent on each other but unalterably separate and mysterious to one another in their separateness. The two great values of comic convention—love and the fuller self—are seen as tragically incompatible.

To sharpen the contrast, Othello is made middle-aged, thick-lipped—everything Desdemona is not. The image of black man and white girl in conjunction, so repellent to some critics that they had to invent a tawny or café-au-lait Moor, is at the center of the play's conception of disjunction in love. It gives visual focus to the other oppositions of war and peace, age and youth, man and woman. This disjunction serves the plot: it assists Iago's initial deception, and it provides most of the tension in the period between the deception and the murder, as Desdemona inopportunely pleads for Cassio, and Othello in turn can communicate his fears only indirectly, through insults and degradations. But beyond this plot function the disjunction constitutes a tragic vision of love itself.

What I am suggesting is that the action of *Othello* moves us not only as a chain of events involving particular people as initiators and victims, but also as an acting out of the tragic implications in any love relationship. Iago is an envious, insecure human being who functions as a perverted magician-manipulator, cunningly altering reality for Othello. But he is also the catalyst who activates destructive forces not of his own creation, forces present in the love itself. His announcement of the "monstrous birth" quoted above has special significance in this regard. Coming at the end of a resolved marriage scene, it implies that the monster will be the product of the marriage. Iago says, "It is engender'd," not "I have engendered it," because he is not parent but midwife. "Hell and night," embodied in this demi-devil who works in the dark, will bring the monster forth, but it is the fruit of love itself.

Stephen Greenblatt on "The Improvisation of Power" †

In Iago's first soliloquy, Shakespeare goes out of his way to emphasize the improvised nature of the villain's plot:

> Cassio's a proper man, let me see now,
> To get this place, and to make up my will,
> A double knavery . . . how, how? . . . let me see,
> After some time, to abuse Othello's ear,
> That he is too familiar with his wife:
> He has a person and a smooth dispose,

† From *Renaissance Self-Fashioning: From More to Shakespeare.* (Chicago: University of Chicago Press, 1980), 37–39. Reprinted by permission.

To be suspected, fram'd to make women false:
The Moor a free and open nature too,
That thinks men honest that but seems to be so:
And will as tenderly be led by the nose . . .
As asses are.
I ha't, it is engender'd; Hell and night
Must bring this monstrous birth to the world's light.

(1.3.390–402)

We will try shortly to cast some light on why Iago conceives of his activity here as sexual; for the moment, we need only to observe all of the marks of the impromptu and provisional, extending to the ambiguity of the third-person pronoun: "to abuse Othello's ear / That he is too familiar with his wife." This ambiguity is felicitous; indeed, though scarcely visible at this point, it is the dark essence of Iago's whole enterprise which is, as we shall see, to play upon Othello's buried perception of his own sexual relations with Desdemona as adulterous.

What I have called the marks of the impromptu extend to Iago's other speeches and actions through the course of the whole play. In Act 2, he declares of his conspiracy, " 'tis here, but yet confus'd; / Knavery's plain face is never seen, till us'd," and this half-willed confusion continues through the agile, hectic maneuvers of the last act until the moment of exposure and silence. To all but Roderigo, of course, Iago presents himself as incapable of improvisation, except in the limited and seemingly benign form of banter and jig. And even here, he is careful, when Desdemona asks him to improvise her praise, to declare himself unfit for the task:

I am about it, but indeed my invention
Comes from my pate as birdlime does from frieze,
It plucks out brain and all: but my Muse labours,
And thus she is deliver'd.

(2.1.125–28)

Lurking in the homely denial of ability is the image of his invention as birdlime, and hence a covert celebration of his power to ensnare others. Like Jonson's Mosca, Iago is fully aware of himself as an improviser and revels in his ability to manipulate his victims, to lead them by the nose like asses, to possess their labor without their ever being capable of grasping the relation in which they are enmeshed. Such is the relation Iago establishes with virtually every character in the play, from Othello and Desdemona to such minor figures as Montano and Bianca. For the Spanish colonialists, improvisation could only bring the Lucayans into open enslavement; for Iago, it is the key to a mastery whose emblem is the "duteous and knee-crooking knave" who dotes "on his own obsequious bondage" (1.1.45–46) [All *Othello* citations are to the Arden Shakespeare edition, ed. M. R. Ridley], a mastery invisible to the servant, a mastery, that is, whose character is essentially ideological. Iago's attitude toward Othello is nonetheless colonial: though he finds himself in a subordinate position, the ensign regards his black general as "an erring barbarian" whose "free and open nature" is a fertile field for exploitation. However galling it may be to him, Iago's subordination is a kind of protection, for it conceals his power and enables him to play upon the ambivalence of Othello's relation to Christian society: the Moor at once represents the institution and the alien, the conqueror and the infidel. Iago can conceal his malicious intentions toward "the thick-lips" behind the mask of dutiful service and hence prolong his improvisation as the Spaniards could not. To be sure, the play suggests, Iago must ultimately destroy the beings he exploits and hence undermine the profitable economy of his own relations, but that destruction may be long deferred, deferred in fact for precisely the length of the play.

If Iago then holds over others a possession that must constantly efface the signs of its own power, how can it be established, let alone maintained? We will find a clue, I think, in what we have been calling [elsewhere] the process of fictionalization that transforms a fixed symbolic structure into a flexible construct ripe for improvisational entry. This process is at work in Shakespeare's play, where we may more accurately identify it as *submission to narrative self-fashioning*. When in Cyprus Othello and Desdemona have been ecstatically reunited, Iago astonishes Roderigo by informing him that Desdemona is in love with Cassio. He has no evidence, of course—indeed we have earlier seen him "engender" the whole plot entirely out of his fantasy—but he proceeds to lay before his gull all of the circumstances that make this adultery plausible: "mark me, with what violence she first lov'd the Moor, but for bragging, and telling her fantastical lies; and she will love him still for prating?" (2.1.221–23). Desdemona cannot long take pleasure in her outlandish match: "When the blood is made dull with the act of sport, there should be again to inflame it, and give satiety a fresh appetite, loveliness in favor, sympathy in years, manners and beauties" (2.1.225–29). The elegant Cassio is the obvious choice: "Didst thou not see her paddle with the palm of his hand?" Iago asks. To Roderigo's objection that this was "but courtesy," Iago replies, "Lechery, by this hand: an index and prologue to the history of lust and foul thoughts" (2.1.251–55). The metaphor makes explicit what Iago has been doing all along: constructing a narrative into which he inscribes ("by this hand") those around him. He does not need a profound or even reasonably accurate understanding of his victims; he would rather deal in probable impossibilities than improbable possibilities. And it is eminently probable that a young, beautiful Venetian gentlewoman would tire of her old, outlandish husband and turn instead to the handsome, young lieutenant: it is, after all, one of the master plots of comedy.

Part 3

KING LEAR

Action and World in *King Lear*

Maynard Mack

The relatively slight attention given in *King Lear* to the psychological processes that ordinarily precede and determine human action suggests that here we are meant to look for meaning in a different quarter from that in which we find it in the earlier tragedies. In *Hamlet*, Shakespeare had explored action in its aspect of dilemma. Whether or not we accept the traditional notion that Hamlet is a man who cannot make up his mind, his problem is clearly conditioned by the unsatisfactory nature of the alternatives he faces. Any action involves him in a kind of guilt, the more so because he feels an already existing corruption in himself and in his surroundings which contaminates all action at the source. "Virtue cannot so inoculate our old stock but we shall relish of it." Hence the focus of the play is on those processes of consciousness that can explain and justify suspension of the will. In *Othello*, by contrast, Shakespeare seems to be exploring action in its aspect of error. Othello faces two ways of understanding love: Iago's and Desdemona's— which is almost to say, in the play's terms, two systems of valuing and two ways of being—but we are left in no doubt that one of the ways is wrong. Even if we take Iago and Desdemona, as some critics do, to be dramatic emblems of conflicting aspects in Othello's own nature, the play remains a tragedy of error, not a tragedy of dilemma. "The pity of it, Iago" is that Othello makes the wrong choice when the right one is open to him and keeps clamoring to be known for what it is even to the very moment of the murder. The playwright's focus in this play is therefore on the corruptions of mind by which a man may be led into error, and he surrounds Iago and Desdemona with such overtones of damnation and salvation as ultimately must attend any genuine option between evil and good.

King Lear, as I see it, confronts the perplexity and mystery of human action at a later point. Choice remains in the forefront of the argument, but its psychic antecedents have been so effectively shrunk down in this primitivized world that action seems to spring directly out of the bedrock of personality. We feel sure no imaginable psychological process could make Kent other than loyal, Goneril other than cruel, Edgar other than "a brother noble." Such characters, as we saw earlier, are qualities as well as persons: their acts have

From *King Lear in Our Time* (Berkeley and Los Angeles: University of California Press, 1965), 92–117. Reprinted by permission of the author.

consequences but little history. The meaning of action here, therefore, appears to lie rather in effects than in antecedents, and particularly in its capacity, as with Lear's in the opening scene, to generate energies that will hurl themselves in unforeseen and unforeseeable reverberations of disorder from end to end of the world.

The elements of that opening scene are worth pausing over, because they seem to have been selected to bring before us precisely such an impression of unpredictable effects lying coiled and waiting in an apparently innocuous posture of affairs. The atmosphere of the first episode in the scene, as many a commentator has remarked, is casual, urbane, even relaxed. In the amenities exchanged by Kent and Gloucester, Shakespeare allows no hint to penetrate of Gloucester's later agitation about "these late eclipses," or about the folly of a king's abdicating his responsibilities and dividing up his power. We are momentarily lulled into a security that is not immediately broken even when the court assembles and Lear informs us that he will shake off all business and "unburthen'd crawl toward death." I suspect we are invited to sense, as Lear speaks, that this is a kingdom too deeply swaddled in forms of all kinds—too comfortable and secure in its "robes and furr'd gowns"; in its rituals of authority and deference (of which we have just heard and witnessed samples as Gloucester is dispatched offstage, the map demanded, and a "fast intent" and "constant will" thrust on our notice by the king's imperious personality); and in its childish charades, like the one about to be enacted when the daughters speak. Possibly we are invited to sense, too, that this is in some sort an emblematic kingdom—almost a paradigm of hierarchy and rule, as indeed the scene before us seems to be suggesting, with its wide display of ranks in both family and state. Yet perhaps too schematized, too regular—a place where complex realities have been too much reduced to formulas, as they are on a map: as they are on that visible map, for instance, on which Lear three times lays his finger in this scene ("as if he were marking the land itself," says Granville-Barker), while he describes with an obvious pride its tidy catalogue of "shadowy forests" and "champains," "plenteous rivers and wide-skirted meads." Can it be that here, as on that map, is a realm where everything is presumed to have been charted, where all boundaries are believed known, including those of nature and human nature; but where no account has been taken of the heath which lies in all countries and in all men and women just beyond the boundaries they think they know?

However this may be, into this emblematic, almost dreamlike situation erupts the mysterious thrust of psychic energy that we call a choice, an act; and the waiting coil of consequences leaps into threatening life, bringing with it, as every act considered absolutely must, the inscrutable where we had supposed all was clear, the unexpected though we thought we had envisaged all contingencies and could never be surprised. Perhaps it is to help us see this that the consequences in the play are made so spectacular. The first consequence is Lear's totally unlooked-for redistribution of his kingdom into two parts instead of three, and his rejection of Cordelia. The second is his totally unlooked-for banishment of his most trusted friend and counselor. The third is the equally unlooked-for rescue of his now beggared child to be the Queen of France; and what the unlooked-for fourth and fifth will be, we already guess from the agreement between Goneril and Regan, as the scene ends, that something must be done, "and i' th' heat." Thereafter the play seems to illustrate, with an almost diagrammatic relentlessness and thoroughness, the unforeseen potentials that lie waiting to be hatched from a single choice and act: nakedness issues out of opulence, madness out of sanity and reason out of madness, blindness out of seeing and insight out of blindness, salvation out of ruin. The pattern of the unexpected is so completely worked out, in fact, that, as we noticed in the preceding chapter, it appears to embrace even such minor devices of the plot as the fact that Edmund, his fortune made by two letters, is undone by a third.

Meantime, as we look back over the first scene, we may wonder whether the gist of the whole matter has not been placed before us, in the play's own emblematic terms, by Gloucester, Kent, and Edmund in that brief conversation with which the tragedy begins. This conversation touches on two actions, we now observe, each loaded with menacing possibilities, but treated with a casualness at this point that resembles Lear's in opening his trial of love. The first action alluded to is the old king's action in dividing his kingdom, the dire effects of which we are almost instantly to see. The other action is Gloucester's action in begetting a bastard son, and the dire effects of this will also speedily be known. What is particularly striking, however, is that in the latter instance the principal effect is already on the stage before us, though its nature is undisclosed, in the person of the bastard son himself. Edmund, like other "consequences," looks tolerable enough till revealed in full: "I cannot wish the fault undone, the issue of it being so proper," says Kent, meaning by proper "handsome"; yet there is a further dimension of meaning in the word that we will only later understand, when Edgar relates the darkness of Edmund to the darkness wherein he was got and the darkness he has brought to his father's eyes. Like other consequences, too, Edmund looks to be predictable and manageable—in advance. "He hath been out nine years," says Gloucester, who has never had any trouble holding consequences at arm's length before, "and away he shall again." Had Shakespeare reflected on the problem consciously—and it would be rash, I think, to be entirely sure he did not—he could hardly have chosen a more vivid way of giving dramatic substance to the unpredictable relationships of act and consequence than by this confrontation of a father with his unknown natural son—or to the idea of consequences come home to roost, than by this quiet youthful figure, studying "deserving" as he prophetically calls it, while he waits upon his elders.

In *King Lear* then, I believe it is fair to say, the inscrutability of the energies that the human will has power to release is one of Shakespeare's paramount interests. By the inevitable laws of drama, this power receives a degree of emphasis in all his plays, especially the tragedies. The difference in *King Lear* is that it is assigned the whole canvas. The crucial option, which elsewhere comes toward the middle of the plot, is here presented at the very outset. Once taken, everything that happens after is made to seem, in some sense, to have been set in motion by it, not excluding Gloucester's recapitulation of it in the subplot. Significantly, too, the act that creates the crisis, the act on which Shakespeare focuses our dramatic attention, is not (like Lear's abdication) one which could have been expected to germinate into such a harvest of disaster. The old king's longing for public testimony of affection seems in itself a harmless folly: it is not an outrage, not a crime, only a foolish whim. No more could Cordelia's death have been expected to follow from her truthfulness or Gloucester's salvation to be encompassed by a son whom he disowns and seeks to kill.

All this, one is driven to conclude, is part of Shakespeare's point. In the action he creates for Lear, the act of choice is cut loose not simply from the ties that normally bind it to prior psychic causes, but from the ties that usually limit its workings to commensurate effects. In this respect the bent of the play is mythic: it abandons verisimilitude to find out truth, like the story of Oedipus; or like the *Rime of the Ancient Mariner*, with which, in fact, it has interesting affinities. Both works are intensely emblematic. Both treat of crime and punishment and reconciliation in poetic, not realistic, terms. In both the fall is sudden and unaccountable, the penalty enormous and patently exemplary. The willful act of the mariner in shooting down the albatross has a nightmarish inscrutability like Lear's angry rejection of the daughter he loves best; springs from a similar upsurge of egoistic willfulness; hurls itself against what was until that moment a natural "bond," and shatters the universe. Nor do the analogies end with this. When the mariner shoots the albatross, the dark forces inside him that prompted his deed project themselves and become the landscape, so to speak, in which he suffers his own nature: it is his own alienation, his own waste land of terror and sterility that he meets. Something similar takes place in Shakespeare's play. Lear, too, as we saw earlier, suffers his own nature, encounters his own heath, his own storm, his own nakedness and defenselessness, and by this experience, like the mariner, is made another man.

To turn from a play's action to its world is not, when the dramatist is Shakespeare, to take up a new subject but to reconsider the old in a new light. The strains of violence and aggression stressed earlier in connection with the play's action could as well be treated as an aspect of its world. The bareness and spareness so often cited as features of its world penetrate equally the character and action. The austerity and rigor that these have in *King Lear* may best be appreciated by comparing Hal and Falstaff, in whom the dramatist's exuberant invention multiplies variety, to Lear and his Fool, where invention plays intensely but always along the same arc; or by recalling

Othello, with all its supernumerary touches of actual domesticity in Desdemona, actual concerns of state in the Moor; or *Hamlet,* with its diversions and digressions among guardsmen, recorders, gossip of city theatres, its mass of historical and literary allusions, its diversities of witty, sophisticated, and self-conscious speech. *Lear,* too, contains diversities of speech—ritual and realistic styles described by W. B. C. Watkins,[1] iterations singled out by Bradley to characterize Cordelia[2] (which are, in fact, characteristic of several of the play's speakers), "oracular fragments of rhapsody" in the mad scenes (the phrase is Granville-Barker's),[3] imperatives, preachments, questionings, and, last but not least, the Fool's wry idiom, vehicle of the hard-won wisdom of the poor, made up largely of proverb, riddle, maxim, fable, and ballad. *Lear* has such diversities, but as Winifred Nowottny argues convincingly in a recent essay, all are marked, even the most passionate and poignant, by a surface "absence of contrivance,"[4] which allows flashes of profound feeling to flare up unexpectedly in the most unpretentious forms of speech, yet seems to tell us at the same time (this is of course the measure of its artfulness in fact) that "feeling and suffering . . . are beyond words." "The play is deeply concerned," she writes, "with the inadequacy of language to do justice to feeling or to afford any handhold against abysses of iniquity and suffering."[5] Here, too, it strikes me, the play is of a piece. As it uses for the most part the barest bones of language to point at experiences that lie beyond the scope of language, so it uses stripped-down constituents of personality (character that is entirely *esse,* that does not alter but develops to be always more completely the thing it was—as in Kent, for whom banishment simply means that he will "shape his old course in a country new," and who at the end of the play will be about answering his master's call once again) to point to complexities of being and of human reality that lie beyond the scope of the ordinary conventions of dramatic character.

But these are matters that come through to us more clearly in the study than onstage. There can be no question that the most powerful single dimension of the play's world for its spectators is its continual reference to and evocation, through eye and ear alike, of the nature and significance of human society. A "sense of sympathy and human relatedness," as Miss Welsford has said, is what the good in this play have or win through to.[6] In the world of *King Lear,* this is the ultimate gift, spring of man's joy and therefore of his pain. When Lear dies, as I mentioned in the beginning, with his whole being launched toward another, with even his last gasp an expression of hope that

---

[1]"The Two Techniques in *King Lear,*" *Review of English Studies,* XVIII (1942), 1–26, reprinted in enlarged form as chap. 3 of his *Shakespeare and Spenser* (1950).

[2]*Lectures on Shakespearean Tragedy* (1904), p. 319; he is corrected on this point by Granville-Barker (*Prefaces to Shakespeare,* 1, 281).

[3]*Ibid.*

[4]"Some Aspects of the Style of *King Lear,*" *Shakespeare Survey,* XIII (1960), 51.

[5]*Ibid.,* p. 52.

[6]*The Fool: His Social and Literary History* (1935), p. 258.

she lives, the image before us is deeply tragic; yet it is also, in the play's terms, a kind of victory. This is a matter we must come back to. What needs to be considered first is the circumstantial "sociality" of the Lear world which defines and gives body to this closing vision of human achievement and its cost.

In writing *King Lear,* Shakespeare's imagination appears to have been so fully oriented toward presenting human reality as a web of ties commutual that not only characterization and action, but language, theme, and even the very *mise en scène* are influenced. The play's imagined settings—divisible into several distinct landscapes as "shadowy forests" and "champains" fade off first into "low farms and poor pelting villages," then into the bare and treeless heath, then into glimpses of high-grown grain at Dover on the brink of the giddy cliff that only exists in Edgar's speech and his father's imagination—are always emphatically social. Even on that literally and emblematically lonesome heath we are never allowed to forget the nearby presence of what Mr. Eliot calls in his *Dry Salvages* "the life of significant soil." Somewhere just beyond the storm's rim and suitably framing the rainswept beggared king, Shakespeare evokes through Tom of Bedlam's speeches a timeless community of farms and villages where the nights are measured between "curfew" and "the first cock," the beggars are "whipp'd from tithing to tithing," the green mantle of the standing pool is broken by the castaway carcasses of the "old rat and the ditch dog," and the white wheat is mildewed by "the foul Flibberti-gibbet," who also gives poor rustics "the web and the pin, squinies the eye and makes the hairlip."[7] Likewise at Dover, around the two old men, one mad, one blind, Shakespeare raises another kind of society, equally well adapted to the movement of the plot, courtly, sophisticated, decadent. A society of adulterers and "simp'ring dames." A society where "a dog's obey'd in office," the beadle lusts for the whore he whips, "the usurer hangs the cozener," and "robes and furr'd gowns hides all."

It is by these surrealist backgrounds and conflations, as we all know, that Shakespeare dilates his family story into a parable of society of all times and places. The characters, too, bear some signs of having been shaped with such a parable in view. As a group, they are significantly representative, bringing before us both extremes of a social and political spectrum (monarch and beggar), a psychic spectrum (wise man and fool), a moral spectrum (beastly behavior and angelic), an emotional spectrum (joy and despair), and, throughout, a "contrast of dimension," as Miss Nowottny has called it,[8] that draws within one compass both the uttermost human anguish which speaks in "She's dead as earth" and the strange limiting "art of our necessities" which speaks in "Undo this button." As individuals, on the other hand, these same characters,

---

[7]Evoked also, of course, is the society of Edgar's imagined corrupt past, a society of "brothels," "plackets," "lenders' books," etc.

[8]*Op. cit.,* p. 56.

especially the younger ones, show a significant and perhaps studied diversification. According to one producer of the play, we meet with "heartless intellect" in Edmund, "impure feelings" in Goneril, "unenlightened will" in Cornwall, "powerless morality" in Albany, "unimaginative mediocrity" in Regan.[9] I should not care myself to adopt these particular descriptions, but they serve to call attention to what everyone has recognized to be a somewhat schematic variety in the play's *dramatis personae*, as if the playwright were concerned to exhibit the widest possible range of human potentiality. This general "anatomy" of mankind, if it is such, is further enhanced by the well-known antiphonal characterizations of Lear and Gloucester and even by the double quality of the old king himself as Titan and (in Cordelia's phrase) "poor *perdu.*" Thus, from the play's opening moments, when we are shown all the powers of the realm collected and glimpse both aspects of the king, we are never allowed to lose sight of the fact that the people in front of us make up a composite image of the state of man, in every sense of the word "state."

Shakespeare's concern with "relation" as the ultimate reality for human beings also expresses itself strongly in the plot of *King Lear* and in the language of social use and habit to which the plot gives rise and which it repeatedly examines. To an extent unparalleled in the other tragedies, the plot of the play depends on and manipulates relations of service and of family—the two relations, as W. H. Auden has reminded us in an arresting essay, from which all human loyalties, and therefore all societies, derive.[10] Family ties, which come about by nature, cannot be dissolved by acts of will: in this lies the enormity of Lear's action in the opening scene and of his elder daughters' actions later. Service ties, however, being contractual, *can* be dissolved by acts of will, only the act must be ratified on both sides. Kent, refusing to dissolve his relation with his master, illustrates the crucial difference between the two types of affiliation. The essentials of the service bond can be restored even though Kent is unrecognized and in disguise. The essentials of the natural bond between Cordelia and Lear, or Edgar and Gloucester, can never be restored apart from mutual recognition and a change of heart.

Ties of service and ties of nature lie closely parallel in *King Lear* and sometimes merge. It has been argued that one way of interpreting the broad outlines of the story would be to say that the lesson King Lear must learn includes the lesson of true service, which is necessarily part of the lesson of true love.[11] Once Lear has banished true love and true service in the persons of Cordelia and Kent, it is only to be expected that he will have trouble with false service and false love in a variety of forms, including Oswald, his

[9]Michael Chekhov, *To the Actor on the Technique of Acting* (1953), p. 134.

[10]"Balaam and His Ass," *The Dyer's Hand* (1962), pp. 107–108.

[11]Jonas Barish and Marshall Waingrow, " 'Service' in *King Lear*," *Shakespeare Quarterly*, IX (1958), 347–355.

daughters, and his knights, and that he should need, once again, the interces-
sion of true service in the form of the disguised Kent. Gloucester, too, we are
told, has to learn to distinguish true service. Beginning by serving badly, he is
badly served in turn by Edmund, and only after he becomes a true servant,
going to Lear's rescue at the risk of his life, is he himself once more served
truly, first by his old tenant, and subsequently by Edgar.

The term "service," with its cognates and synonyms, tolls in the language of
King Lear like that bell which reminded John Donne we are all parts of a
single continent, but it is only one of a host of socially oriented terms to do so.
Almost as prominent, and equally pertinent to the playwright's concern with
human relatedness, are the generic terms of social responsibility: "meet," "fit,"
"proper," "due," "duty," "bond," and the generic appellations of social status
and social approbation and disapprobation: "knave," "fool," "villain," "rogue,"
"rascal," "slave," and many more. Often these last are simply vehicles of the
willfulness that crackles in this frantic disintegrating realm where kings are
beggars, but several of them carry in solution anxious questions about the ties
that hold together the human polity, which from time to time the action of the
play precipitates out. When Cornwall, challenged by his own servant after
Gloucester's blinding, exclaims incredulously "My villain!" and Regan adds
scornfully "A peasant stand up thus!" the ambiguities that may attach to
servitude are brought into question with a precision that enables us to
appreciate the immediately following references to Gloucester as "treacherous
villain" and "eyeless villain," and to the now slain rebel servant as "this slave."
In the Byam Shaw production, as Muriel St. Clare Byrne describes it, a
highly imaginative *exeunt* was adopted for Regan and Cornwall at this moment, which must have brought home to any audience the implications of a
world in which language could be so perversely and solipsistically misused.
"Mortally wounded, terror and pain in voice and gesture, Cornwall turned to
his wife: 'Regan, I bleed apace. Give me your arm.' Ignoring him, almost
disdainfully, she swept past to the downstage exit. He staggered back, groping
for support; no one stirred to help him. Open-mouthed, staring-eyed, death
griping his heart, he faced the dawning horror of retribution as the jungle law
of each for himself caught up on him and he knew himself abandoned even by
his wife."[12]

Two other "titles" that the play first manipulates and then explores in
visually expressive episodes are "gentleman" and "fellow." Kent is introduced
to us and to Edmund as "this noble gentleman" in the first lines of the play, a
title which he later amplifies into "gentleman of blood and breeding." Oswald
is also introduced to us first as a gentleman—"my gentleman"—by Goneril,
and receives the title again at a significant moment when Edgar, speaking as a
peasant, has to defend his father's life against him. In II,ii, these two very
different definitions of gentility, Oswald and Kent, clash outside Gloucester's
castle. The "gentleman of blood and breeding" puts Goneril's "gentleman" to

[12]*King Lear* at Stratford-on-Avon, 1959," *Shakespeare Quarterly*, XI (1960), 198.

rout by power of nature, but by power of authority—that great graven image of authority which, as Lear says later in a reference likely to recall this episode, makes "the creature run from the cur"—he is ejected (and punished) in favor of one whose true titles, Kent tells us, make him no gentleman, but "the composition of a knave, beggar, coward, pandar, and the son and heir of a mongrel bitch."

Or again, the play asks (and this is perhaps its most searching exploration visually as well as verbally), what is it that makes a man a "fellow"? Is it being born to menial status, as for the many servingmen to whom the word is applied? Is it total loss of status, as for Edgar, Kent, and Lear, to each of whom the word is also applied? Or is it simply being man—everyone's fellow by virtue of a shared humanity? During the heath scenes, when Lear, Kent, Edgar, and the Fool become fellows in misery as well as in lack of status, this question too is given a poignant visual statement. Gloucester, coming to relieve Lear, rejects one member of the motley fellowship, his own son Poor Tom: "In, fellow, there into the hovel." But Lear, who has just learned to pray for all such naked fellows, refuses to be separated from his new companion and finally is allowed to "take the fellow" into shelter with him. For, as Edgar will ask us to remember in the next scene but one,

> the mind much sufferance doth o'erskip,
> When grief hath mates, and bearing fellowship.

Questions like these point ultimately to larger and more abstract questions, over which the action of the play, like Hamlet's melancholy, "sits on brood." One of these has to do with the moral foundations of society. To what extent have our distinctions of degree and status, our regulations by law and usage, moral significance? To what extent are they simply the expedient disguises of a war of all on all, wherein humanity preys on itself (as Albany says) "Like monsters of the deep"? This anxiety, though it permeates the play, is pressed with particular force in the utterances of the mad king to Gloucester in the fields near Dover. Here, as so often in Shakespeare, we encounter an occasion when the barriers between fiction and reality are suddenly collapsed, and the Elizabethan audience was made to realize, as we are, that it was listening to an indictment far more relevant to its own social experience than to any this king of ancient Britain could be imagined to have had. Furthermore, here onstage, as during the scene on the heath, a familiar convention was again being turned upside down and made electric with meaning. A king of the realm—like their own king, guarantee of its coinage ("they cannot touch me for coining"), commander of its troops ("There's your press money"), chief object of its *paideia* ("They flattered me like a dog"), fountain of its justice ("I pardon that man's life"), center of its reverence ("O! let me kiss that hand")—was not only presented mad, crowned with weeds, but in his madness registered for all to hear the bankruptcy of the very body politic (and body moral) of which he was representative and head:

Plate sin with gold,
And the strong lance of justice hurtless breaks;
Arm it in rags, a pigmy's straw does pierce it.
None does offend, none, I say none; I'll able 'em:
Take that of me, my friend, who have the power
To seal th' accuser's lips. Get thee glass eyes;
And, like a scurvy politician, seem
To see the things thou dost not.

No one, I suspect, who had responded to the role of the king in Shakespeare's history plays, or the king's role in contemporary drama generally, could miss the shock in these lines, coming as they did from "the thing itself." If we suppose, further, that the structural conventions of the Elizabethan theatre, with its "very solid three-dimensional symbols of order" representing "home, city, and king,"[13] sometimes induced in observers a deeper identification, a sense that they were witnessing in the career of the stage monarch a "sacred combat" or ritual struggle that enacted the corporate (and individual) quest for well-being and self-knowledge in the person of the king, we may guess that the shock of this reversal was profound indeed. But we need not suppose so much. Even the most casual playgoer, who had looked about him reflectively in Jacobean England, must have experienced a shudder of self-recognition as Lear's "sermon" proceeded. The gulf between medieval social ideals and contemporary actualities was imposing by Shakespeare's time a significant strain on sensitive minds, the kind of strain that (in a way we are painfully familiar with in our own age) can madden men, as in a sense it has maddened Lear. "The ideal was still Christian," writes Crane Brinton, who has put the matter as pithily as anyone, "still an ideal of unity, peace, security, organization, status; the reality was endemic war, divided authority even at the top, [and] a great scramble for wealth and position."[14]

Lear's vision of society in Dover fields is a vision of this gulf. To a limited extent it relates to his own sufferings, but principally to the society for which it was written, and, I would wish to add, to all societies as such. Under the masks of discipline, Lear's speeches imply, in any imaginable society on earth, there will always lurk the lust of the simpering dame, the insolence of the dog in office, the hypocrisy of the usurer who hangs the cozener, the mad injustice of sane men's choices, like Lear's in disowning Cordelia. Institutions are necessary if society is to exist at all; but as the play here eloquently points out, and as Lear from this point on himself knows, they are not enough.[15] What human relatedness truly means, stripped of its robes and furr'd gowns and all marks of status and images of authority, we are shown in the ensuing

[13]G. R. Kernodle, "The Open Stage: Elizabethan or Existentialist," *Shakespeare Survey*, XII (1959), 3.
[14]*Ideas and Men* (1950), p. 269.
[15]See particularly on this point Arthur Sewell, *Character and Society in Shakespeare* (1951), pp. 110 ff.

scenes of mutual humility and compassion between Lear and Cordelia, Edgar and Gloucester.

A second question that the play keeps bringing before our imaginations in its social dimension is the problem of human identity. It sees this, in part, as a function of status, and it is doubtless not without meaning that so many of the play's persons undergo drastic alterations in the "statistical" sphere. Cordelia is deprived of her place in state and family; Kent, of his earldom; Edgar, of his sonship and patrimony; Gloucester, of his title and lands; Lear, of the whole fabric of familiar relations by which he has always known himself to be Lear and through the loss of which he falls into madness. Yet the matter is also presented to us at a deeper level than that of status. When, at Goneril's Lear cries out, "This is not Lear. . . . Who is it that can tell me who I am?" or, on the heath, staring at Edgar's nakedness, "Is man no more than this?" we realize that his questionings cast a shadow well beyond the limits of the immediate situation as he understands it, a shadow that involves the problem of human identity in its ultimate sense, which has lost none of its agonizing ambiguity with the passage of three centuries. *Is* man, in fact, no more than "this"?—a poor bare forked animal in the wind and rain—or is man a metaphysical conception, a normative term, which suffers violence whenever any human being has been reduced to the condition of "bare fork'd animal," whenever "man's life is cheap as beast's" because the "need" has been too much "reasoned," whenever "man's work" (as with Edmund's officer) excludes drawing a cart or eating dried oats but not the murder of his own kind? As the waters rise against our foothold on the cliff of chalk, this has become our question too.

The ultimate uncertainty in *King Lear* to which all others point is, as always in tragedy, the question of man's fate. With its strong emphasis on inexorable and unimaginable consequences unwinding to make a web to which every free and willful act contributes another toil, *King Lear* may claim a place near the absolute center, "the true blank" (so Kent might call it), of tragic experience. "The tragedy of Adam," writes Northrop Frye, following Milton in tracing "the archetypal human tragedy" in the narrative of Genesis, "resolves, like all other tragedies, in the manifestation of natural law. He enters a world in which existence is itself tragic, not existence modified by an act, deliberate or unconscious."[16] This is the form of tragedy I think we all sense at the basis of *King Lear,* and the reason why its windows opening on the pilgrimage and *psychomachia* of a king who is also Rex Humanitas are so relevant to its theme. Existence is tragic in *King Lear* because existence is inseparable from relation; we are born from and to it; it envelops us in our loves and lives as parents, children, sisters, brothers, husbands, wives, servants, masters, rulers, subjects—the web is seamless and unending. When

---

[16]*Anatomy of Criticism* (1957), pp. 212, 213.

we talk of virtue, patience, courage, joy, we talk of what supports it. When we talk of tyranny, lust, and treason, we talk of what destroys it. There is no human action, Shakespeare shows us, that does not affect it and that it does not affect. Old, we begin our play with the need to impose relation—to divide our kingdom, set our rest on someone's kind nursery, and crawl toward our death. Young, we begin it with the need to respond to relation—to define it, resist it even in order to protect it, honor it, or destroy it. Man's tragic fate, as *King Lear* presents it, comes into being with his entry into relatedness, which is his entry into humanity.

In the play's own terms this fate is perhaps best summarized in the crucial concept of "patience." By the time he meets Gloucester in Dover fields, Lear has begun to learn patience; and patience, as he defines it now, is not at all what he had earlier supposed. He had supposed it was the capacity to bear up under the outrages that occur in a corrupt world to oneself; and so he had cried, when Regan and Goneril joined forces against him, "You heavens, give me that patience, patience I need!" Now, with his experience of the storm behind him, his mind still burning with the lurid vision of a world where "None does offend, none," because all are guilty, he sees further. His subject is not personal suffering in what he here says to Gloucester; his subject is the suffering that is rooted in the very fact of being human, and its best symbol is the birth cry of every infant, as if it knew already that to enter humanity is to be born in pain, to suffer pain, and to cause pain.

> Thou must be patient; we came crying hither:
> Thou know'st the first time that we smell the air
> We waul and cry.

Or as George Gascoigne had put it, giving an old sentiment a new turn in his translation of Innocent III's *De Contemptu Mundi:* "We are all borne crying that we may thereby expresse our misery; for a male childe lately borne pronounceth A [for Adam] and a woman childe pronounceth E [for Eve]: So that they say eyther E or A: as many as discend from Eva. . . . Eche of these soundes is the voyce of a sorrowful creature, expressing the greatnesse of his grefe."[17]

Lear's words to Gloucester, I take it, describe this ultimate dimension of patience, in which the play invites us to share at its close. It is the patience to accept the condition of being human in a scheme of things where the thunder will not peace at our bidding; where nothing can stay the unfolding consequences of a rash act, including the rash acts of bearing and being born;

> where the worst is not
> So long as we can say 'This is the worst';

yet where the capacity to grow and ripen—in relation and in love—is in some

---

[17]*Complete Works*, ed. J. W. Cunliffe (1910), 2, 220.

mysterious way bound up with the capacity to lose, and to suffer, and to endure:

Men must endure
Their going hence, even as their coming hither:
Ripeness is all.

From one half of this tragic knowledge, Lear subsequently wavers—as Gloucester wavers from what Edgar thought he had learned at Dover Cliff. Lear would need no crumbs of comfort after the battle if his sufferings could at last be counted on to bring rewards—if, for example, he could pass his declining years in peace and happiness with Cordelia. He wants to believe that this is possible. He has made the choice that he should have made in the beginning. He has allied himself with those who in the world's sense are fools; and he is prepared to accept the alienation from the world that this requires, as the famous passage at the opening of the last scene shows. In this passage he puts aside Goneril and Regan forever; he does not even want to see them. He accepts eagerly the prison which marks his withdrawal from the world's values, for he has his own new values to sustain:

We two alone will sing like birds i' th' cage:
When thou dost ask me blessing, I'll kneel down
And ask of thee forgiveness: so we'll live,
And pray, and sing, and tell old tales, and laugh
At gilded butterflies, and hear poor rogues
Talk of court news; and we'll talk with them too,
Who loses and who wins, who's in, who's out:
And take upon 's the mystery of things
As if we were God's spies.

They will be in the world, but not of it. On this kind of sacrifice, he adds, "the Gods themselves throw incense."

But to speak so is to speak from a knowledge that no human experience teaches. If it could end like this, if there were guaranteed rewards like this for making our difficult choices, the play would be a melodrama, and our world very different from what it is. So far as human wisdom goes, the choice of relatedness must be recognized as its own reward, leading sometimes to alleviation of suffering, as in the case of Gloucester's joy in Edgar, but equally often to more suffering, as in the case of Lear. For Lear, like many another, has to make the difficult choice only to lose the fruits of it. Not in his own death—as Kent says, "he hates him That would upon the rack of this tough world Stretch him out longer"—but in Cordelia's. Cordelia, our highest choice, is what we always want the gods to guarantee. But to this the gods will not consent. Hence when Albany exclaims, at Edmund's confession that he has ordered Cordelia's death, "The gods defend her," the gods' answer to that is, as Bradley pointed out long ago, "Enter Lear, with Cordelia in his arms."[18]

---

[18]*Op. cit.*, p. 326.

In his last speech, the full implications of the human condition evidently come home to Lear. He has made his choice, and there will be no reward. Again and again, in his repetitions, he seems to be trying to drive this final tragic fact into his human consciousness, where it never wants to stick:

No, no, no life!
Why should a dog, a horse, a rat have life
And thou no breath at all? Thou'lt come no more,
Never, never, never, never, never!

He tries to hold this painful vision unflinchingly before his consciousness, but the strain, considering everything else he has been through, is too great: consciousness itself starts to give way: "Pray you, undo this button: thank you, Sir." And with it the vision gives way too: he cannot sustain it; he dies, reviving in his heart the hope that Cordelia lives: "Look on her, look, her lips, Look there, look there!"

We are offered two ways of being sentimental about this conclusion, both of which we must make an effort to eschew. One is to follow those who argue that, because these last lines probably mean that Lear dies in the joy of thinking Cordelia lives, some sort of mitigation or transfiguration has been reached which turns defeat into total victory. "Only to earthbound intelligence," says Professor O. J. Campbell, "is Lear pathetically deceived in thinking Cordelia alive. Those familiar with the Morality plays will realize that Lear has found in her unselfish love the one companion who is willing to go with him through Death up to the throne of the Everlasting Judge."[19] I think most of us will agree that this is too simple. Though there is much of the Morality play in *Lear*, it is not used toward a morality theme, but, as I have tried to suggest in this essay, toward building a deeply metaphysical metaphor, or myth, about the human condition, the state of man, in which the last of many mysteries is the enigmatic system of relatedness in which he is enclosed.

The other sentimentality leads us to indulge the currently fashionable existentialist *nausée*, and to derive from the fact that Lear's joy is mistaken, or, alternatively, from the fact that in the Lear world "even those who have fully repented, done penance, and risen to the tender regard of sainthood can be hunted down, driven insane, and killed by the most agonizing extremes of passion,"[20] the conclusion that "we inhabit an imbecile universe."[21] Perhaps we do—but Shakespeare's *King Lear* provides no evidence of it that till now we lacked. That love, compassion, hope, and truth are "subjects all," not only to "envious and calumniating time," but to purest casualty and mischance has

---

[19]"The Salvation of Lear," *ELH*, XV (1948), 107.
[20]J. Stampfer, "The Catharsis of *King Lear*," *Shakespeare Survey*, XIII (1960), 4.
[21]*Ibid.*, p. 10.

been the lament of poets since Homer. Shakespeare can hardly have imagined that in *King Lear's* last scene he was telling his audiences something they had never known, or was casting his solemn vote on one side or other of the vexing philosophical and theological questions involved in the suffering of the innocent and good. The scene has, besides, his characteristic ambiguity and balance. No world beyond this one in which "all manner of things will be well" is asserted; but neither is it denied: Kent happens to take it for granted and will follow his master beyond that horizon as he has beyond every other: "My master calls me, I must not say no." Edgar has come to soberer assessments of reality than he was given to making in the forepart of the play, but his instinctive kindness (we may assume) is unabated and has survived all trials. Lear's joy in thinking that his daughter lives (if this is what his words imply) is illusory, but it is one we need not begrudge him on his deathbed, as we do not begrudge it to a dying man in hospital whose family has just been wiped out. Nor need we draw elaborate inferences from its illusoriness about the imbecility of our world; in a similar instance among our acquaintances, we would regard the illusion as a godsend, or even, if we were believers, as God-sent.

In short, to say, with an increasing number of recent critics, that "the remorseless process of *King Lear*" forces us to "face the fact of its ending without any support from systems of moral . . . belief at all"[22] is to indulge the mid-twentieth-century *frisson du néant* at its most sentimental. We face the ending of this play, as we face our world, with whatever support we customarily derive from systems of belief or unbelief. If the sound of David crying "Absalom, my son," the image of Mary bending over another broken child, the motionless form of a missionary doctor whose martyrdom is recent, not to mention all that earth has known of disease, famine, earthquake, war, and prison since men first came crying hither—if our moral and religious systems can survive this, and the record suggests that for many good men they do and can, then clearly they will have no trouble in surviving the figure of Lear as he bends in his agony, or in his joy, above Cordelia. Tragedy never tells us what to think; it shows us what we are and may be. And what we are and may be was never, I submit, more memorably fixed upon a stage than in this kneeling old man whose heartbreak is precisely the measure of what, in our world of relatedness, it is possible to lose and possible to win. The victory and the defeat are simultaneous and inseparable.

If there is any "remorseless process" in *King Lear*, it is one that begs us to seek the meaning of our human fate not in what becomes of us, but in what we become. Death, as we saw, is miscellaneous and commonplace; it is life whose quality may be made noble and distinctive. Suffering we all recoil from; but we know it is a greater thing to suffer than to lack the feelings and virtues that make it possible to suffer. Cordelia, we may choose to say,

[22]Nicholas Brooke, *Shakespeare: King Lear* (1963), p. 60.

accomplished nothing, yet we know it is better to have been Cordelia than to have been her sisters. When we come crying hither, we bring with us the badge of all our misery; but it is also the badge of the vulnerabilities that give us access to whatever grandeur we achieve.

The Avoidance of Love: A Reading of *King Lear*

Stanley Cavell

In a fine paper published a few years ago, Professor Paul Alpers notes the tendency of modern critics to treat metaphors or symbols rather than the characters and actions of Shakespeare's plays as primary data in understanding them, and undertakes to disconfirm a leading interpretation of the symbolic sort which exactly depends upon a neglect, even a denial, of the humanness of the play's characters.[1] If I begin by finding fault with his reading, I put him first to acknowledge my indebtedness to his work. His animus is polemical and in the end this animus betrays him. For he fails to account for the truth to which that leading interpretation is responding, and in his concern to insist that the characters of the play are human beings confronting one another, he fails to characterize them as specific persons. He begins by assembling quotations from several commentators which together compose the view he wishes to correct—the view of the "sight pattern":

> In *King Lear* an unusual amount of imagery drawn from vision and the eyes prompts us to apprehend a symbolism of sight and blindness having its culmination in Gloucester's tragedy. . . . The blinding of Gloucester might well be gratuitous melodrama but for its being imbedded in a field of meanings centered in the concept of *seeing*. This sight pattern relentlessly brings into the play the problem of seeing and what is always implied is that the problem is one of insight. . . . It is commonly recognized that just as Lear finds "reason in madness" so Gloucester learns to "see" in his blindness. . . . The whole play is built on this double paradox.[2]

From *Disowning Knowledge: In Six Plays of Shakespeare.* (New York and Cambridge: Cambridge University Press, 1987), 44–72. Reprinted by permission. The original essay has been reduced for inclusion here.

[1]"*King Lear* and the Theory of the Sight Pattern," in R. Brower and R. Poirier, eds., *In Defense of Reading* (New York: Dutton, 1963), pp. 133–52.

[2]Alpers gives the references for the elements of his quotation as follows: J. I. M. Stewart, *Character and Motive in Shakespeare* (New York: Longman, Green, 1949), pp. 20–1; R. B. Heilman, *This Great Stage* (Baton Rouge: Louisiana State University Press, 1948), p. 25; L. C. Knights, *Some Shakespearean Themes* (London, Chatto and Windus, 1959), p. 107; *King Lear*, ed. K. Muir (Cambridge: Harvard University Press, 1952, Arden edition), p. lx.

But when Alpers looks to the text for evidence for this theory he discovers that there is none. Acts of vision and references to eyes are notably present, but their function is not to symbolize moral insight; rather, they insist upon the ordinary, literal uses of eyes: to express feeling, to weep, and to recognize others. Unquestionably there is truth in this. But the evidence for Alpers's view is not perfectly clear and his concepts are not accurately explored in terms of the events of the play. The acts of vision named in the lines he cites are those of giving *looks* and of *staring*, and the function of these acts is exactly *not* to express feeling, or else to express cruel feeling. Why? Because the power of the eyes to see is being used in isolation from their capacity to weep, which seems the most literal use of them to express feeling.

Alpers's dominant insistence upon the third ordinary use of the eyes, their role in recognizing others, counters common readings of the two moments of recognition central to the "sight pattern": Gloucester's recognition of Edgar's innocence and Lear's recognition of Cordelia. "The crucial issue is not insight, but recognition" (Alperts, p. 149): Gloucester is not enabled to "see" because he is blinded, the truth is heaped upon him from Regan's luxuriant cruelty; Cordelia need not be viewed symbolically, the infinite poignance of her reconciliation with Lear is sufficiently accounted for by his literal recognition of her.—But then it becomes incomprehensible why or how these children have *not* been recognized by these parents; they had not become literally invisible. They are in each case banished, disowned, sent out of sight. And the question remains: What makes it possible for them to be *received* again?

In each case, there is a condition necessary in order that the recognition take place: Gloucester and Lear must each first recognize himself, and allow himself to be recognized, revealed to another. In Gloucester, the recognition comes at once, on hearing Regan's news:

> O my follies! Then Edgar was abused.
> Kind Gods, forgive me that, and prosper him!
> (3.7.90–1)

In each of these two lines he puts his recognition of himself first. Lear's self-revelation comes harder, but when it comes it has the same form:

> Do not laugh at me;
> For, as I am a man, I think this lady
> To be my child Cordelia.
> (4.7.68–70)

He refers to himself three times, then "my child" recognizes her simultaneously with revealing himself (as her father). Self-recognition is, phenomenologically, a form of insight; and it is because of its necessity in recognizing others that critics have felt its presence here.

Lear does not attain his insight until the end of the fourth act, and when he does it is climactic. This suggests that Lear's dominating motivation to this point, from the time things go wrong in the opening scene, is to *avoid being recognized.* The isolation and avoidance of eyes is what the obsessive sight imagery of the play underlines. This is the clue I want to follow first in reading out the play.

If the blinding is unnecessary for Gloucester's true seeing of Edgar, why is Gloucester blinded? Alpers's suggestion, in line with his emphasis on the literal presence of eyes, is that because the eyes are physically the most precious and most vulnerable of human organs, the physical assault on them best dramatizes the human capacity for cruelty. But if the symbolic interpretation seems hysterical, this explanation seems overcasual, and in any case does not follow the words. Critics who have looked for a *meaning* in the blinding have been looking for the right thing. But they have been looking for an aesthetic meaning or justification; looking too high, as it were. It is aesthetically justified (it is "not an irrelevant horror" [Muir, p. lx]) just because it is morally, spiritually justified, in a way which directly relates the eyes to their power to see.

Gloucester:	. . . but I shall see
	The winged vengeance overtake such
	children.
Cornwall:	See't shalt thou never.

(3.7.64–6)

And then Cornwall puts out one of Gloucester's eyes. A servant interposes, wounding Cornwall; then Regan stabs the servant from behind, and his dying words, meant to console or establish connection with Gloucester, ironically recall Cornwall to his interrupted work:

First Servant:	O! I am slain. My Lord, you have one eye left
	To see some mischief on him. Oh! *Dies.*
Cornwall:	Lest it see more, prevent it. Out, vile jelly!

(3.7.80–2)

Of course the idea of punishment by plucking out eyes has been implanted earlier, by Lear and by Goneril and most recently by Gloucester himself, and their suggestions implicate all of them spiritually in Cornwall's deed. But Cornwall himself twice gives the immediate cause of his deed, once for each eye: to prevent Gloucester from seeing, and in particular to prevent him from seeing *him.* That this scene embodies the most open expression of cruelty is true enough; and true that it suggests the limitlessness of cruelty, once it is given its way—that it will find its way to the most precious objects. It is also true that the scene is symbolic, but what it symbolizes is a function of what it means. The physical cruelty symbolizes (or instances) the psychic cruelty which pervades the play; but what this particular act of cruelty means is that cruelty cannot bear to be seen. It literalizes evil's ancient love of darkness.

This relates the blinding to Cornwall's needs; but it is also related to necessities of Gloucester's character. It has an aptness which takes on symbolic value, the horrible aptness of retribution. (It is not merely literary critics who look for meaning in suffering, attempting to rationalize it. Civilizations have always done it, in their myths and laws; we do it in our dreams and fears of vengeance. They learned to do it from gods.) For Gloucester has a fault, not particularly egregious, in fact common as dirt, but in a tragic accumulation in which society disgorges itself upon itself, it shows clearly enough; and I cannot understand his immediate and complete acquiescence in the fate which has befallen him (his acknowledgment of his folly, his acceptance of Edgar's innocence, and his wish for forgiveness all take just twenty syllables) without supposing that it strikes him as a retribution, forcing him to an insight about his life as a whole. Not, however, necessarily a true insight. He has revealed his fault in the opening speeches of the play, in which he tells Kent of his *shame*. (That shame is the subject of those speeches is emphasized by Coleridge; but he concentrates, appropriately enough, on *Edmund's* shame.) He says that now he is "braz'd to it," that is, used to admitting that he has fathered a bastard, and also perhaps carrying the original sense of soldered fast to it. He recognizes the moral claim upon himself, as he says twice, to "acknowledge" his bastard; but all this means to him is that he acknowledge that he has a bastard for a son. He does not acknowledge *him*, as a son or a person, with *his* feelings of illegitimacy and being cast out. *That* is something Gloucester ought to be ashamed of; his shame is itself more shameful than his one piece of licentiousness. This is one of the inconveniences of shame, that it is generally inaccurate, attaches to the wrong thing. . . .

That Gloucester still feels shame about his son is shown not just by his descriptions of himself, but also by the fact that Edmund "hath been out nine years, and away he shall again" (1.1.32), and by the fact that Gloucester has to joke about him: Joking is a familiar specific for brazening out shame, calling enlarged attention to the thing you do not want naturally noticed. (Hence the comedian sports disfigurement.) But if the failure to recognize others is a failure to let others recognize you, a fear of what is revealed to them, an avoidance of their eyes, then it is exactly shame which is the cause of his withholding of recognition. (It is not simply his legal treatment that Edmund is railing against.) For shame is the specific discomfort produced by the sense of being looked at; the avoidance of the sight of others is the reflex it produces. Guilt is different; there the reflex is to avoid discovery. As long as no one *knows* what you have done, you are safe; or your conscience will press you to confess it and accept punishment. Under shame, what must be covered up is not your deed, but yourself. It is a more primitive emotion than guilt, as inescapable as the possession of a body, the first object of shame.—Gloucester suffers the same punishment he inflicts: In his respectability, he avoided eyes; when respectability falls away and the disreputable come into power, his eyes are avoided. In the fear of Gloucester's poor eyes there is the promise that cruelty can be overcome, and instruction about how it can be overcome. That is the content which justifies the scene of his blinding, aesthetically, psychologically, morally.

This raises again the question of the relation between the Gloucester subplot and the Lear plot. The traditional views seem on the whole to take one of two lines: Gloucester's fate parallels Lear's in order that it become more universal (because Gloucester is an ordinary man, not a distant king, or because in happening to more than one it may happen to any); or more concrete (since Gloucester suffers physically what Lear suffers psychically). Such suggestions are not wrong, but they leave out of account the specific climactic moment at which the subplot surfaces and Lear and Gloucester face one another.

> *Edgar:*   I would not take this from report; it is,
>   And my heart breaks at it.
>   (4.6.142–3)

I have felt that, but more particularly I have felt an obscurer terror at this moment than at any other in the play. The considerations so far introduced begin, I think, to explain the source of that feeling.

Two questions immediately arise about that confrontation: (1) This is the scene in which Lear's madness is first broken through; in the next scene he is reassembling his sanity. Both the breaking through and the reassembling are manifested by his *recognizing* someone, and my first question is: Why is it Gloucester whom Lear is first able to recognize from his madness, and in recognizing whom his sanity begins to return? (2) *What* does Lear see when he recognizes Gloucester? What is he confronted by?

1. Given our notion that recognizing a person depends upon allowing oneself to be recognized by him, the question becomes: Why is it Gloucester whose recognition Lear is first able to bear? The obvious answer is: Because Gloucester is blind. Therefore one can be, can only be, *recognized by him without being seen*, without having to bear eyes upon oneself.

Leading up to Lear's acknowledgment ("I know thee well enough") there is that insane flight of exchanges about Gloucester's eyes; it is the only active cruelty given to Lear by Shakespeare, apart from his behavior in the abdication scene. But here it seems uncaused, deliberate cruelty inflicted for its own sake upon Gloucester's eyes. . . .

Lear is picking at Gloucester's eyes, as if to make sure they are really gone. When he is sure, he recognizes him:

> If thou wilt weep my fortunes, take my eyes;
> I know thee well enough; thy name is Gloucester.
>   (4.6.178–9)

(Here "take my eyes" can be read as a crazy consolation: Your eyes wouldn't have done you any good anyway in this case; you would need to see what I have seen to weep my fortunes; I would give up my eyes not to have seen it.)

This picking spiritually relates Lear to Cornwall's and Regan's act in first blinding Gloucester, for Lear does what he does for the same reason they do—in order not to be seen by this man, whom he has brought harm. (Lear exits from this scene running. From what? From "A Gentleman, with Attendants." His first words to them are: "No rescue? What! A prisoner?" But those questions had interrupted the Gentleman's opening words to him, "Your most dear daughter—". Lear runs not because in his madness he cannot distinguish friends from enemies but because he knows that recognition of himself is imminent. Even madness is no rescue.)

2. This leads to the second question about the scene: What is Lear confronted by in acknowledging Gloucester? It is easy to say: Lear is confronted here with the direct consequences of his conduct, of his covering up in rage and madness, of his having given up authority and kingdom for the wrong motives, to the wrong people; and he is for the first time confronting himself. What is difficult is to show that this is not merely or vaguely symbolic, and that it is not merely an access of knowledge which Lear undergoes. Gloucester has by now become not just a figure "parallel" to Lear, but Lear's double; he does not merely represent Lear, but is psychically identical with him. So that what comes to the surface in this meeting is not a related story, but Lear's submerged mind. This, it seems to me, is what gives the scene its particular terror, and gives to the characters what neither could have alone. In this fusion of plots and identities, we have the great image, the double or mirror image, of everyman who has gone to every length to avoid himself, caught at the moment of coming upon himself face to face. (Against this, "take my eyes" strikes psychotic power.) . . .

The question, as generally asked, is: Why does Edgar wait, on seeing his father blind, and hearing that his father knows his mistake, before revealing himself to him? The answers which suggest themselves to that question are sophisticated, not the thing itself. For example: Edgar wants to clear himself in the eyes of the world before revealing himself. (But he could still let his *father* know. Anyway, he does tell his father before he goes to challenge Edmund.) Edgar "wants to impose a penance on his father, and to guarantee the genuineness and permanence of the repentance" (Muir, 1). (This seems to me psychologically fantastic; it suggests that the first thing which occurs to Edgar on seeing his father blinded is to exact some further punishment. Or else it makes Edgar into a monster of righteousness; whereas he is merely self-righteous.) Edgar wants to cure his father of his desire to commit suicide. (But *revealing himself* would seem the surest and most immediate way to do that.) And so on. My dissatisfaction with these answers is not that they are psychological explanations, but that they are explanations of the wrong thing, produced by the wrong question: Why does Edgar *delay*? "Delay" implies he is going to later. But we do not *know* (at this stage) that he will; we do not so much as know that he intends to. In terms of our reading of the play so far, we are alerted to the fact that what Edgar does is most directly described as *avoiding recognition. That* is what we want an explanation for. . . .

To hold to the fact that Edgar is avoiding recognition makes better sense to me of that grotesque guiding of Gloucester up no hill to no cliff to no suicide than any other account I know. The special quality of this scene, with its purest outbreak of grotesquerie, has been recognized at least since Wilson Knight's essay of 1930.[3] But to regard it as *symbolic* of the play's emphasis on the grotesque misses what makes it so grotesque, and fails to account for the fact that Edgar and Gloucester find themselves in this condition. It is grotesque because it is so *literal* a consequence of avoiding the facts. It is not the emblem of the Lear universe, but an instance of what has led its minds to their present state: There are no lengths to which we may not go in order to avoid being revealed, even to those we love and are loved by. Or rather, especially to those we love and are loved by; to other people it is *easy* not to be known. That grotesque walk is not full of promise for our lives. It is not, for example, a picture of mankind making its way up Purgatory[4]; for Gloucester's character is not purified by it, but extirpated. It shows what people will *have* to say and try to mean to one another when they are incapable of acknowledging to one another what they have to acknowledge. To fill this scene with nourishing, profound meaning is to see it from Edgar's point of view; that is, to avoid what is there. . . .

If one wishes a psychological explanation for Edgar's behavior, the question to be answered is: Why does Edgar avoid his father's recognition? Two answers suggest themselves. (1) He is himself ashamed and guilty. He was as gullible as his father was to Edmund's "invention." He failed to confront his father, to trust his love, exactly as his father had failed him. He is as responsible for his father's blinding as his father is. He wants to make it up to his father before asking for his recognition—to make it up instead of repenting, acknowledging; he wants to *do* something instead of stopping and seeing. So he goes on doing the very thing which needs making up for. (2) He cannot bear the fact that his father is incapable, impotent, maimed. He wants his father still to be a father, powerful, so that *he* can remain a child. For otherwise they are simply two human beings in need of one another, and it is not usual for parents and children to manage that transformation, becoming for one another nothing more, but nothing less, than unaccommodated men. That is what Lear took Edgar to be, but that was a mad, ironic compliment; to become natural again, human kind needs to do more than remove its clothes; for we can also cover up our embarrassment by nakedness. We have our inventions, our accommodations. . . .

We now have elements with which to begin an analysis of the most controversial of the *Lear* problems, the nature of Lear's motivation in his opening (abdication) scene. The usual interpretations follow one of three main

---

[3]"*King Lear* and the Comedy of the Grotesque," one of the studies composing *The Wheel of Fire*, originally published by Oxford University Press, 1930; published in the fifth revised edition by Meridian Books, New York, 1957.

[4]Suggested by R. W. Chambers, *King Lear*, 1940; cited by Muir, p. 1.

lines: Lear is senile; Lear is puerile; Lear is not to be understood in natural terms, for the whole scene has a fairy-tale or ritualistic character which simply must be accepted as the premise from which the tragedy is derived. Arguments ensue, in each case, about whether Shakespeare is justified in what he is asking his audience to accept. My hypothesis will be that Lear's behavior in this scene is explained by—the tragedy begins because of—the same motivation which manipulates the tragedy throughout its course, from the scene which precedes the abdication, through the storm, blinding, evaded reconciliations, to the final moments: by the attempt to avoid recognition, the shame of exposure, the threat of self-revelation.

Shame, first of all, is the right kind of candidate to serve as motive, because it is the emotion whose effect is most precipitate and out of proportion to its cause, which is just the rhythm of the *King Lear* plot as a whole. And with this hypothesis we need not assume that Lear is either incomprehensible or stupid or congenitally arbitrary and inflexible and extreme in his conduct. Shame itself is exactly arbitrary, inflexible, and extreme in its effect. It is familiar to find that what mortifies one person seems wholly unimportant to another: Think of being ashamed of one's origins, one's accent, one's ignorance, one's skin, one's clothes, one's legs or teeth. . . . It is the most isolating of feelings, the most comprehensible perhaps in idea, but the most incomprehensible or incommunicable in fact. Shame, I've said, is the most primitive, the most private, of emotions; but it is also the most primitive of *social* responses. With the discovery of the individual, whether in Paradise or in the Renaissance, there is the simultaneous discovery of the isolation of the individual; his presence to himself, but simultaneously to *others*. Moreover, shame is felt not only toward one's own actions and one's own being, but toward the actions and the being of those with whom one is identified—fathers, daughters, wives. . . , the beings whose self-revelations reveal oneself. Families, any objects of one's love and commitment, ought to be the places where shame is overcome (hence happy families are all alike); but they are also the place of its deepest manufacture, and one is then hostage to that power, or fugitive. . . .

That Lear is ashamed, or afraid of being shamed by a revelation, seems to be the Fool's understanding of his behavior. It is agreed that the Fool keeps the truth present to Lear's mind, but it should be stressed that the characteristic mode of the Fool's presentation is *ridicule*—the circumstance most specifically feared by shame (as accusation and discovery are most feared by guilt). Part of the exquisite pain of this Fool's comedy is that in riddling Lear with the truth of his condition he increases the very cause of that condition, as though shame should finally grow ashamed of itself, and stop. The other part of this pain is that it is the therapy prescribed by love itself. We know that since Cordelia's absence "the fool hath much pin'd away" (1.4.78), and it is generally assumed that this is due to his love for Cordelia. That need not be denied, but it should be obvious that it is directly due to his love for Lear; to his having to see the condition in Lear which his love is impotent to prevent, the condition moreover which his love has helped to cause, the precise condition therefore which his love is unable to comfort, since its touch wounds. This is why the Fool dies or disappears; from the terrible relevance, and the horrible irrelevance, of his own passion. This is the point of his connection with Cordelia, as will emerge.

I call Lear's shame a hypothesis, and what I have to say here will perhaps be hard to make convincing. But primarily it depends upon not imposing the traditional interpretations upon the opening events. Lear is puerile? Lear senile? But the man who speaks Lear's words is in possession, if not fully in command, of a powerful, ranging mind; and its eclipse into madness only confirms its intelligence, not just because what he says in his madness is the work of a marked intelligence, but because the nature of his madness, his melancholy and antic disposition, its incessant invention, is the sign, in fact and in Renaissance thought, of genius; an option of escape open only to minds of the highest reach. How then can we understand such a mind seriously to believe that what Goneril and Reagan are offering in that opening scene is love, proof of his value to them; and to believe that Cordelia is withholding love? We cannot so understand it, and so all the critics are right to regard Lear in this scene as psychologically incomprehensible, or as requiring from them some special psychological makeup—if, that is, we assume that Lear believes in Goneril and Regan and not in Cordelia. But we needn't assume that he believes anything of the kind.

We imagine that Lear *must* be wildly abused (blind, puerile, and the rest) because the thing works out so badly. But it doesn't *begin* badly, and it is far from incomprehensible conduct. It is, in fact, quite ordinary. A parent is bribing love out of his children; two of them accept the bribe, and despise him for it; the third shrinks from the attempt, as though from violation. Only this is a king, this bribe is the last he will be able to offer; everything in his life, and in the life of his state, depends upon its success. We need not assume that he does not know his two older daughters, and that they are giving him false coin in return for his real bribes, though perhaps like most parents he is willing not to notice it. But more than this: There is reason to assume that the open possibility—or the open fact—that they are *not* offering true love is exactly what he wants. Trouble breaks out only with Cordelia's "Nothing," and her broken resolution to be silent.—What does he want, and what is the meaning of the trouble which then breaks out?

Go back to the confrontation scene with Gloucester:

If thou wilt weep my fortunes, take my eyes.

The obvious rhetoric of those words is that of an appeal, or a bargain. But it is also warning, and a command: If you weep for me, the same thing will happen to me that happened to you; do not let me see what you are weeping for. Given the whole scene, with its concentrated efforts at warding off Gloucester, that line says explicitly what it is Lear is warding off: Gloucester's sympathy, his love. And earlier:

Gloucester: O! Let me kiss that hand.
Lear: Let me wipe it first, it smells of mortality.
                                                         (4.6.134–5)

Mortality, the hand without rings of power on it, cannot be lovable. He feels unworthy of love when the reality of lost power comes over him. That is what his plan was to have avoided by exchanging his fortune for his love at one swap. He cannot bear love when he has no reason to be loved, perhaps because of the helplessness, the passiveness which that implies, which some take for impotence. And he wards it off for the reason for which people do ward off being loved, because it presents itself to them as a demand:

Lear: No. Do thy worst, blind Cupid; I'll not love.
                                                         (4.6.139)

Gloucester's presence strikes Lear as the demand for love; he knows he is being offered love; he tries to deny the offer by imagining that he has been solicited (this is the relevance of "blind Cupid" as the sign of a brothel); and he does not want to pay for it, for he may get it, and may not, and either is intolerable. Besides, he has recently done just that, paid his all for love. The long fantasy of his which precedes this line ("Let copulation thrive. . . . There is the sulphurous pit—burning, scalding, stench, consumption . . .") contains his most sustained expression of disgust with sexuality (4.6.116 ff.)—as though furiously telling himself that what was wrong with his plan was not the debasement of love his bargain entailed, but the fact that love itself is inherently debased and so unworthy from the beginning of the bargain he had made for it. That is a maddening thought; but still more comforting than the truth. For some spirits, to be loved knowing you cannot return that love is the most radical of psychic tortures.

This is the way I understand that opening scene with the three daughters. Lear knows it is a bribe he offers, and—part of him anyway—wants exactly what a bribe can buy: (1) false love and (2) a public expression of love. That is, he wants something he does not have to return *in kind*, something which a division of his property fully pays for. And he wants to *look* like a loved man— for the sake of the subjects, as it were. He is perfectly happy with his little plan, until Cordelia speaks. Happy not because he is blind, but because he is getting what he wants, his plan is working. Cordelia is alarming precisely because he *knows* she is offering the real thing, offering something a more opulent third of his kingdom cannot, must not, repay; putting a claim upon him he cannot face. She threatens to expose both his plan for returning false love with no love, and expose the necessity for that plan—his terror of being loved, of needing love.

Reacting to oversentimental or over-Christian interpretations of her character, interpreters have made efforts to implicate her in the tragedy's source,
convincing her of a willfulness and hardness kin to that later shown by her
sisters. But her complicity is both less and more than such an interpretation
envisages. That interpretation depends, first of all, upon taking her later
speeches in the scene (after the appearance of France and Burgundy) as
simply uncovering what was in her mind and heart from the beginning. But
why? Her first utterance is the aside:

What shall Cordelia speak? Love, and be silent.

This, presumably, has been understood as indicating her decision to refuse
her father's demand. But it needn't be. She asks herself what she can say;
there is no necessity for taking the question to be rhetorical. She wants to
obey her father's wishes (anyway, there is no reason to think otherwise at this
stage, or at any other); but how? She sees from Goneril's speech and Lear's
acceptance of it what it is he wants, and she would provide it if she could. But
to pretend publicly to love, where you do not love, is easy; to pretend to love,
where you really do love, is not obviously possible. She hits on the first
solution to her dilemma: Love, and be silent. That is, love *by being* silent.
That will do what he seems to want, it will avoid the expression of love, keep
it secret. She is his joy; she knows it and he knows it. Surely that is enough?
Then Regan speaks, and following that Cordelia's second utterance, again
aside:

Then poor Cordelia!
And yet not so; since I am sure my love's
More ponderous than my tongue.
(1.1.76–8)

Presumably, in line with the idea of a defiant Cordelia, this is to be inter-
preted as a reaffirmation of her decision not to speak. But again, it needn't be.
After Lear's acceptance of Regan's characteristic outstripping (she has no ideas
of her own; her special vileness is always to increase the measure of pain
others are prepared to inflict; her mind is itself a lynch mob) Cordelia may
realize that she will *have* to say something. "More ponderous than my tongue"
suggests that she is going to move it, not that it is immovable—which would
make it more ponderous than her love. And this produces her second groping
for an exit from the dilemma: to speak, but making her love seem less than it
is, out of love. Her tongue will move, and obediently, but against her
condition—then poor Cordelia, making light of her love. And yet *she* knows
the truth. Surely that is enough?

But when the moment comes, she is speechless: "Nothing, my lord." I do
not deny that this can be read defiantly, as can the following "You have begot
me, bred me, lov'd me" speech. She is outraged, violated, confused, so
young; Lear is torturing her, claiming her devotion, which she wants to give,

but forcing her to help him betray (or not to betray) it, to falsify it publicly. . . .

The truth, is, she *could* not flatter; not because she was too proud or too principled, though these might have been the reasons, for a different character; but because nothing she could have done would have *been* flattery—at best it would have been *dissembled flattery.* There is no convention for doing what Cordelia was asked to do. It is not that Goneril and Regan have taken the words out of her mouth, but that here she cannot say them, because for her they are true ("Dearer than eye-sight, space and liberty"). She is not disgusted by her sisters' flattery (it's nothing new); but heartbroken at hearing the words she wishes she were in a position to say. So she is sent, and taken, away. Or half of her leaves; the other half remains, in Lear's mind, in Kent's service, and in the Fool's love.

(I spoke just now of "one's" gratitude and relief toward France. I was remembering my feeling at a production given by students at Berkeley during 1946 in which France—a small part, singled out by Granville-Baker as particularly requiring an actor of authority and distinction—was given his full sensitivity and manliness, a combination notably otherwise absent from the play, as mature womanliness is. The validity of such feelings as touchstones of the accuracy of a reading of the play, and which feelings one is to trust and which not, ought to be discussed problems of criticism.) . . .

The final scene opens with Lear and Cordelia repeating or completing their actions in their opening scene; again Lear abdicates, and again Cordelia loves and is silent. Its readers have for centuries wanted to find consolation in this end: Heavy opinion sanctioned Tate's Hollywood ending throughout the eighteenth century, which resurrects Cordelia; and in our time, scorning such vulgarity, the same impulse fastidiously digs itself deeper and produces redemption for Lear in Cordelia's figuring of transcendent love. But Dr. Johnson is surely right, more honest and more responsive: Cordelia's death is so shocking that we would avoid it if we could—if we have responded to it. And so the question, since her death is restored to us, is forced upon us: Why does she die? And this is not answered by asking, What does her death mean? (cp. Christ died to save sinners); but by answering, What killed her? (cp. Christ was killed by us, because his news was unendurable).

Lear's opening speech of this final scene is not the correction but the repetition of his strategy in the first scene, or a new tactic designed to win the old game; and it is equally disastrous.

Cordelia: Shall we not see these daughters and these sisters?
Lear: No, no, no, no!

(5.3.7–8)

He cannot finally face the thing he has done; and this means what it always does, that he cannot bear being seen. He is anxious to go off to prison, with

Cordelia; his love now is in the open—that much circumstance has done for him; but it remains imperative that it be confined, out of sight. . . .

It can be said that what Lear is ashamed of is not his need for love and his inability to return it, but of the *nature* of his love for Cordelia. It is too far from plain love of father for daughter. Even if we resist seeing in it the love of lovers, it is at least incompatible with the idea of her having any (other) lover. . . .

I do not wish to suggest that "avoidance of love" and "avoidance of a particular kind of love" are alternative hypotheses about this play. On the contrary, they seem to me to interpret one another. Avoidance of love is always, or always begins as, an avoidance of a particular kind of love: Human beings do not just naturally not love, they learn not to. And our lives begin by having to accept under the name of love whatever closeness is offered, and by then having to forgo its object. And the avoidance of a particular love, or the acceptance of it, will spread to every other; every love, in acceptance or rejection, is mirrored in every other. It is part of the miracle of the vision in *King Lear* to bring this before us, so that we do no care whether the *kind* of love felt between these two is forbidden according to humanity's lights. We care whether love is or is not altogether forbidden to us, whether we may not altogether be incapable of it, of admitting it into our world. We wonder whether we may always go mad between the equal efforts and terrors at once of rejecting and of accepting love.

Lear's Theatre Poetry

Marvin Rosenberg

Of course *Lear* can be staged. It has been, and will continue to be.
Criticism's only sane posture, in fact, is to insist that it must be staged, if the
full dimensions of Shakespeare's art are to be perceived sensually as well as
cognitively, as the playwright intended.

The staging is not easy. The scenic demands are considerable; the demands
on the actor ultimate. Not a single character can be conveniently synthesized
into a type: each is designed as a polyphony, to use Mikhoels' word, each is
made of mixed and even contradictory qualities. Lear most of all; we have seen
that the fissioning of his opposing attributes almost bursts the limits of
character possibility. He is all the four streams—and all the tributaries—of
characterization we followed: titan king, tough king, mad king, everyman
king. These four were only singled out for the convenience of discussion,
because they seemed to dominate actors' conceptions: something of all of
them—and more—informed such distinguished performances as by Scofield,
Devrient, Salvini, Carnovsky, Gielgud. Similarly, the conflicting impulses,
ideas, and even physical acts of Lear must, like the play itself, back-forth in
tidal flow; to deny the dialectic to the character on the stage—or in criticism—is to congeal the whole mighty ocean of the play. This form, as much
as what the play says and does, contributes to its power continuously to
arouse.

The temptation to congeal, simplify, fit all into an easily graspable pattern,
is great; particularly with the lesser characters. But they too are constella-
tions—Redgrave's word; we have seen how multiple, countering motivations
and qualities shape their designs: the best are somewhere discolored, the
worst show moldings of dignity and understandable motivation.

To resist closure, to keep the dialectic of the characters—and the play—
open-ended, is hard enough for the imagining mind; harder in the theatre
where the dynamic designs must be enclosed in physical shapes. But only in
the theatre, for the same reason, can the whole be realized. Actors can meet
the challenge: can, with their faces and bodies, project the play's ambiguities
(as these ambiguities may be intuited by them, or made present to them by
scholar-critics). Shakespeare counted on this: hence so much of *Lear*'s lan-

From *The Masks of King Lear* (Berkeley and Los Angeles: University of California Press, 1972),
336–45. Reprinted by permission of the author.

guage is nonverbal, designed for the actor's face and body rather than his tongue. Often, at crucial points, the play's meaning depends on subtextual gesture that may deny, undercut, play against the words. Thus, to recapitulate, Lear's furious angers may issue from a body partly aching for love. The ambivalence of Edgar's curious treatment of Gloster must have, to make sense, nuances of accompanying physical expression. Cordelia's inner resistances are barely indicated in words, are meaningful only in terms of a *persona* projecting them. This of course is why so many arguments flower over these and the other character designs: because so much has to be said without words, and what that is must be intuited. The art of the great actor, as Shakespeare knew, is to say these things superbly, even when, with face and body, as with the words, more than one thing must be said at a time.

What Shakespeare says with faces and bodies—and things—involves a special kind of poetry. Sometimes *Lear's* physical language matches the verbal, as where bodies are wrenched and pierced. Sometimes the physical must say what the words suggest: as when Lear, Fool, Kent, Edgar, Gloster must indicate as a continuing background through Act 3 the intense cold, the acute bodily discomfort, of heath and hovel. But beyond this, *Lear's* language of gesture has a cumulative symbolic content and texture that command the eye and mind to a special poetic experience as subtle and deeply stirring in its way as the ear-mind's experience of the words (though of course the two complement each other, cannot be separated except for discussion). The whole of this fluid tapestry can be made present only to the seeing eye; the reading mind cannot encompass it. The past pages have traced the artistry of *Lear's* visual imagery; I will summarize here, building on my definition of dramatic poetry:

> an organic structure of verbal symbols, with associated sounds, rich in denotative detail and connotative reverberation and ambiguity, often presented in recurrent, rhythmic patterns and changing perspectives that accumulate and extend the power of the whole to stimulate feeling, thought, and kinesthetic response in its audience.

How does this definition apply to *Lear's* visual imagery (in association with its imagery of sound: the non-verbal poetry of cries, howls, barks, trumpets and other music)? The best way to approach Shakespeare's composition of spectacle is for us to imagine the play as a mime with linked non-verbal sounds. This will enable us to discern, in relief, the poem of Shakespeare's gestures.

For an easy bridge to this imagining, I will concentrate on a single motif in the *Lear* language: the familiar motif of seeing. We have followed the orchestration of the idea through the network of such words as see, *sight, blindness, look, looking glass,* and have sensed the growing reverberative implications for perception, understanding, insight, knowing, and their opposites. These implications converge in Gloster's focal speech

I see it feelingly.

On one level, the blind man actually reaches out to Lear, and so sees him in his touch. But Gloster's way of seeing, as well as his words, suggests that he feels he has insight, he understands what is not visible, he does so with his feelings, and he does so very well. A further shadow persists— Gloster does not, even inwardly, really see well. The words say some of this but here as elsewhere words fail in *Lear;* and sight-sound imagery must complete the communication, especially when latent, subconscious impulses must be conveyed.

The scene resonates with visual, as well as verbal, echoes. Shakespeare created a string of "speaking pictures," every line and shape of which said something to the mind. We in this century are learning to demonstrate experimentally what visual artists like Shakespeare have always understood: that the eye thinks, it selects what things or what parts of things it will see, and brings to their interpretation a tremendous store of funded information and preconception. The hieroglyph, the pictograph, in our day the cartoon, more relevantly the Elizabethan emblem are examples of single visual symbolic structures that carry implications far beyond their components. The very components are eloquent. A simple straight line implies one thing; torture the line, and it says something else. Once figures become representational, as in Shakespeare's work they are, they are burdened with social meaning. Some attempts have been made to reduce Shakespeare's speaking pictures to the terms of contemporary emblems; but as an artist he was always breaking and restructuring the familiar. Thus he provided many royal tableaux, but even in the histories they were visually tensed and discolored with ambiguities of character and situation. More: as he shifted perspectives with his startling visual designs, he also used these images— as he used verbal images—in rhythmic and recurrent patterns. The images changed in light, line, color, and shape, their implications and ambiguities widened as the plays progressed. Thus, in our *Lear* mime, the first royal tableau will be refracted in succeeding images that hollow, mock, and grotesquely invert the initial experience.

Let us return to the specific visualized act of seeing. In our life, the act is so central to our way of knowing our world, and particularly the people in it, that any theatre representation is charged with allusion. Shakespeare exploited the act from his very first plays. Even in *Comedy of Errors,* many "see" words and acts help centrally to complicate and solve the puzzle of mistaken identity. In later plays, as deception grows inward, and more inward, words of seeing and insight are more subtly mated and polarized, and associated with visual images that confuse reality and appearance. The "ocular proof" Iago promises is meant to deceive. Macbeth's speech to the knife is loaded with *see* words—he believes the knife is there because he *sees* it— but it is not there.

On the stage, the simple act of looking may be powerfully dramatic. For one character to lock eyes with another, or avoid this, in silence or in speech, may be rich in ambiguity, stir deep responses. No words are needed to convey the potential of an exchange of speaking looks, as—to give an obvious example—between Edmund and Goneril. In a great actor's face the complex of feeling can converge in such singleness of passions as to be frightening; conversely, his fluid face may reveal multiple-layered, struggling impulses. For Lear to look, to see, to try to understand and identify, is peculiarly characteristic; and each seeing adds to the others, extends the implication of the visual imagery.

In the first scene this will become apparent as Lear glances at the other characters while addressing them. Here the playwright is partly, as craftsman, identifying the characters for the audience; but he is also saying something about them, and their relationship to Lear, and he is developing Lear's special way of scrutinizing those he addresses. As we observed, Lear himself has something to say about that later on: in his madness, asked if he is the king, he notes a distinguishing characteristic:

> Ay, every inch a king.
> When I do stare, see how the subject quakes.

At some level of his consciousness, Lear always tests, with his look, the submission of his subjects. This will be apparent, without words, in the special and different way he *looks* in the first scene at the subservient Gloster, the "fiery" Cornwall, the uncertain Albany, the masked Regan and Goneril, the withdrawn Cordelia. His act of scrutinizing will set off ripples of ambiguity in the recurrent motifs of appearance and reality, of disguise and disclosure, of the success and failure of this primary way of knowing.

In a *Lear* mime, we would observe at once a quality that, we saw, actors of Lear have sometimes accentuated in the play—the mystery of Lear's seeing— by seeming to look at the surrounding court, and all else, with an almost painful intensity, as if indeed Lear's physical capacity to see was strained—as in fact it would fail. Some actors also seemed to look beyond what they saw, as if trying to discern something not present, as if looking into another world. In the first scene, a mime audience would not need Lear's words to know that Lear will believe what he sees; and that what he sees in Goneril and Regan satisfies him. What he sees in Cordelia—however hard he looks—does not satisfy him. Then he makes a negative seeing gesture, often to be repeated — *out of my sight.* He will look elsewhere, cover his eyes, wave away what is present—if he does not like it, he will not see what is there.

On the other hand, he will be seen to communicate with what is not before him. He will look upward toward invisible powers, and seem to command them, as he would command the people around him. Here he seems indeed to see into a world beyond reason—a vision that will be inverted ironically later.

The visual imagery of Lear's scrutiny of his world is echoed and orchestrated in mime with the disguised figures he encounters: first the banished Kent, whom he examines so closely in 1.4. Shakespeare's design of suspense, we saw, includes the possibility that Lear will recognize this disguised old friend, now called enemy, who must die if discovered: so the scrutiny functions in the action as well as the character. The seeing symbolism partly is extended by Lear's need to assure himself of his own identity, to know he is there. This is central to his confrontations with Oswald, Fool, Goneril. *Who am I sir? Dost thou call me Fool, boy? Does Lear walk thus? Speak thus?* In a mime, we would know, without speech, that Lear is looking for some assurance of who he is. It is himself he is trying to see.

Slowly Lear's way of seeing changes; the rhythm alters. When he banished Cordelia, he looked confidently to unseen powers of night and day to endorse his oath of excommunication. When he calls on the unseen to curse Goneril, he looks with appeal and his eyes are misted now; physically he cannot see so well because of tears (Shakespeare often links *eye* and *tear*), his eyes betray him, he may be seen to threaten them with plucking out; and yet on his face a new seeing is visible, that reflects, *I did her wrong.*

Charged as his glance is with anger and contempt, when he confronts Kent in the stocks, when Gloster servilely keeps him outside the castle door, he yet looks with some insecurity at the approach of Regan, and with even more when Goneril appears. His face reflects many ways of seeing at once because he is designed to experience many feelings at once. He is reduced to glancing helplessly from one to the other daughter as they beat down the number of the knights. And when next he speaks to the unseen powers, he is much less certain, his questing eyes beseech support. Again these organs of his sight cloud with tears; but we see that Lear has nevertheless begun to see reality beneath surfaces.

In the storm, he defies the invisible powers, but also defends himself against them, asks for pity—*you see me here*, he gestures—for what he sees as himself: poor, weak, despised, infirm. Raindrops join teardrops in blurring his sight; and yet a better vision becomes possible to him, the light of it shows on his face, and he kneels to pray. For a moment we see that in this dark night Lear *sees better.*

Then his eyes find Mad Tom, and he slides into madness; and the mime emphasizes a curious, ironic change that happens in his seeing. He sees things no man else sees, but he seems to see them more sharply, more craftily than he ever saw before. The whole base of his knowing, and of ours, as we experience with him, is altered—herein lies much of the power of mad scenes. Lear examines Mad Tom with the same care he gave to the scrutiny of Kent; yet he sees him in a different way. The uncertainties of the rational seeing are replaced by the certainties of the irrational. With this, values are reversed. Where before we saw that Lear saw beauty in robes and furred gowns, he now discovers it in rags and nakedness.

Before, he spoke to invisible powers he saw in space; now, mad, he speaks to invisible hallucinations he sees in space. Handy-dandy—a god or hallucination—is one any more real than the other? And behind this ambiguity lurks another: the eyes that seem to see Edgar, and then Gloster, for what they are not may, on some level, see them for what they are. The line between reason and unreason, we observed, may dissolve in cunning, or accident, or naturally. These uncertainties are latent in the text; they are made visual in Lear's looking, for instance, at Gloster in 4.4., the face to face searching of the bloody sockets as Gloster peers sightlessly—seeingly—into Lear's eyes. What is it that the empty eyes see that shocks Lear into admitting some awareness of reality?[1] Silences—those punctuation marks of visual language that are often more powerful than any words or acts in the dramatic art—accent the process of Lear's mad seeing, his staring.

> Ay, every inch a king.

This is a mock king, a fool king, in a crown of weeds; one subject now, Gloster, may quake before him. When he was a real king, the subjects whom he wanted to quake did not. The stare, now, stirs ironic reverberations of the earlier unavailing look.

The mad king weeps, but the tears do not clear his sight now. Only when the great rage is stilled can he open his eyes in reason again; and then he can hardly believe what he sees. He touches Cordelia's weeping eyes, in an echo of his gesture to Gloster—eyes are for weeping, as well as seeing, whether blind or not. He must try to reestablish a base in knowing, try to see himself again, try to believe the hands he holds up before his eyes are his own.

When Cordelia is dead, he assults with his eyes—and voice—the heavens themselves; tired eyes now, tired voice, so he must assail the men who do not help him:

> Had I your tongues and eyes, I'd use them so
> That heaven's vault should crack.

The eyes are failing, for sight as well as stare, he can hardly see what to believe, cannot recognize an old friend. A dull sight.

He dies on an ambiguity. He sees something—points—(we don't need the words, *Look there, look there*) and only the visual and subverbal poetry sustains the action now, all else fades away. What Lear sees in Cordelia's face—vision, illusion, joy, horror, or a mixture of all of them—can be known *only* by what his face tell us his eyes see. And somehow, this will be another refraction of the whole preceding, accumulating visual imagery of seeing-knowing.

---

[1]Gloster's own failure to see is painfully visual. He does not, in fact, *see feelingly*. Without eyes, he is seen to be nearly helpless. He cannot tell the identity of his guide, though his happiness depends on it. He cannot know high ground from low, can be led anywhere, deceived anyhow. Edgar, for ambiguous purposes of his own that can only be conveyed by physical imagery, baffles Gloster's attempts to perceive reality through ears and touch. If eyes are no guarantee of seeing, neither is blindness.

Seeing involves an act. Some inanimate visual images in the play carry a heavy load of symbolism almost by themselves. One of these is the crown. It is hardly mentioned; and yet it is a centrally significant image in the ironic reversal in which the most powerful are seen to be degraded, robes and furred gowns exchanged for rags, the regal gestures once made with a royal sceptre now parodied by a disheveled madman with a baton of straw. In the complex interweaving of change and loss of garments, where fugitives disguise themselves downward to lower station or divest themselves of opulence while upstarts take on the gorgeous dress and ornaments of higher rank, the crown is a pivotal symbol.

Lear wears it in the first scene. He might continue to wear it as one of the "additions" to a king, and if so, with so much more irony does he carry this ornament charged with authority, now meaningless. More likely he does not wear it again, hunting, or riding in the night toward Regan; he dashes out into the storm, and runs unbonneted. The next reference is to the weedy circlet he will be seen to wear in 4.4.; but there may be other visual allusions to it. To Mikhoels, we observed, the crown's presence was felt most in its absence; after the first scene, when he had let it go, he would reach up, in a habitual gesture, to reassure himself that it was there—and it was not. So Klöpfer, in the trial scene (3.4.), took up a three-legged copper pot, and put it upside down on his head, so that its legs simulated a crown, a simulated power image for simulated authority. The flowered madman's crown, made of plants related to mindsickness, is the primary visual symbol of the irony of surface values. Lear's gestures as he asserts his mad kingship may be exactly the same as those he made in 1.1.—gestures of magnanimity, authority, power, rage— but now they make only a grotesque charade.

The reappearance and shifting of the real crown can convey the ambiguities of power's meaning. We followed this clearly enough through the play, but a mime would accentuate it. Cordelia may be seen to restore a crown to Lear in 4.7.—she is concentrating on making him feel his royal strength again. He may be seen to wear it in the brief passing over with the army at the beginning of Act 5, before he and Cordelia are captured. Then Edmund, their captor, takes it, and tries it— and in this brief gesture makes visual the whole scheme of the king's fall intersecting the bastard's rise to within one planned murder—Albany's—of a kingship. The crown will fit Edmund; but Albany will take it from him, and again a resonant symbolic visual act will be performed: Albany will try to give the crown back to Lear, but now to the true king the piece of metal is as nothing. Albany will momentarily try it himself; but being—in Edmund's Quarto speech—full of abdication and self-reproving, in a ghastly repetition of the first scene—as indeed the whole ending is visually a symbolic reprise of the assembled court at the beginning—Albany will offer to divide the crown between two rulers, Edgar and Kent. Kent will be seen to reject it, perhaps with some shock at Albany's obtuseness; Edgar will accept reluctantly the ultimate symbol of power; in the context of this royal tableau of corpses, he is king of the dead.

None of these kaleidoscopic "speaking pictures" can be taken as moral or philosophical statements. They are poetic images, open ended, reverberant, ambiguous. The crown is seen to be real, and carries real authority; it may also be utterly without value, or dangerous, blinding, subversive. The very power the crown symbolizes is, in its absoluteness, disastrously linked to infantile fantasy: anyone but a child can see that he is not everything. Yet the crown must be worn.

For discussion, I have isolated the developing images of a symbolic act and of a symbolic thing. In fact, they cannot be separated from each other, as they cannot be separated from the interwoven verbal images. Lear's seeing is one aspect of a total character design that reflects one larger design in the play: the necessity and difficulty of seeing to know. Characters strain to see in the dark, in the storm. Again and again they look off to see what mystery, what danger, approaches. No language is needed to convey to us the persistent alarm as to identity: *What's he? Who's there? What are you there?* One of the oldest techniques of the theatre craftsman, to compel the actors—and hence the audience—to look toward an entrance in anticipation or dread, is repeatedly employed in appearances by Edgar, Goneril, Regan, Mad Tom, Gloster, Gentleman. All actors, like Lear, try to look, see, know. What they see may, in a purely visual stroke, defeat their hopes: most obviously, again, Albany, in a prayerful gesture to the gods, begs Cordelia's safety, Lear enters bearing her corpse. Lear may die with his eyes open, unseeing, and someone must close them—a final irony.

Seeing and knowing are never certain in *Lear*, for the play's dialectic insists on ambiguity. Lear's character design, sustained by conflicting and even contradictory qualities, emerges in all its visual manifestations. In a clear light of mime we would see that Lear sees and does not see. He wishes others banished from his sight, and he wishes them by him. When sane, he sometimes looks as if mad; when mad, as if sane. His gestures—as well as his words—would be qualified by what we see him do: when his refusal to see is frustrated —as it invariably is—it is associated with another pervasive visual image: of flight. We saw that men constantly flee pursuit in *Lear*, but he who flees most is Lear himself, who first ordered Kent to fly. A mime would stress how much Lear flees, psychically as well as physically. Lear tries to banish the resistance of others from his sight, but, failing, he always flees confrontation—until finally Cordelia has caught him, and they kneel to each other.

Each repetition of a visual image takes on new meaning in a context that becomes more dense and complex as perspectives accumulate. How Lear kneels in serious prayer refracts the implications of his daughters' initial kneeling to him, of the kneeling of his courtiers, of his mock kneeling to Regan, of Gloster's blind kneeling to him, of his kneeling with Cordelia, of his kneeling over her dead body. So with other symbolic acts, such as putting on or off clothes, weeping, threatening, playing animal, fleeing pursuit, suffering pain, dying.

These images then, and their associated sounds, support an organic structure of symbols rich in denotative detail and connotative reverberation and
ambiguity, in rhythmic and recurrent patterns and changing perspectives that
accumulate and extend the power of the whole to stimulate feeling, thought,
and kinesthetic response in its audience. They can only be known in performance: the mind's eye, imagining Lear's physical action, can never recreate the
totality of the visual poetry that the eye's mind, in the theatre, experiences
and organizes.

The Father and the Bride

Lynda E. Boose

The aristocratic family of Shakespeare's England was, according to social historian Lawrence Stone, "patrilinear, primogenitural, and patriarchal." Parent-child relations were in general remote and formal, singularly lacking in affective bonds and governed solely by a paternal authoritarianism through which the "husband and father lorded it over his wife and children with the quasi-authority of a despot" (*Crisis* 271). Stone characterizes the society of the sixteenth and early seventeenth centuries as one in which "a majority of individuals . . . found it very difficult to establish close emotional ties to any other person" (*Family* 99)[1] and views the nuclear family as a burdensome social unit, valued only for its ability to provide the means of patrilineal descent. Second and third sons counted for little and daughters for even less. A younger son could, it is true, be kept around as a "walking sperm bank in case the elder son died childless," but daughters "were often unwanted and might be regarded as no more than a tiresome drain on the economic resources of the family" (Stone, *Family* 88, 112).[2]

Various Elizabethan documents, official and unofficial, that comment on family relations support Stone's hypothesis of the absence of affect.[3] Yet were we to turn from Stone's conclusions to those we might draw from Shakespeare's plays, the disparity of implication—especially if we assume that the plays to some extent mirror the life around them—must strike us as significant. Shakespeare's dramas consistently explore affective family dynamics with an intensity that justifies the growing inference among Shakespearean scholars that the plays may be primarily "about" family relations and only

Adapted from a longer essay in *PMLA* 97 (1982), 325–47. Reprinted by permission of the Modern Language Association of America.

[1]Stone accounts for the drama and poetry of the sixteenth and early seventeenth centuries by modifying his "rather pessimistic view of a society with little love and generally low affect" to allow for "romantic love and sexual intrigue . . . in one very restricted social group . . . that is the households of princes and great nobles" (*Family* 103–04). This qualification does not extend to his view of parent-child relationships.

[2]Stone also points out that the high infant-mortality rate, "which made it folly to invest too much emotional capital in such ephemeral beings," was as much responsible for this lack of affective family ties as were any economic motives (*Family* 105).

[3]As Christopher Hill suggests in his review of Stone's *Family,* much of the evidence used could well imply its opposite: "The vigour of the preachers' propaganda on behalf . . . of breaking children's wills, suggests that such attitudes were by no means so universally accepted as they would have wished" (461).

secondarily about the macrocosm of the body politic.[4] Not the absence of affect but the possessive overabundance of it is the force that both defines and threatens the family in Shakespeare. When we measure Stone's assertions against the Shakespeare canon, the plays must seem startlingly ahistorical in focusing on what would seem to have been the least valued relationship of all: that between father and daughter.

While father and son appear slightly more often in the canon, figuring in twenty-three plays, father and daughter appear in twenty-one dramas and in one narrative poem. As different as these father-daughter plays are, they have one thing in common: almost without exception the relationships they depict depend on significant underlying substructures of ritual. Shakespeare apparently created his dramatic mirrors not solely from the economic and social realities that historians infer as having dictated family behavior but from archetypal models, psychological in import and ritual in expression. And the particular ritual model on which Shakespeare most frequently drew for the father-daughter relationship was the marriage ceremony.[5]

In an influential study of the sequential order or "relative positions within ceremonial wholes," Arnold van Gennep isolated three phases in ritual enactment that always recur in the same underlying arrangement and that form, in concert, "the pattern of the rites of passage": separation, transition, and reincorporation.[6] The church marriage service—as familiar to a modern audience as it was to Shakespeare's—contains all three phases. When considered by itself, it is basically a separation rite preceding the transitional phase of consummation and culminating in the incorporation of a new family unit. In Hegelian terms, the ceremonial activities associated with marriage move from thesis through antithesis to synthesis; the anarchic release of fertility is positioned between two phases of relative stasis. The ritual enables society to allow for a limited transgression of its otherwise universal taboo against human eroticism. Its middle movement is the dangerous phase of transition and transgression; its conclusion, the controlled reincorporation into the stability of family. But before the licensed transgression can take place—the transgression that generates the stability and continuity of society itself—the ritual must separate the sanctified celebrants from the sterile forces of social interdiction. The marriage ritual is thus a pattern of and for the community that surrounds it, as well as a rite of passage of and for the individuals who enact it. It serves as an especially effective substructure for the father-

<hr/>

[4]One could chart the new emphasis on the family by reviewing the Shakespeare topics at recent MLA conventions.

[5]Margaret Loftus Ranald has done substantial work on the legal background of marriage in Shakespeare plays. I have found no marriages (or funerals) staged literally in the plays of Shakespeare or of his contemporaries.

[6]Van Gennep built his study on the work of Hartland, Frazer, Ciszewski, Hertz, Crowley, and others who had noted resemblances among the components of various disparate rites. His tripartite diachronic structure provides the basis for Victor W. Turner's discussions in the essay Liminality and Communitas" (*Ritual Process* 94–203).

daughter relation because within its pattern lies the paradigm of all the conflicts that define this bond at its liminal moment of severance. The ceremony ritualizes two particularly significant events: a daughter and a son are being incorporated into a new family unit, an act that explicitly breaks down the boundaries of two previously existing families; yet, at the same time, the bonds being dissolved, particularly those between father and daughter, are being memorialized and thus, paradoxically, reasserted. In early comedies like *The Taming of the Shrew*, Shakespeare followed the Roman design of using the father of the young male lover as the *senex iratus*, a blocking figure to be circumvented. The mature comedies, tragedies, and romances reconstruct the problems of family bonds, filial obedience, and paternal possessiveness around the father and daughter, the relation put into focus by the marriage ceremony. When marriage activities are viewed from the perspective of their ritual implications, the bride and groom are not joined until the transitional phase of the wedding-night consummation; before that, a marriage may be annulled. What the church service is actually all about is the separation of the daughter from the interdicting father.

The wedding ceremony of Western tradition has always recognized the preeminence of the father-daughter bond. Until the thirteenth century, when the church at last managed to gain control of marriage law, marriage was considered primarily a private contract between two families concerning property exchange. The validity and legality of matrimony rested on the *consensus nuptialis* and the property contract, a situation that set up a potential for conflict by posing the mutual consent of the two children, who owed absolute obedience to their parents, against the desires of their families, who must agree beforehand to the contract governing property exchange. However true it was that the couple's willing consent was necessary for valid matrimony and however vociferously the official conduct books urged parents to consider the compatibility of the match, fathers like Cymbeline, Egeus, and Baptista feel perfectly free to disregard these requirements. Although lack of parental consent did not affect the validity of a marriage and, after 1604, affected the legality only when a minor was involved,[7] the family control over the dowry was a powerful psychological as well as economic weapon. Fathers like Capulet, Lear, and Brabantio depend on threats of disinheritance to coerce their children. When their daughters nonetheless wed without the paternal blessing, the marriages are adversely affected not because any legal

---

[7]The church canons of 1604 seem to have confused the situation further by continuing to recognize the validity of the nuptial pledge but forbidding persons under twenty-one to marry without parental consent; this ruling would make the marriage of minors illegal but nonetheless binding for life and hence valid (Stone, *Family* 32). Until the passage of Lord Hardwicke's Marriage Act in 1753, confusion was rife over what constituted a legal marriage and what a valid one. In addition to bringing coherence to the marriage laws, this act was designed to protect increasingly threatened parental interests by denying the validity as well as the legality of a religious ceremony performed without certain conditions, including parental consent for parties under twenty-one (Stone, *Family* 35–36).

statutes have been breached but because the ritual base of marriage has been circumvented and the psychological separation of daughter from father thus rendered incomplete. For in Shakespeare's time—as in our own—the ceremony acknowledged the special bond between father and daughter and the need for the power of ritual to release the daughter from its hold.

As specified in the 1559 *Book of Common Prayer*, the marriage ritual enjoins that the father (or, in his absence, the legal guardian)[8] deliver his daughter to the altar, stand by her in mute testimony that there are no impediments to her marriage, and then witness her pledge henceforth to forsake all others and "obey and serve, love honor and keep" the man who stands at her other side. To the priest's question, "Who giveth this woman to be married unto this man?"—a question that dates in English tradition back to the York manual (*Book of Common Prayer* 290—99; 408, n.)—the father must silently respond by physically relinquishing his daughter, only to watch the priest place her right hand into the possession of another man. Following this expressly physical symbolic transfer, the father's role in his daughter's life is ended; custom dictates that he now leave the stage, resign his active part in the rite, and become a mere observer. After he has withdrawn, the couple plight their troths, and the groom receives the ring, again from the priest. Taking the bride's hand into his, the groom places the ring on her finger with the words, "With this ring I thee wed, with my body I thee worship, and with all my worldly goods I thee endow," thus solemnizing the transfer in its legal, physical, and material aspects.[9]

Before us we have a tableau paradigmatic of the problematic father-daughter relation: decked in the symbols of virginity, the bride stands at the altar between her father and husband, pulled as it were between the two important male figures in her life. To resolve the implied dilemma, the force of the priest and the community presides over and compels the transfer of an

---

The concern for parental approval has always focused on, and in fact ritualized, the consent of the bride's father. In 1858, the Reverend Charles Wheatly, a noted authority on church law, attributed the father's giving away his daughter as signifying the care that must be taken of the female sex, "who are always supposed to be under the tuition of a father or guardian, whose consent is necessary to make their acts valid" (496). For supportive authority Wheatly looks back to Richard Hooker, whose phrasing is substantially harsher. Hooker felt that the retention of the custom "hath still this vse that it putteth we men in mind of a dutie whereunto the verie imbecillitie of their [women's] nature and sex doth binde them, namely to be alwaies directed, guided and ordered by others . . ." (215).

8Given the high parent mortality rate, a number of brides necessarily went to the altar on the arms of their legal guardians. Peter Laslett notes that in Manchester between 1553–1657 over half of the girls marrying for the first time were fatherless (103), but some historians have criticized his reliance on parish registers as the principal demographic barometer.

9The groom's pledge suggests the wedding ring's dual sexual and material symbolism. Historically, the ring symbolizes the dowry payment that the woman will receive from her husband by the entitlement of marriage; it apparently superseded the custom of placing tokens of espousal on the prayer book (see *Book of Common Prayer* 408). It also signifies the physical consummation, a point frequently exploited in Renaissance drama and also implied by the rubrics in the older Roman Catholic manuals, which direct the placing of the ring.

untouched daughter into the physical possession of a male whom the ceremony authorizes both as the invested successor to the father's authority and as the sanctified transgressor of prohibitions that the father has been compelled to observe.[10] By making the father transfer his intact daughter to the priest in testimony that he knows of no impediments to her lawful union, the service not only reaffirms the taboo against incest but implicitly levels the full weight of that taboo on the relationship between father and daughter. The groom's family does not enter into the archetypal dynamics going on at this altar except through the priest's reference to marriage as the cause why a man "shall leave father and mother and shall be joined unto his wife." The mother of the bride is a wholly excluded figure—as indeed she is throughout almost the entire Shakespeare canon. Only the father must act out, must dramatize his loss before the audience of the community. Within the ritual circumscription, the father is compelled to give his daughter to a rival male; and as Georges Bataille comments:

> The gift itself is a renunciation. . . . Marriage is a matter less for the partners than for the man who gives the woman away, the man whether father or brother who might have freely enjoyed the woman, daughter or sister, yet who bestows her on someone else. This gift is perhaps a substitute for the sexual act; for the exuberance of giving has a significance akin to that of the act itself; it is also a spending of resources.[11]

(218)

[10]The ceremonial transfer of the father's authority to the husband is acknowledged by the Reverend John Shepherd in his historical commentary accompanying the 1853 *Family Prayer Book*: ". . . the ceremony shows the father's consent; and that the authority, which he before possessed, he now resigns to the husband" (Brownell 465). By implication, however, the ceremony resolves the incestuous attraction between father and daughter by ritualizing his "gift" of her hand, a signification unlikely to be discussed in the commentary of church historians. When first the congregation and next the couple are asked to name any impediments to the marriage, there are, Wheatly says, three specific impediments the church is charging all knowledgeable parties to declare: a preceding marriage or contract, consanguinity or affinity, and want of consent (483).

[11]The sections on the celebration of "Festiuall daies" and times of fast that precede Hooker's defense of the English "Celebration of Matrimonie" are especially helpful in understanding Elizabethan ritual, for in these sections Hooker expands his defense of the Anglican rites into an explanation of, and rationale for, the whole notion of ritual. Having first isolated three sequential elements necessary for festival—praise, bounty, and rest—he goes on to justify "bountie" in terms remarkably compatible with the theories of both Bataille and Lévi-Strauss on the essential "spending-gift" nature of marriage. To Hooker, the "bountie" essential to celebration represents the expression of a "charitable largenesse of somewhat more then common bountie. . . . Plentifull and liberall expense is required in them that abounde, partly as a signe of their owne ioy in the goodnesse of God towards them" (292, 293). Bounty is important to all festival rites, but within the marriage rite this "spending" quality incorporates the specific idea of sexual orgasm as the ultimate and precious expenditure given the bride by her husband, a notion alluded to in Bataille and one that functioned as a standard Elizabethan metaphor apparent in phrases like "Th' expense of spirit" (sonnet 129) or Othello's comment to Desdemona, "The purchase made, the fruits are to ensue; / That profit's yet to come 'tween me and you" (2.3.9–10). The wedding ceremony ritualizes this notion of bounty as the gift of life by having the father give the groom the family treasure, which the father cannot "use" but can only bequeath or hoard. The groom, who ritually places coins or a gold ring on the prayer book as a token "bride price," then fully "purchases" the father's treasure through his own physical expenditure, an act that guarantees the

By playing out his role in the wedding ceremony, the father implicitly gives the blessing that licenses the daughter's deliverance from family bonds that might otherwise become a kind of bondage. . . .

Within the father-daughter plays, the daughter's association of father with husband is so strong that even when a woman as independent as Rosalind or Viola first thinks about the man she will eventually marry, her thoughts immediately call to mind her father. Her movement toward conjugal love unconsciously resuscitates a mental movement back to the father to whom she will remain emotionally as well as legally bound until the ritual of marriage transfers her loyalties from one domain to the other. The lack of narrative logic in the association emphasizes its subconscious quality. . . .

In tragedies like *Lear, Othello,* and *Romeo and Juliet,* the father's failure to act out his required role has a special significance, one that we can best apprehend by looking not at the logic of causal narrative progression but at the threat implied by the violation of ritual. Even when marriage is sanctified by the presence of a priest, as it is in *Romeo and Juliet,* the absence of the father becomes crucial. In *Romeo,* the significance is dramatically projected through ritual structures in which Capulet repeatedly "gives away" his daughter without her consent and Juliet is repeatedly "married" without the blessing of her father, a father who ironically has been "a careful father" in choosing a harmonious match compatible with the best interests of the daughter he obviously cherishes. . . .

Once a ritual has been invoked, has in effect drawn a circle of archetypal reference around the moment and space, any events from the nonsacramental surrounding world that interrupt or counter its prescribed direction take on special, portentous significance.[12] By interrupting or converting the invoked

---

father's "interest" through future generations. This money-sex image complex is pervasive and important in many of Shakespeare's plays. The pattern and its relation to festival are especially evident in Juliet's ecstatic and impatient speech urging night to come and bring her husband:

O, I have bought the mansion of a love,
But not possess'd it, and though I am sold,
Not yet enjoy'd. So tedious is this day
As is the night before some festival.
(3.2.26–29)

In another context, this pattern enables us fully to understand Shylock's miserly refusal to give or spend and the implication of his simultaneous loss of daughter and hoarded fortune. His confusion of daughter and ducats is foreshadowed when he recounts the story of Jacob and equates the increase of the flock through the "work of generation" to the increase of money through retentive "use." To Antonio's question, "Or is your gold and silver ewes and rams?" Shylock responds, "I cannot tell, I make it breed as fast" (*MV* 1.3.95–96).

[12]Hooker also makes the point that the sacramentality invoked by ritual is profaned when festival celebration overflows the measure or when the form of ceremony becomes parodic. Hooker asserts that the festivals of the "Israelites and heathens," though they contained the necessary elements, "failed in the ende it self, so neither could they discerne rightly what forme and measure Religion therein should obserue. . . . they are in every degree noted to haue doen amisse, their Hymnes or songs of praise were idolatrie, their bountie excesse, and their rest wantonnesse" (294). On the use of ritual as the human means to recover the sacred dimension of existence, see Eliade:

ritual to parody, such profane invasions rupture its sacramental context. . . .

In *Othello*, the father-daughter rupture is dramatized as a structural parody of the church service. The Desdemona-Brabantio scene and the Lear-Cordelia confrontation, two versions of the same ritual model, have obvious similarities.[13] The opening scene of *King Lear*, however, is infused with the additional tension of colliding, incompatible ritual structures: the attempt of the man who is both king and father to substitute the illegitimate transfer of his kingdom for the legitimate one of his daughter.

In *King Lear*, the father's grudging recognition of the need to confer his *daughter* on younger strengths while he unburdened crawls toward death should be understood as the basal structure underlying his divestiture of his kingdom. Lear has called his court together in the opening scene because he must at last face the postponed reckoning with Cordelia's two princely suitors, who "Long in our court have made their amorous sojourn, / And here are to be answer'd" (1.1.47–48). But instead of justly relinquishing his daughter, Lear tries to effect a substitution of paternal divestitures: he portions out his kingdom as his "daughters' several dowers," attaching to Cordelia's share a stipulation designed to thwart her separation. In substituting his public paternity for his private one, the inherently indivisible entity for the one that biologically must divide and recombine, Lear violates both his kingly role in the hierarchical universe and his domestic one in the family. Nor is it accident—as it was in *Hamlet* 5.1—that brings these two incompatible rituals into collision in *Lear* 1.1. It is the willful action of the king and father, the lawgiver and protector of both domain and family, that is fully responsible for this explosion of chaos.

Yet of course Lear's bequest of his realm is in no way an unconditional transfer of the kingdom from one rulership to another. Instead, Lear wants to retain the dominion he theoretically casts off and to "manage those authorities / That he hath given away" (1.3.17–18). Likewise, the bequest of his daughter is actually an attempt to keep her, a motive betrayed by the very words he uses. When he *dis*claims "all my paternal care" and orders Cordelia "as a stranger to my heart and me / Hold thee from this for ever" (1.3.113, 115–16),

Driven from religious life in the strict sense, the *celestial sacred* remains active through symbolism. A religious symbol conveys its message even if it is no longer consciously understood in every part. For a symbol speaks to the whole human being and not only to the intelligence. . . . Hence the supreme function of the myth is to "fix" the paradigmatic models for all rites and significant human activities. . . . By the continuous reactualization of paradigmatic divine gestures, the world is sanctified.

(129, 98–99)

Unquestionably, the late C. L. Barber's study is the best book to date on the relation of Shakespeare's plays to underlying patterns of ritual.

13C. L. Barber also notes the ritual connection: "*Lear* begins with a failure of the passage that might be handled by the marriage service, as it is structured to persuade the father to give up his daughter. Regan and Goneril, though married, pretend to meet Lear's demand on them in all-but-incestuous terms. Cordelia defends herself by reference to the service" (in Schwartz and Kahn 197).

his verb holds to his heart rather than expels from it the daughter he says is "adopted to our hate" (1.3.203), another verbal usage that betrays his retentive motives. His disastrous attempts to keep the two dominions he sheds are structurally linked through the parodic divestiture of his kingdom as dowry. In recognition of the family's economic interest in marriage, the terms of sixteenth-century dowries were required to be fully fixed before the wedding, thus making the property settlement a precondition for the wedding.[14] But Lear the father will not freely give his daughter her endowment unless she purchases it with pledges that would nullify those required by the wedding ceremony. If she will not love him all, she will mar her fortunes, lose her dowry, and thus forfeit the symbolic separation. And yet, as she asserts, she cannot marry if she loves her father all. The circularity of Lear's proposition frustrates the ritual phase of separation: by disinheriting Cordelia, Lear casts her away not to let her go but to prevent her from going. In Lévi-Strauss' terms, Lear has to give up Cordelia because the father must obey the basic social rule of reciprocity, which has a necessarily communal effect, functioning as a "distribution to undo excess." Lear's refusal is likewise communal in its effect, and it helps create the universe that he has "ta'en too little care of."

Insofar as Burgundy's suit is concerned, Lear's quantitatively constructed presumption works. Playing the mime priest and intentionally desecrating the sacramental ritual question he imitates, Lear asks the first bridegroom-candidate:

> Will you, with those infirmities she owes,
> Unfriended, new adopted to our hate,
> Dow'r'd with our curse, and stranger'd with our oath,
> Take her, or leave her?
>
>   (1.1.202–05)

Burgundy's hedged response is what Lear anticipates—this suitor will gladly "take Cordelia by the hand" only if Lear will give "but that portion which yourself propos'd" (1.1.243, 242). Shrewdly intuiting that France cannot be dissuaded by so quantitative a reason as "her price is fallen," Lear then adopts a strategy based on qualitative assumptions in his attempt to discourage the rival he most greatly fears. Insisting to France that

>   For you, great King
> I would not from your love make such a stray
> To match you where I hate; therefore beseech you
> T'avert your liking a more worthier way
>
>   (1.1.208–11)

---

[14]*Measure for Measure* provides the most dramatic testimony to the importance of fixing the dowry provisions before the wedding. Although Juliet is nearly nine months pregnant and although she and Claudio believe themselves spiritually married, they have not legalized the wedding in church because of still unresolved dowry provisions.

Lear tries to avoid even making the required ritual offer. By calling his own daughter "a wretch whom Nature is asham'd / Almost t'acknowledge hers" (1.1.212–13), Lear implies by innuendo the existence of some unnatural impediment in Cordelia that would make her unfit to marry and would thus prevent her separation. Effectively, the scene presents an altar tableau much like that in *Much Ado*, with a bride being publicly pronounced unfit for marriage. In *Lear*, however, it is the father rather than the groom who defames the character of the bride, and his motives are to retain her rather than to reject her. In this violated ceremony, the slandered daughter—instead of fainting—staunchly denies the alleged impediments by demanding that her accuser "make known / It is no vicious blot . . . No unchaste action, or dishonored step, / That hath deprived me of your grace and favor" (1.1.226–29). And here the groom himself takes up the role implicit in his vows, defending Cordelia's suborned virtue by his statement that to believe Lear's slanders would require "a faith that reason without miracle / Should never plant in me" (1.1.222–23). The physical separation of the daughter from the father is finally achieved only by France's perception that "this unpriz'd precious maid . . . is herself a dowry" (1.1.259, 241); France recognizes the qualitative meaning of the dowry that Burgundy could only understand quantitatively.

In Cordelia's almost archetypal definition of a daughter's proper loyalties (1.1.95–104), Shakespeare uses a pun to link the fundamental predicament of the daughter—held under the aegis of the father—to its only possible resolution in the marriage troth: "That lord whose hand must take my plight shall carry / Half my love with him" (1.1.101–02), says Cordelia. When France later addresses his bride as "Fairest Cordelia, that art most rich being poor, / Most choice forsaken, and most lov'd despis'd" (1.1.250–51), he echoes the husband's traditional pledge to love "for richer, for poorer" the daughter who has "forsaken all others." And France himself then endows Lear's "dow'rless daughter" with all his worldly goods by making her "queen of us, of ours, and our fair France" (1.1.256–57). His statement "Be it lawful I take up what's cast away" (1.1.253) even suggests a buried stage direction through its implied allusion to the traditional conclusion of the *consensus nuptialis* as explained in the Sarum and York manuals: the moment when the bride, in token of receiving a dowry of land from her husband, prostrates herself at her husband's feet and he responds by lifting her up again (*Rathen* 36, Legg 190, Howard 306–07).

The visual and verbal texts of this important opening scene allude to the separation phase of the marriage ritual; the ritual features are emphasized because here, unlike the similar scene in *Othello*, the daughter's right to choose a husband she loves is not at issue. Because the ritual is sacred, Cordelia dispassionately refuses to follow her sisters in prostituting it. Lear, in contrast, passionately destroys his kingdom in order to thwart the fixed movement of the ritual pattern and to convert the pattern's linear progression away from the father into a circular return to him.[15] The discord his violation engenders continues to be projected through accumulating ritual substructures: in a parody of giving his daughter's hand, Lear instead gives her "father's heart from her" (1.1.126); in a parody of the ring rite, Lear takes the golden round uniting king and country and parts it, an act that both dramatizes the consequences of dividing his realm and demonstrates the anguish he feels at losing his daughter to a husband.

Once Lear has shattered the invoked sacred space by collapsing two incompatible rituals into it, he shatters also all claims to paternal authority. From this scene onward, the question of Lear's paternal relation to his daughters and his kingdom pervades the drama through the King's ceremonial invocations of sterility against the daughters he has generated and the land he has ruled. In the prototype of a harmonious wedding that concludes *As You Like It*, Hymen—who "peoples every town"—defines Duke Senior's correct paternal role as that of the exogamous giver of the daughter created in heaven:

> Hymen from heaven brought her,
>   Yea, brought her hither,
> That thou mightst join her hand with his
> Whose heart within his bosom is.
>   (5.4.112–15)[16]

Hymen characterizes the generating of children as a gift from heaven, an essential spending of the self designed to increase the world. By contrast, Lear's image of the father is the "barbarous Scythian, / Or he that makes his generation messes / To gorge his appetite" (1.1.116–18). The definition is opposite to the very character of ritual. It precludes the possibility of transformation, for the father devours the flesh he begets. Here, generation becomes primarily an autogamous act, a retention and recycling of the procreative energies, which become mere extensions of private appetite

---

[15]Alan Dundes points out the psychological dimensions of various folktale types underlying a number of Shakespeare's plays; significantly, the central figure in the folktale is usually the daughter-heroine. The theme of incest, which Freud himself recognized as a powerful undercurrent in *King Lear*, is manifest in the folktale father who demands that his daughter marry him; Shakespeare transforms the overt demand into a love test requiring that she love her father all (358). In Dundes' interpretation, the more obvious father-daughter incest wish is actually an Electral daughter-father desire that has been transformed through projection. Dundes also lists other discussions of the father-daughter incest theme in *King Lear* (359).

[16]Hymen's verses emphasize the religious sense of the marriage ritual. In this context the genetic father is only a surrogate parent, appointed by the heavenly parent to act out the specific role of bequeathing the daughter to a new union; Hymen himself functions as the mythic priest, the agent authorized by heaven to oversee the transfer. Wheatly's notes reflect this same sense of the religious meaning of the roles played by father and priest: ". . . the woman is to be given not to the man, but to the Minister; for the rubric orders, that the minister shall receive her *at her father's or friend's hands*; which signifies, to be sure, that the father resigns her up to God, and that it is God, who, by His Priest, now gives her in marriage . . ." (497).

feeding on its own production. The unnatural appetite of the father devouring his paternity is implicit even in the motive Lear reveals behind his plan to set his rest on Cordelia's "kind nursery" (1.1.124), an image in which the father pictures himself as an infant nursing from his daughter. The implied relationship is unnatural because it allows the father to deflect his original incestuous passions into Oedipal ones, thus effecting a newly incestuous proximity to the daughter, from whom the marriage ritual is designed to detach him. And when this form of appetite is thwarted by France's intervention, Lear effects yet another substitution of state for daughter: having ordered Cornwall and Albany to "digest the third" part of his kingdom, he and his gluttonous knights proceed to feed off it and through their "Epicurism and lust / Make . . . it more like a tavern or a brothel / Than a grac'd palace" (1.4.244–46). Compelled by nature to give up his daughter, he unnaturally gives up his kingdom; when his appetites cannot feed on her, they instead devour the paternity of his land.

The father devouring his own flesh is the monstrous extension of the circular terms of Lear's dowry proposal. The image belongs not only to the play's pervasive cluster of monsters from the deep but also to its dominant spatial pattern of circularity. Within both the narrative movement and the repeated spatial structure inside the drama, the father's retentive passions deny the child's rite of passage. When Cordelia departs from the father's realm for a new life in her husband's, ostensibly fulfilling the ritual separation, the journey is condemned to futility at its outset, for Cordelia departs dowered with Lear's curse: "Without our grace, our love, our benison" (1.1.265). Although the bride and groom have exchanged vows, the denial of the father's blessing renders the separation incomplete and the daughter's future blighted. Cordelia, like Rosalind, must therefore return to be reincorporated with her father before she can undergo the ritual severance that will enable her to progress. She thus chooses father over husband, returning to Lear to ask his blessing: "look upon me, sir, / And hold your hand in benediction o'er me" (4.7.56–57). In lines that indicate how futile the attempt at incorporation has been when the precedent rites of passage have been perverted, Cordelia asserts, "O dear father, / It is thy business that I go about" (4.4.23–24), and characterizes her life with France as having been one of constant mourning for the father to whom she is still bound.

Shakespeare rewrote the source play *Leir* to make Cordelia remain in England alone (rather than with France at her side) to fight, lose, and die with her father, a revision that vividly illustrates the tragic failure of the family unit to divide, recombine, and regenerate. The only respite from pain the tragedy offers is the beauty of Lear's reunion with Cordelia, but that reunion takes place at the cost of both the daughter's life and the future life of the family. And for all the poignancy of this reunion, the father's intransigence—which in this play both initiates and conditions the tragedy—remains unchanged: it is still writ large in his fantasy that he and his daughter will be forever

imprisoned together like birds in a cage.[17] At the end of the play, excluding
any thought of Cordelia's new life with France, Lear focuses solely on the
father-daughter merger, which he joyfully envisions enclosed in a perpetuity
where no interlopers—short of a divine messenger—can threaten it: "He that
parts us shall bring a brand from heaven, / And fire us hence like foxes"
(5.3.22–23). The rejoining is the precise opposite of that in *As You Like It*. To
Rosalind's question, "if I bring in your Rosalind, / You will bestow her on
Orlando here?" Duke Senior responds, "That would I, had I kingdoms to give
with her" (*AYL* 5.4.6–7, 8). In the Duke's characterization of Orlando's newly
received endowment as "a potent Dukedom" (5.4.169), the implied fertility of
both kingdom and family is ensured through the father's submission to the
necessary movement of ritual. In *King Lear*, the father who imagined that he
"gave his daughters all" extracts from his daughter at the end of the play the
same price he demanded in the opening scene—that she love her father all.
The play's tragic circles find their counterpart in its ritual movements.
Cordelia returns to her father, and the final scene stages the most sterile of
altar tableaux: a dead father with his three dead daughters, the wheel having
come full circle back to the opening scene of the play. Initially barren of
mothers, the play concludes with the death of all the fathers and all the
daughters; the only figures who survive to emphasize the sterility of the final
tableau are Albany, a widower, and Edgar, an unmarried son. . . .

Works Cited

Barber, C. L. *Shakespeare's Festive Comedy*. Princeton: Princeton Univ. Press, 1959.
Bataille, Georges. *Death and Sensuality: A Study of Eroticism and the Taboo.* 1962;
    rpt. New York: Arno, 1977.
Berkowitz, David. *Renaissance Quarterly* 32(1979):396–403.
The Book of Common Prayer, 1559. Ed. John E. Booty. Charlottesville: Univ. of
    Virginia Press, 1967.
Boose, Lynda E. "Othello's Handkerchief: 'The Recognizance and Pledge of Love.'"
    English Literary Renaissance 5(1975):360–74.
Brownell, Thomas Church, ed. *The Family Prayer Book; or*, The Book of Common
    Prayer *according to the Use of the Protestant Episcopal Church.* New York: Stanford
    and Swords, 1853.
The Church and the Law of Nullity of Marriage. Report of a commission appointed by
    the archbishops of Canterbury and York in 1949. London: Society for Promoting
    Christian Knowledge, 1955.
Demos, John. *New York Times Book Review,* 25 Dec. 1977, 1.
Dundes, Alan. "'To Love My Father All': A Psychoanalytic Study of the Folktale
    Source of *King Lear.*" *Southern Folklore Quarterly* 40(1976):353–66.

[17]See Barber's essay in Schwartz and Kahn, esp. pp. 198–221. Barber additionally provides a
striking iconographic association, noting the image of Lear with Cordelia in his arms as being
effectively "a *pietà* with the roles reversed, not Holy Mother with her Dead Son, but father with
his dead daughter" (200).

Eliade, Mircea. *The Sacred and the Profane.* Trans. Willard R. Trask. New York: Harcourt, 1959.

Evans, G. Blakemore, ed. *The Riverside Shakespeare.* Boston: Houghton, 1974.

Flandrin, Jean-Louis. *Families in Former Times: Kinship, Household and Sexuality.* Trans. Richard Southern. Cambridge: Cambridge Univ. Press, 1979.

Frey, Charles. " 'O sacred, shadowy, cold, and constant queen': Shakespeare's Imperiled and Chastening Daughters of Romance." *South Atlantic Bulletin* 43(1978):125–40.

The Geneva Bible. 1560; facsim. rpt. Madison: Univ. of Wisconsin Press, 1961.

Harding, D. W. "Father and Daughter in Shakespeare's Last Plays." *TLS*, 30 Nov. 1979, 59–61.

Hill, Christopher. "Sex, Marriage and the Family in England." *Economic History Review,* 2nd ser., 31(1978):450–63.

Hooker, Richard. *Of the Lawes of Ecclesiasticall Politie.* 1594; facsim. rpt. Amsterdam: Theatrum Orbis Terrarum, 1971.

Howard, George Elliott. *A History of Matrimonial Institutions.* London: T. Fisher Unwin, 1904.

Hoy, Cyrus. "Fathers and Daughters in Shakespeare's Romances." In *Shakespeare's Romances Reconsidered.* Ed. Carol McGinnis Kay and Henry E. Jacobs. Lincoln: Univ. of Nebraska Press, 1978, 77–90.

Kelly, Henry Ansgar. *The Matrimonial Trials of Henry VIII.* Stanford, Calif.: Stanford Univ. Press, 1976.

Laslett, Peter. *The World We Have Lost.* 2nd ed. 1965; rpt. London: Methuen, 1971.

LeClercq, R. V. "Crashaw's Epithalamium: Pattern and Vision." *Literary Monographs* 6. Madison: Univ. of Wisconsin Press, 1975, 73–108.

Legg, J. Wickham. *Ecclesiological Essays.* London: De La More Press, 1905.

Lévi-Strauss, Claude. *The Elementary Structures of Kinship.* Trans. James Harle Bell. Ed. John Richard von Sturmer and Rodney Needham. Paris, 1949; rpt. Boston: Beacon, 1969.

McCown, Gary M. " 'Runnawayes Eyes' and Juliet's Epithalamion." *Shakespeare Quarterly* 27(1976):150–70.

Noble, Richmond. *Shakespeare's Use of the Bible and* The Book of Common Prayer. London: Society for the Promotion of Biblical Knowledge, 1935.

Partridge, Eric. *Shakespeare's Bawdy.* 1948; rpt. New York: Dutton, 1969.

Rabkin, Norman. *Shakespeare and the Problem of Meaning.* Chicago: Univ. of Chicago Press, 1981.

Ranald, Margaret Loftus. " 'As Marriage Binds, and Blood Breaks': English Marriage and Shakespeare." *Shakespeare Quarterly* 30(1979):68–81.

The Rathen Manual. Ed. Duncan MacGregor. Aberdeen: Aberdeen Ecclesiological Society, 1905.

Schoenbaum, S. *William Shakespeare: A Compact Documentary Life.* Oxford: Oxford Univ. Press, 1975.

Schwartz, Murray M., and Coppélia Kahn, eds. *Representing Shakespeare: New Psychoanalytic Essays.* Baltimore: Johns Hopkins Univ. Press, 1980.

The Statutes of the Realm. London: Record Commissions, 1820–28; facsim. ed. 1968.

Stone, Lawrence. *The Crisis of the Aristocracy: 1558–1660.* Abridged ed. London: Oxford Univ. Press, 1971.

———. *The Family, Sex and Marriage in England: 1500–1800.* New York: Harper, 1977.

Thomas, Keith. *TLS*, 21 Oct. 1977, 1226.

Tufte, Virginia. *The Poetry of Marriage.* Los Angeles: Tinnon-Brown, 1970.

Turner, Victor W. *The Ritual Process: Structure and Anti-Structure.* Chicago: Aldine, 1969.

Van Gennep, Arnold. *The Rites of Passage.* Trans. Monika B. Vizedom and Gabrielle L. Caffee. 1908; rpt. London: Routledge and Kegan Paul, 1960.

Wheatly, Charles. *A Rational Illustration of* The Book of Common Prayer *according to the Use of the Church of England.* Cambridge: Cambridge Univ. Press, 1858.

"The Base Shall Top Th'Legitimate": The Bedlam Beggar and the Role of Edgar in *King Lear*

William C. Carroll

Edgar's passage through *King Lear* is relatively clear in its outlines—from naive son to outcast beggar to restored son, heir, and finally, perhaps, king. It is the curve of a romance plot, though it never feels like one. The nature of Edgar's inner changes, on the other hand, is an entirely different question; whether he possesses what may be called a consistent inner self has been widely debated. Much of the difficulty in discussing Edgar stems from the series of roles he plays in the middle of the play which seem embodiments (if that is possible) of negation and self-alienation, most cryptically expressed in a string of orphic negatives, from "Edgar I nothing am" (2.3.21) through "in nothing am I chang'd / But in my garments" (4.6.9–10) to "Know, my name is lost" (5.3.121).[1] The play's eerie calculus transforms these negatives into the positive assertion of identity that Edgar makes to Edmund at the end of the play: "My name is Edgar, and thy father's son" (5.3.169)—and yet even this positive assertion is characteristically ambiguous. We will never be able to

From *Shakespeare Quarterly*, 38 (1987). Reprinted by permission.

This research was assisted by a grant from the American Council of Learned Societies under a program funded by the National Endowment for the Humanities.

[1]Textual quotations are from the Arden *King Lear*, ed. Kenneth Muir (New York: Random House, 1964). Muir bases his text on the Folio, but includes much from the Quarto in what is now termed a "hybrid" or "conflated" text. I have used the Muir edition because it is readily available. The problem of the "two-text" *Lear* is not my subject here, although the character of Edgar undergoes relatively significant alterations in the Folio version of the play; see Michael Warren's article, "Quarto and Folio *King Lear* and the Interpretation of Albany and Edgar," in *Shakespeare: Pattern of Excelling Nature*, eds. David Bevington and Jay L. Halio (Newark: Univ. of Delaware Press, 1978), pp. 95–107, as well as Peter Blayney, *The Texts of* King Lear *and Their Origins* (Cambridge: Cambridge Univ. Press, 1982), and *The Division of the Kingdoms*, eds. Gary Taylor and Michael Warren (Oxford: Clarendon Press, 1983). The alterations in Edgar's part—such as the deletion of his soliloquy at the end of 3.4.—do not in general affect my argument in this paper, and I have indicated in the notes where I have diverged from Muir's text, and/or where there is a significant distinction between Folio and Quarto readings. For an analysis of the interpretive implications of the two-text theory, particularly in the case of Edgar, see my essay "New Plays vs. Old Readings: *The Division of the Kingdoms* and Folio Deletions in *King Lear*," in *Studies in Philology*.

explain everything about Edgar—the mystery of things is too great in his case—but his role in the play becomes clearer when we look more closely at his disguise as Poor Tom, the Bedlam beggar, and when we realize that the play's persistent interrogation of the human body's place in the natural and social orders is culminated in Poor Tom's suffering body. We will also see how a link between Poor Tom and Edmund helps clarify Edgar's situation in the play.

My emphasis on Edgar here is not a detour from the main line of the play, for Edgar is the chief point of contact between the Lear and the Gloucester plots. Edgar even received equal billing in the first published version of the play, the 1608 Quarto, whose title page reads: "M. William Shak-speare: His True Chronicle Historie of the life and death of King LEAR and his three Daughters. *With the unfortunate life of* EDGAR, *sonne* and heire to the Earle of Gloster, and his sullen and assumed humor of TOM of Bedlam."[2] If Shakespeare did not compose this title—and he probably did not—at least whoever composed it recognized the importance, and the notorious appeal, of Edgar. Moreover, the paired antithetical attributes given to Edgar on the title page— the "sonne and heire" on the one hand, and the "sullen and assumed humor of Tom of Bedlam" on the other—mark the boundaries of cultural possibility for Edgar.

I

The first reference to Edgar in the play is Gloucester's response to Kent's praise of Edmund: "But I have a son, Sir, by order of law, some year elder than this, who yet is no dearer in my account" (1.1.19–21). This as yet unnamed son—for whom the phrase "by order of law" takes the place of a name—has a legal but avowedly not an emotional advantage in his father's affections over his bastard brother Edmund. The next reference to Edgar— his very naming in the play—is in Edmund's opening soliloquy, where he is called "Legitimate Edgar" (1.2.16), as if the epithet were part of his name. Certainly for the "sonne and heire," created "by order of law," the central fact of his nature seems to be that he is "legitimate." Fine word, legitimate. Edgar's nature seems essentially indistinguishable from the order of law, but in depicting Edgar's dispossession and abasement, the play will suggest that "legitimacy" might be a legal, not a biological category; written, not natural. If one is "got 'tween the lawful sheets" (4.6.119), the adjective "lawful"—a social construct—counts for more than the verb. The ideas of legitimacy and inheritance seem by turn incorporated in the natural body and arbitrarily empowered by the social order. The issue of legitimacy is most clearly

    [2]Quarto quotations are from *King Lear 1608 (Pied Bull Quarto)*, ed. W. W. Greg (Oxford: Clarendon Press, 1939).

articulated in the relationship between Edgar, the "sonne and heire to the Earle of Gloster," and Edmund, got "in the lusty stealth of nature."

Edgar's role as son and heir—the two are not exactly synonymous, we see, since Edmund is also a son but not an heir—figures as the very key Edmund will use to unlock his father's fears; Edmund will himself enact the fantasy of father-replacement which Gloucester would have expected from Edgar. What Edmund wants to do is become someone else, almost anyone else, because he cannot stand himself. His goal is to become Edgar, and he does; and then he becomes his father as well, dispossessing him as he himself was dispossessed. Edmund therefore does not really want to overthrow the legal order when he asks "Wherefore should I / Stand in the plague of custom, and permit / The curiosity of nations to deprive me . . .?" (1.2.2–4), but he wishes rather to render the social order arbitrary, dissociated from the order of nature, and to stand where the order of law has instead placed his brother. Throughout the play, he will speak and write in the stolen or forged voices of his brother and father, endeavoring to replace them by becoming them.

The key moment in Edmund's displacement of Edgar as heir occurs in the famous passage in 1.2., after his now-deluded father leaves the stage and Edmund mocks Gloucester's superstitious empiricism:

> My father compounded with my mother under the dragon's tail, and my nativity was under *Ursa major*; so that it follows I am rough and lecherous. Fut! I should have been that I am had the maidenliest star in the firmament twinkled on my bastardizing. Edgar—[s.d. *Enter* Edgar].
>
> (1.2.128–33)

Precisely as the subject turns to Edmund's bastardizing, pat he comes, Edgar the true son and heir, as if summoned up as the bodily proof of Edmund's bastardy, and as the model of what Edmund would be. The deepest irony in this scene now follows, in the full text of Edmund's aside on Edgar's entrance: "Edgar—and pat he comes, like the catastrophe of the old comedy: my cue is villanous melancholy, with a sigh like Tom o' Bedlam. O! these eclipses do portend these divisions. *Fa, sol, la, mi*" (1.2.140–44). Edmund thus names, by first impersonating, the theatrical role into which Edgar will cast himself, displaced from old comedy to new tragedy, his biological identity subverted into a marginal fiction.[3] Himself speaking *as* Tom o'Bedlam, Edmund sees his own way to "eclipse" the *sol*, the true son, reversing sides of the biological distinction between them. Edmund has therefore *named* both the true son and heir—"Legitimate Edgar"—and his displacement, the pathetic figure of exile—"Tom o'Bedlam"—whose name is not so much a unique name as a

---

[3]The Quarto here reads "them of Bedlam" rather than the "*Tom* o'Bedlam" of the Folio; if "them" is not simply a compositor's misreading, this revision may suggest an attempt to equate Edmund's assumed voice and Edgar's enforced role even more closely. Edmund's own heritage as a Vice figure and the tradition of the Vice's histrionic powers are fully outlined in Bernard Spivack, *Shakespeare and the Allegory of Evil* (New York: Columbia Univ. Press, 1958).

generic label, because Poor Tom is all that is left over when "Legitimate Edgar" vanishes. Indeed, the change in epithets—from "legitimate" to "poor"—signals how Edgar falls from hierarchical privilege to marginality.

Edmund's forgeries quickly work their way on Gloucester, who asks of Edgar incredulously, "Would he deny his letter?" He does not wait for Edmund to reassure him, but rushes to the awful conclusion, "I never got him" (2.1.78). Edgar's biological identity as son—the fact that he was "got" by Gloucester—is renounced, as is Lear's bond to Cordelia, as if it were merely an arbitrary convenience, a matter of the "letter" rather than of blood, and so Edmund becomes the son and heir now. Edmund has indeed produced Edgar's very "character" (1.2.63), taken over his voice, his role, his name, and now his place in his father's eyes; that is one reason why Gloucester will have to lose them. When Edmund gains "no less than all" (3.3.26), his brother and his father are left with no more than nothing.

Edmund's sudden hierarchical rise represents a triumph over his earlier obsession with merely biological reproduction; in forging Edgar's "character," Edmund forces his father to renounce what is natural and to engage in a kind of social reproduction instead—to *name* his (other) son *as heir*. Legitimacy has now been decoupled from the natural body, the "order of law" set aside as arbitrary. It is at precisely this point, however, that we may ask what, exactly, does Edmund gain at the moment of this triumph? The answer is that *Edmund* gains "nothing." He has become at best a ventriloquist, speaking someone else's words, bearing someone else's name. He succeeds (in all senses of the term) only *as* Edgar. Moreover his accession to this particular form of power stems from a violent deviation from the very system that mediates this power. Edmund's project is doomed by self-annihilating contradictions from its inception. Edgar, on the other hand, falls from his status as the son "by order of law" to that of an outlaw exposed to "the winds and persecutions of the sky" (2.3.12), from privilege to persecution.[4] When the legitimate body of the son and heir is displaced, the play reveals a translation of son and heir into man as mere body, as Poor Tom.

II

Long before we see Poor Tom's naked, suffering body, the play has emphasized the ways in which the physical body functions as a contradictory signifier. The play opens with Gloucester displaying Edmund—the body that is both the result of and the public sign of Gloucester's physical and spiritual

---

[4]The play links Gloucester's and Edgar's descents in several ways, and their roles as reflectors of Lear's suffering have been frequently documented; see, e.g., A. C. Bradley, *Shakespearean Tragedy* (1904; rpt. New York: Fawcett, 1968), pp. 215–16; Maynard Mack, King Lear *In Our Time* (Berkeley: Univ. of California Press, 1965), pp. 71–73; and Sigurd Burckhardt, *Shakespearean Meanings* (Princeton: Princeton Univ. Press, 1968), p. 238.

sin. But the physical results here are deceiving, already divided from the moral, for Edmund is handsome (Kent: "the issue of it being so proper," [1.1.17–18]); Edmund will in fact employ the appearance of his body as proof of his fitness to be true son and heir, using nature, ironically, to justify or determine the order of law:

> Why bastard? Wherefore base?
> When my dimensions are as well compact,
> My mind as generous, and my shape as true,
> As honest madam's issue?
>
> (1.2.6–9)

Indeed, he argues, he is superior to the "whole tribe of fops" (1.2.14) who are "legitimate" because he was created "in the lusty stealth of nature" (1.2.11) and therefore takes "more composition and fierce quality" than those conceived legitimately.

Throughout the play, Edmund will rely on his body—and particularly its sexual attractiveness, its "fierce quality"—as much as his wit to advance him. Goneril and Regan feud over him, each worrying whether he has found the "way / To the forfended place" (5.1.10–11) with the other, each claiming him before the other in a public scene. Edmund then re-enacts with them the same fatal quantification and attempted division of love—though now in a grotesque physical mockery—which he has himself suffered, and which Lear has already perpetrated in the opening scene:

> To both these sisters have I sworn my love;
> Each jealous of the other, as the stung
> Are of the adder. Which of them shall I take?
> Both? one? or neither? Neither can be enjoy'd
> If both remain alive. . . .
>
> (5.2.55–59)

Edmund would have to give each half his "love," but the play keeps showing, as even he realizes, that love, by whatever name, cannot be divided. Edmund's method destabilizes the relation between the natural and the social, between his body and its place in a social hierarchy.

When Edmund has been fatally wounded by Edgar, and the news brought that Goneril and Regan are dead, there follows what is sometimes felt to be an awkward piece of Shakespearean staging, Albany's command to "Produce the bodies, be they alive or dead" (5.3.230); Goneril's and Regan's corpses are brought onstage several lines later. This staging can be defended as necessary to produce a terrible symmetry between the opening and the final scenes of the play—once Cordelia's body is brought in, all three of the daughters are onstage together again, with all the horrible ironies associated. I find this argument persuasive, but would argue as well that it is the presence of the *body* that is essential here, the physical fact that drives home the point. Moreover, Albany goes on with another, even stranger command to "Cover their faces" (5.3.242), so that only their bodies remain visible. When Cordelia's body is carried on, by contrast, her face is *not* covered, for we always need to see Cordelia's lips, and she always represents more than simply her body: her words are all. With Goneril and Regan, however, we are left with the bodies *qua* bodies, for that is all they were and are. Edmund's body, on the other hand, is borne off the stage just as Cordelia's is brought on. His offstage death befits the disappearance of his role; no longer the Earl of Gloucester, his identity as son and heir taken back by Edgar, his body simply vanishes. His death is like his marginal social status, "but a trifle" (5.3.295).

The play's emphasis on the bodies of Edmund, Gloucester, Goneril and Regan—Nature in its basest form—leads us inevitably to the body of Edgar as well: as the outcast beggar, he incarnates everything antithetical to the "order of law" represented in his initial identity. The name of loss and exile, of suffering and abasement, is Poor Tom. When Edmund becomes the son and heir, Edgar is left with nothing but his own body—the residue remaining once all the "bonds" of life and social order have been stripped away. Caroline Spurgeon long ago noted that perhaps the key recurring image in *King Lear* was that "of a human body in anguished movement, tugged, wrenched, beaten, pierced, stung, scourged, dislocated, flayed, gashed, scalded, tortured and finally broken on the rack."[5] Such a body is quite literally before us in the middle of the play in the figure of Poor Tom.

III

Much recent commentary has been very critical of Edgar's actions while in the disguise of Poor Tom, though there are still strong defenders of Edgar's essential goodness throughout.[6] Still, even those who find fault with Edgar

[5]Caroline F. E. Spurgeon, *Shakespeare's Imagery And What It Tells Us* (New York: Macmillan, 1935), p. 339.
[6]A representative negative view of Edgar may be found in Marvin D. Rosenberg, *The Masks of King Lear* (Berkeley: Univ. of California Press, 1972); Rosenberg questions Edgar's stated motives throughout while arguing for the presence of "motives of revenge and punishment" (p. 266); "Edgar," he says, "hates well" (p. 245). To S. L. Goldberg (*An Essay on* King Lear [Cambridge: Cambridge Univ. Press, 1974]), "Edgar is the most lethal character in the play" (p. 121). For Stanley Cavell, *Must We Mean What We Say?* (New York: Scribner's, 1969), "Edgar's capacity for cruelty [is] the *same* cruelty as that of the evil characters" (p. 283). The sentimentalizing tradition of the ideal Edgar is of much longer standing but equally one-sided. To Edgar A. Peers, *Elizabethan Drama and Its Mad Folk* (Cambridge: Heffer, 1914), "Edgar is Shakespeare at his best and truest—he rings true—we may even say that he stands for Truth itself" (p. 173). In *Prefaces to Shakespeare First Series* (London: Sidgwick & Jackson, 1927), Harley Granville-Barker concludes that Edgar became "a man of character indeed, modest, of a discerning mind, and, in this pagan play, a very Christian gentleman" (p. 213). Two recent essays have presented a more complex, and to me a more persuasive view of Edgar: Janet Adelman, "Introduction" to *Twentieth Century Interpretations of* King Lear (Englewood Cliffs, N.J.: Prentice-Hall, 1978), and Harry Berger, Jr., "Text Against Performance: The Gloucester Family Romance," in *Shakespeare's "Rough Magic": Renaissance Essays in Honor of C. L. Barber*, eds. Peter Erickson and Coppélia Kahn (Newark: Univ. of Delaware Press, 1985).

have tended to sentimentalize or even ignore the meaning of the disguise as Poor Tom. To understand how nasty and repulsive Tom o'Bedlam might have seemed to Shakespeare's audience, and to see at least one reason why Shakespeare chose this particular disguise for Edgar rather than some other, we need to separate Poor Tom from Edgar.[7] For most of Shakespeare's audience, Tom o'Bedlam would not have been a figure to pity, but one to flee; not a Dickensian figure reduced in circumstances by an unjust social order, but something of a charlatan. That Tom *becomes* pitiable and a figure eliciting our sympathy is more the result of our seeing Edgar *within* Tom; on the surface, Tom o'Bedlam is a figure of disturbing deformity. As Michael Goldman has noted, Edgar is the kind of beggar "that you pay . . . to go away . . . and certainly not the decent young man down on his luck that actors frequently portray him to be. He is the kind that sticks his stump in your face."[8] If we can overcome the terror of the body that Tom represents, and even care for his welfare, as Lear learns to do, so much greater the triumph.

Poor Tom is, of course, a lunatic beggar, an escaped or released inmate of Bethlehem (or Bedlam) Hospital.[9] Yet for Elizabethans he was also a stereotype of the con man, one who "fayned himself mad," "fayned himself a bedlam inmate," his mug-shot a regular feature in the sixteenth-century equivalent of the post office—the dozens of books, pamphlets, and royal decrees on the rogues and vagabonds of the kingdom.[10] Also known as an "Abraham" or

[7]Most accounts of Poor Tom take the connection (or lack of it) between Edgar and Poor Tom as their subject; see, e.g., Janet Adelman: "Despite Edgar's attempt to keep himself separate from Poor Tom, the likeness between Edgar and Poor Tom is finally as striking as the difference" (*Twentieth Century Interpretations of* King Lear, [p. 15]); and Russell A. Peck, "Edgar's Pilgrimage: High Comedy in King Lear," *Studies in English Literature*, 7 (1967): "Edgar capitalizes on this mad role of the sin-infected man to make of his 'Poor Tom of Bedlam' identity a kind of scapegoat" (p. 228).

[8]Michael Goldman, *Shakespeare and the Energies of Drama* (Princeton: Princeton Univ. Press, 1972), pp. 97–98. Goldman insists that on the stage "Edgar must be filthy, grotesque, very nearly naked, and bear on his body evidence of horrible mutilation" (p. 97). Cf. Marvin Rosenberg (*Masks of* King Lear, cited in note 6) on the theatrical necessity of Edgar's nakedness: "The visible, anguished, animal body enduring physical pain is again central to the ritual design, though its caperings and language may be grotesquely comic" (p. 217).

[9]A convenient short history of the hospital may be found on pages 1–39 of Robert R. Reed, Jr., *Bedlam on the Jacobean Stage* (1952; rpt. New York: Octagon, 1970).

[10]See Frank Aydelotte, *Elizabethan Rogues and Vagabonds* (1913; rpt. New York: Barnes & Noble, 1967), and Frank W. Chandler, *The Literature of Roguery* (New York: Houghton Mifflin, 1907) for general background. The historical context of beggars and vagabonds in Tudor England is concisely set forth by G. R. Elton, *England Under the Tudors* (London: Methuen, 1974), pp. 188–90 and 260–61; and by D. M. Palliser, *The Age of Elizabeth 1547–1603* (London: Longman, 1983), pp. 93–94 and 119–25. The most useful book-length study of the wandering homeless is A. L. Beier, *Masterless Men: The Vagrancy Problem in England 1560–1640* (London: Methuen, 1985).

The larger questions of the relation between "literary" and "historical" texts—the questions surrounding the work of recent historicist criticism—are beyond the scope of this paper; these issues are addressed at length in my forthcoming study, *Vagrancy and Marginality in Elizabethan Literature*. In brief, the representation of the Bedlam beggar, in my view, illustrates what Jean Howard has recently described as one of the central tenets of historicist criticism: "Rather than passively reflecting an external reality, literature is an agent in constructing a culture's sense of

"Abram" man,[11] he appears—along with other vagabonds and rogues such as "Rufflers," "Palliards," "Swadders," "Mortes," "Doxes," and "Kinching cooes"— in such works as John Awdeley's *The Fraternitye of Vacabondes* (1561), Thomas Harman's *A Caveat or Warening for Common Cursetors* (1566), William Harrison's "Description of England" (prefixed to the 1577 and 1587 editions of Holinshed's *Chronicles*), and in Thomas Dekker's *The Belman of London* (1608) and *O per se O* (1612), among many other places. For Awdeley, "An Abraham man is he that walketh bare armed, and bare legged, fayneth hym selfe mad, and caryeth a packe of wool, or a stycke with baken on it, or such lyke toy, and nameth himselfe poore Tom."[12] Harman begins his description in similar terms: "These Abrahom men be those that fayne themselues to haue beene mad, and haue bene kept eyther in Bethelem or in some other pryson a good tyme, *and* not one amongst twenty that euer came in pryson for any such cause: yet wyll they saye howe pitiously and most extreamely they haue bene beaten, and dealt with all. . . . [F]or feare[,] the maydes wyll geue theym [money] largely to be ryd of theym."[13]

In many contemporary accounts, these men are a species of actor— costumes, rhetoric, feigned gestures, and familiar street plots remain the same within the individual variation.[14] "Every one of these *Abrams* hath a seuerall gesture in playing his part," Dekker reports in *O per se O*: "Some make an horrid noyse, hollowly sounding: some whoope, some hollow, some

reality. It is part of a much larger symbolic order through which the world at a particular historical moment is conceptualized and through which a culture imagines its relationship to the actual conditions of its existence" ("The New Historicism in Renaissance Studies," *English Literary Renaissance*, 16 [1986], 13–43, esp. p. 25). Michael MacDonald, in his important study *Mystical Bedlam: Madness, Anxiety, and Healing in Seventeenth-Century England* (Cambridge and New York: Cambridge Univ. Press, 1981), offers a concrete instance of Howard's generalization in the case of the cultural representation of madness, showing how "Abraham men, beggars who pretended to be Bedlamites, and Mad Toms" along with "the popularity of stage lunatics and real madmen and the proliferation of words and phrases describing or invoking insanity" reflected "the diffusion of generally understood stereotypes of insanity" (p. 122). Most of the examples I employ in this essay are literary or quasi-journalistic—the rogue pamphlets are notoriously unreliable—but comparable archival evidence is plentiful.

[11]The usual explanation for the term "Abraham" is that it "may come from a ward in the hospital" (Beier, p. 115); the earliest usage registered by the OED is from Awdeley (1561). The most authoritative history of the hospital, however—Patricia Allderidge, "Management and Mismanagement at Bedlam, 1547–1633," in *Health, medicine, and mortality in the sixteenth century*, ed. Charles Webster (Cambridge: Cambridge Univ. Press, 1979), pp. 141–64—makes no reference to the existence of such a ward. Since the hospital had only two areas where patients slept at this time, the term "ward" seems a little grandiose; Allderidge reproduces the original groundplan of the hospital on page 146 of her essay.

[12]*The Rogues and Vagabonds of Shakespeare's Youth:* [John] Awdeley's *The Fraternitye of Vacabondes* and [Thomas] Harman's *A Caveat or Warening for Common Cursetors*, eds. Edward Viles and F. J. Furnivall (London: Chatto and Windus, 1907), p. 3.

[13]*Rogues and Vagabonds*, p. 47.

[14]Dekker describes the costume: "hee goes without breeches, a cut Jerkin with hanging sleeves (in imitation of our Gallants,) but no Sattin or Chamblet elbowes, for both his legges and armes are bare. . . . A face staring like a Sarasin, his hayre long and filthily knotted . . . a good . . . Staffe of growne Ash, or else Hazell, in his . . . Hand" (*O per se O* [London: John Busbie, 1612]).

shewe onely a kind of wild distracted ugly looke. . . ." The cumulative effect, Dekker says, is that these men, "walking up and downe the Countrey, are more terribly to women and Children, than the name of *Raw-head* and *Bloudy-bones, Robbin Good-fellow,* or any other Hobgobling. Crackers tyed to the Dogges tayle, make not the poore Curre runne faster, then these *Abram Ninnies* doe the silly Village[r]s of the Countrey, so that when they come to any doore a begging, nothing is denyed them."[15]

Both the rogue pamphlets and official documents frequently mention the mutilated bodies of these "Bedlamites," and warn against their fraud. Thus in *The Belman of London,* Dekker describes one of them who

> sweares hee hath beene in Bedlam, and will talke frantickly of purpose: you see pinnes stuck in sundrie places of his naked flesh, especially in his armes, which paine hee gladly puts himselfe to . . . onely to make you beleeve hee is out of his wits: he calls himselfe by the name of *Poore Tom,* and comming neere any body cries out *Poore Tom* is a colde.[16]

Some contemporaries even provided, in a debunking if voyeuristic spirit, recipes and advice on temporary self-mutilation; Harrison describes the "making of corrosives, and applying the same to the more fleshie parts of their bodies: and also laying of Ratsbane, Sperewoort, Crowfoote, and such like unto their whole members, thereby to raise piteous and odious sores, and moove [the harts of] the goers by such places where they lie, to lament their miserie, and [thereupon] bestowe large almes upon them."[17] In *O per se O,* Dekker observes that some of them

> have the Letters E. and R. upon their armes: some have Crosses, and some other marke, all of them carrying a blew colour. . . . Which markes are printed upon their flesh, by tying their arme hard with two strings three or foure inches asunder, and then with a sharpe Awle pricking or raizing the skinne, to such a figure or print as they best fancy. They rub that place with burnt paper, pisse and Gunpowder, which being hard rubd in, and suffered to dry, stickes in the flesh a long time after. When these marks faile, they renew them at pleasure. If you examine them how these Letters or Figures are printed upon their armes, they will tell you it is the Marke of Bedlam, but the truth is, they are made as I have reported.[18]

The self-mutilations of fraudulent beggars are deeply ironic, for these marks become the self-confirming stigmata of those excluded from society; they write their humiliation at large on their skins as an acceptance of what the social order has already inscribed them to be.[19]

[15]*O per se O.*

[16]Thomas Dekker, *The Belman of London* (London: Nathaniel Butter, 1608).

[17]Raphael Holinshed, *The Firste volume of the Chronicles of England, Scotlande, and Irelande* (London: Lucas Harrison, 1577).

[18]*O per se O.*

[19]In a yet more disturbing irony, the punishment for being arrested and convicted as a vagabond was a further but real and lasting mutilation of the body. The marks of the sovereign were to be inscribed on the body of the beggar, frequently as a hole "burned thorow the gristell of

Two points stand out in this strange eventful social history. First, Poor Tom o'Bedlam or the Abraham man was a widely known figure, a social stereotype of the underclass; he is described, and reviled, in both popular and legal literature from the mid-sixteenth century on. If he later becomes sentimental-ized (the "Loving Mad Tom" of the ballads[20]), there is no doubt that he began life primarily as a fraud: he "fayneth hym selfe mad" (Awdeley); "not one amongst twenty that ever came in pryson for any such cause" (Harman). Rather than eliciting pity, these vagabonds seemed to excite something more in the way of amusement, fear, and contempt.

The phenomenon of the fraudulent Bedlamite apparently endured late into the seventeenth century: the governors of Bethlehem Hospital found it necessary, in 1675, to state in public notice,

> Whereas several vagrant persons do wander about . . . pretending themselves to be lunatics under cure in the Hospital of Bethlem commonly called Bedlam, with brass plates about their arms and inscriptions thereon: These are to give notice that there is no such liberty given . . . , neither is any such plate as a distinction or mark put upon any lunatic during their being there, or when discharged thence. And that the same is a false pretence, to colour their wandering and begging, and to deceive the people. . . .[21]

It would not be too much to say, in the end, that the role of Poor Tom was usually conceived of by the culture at large as a theatrical fiction.[22]

The second point that stands out in the history of Poor Tom, and that takes on the utmost importance in *King Lear*, is the emphasis, through Tom, on the body. Poor Tom of Bedlam is, after all, allegedly someone who has lost his mind, and so has only his body left, his language fractured into disordered fragments. The multilations of his body reflect this disorder and monstrosity. Above all, Poor Tom *used* his body as a means of forcing his will on the populace, by assaulting men's senses: people gave them money partly out of

---

the right eare," as Harrison noted (Holinshed, fol. 107r). A second offense meant the other ear, a third the punishment of death. The feigned wounds became the cause and the proleptic sign of real ones, and the real mutilations both the sign of and the punishment for the crime, in a reciprocal economy of pain which eerily anticipates Kafka's "In the Penal Colony." For a stimulating related study which takes up similar questions of punishment and signification, see Michel Foucault's *Discipline and Punish: The Birth of the Prison* (New York: Vintage, 1979), esp. pp. 3–69.

    [20]See *Loving Mad Tom: Bedlamite Verses of the XVI and XVII Centuries*, ed. Jack Lindsay (1927; rpt. New York: Augustus M. Kelley, 1970).

    [21]Quoted in Gamini Salgado, *The Elizabethan Underworld* (London: J. M. Dent, 1977), p. 198.

    [22]Approaching the play from his analysis of Harsnett and the fraudulent Catholic exorcisms of 1585–86, Stephen Greenblatt notes that "Shakespeare appropriates for Edgar . . . a documented fraud," a "model of inauthenticity" ("Shakespeare and the Exorcists," in *Shakespeare and the Question of Theory*, eds. Patricia Parker and Geoffrey Hartmam [London: Methuen, 1985], p. 175). After reviewing archival and historical documents, however, Beier (cited in note 10, above) cautions that "Such contradictory evidence suggests that it would be unwise to accept the literary portrayal of all Tom O'Bedlam men as impostors," p. 117; see his discussion, pp. 110–19.

sympathy, but "largely to be ryd of them," Harman notes; "when they come to any doore a begging," Dekker concurs, "nothing is denied them."

Nothing is denied them: no wonder Edgar, who has become nothing by being denied, finds Poor Tom such an appropriate disguise. Against these contemporary accounts of Poor Tom, let me now quote Edgar's soliloquy as he turns himself into a Shakespearean Poor Tom:

> Whiles I may 'scape,
> I will preserve myself; and am bethought
> To take the basest and most poorest shape
> That ever penury, in contempt of man,
> Brought near to beast; my face I'll grime with filth,
> Blanket my loins, elf all my hairs in knots,
> And with presented nakedness outface
> The winds and persecutions of the sky.
> The country gives me proof and precedent
> Of Bedlam beggars, who, with roaring voices,
> Strike in their numb'd and mortified bare arms
> Pins, wooden pricks, nails, sprigs of rosemary;
> And with this horrible object, from low farms,
> Poor pelting villages, sheep-cotes, and mills,
> Sometime with lunatic bans, sometime with prayers,
> Enforce their charity. Poor Turlygod! poor Tom!
> That's something yet: Edgar I nothing am.
> (2.3.5–21)

Edgar's self-description follows the tradition closely, as he takes on the part with all its theatrical implications—grimed face, presented nakedness, roaring voice—and disappears into "nothing," into Tom's body. The gap between Tom's "basest and most poorest shape" and Edmund's "shape as true, / As honest madam's issue" seems absolute.

During the heath scene, Lear says to, or of, Tom, "Thou wert better in a grave than to answer with thy uncover'd body this extremity of the skies" (3.4.103–5). For Lear, though not for those aware of who Tom is, the beggar's shivering, near-naked body is "the thing itself; unaccommodated man[,] . . . a poor, bare, forked animal" (3.4.109–11). Lear's vision is powerful but incomplete: when he asks of Tom, "Is man no more than this?" we want to reply "Yes, much more," for the entire role of Poor Tom, as we have seen, is a complicated fiction. Tom is *always* "more than this," because he is always Edgar-as-Tom, and Edgar-as-Tom's suffering is in part a *performance* of marginality, exclusion, and dispossession. What seems to be the basest shape of nature is also seen by the audience to be a social construct: a stereotypical beggar's role fantastically performed by an Edgar who far out-tops even his brother's histrionic genius.

Yet "sophisticated" as he is, Edgar nevertheless still feels, in all its real pain, the role he performs. The burden of both playing and being such a creature as Poor Tom is very heavy for Edgar, the more so because Edgar's impersonation of Poor Tom is a particularly graphic and horrifying instance. "What are you there?" Gloucester asks, and Edgar tells him, with a vengeance:

> Poor Tom; that eats the swimming frog, the toad, the todpole, the wall-newt, and the water; that in the fury of his heart, when the foul fiend rages, eats cow-dung for sallets; swallows the old rat and the ditch-dog; drinks the green mantle of the standing pool; who is whipp'd from tithing to tithing, and stock-punish'd, and imprison'd; who hath had three suits to his back, six shirts to his body,
> *Horse to ride, and weapons to wear,*
> *But mice and rats and such small deer,*
> *Have been Tom's food for seven long year.*
>   (3.4.132–43)[23]

Tom seems little more than an embodied mouth here, a paradigm of mere appetite ingesting the scum of nature. This relentless emphasis on the physical body—what it eats, how it is punished, what it wears—marks Tom's complete fall to the bottom of the lake of darkness, making Lear's belief that "our basest beggars / Are in the poorest thing superfluous" (2.4.266–67) seem optimistic by comparison. To be Tom at all is to feign *and* to endure grotesque physical torment.

The play's insistence on the suffering of the body is not confined to the Gloucester plot, to be sure, but it is represented most intensely there. Certainly Lear, Kent, and Cordelia endure their own physical tortures. As terrible as it is to shut an old man out in a storm, however, Lear's greatest punishments, in keeping with the nature of his transgression, are suffered in the heart. "We are not ourselves," he says, "When Nature, being oppress'd, commands the mind / To suffer with the body" (2.4.107–9). When an image of bodily torture, such as the rack, is used with respect to Lear, it is the "rack of this tough world" (5.3.314), but it is Gloucester who is physically bound, tormented, and blinded. When Lear feels as if he is "bound / Upon a wheel of fire, that mine own tears / Do scald like molten lead" (4.7.46–48), his suffering is internalized, the image figurative, though no less powerful or "real." And when Lear is cut, he is "cut to th' brains" (4.6.195), in an exquisite agony of suffering and despair, but it is Poor Tom who would actually lacerate his "numb'd and mortified bare arms," and Edmund who will enact the "queasy question" (2.1.18) by cutting his own arm while claiming that Edgar "With his prepared sword . . . charges home / My unprovided body, lanch'd mine arm" (2.1.51–52). Lear's insight that "When the mind's free / The body's delicate"

23The verbal links to other characters in the play—Kent is also "stock-punish'd" in 2.2., Oswald is called "three-suited" at 2.2.14—again make Edgar's experience refract that of others.

(3.4.11–12) is transformed, for Edgar, into overwhelming bodily pain as a cause, consequence, and sign of mental suffering.

The great irony of the figure of Poor Tom is that while it is his body that endures mutilation and deprivation, it is Edgar's spirit that is trapped within, and Edgar—who would "the pain of death . . . hourly die / Rather than die at once" (5.3.185–86)—suffers spiritually. Most of us have always seen Tom as the embodiment of Edgar's suffering even as he is also a way of escaping it,[24] but we should also recognize, as noted earlier, how Poor Tom is in a sense the *cause* of Edgar's suffering. Edgar's suffering is both released and caused by his performance of Tom's suffering.

To be Poor Tom is Edgar's trial. And in becoming, as it were, all body, subjected to nature, Edgar is forced to live out a grotesque version of what it must be like to be Edmund. Poor Tom's sufferings are therefore not only Edgar's—it is clear how his own personal pain is transmitted through this hideous disguise—but they are Edmund's as well. Displacement links them together, as does their fate to be nothing more than natural bodies, forbidden by law or culture from any place in the social hierarchy. The link between Edmund and Poor Tom is thus both implicit (Poor Tom appears only when Edmund has displaced Edgar, and disappears when the son and heir is reunited with his father) and explicit (Edmund first performs the voice of Poor Tom). Facing yet another banishment by his father—"He hath been out nine years, and away he shall again" (1.1.32–33). Edmund has carefully engineered his plot so that he and his brother will be forced to exchange places: the category of "sonne and heire" and social outcast will be reversed; "the base / Shall top th'legitimate" (1.2.20–21) only to replace it. Edgar has not chosen to be cast out, but (though no explicit motive is articulated for him) he has chosen this enforced role—and it fits him perfectly.

IV

The place where Edgar is freed and Poor Tom vanishes is Dover Cliff. Poor Tom o'Bedlam is both "some fiend," as Edgar says (4.6.72), and "a poor unfortunate beggar" (4.6.68), as Gloucester says, and in 4.6 Edgar is released from the "fiend." The process begins with Gloucester's unexpected tenderness, when he asks the Old Man leading him to "bring some covering for this naked soul, / Which I'll entreat to lead me" (4.1.44–45). The significance of the clothing theme, as R. B. Heilman and others have shown,[25] is reflected on

---

[24]Adelman argues that Edgar "tries more insistently than any other character to gain some distance on suffering, and hence relief from it" (p. 3), and that "Edgar's disguises throughout are emblematic partly of Edgar's own distance from what he can recognize as himself" (p. 19).

[25]See R. B. Heilman, *This Great Stage* (1948; rpt. Westport, Conn.: Greenwood Press, 1963), pp. 67–87.

several interpretive levels, but I am interested in it here on the most literal of levels: the "naked soul" will be clothed, the body veiled.

Although he continues on as Poor Tom through much of 4.6, Edgar almost immediately, upon Gloucester's request to the Old Man, begins to emerge from the body of Poor Tom. It is not Tom the "fiend" but the poor unfortunate beggar "whom the heav'ns' plagues / Have humbled to all strokes" (4.1.64–65) who stands in Gloucester's imagination, a Poor Tom whom the devils have released and who therefore has begun the process of turning back into Edgar. That process of self-return is dramatically accelerated in 4.6., beginning with Edgar's entrance wearing clothes. To Gloucester's sense that Edgar's "voice is alter'd," he deviously and ambiguously replies, "You're much deceiv'd; in nothing am I chang'd / But in my garments" (4.6.9–10).

Most discussions of the Dover Cliff scene have focused either on the nature of Edgar's motivation toward his father—"Why I do trifle thus with his despair / Is done to cure it" (4.6.33–34), he says—or on the staging of the scene and its illusory quality.[26] I would like to consider the scene also as a "cure" or final exorcism of Poor Tom. In one way, the cure has already occurred: Tom has spoken of the five fiends once in his body, now apparently gone, and has entered 4.6. with new clothing and altered speech. The famous image Edgar creates of the view from the cliff—"The crows and choughs that wing the midway air / Show scarce so gross as beetles"—contains perhaps more detail than even Gloucester needs to convince him of where he stands (he has condemned his true son on less). The perspective Edgar imagines which makes a man seem "no bigger than his head," and the "fishermen that walk upon the beach / Appear like mice" is created, I think, as much for Edgar's own sake as it is for Gloucester's. This view of man "brought near to beast," in which there is no sign of a human figure but only crows, choughs, beetles, and mice, represents both Gloucester's view of the world as he prepares to attempt suicide and Edgar's experience as Poor Tom. When Edgar says "I'll look no more, / Lest my brain turn, and the deficient sight / Topple down headlong," he is not only trying to convince Gloucester that they are "within a foot / Of th'extreme verge," but also speaking for himself as he turns away from the role of Tom.

After Gloucester's dramatic "fall," Edgar asks his father the same question—"What are you, sir?" (4.6.48)—that his father had directed at him when he was Poor Tom—"What are you there? Your names?" (3.4.131). The

26On the staging, see among others Harry Levin, "The Heights and the Depths: A Scene from *King Lear," More Talking of Shakespeare*, ed. John Garrett (London: Longman, 1959); Alvin Kernan, "Formalism and Realism in Elizabethan Drama: The Miracles of *King Lear," Renaissance Drama*, 9 (1966), 59–66; Marvin Rosenberg, *The Masks of King Lear*, pp. 264–65; Alan C. Dessen, "Two Falls and a Trap: Shakespeare and the Spectacles of Realism," *ELR*, 5 (1975), 291–307; and Derek Peat, " 'And that's true too': *King Lear* and the Tension of Uncertainty," *Shakespeare Survey*, 33 (1980), 43–53. On the cliff scene's iconoclastic nature, see the stimulating discussion by James R. Siemon, *Shakespearean Iconoclasm* (Berkeley: Univ. of California Press, 1985), pp. 269–73.

fall from top to bottom, "so many fathom down" (4.6.50), is also a refraction of Edgar's fall, who as Poor Tom was "fathom and half" down. For Edgar, the fall as Poor Tom is over, his life also a miracle. When Edgar describes the figure he was, fictively standing at the top of the cliff, he turns out to have been a kind of cosmological monster:

> As I stood here below methought his eyes
> Were two full moons; he had a thousand noses,
> Horns whelk'd and wav'd like the enridged sea:
> It was some fiend. . . .
>
> (4.6.69–72)

That is what it felt like to be Poor Tom: to live in the body of a nightmare. The "fiend" left behind on the cliff is gone forever. When Gloucester turns the iterated question of identity back on Edgar later in the scene—"Now, good sir, what are you?" (4.6.221)—Edgar's response completes the full transition from the fiend to a man, his reply evocative of both his father's and of Lear's new-found capacities to *feel*: "A most poor man, made [lame by] Fortune's blows; / Who, by the art of known and feeling sorrows, / Am pregnant to good pity."[27]

Edgar's transition from the role of suffering madman to his father's active guide receives an immediate test in the challenge of Oswald, who enters the scene exactly at the moment that Edgar's identity has shifted: pat he comes like the catastrophe of the old morality. Now Edgar plays a "bold peasant" to Oswald and adopts a country dialect. He has risen on the social scale above the level of beast and beggar, but he remains displaced from the court, where he was heir to an earl; "good gentleman," he humbly asks Oswald, "let poor volk pass," but the poor have no rights of passage in this play. Edgar's judgment upon Oswald, whom he easily kills, is that he was "a serviceable villain"—the adjective of course linking Oswald with Edmund. Throughout the play Oswald has represented one of the deepest perversions of human bonds, the destruction of "service" in its widest sense, and Poor Tom has described his own history in terms that recall Oswald and Edmund in particular:

> A servingman, proud in heart and mind; that curl'd my hair, wore gloves in my cap, serv'd the lust of my mistress' heart, and did the act of darkness with her; swore as many oaths as I spake words, and broke them in the sweet face of Heaven; one that slept in the contriving of lust, and wak'd to do it. Wine lov'd I deeply, dice dearly, and in woman out-paramour'd the Turk: false of heart, light of ear, bloody of hand; hog in sloth, fox in stealth, wolf in greediness, dog in madness, lion in prey.
>
> (3.4.85–95)

Poor Tom's self-description emphasizes the body in all ways—the vanity of

---

[27]I prefer the Quarto's "lame by" to the Folio's "tame to" because it reinforces the subplot's emphasis on the physical body.

physical appearance, the urgings of the sensual appetite, the bestial identification. He describes his life as a Fall: from serving-man to beggar, from the
court to the heath, from vanity to madness, from a place in the hierarchy to
the level of the beasts.[28] Edgar-as-Tom's description of his earlier life as son
and heir transforms it into its opposite, that of a "servingman," his former
position of hierarchical privilege now seen to be really one of subservience. In
slaying Oswald, Edgar destroys yet another parodic alter ego of Edmund.

V

The final confrontation between the true son and heir and the new son and
heir occurs in a scene of ritual combat; as in any doppelgänger tale, one must
be vanquished. Summoned by the third sound of the trumpet, Edgar appears
as an unknown but noble soldier. As we might expect, only his body can be
seen, for his face is covered, his anonymity and facelessness a reflection of
Edmund's own marginality and emptiness. Edmund knows better than to
trust a fair shape, but does so anyway, seeming to find something naturally
noble in the figure before him:

> In wisdom I should ask thy name;
> But since thy outside looks so fair and war-like,
> And that thy tongue some say of breeding breathes,
> What safe and nicely I might well delay
> By rule of knighthood, I disdain and spurn. . . .
> (5.3.141–45)

Had Edmund indeed asked him his name, it would have done little good.
Edgar's response to the herald's now familiar question of identity, "What are
you? / Your name? your quality?" is necessarily cryptic, reflecting his still
indeterminate place in any hierarchy:

> Know, my name is lost;
> By treason's tooth bare-gnawn, and canker-bit:
> Yet am I noble as the adversary
> I come to cope.
> (5.3.121–24)

The distinction made between his name and the knowledge of his own
nobility is not merely paradoxical, for now his name "by order of law"—with
his father dead offstage—is the Earl of Gloucester, a name, however, now
appropriated by Edmund. Moreover, his name is clearly something separable
from his body: it can be "lost," and found again. When Edmund forgives his

---

[28]As several readers have noticed, Kent's verbal attack on Oswald in 2.2. corresponds closely
to Tom's self-description; see, e.g., Leo Kirschbaum, "Banquo and Edgar: Character or Function,"
Essays in Criticism, 7 (1957), 1–21, esp. p. 15.

still unknown assailant after their battle and pronounces his own death, Edgar is at last allowed to reclaim his status as the son and heir:

> Let's exchange charity.
> I am no less in blood than thou art, Edmund;
> If more, the more th'hast wrong'd me.
> My name is Edgar, and thy father's son.
>   (5.3.166–69)

But if Edgar is "no less in blood" than his brother, then Edmund's chief motive for doing evil has been a colossal mistake; of course Edgar is "more" in blood, in nature, yet he speaks here as if he might be less—as if he were Edmund. He speaks, then, no longer from a privileged but from a marginal position, reclaiming his name as if it were only a piece of missing property— we might recall, for contrast, Hamlet's more forceful, "This is I, / Hamlet the Dane!"

The uniqueness of Edgar's proper name—already compromised in the repetition of the "Ed" sound in Edmund's—is further diluted by the odd grammar of his speech, so that his *full* name is really two things: "Edgar and thy father's son." In this formulation, the uniqueness of "Edgar" is subverted by the ambiguity of "thy father's son," since Edmund himself fulfills that category as well. Edgar's claim, moreover, is expressed in the most indirect way possible: he tells Edmund that he, Edgar, is "thy father's son." While this establishes a human and fraternal bond with Edmund, it is also a displace-ment of his identity, through the father and the half-brother, elevating Edmund to co-equal status and implying that Gloucester was first Edmund's father. Again, it sounds as if it is the claim Edmund would make, as Edgar seems to give away the very principles that made him son and heir. It is as if Edgar has realized the arbitrariness within the system of social privilege, and can no longer claim his body as an absolute against which the social order must be measured; rather the reverse seems the case now. He has *been* Poor Tom long enough to know the pain of dispossession, and in returning as Edgar he seems vastly more tentative now. The apparent allegorical clarity of the ritual battle with Edmund is soon complicated by Edmund's change of heart, and by Edgar's ineffectualness at the end of the play.

Edgar's self-denial does not extend much further, however. His experience of dispossession has perhaps allowed him a deeper vision of the world, but it has also embittered him, so that his moral judgment on Edmund and Gloucester is harsh indeed:

> The Gods are just, and of our pleasant vices
> Make instruments to plague us;
> The dark and vicious place where thee he got
> Cost him his eyes.
>   (5.3.170–73)

Edmund's ready agreement—"Th'hast spoken right, 'tis true"—may surprise more liberal modern audiences, but by this point we should really expect that the subplot will insist on an unforgiving economy of the body, in which a bodily sin redounds upon the body, one dark place leading to another.

Edgar is our guide to one kind of suffering throughout the play—the pain of the body—his body as Poor Tom not just an instance of but also an enforced performance of extreme pain and deprivation. There is nothing at all ironic in this role, and yet the nature of Poor Tom has reflected ironically on Lear. Poor Tom's only function is to beg, but more than that, to use the horror of his deformity and degradation to make us feel guilty, to make us question the integrity of our own bodies; such beggars, Edgar said, would "Enforce their charity" (2.3.20). This formulation presents undoubtedly the most powerful oxymoron in the play—the idea that anyone could "enforce" charity.[29]

As Poor Tom, Edgar has *performed* the role of suffering and marginalization, but has also profoundly experienced it, just as the counterfeit madmen of the period may have feigned self-mutilations that were essentially indistinguishable from the real thing. This disguise is an escape for Edgar, because it saves his life; it is a release for him, because he can allow his own bitter fury to be anonymously released through the madman's voice; it is a deep necessity, because through it he can beg for the love that has been denied him; and finally, it is a torment to him, as much the cause as the relief of his suffering. To be dispossessed, to be stripped of all social bonds, to be reduced to the basest and most poorest shape, to surrender one's body to the winds and persecutions of the sky—this experience of alienation forces Edgar to *feel* what it must, in part, be like to *be* his bastard brother, Edmund. These half-brothers exchange the voice of dispossession in the course of the play: as Edgar disappears into Tom when Edmund becomes Earl of Gloucester, so Edmund disappears altogether when Edgar becomes Earl of Gloucester.

At the very end, the biological order of succession has been shattered, and the legal order of succession is abrogated. No one looks much like a king: Lear is dead, Kent dying, Albany blindly ineffectual, Edgar mostly a bystander, succeeding to the throne—if that, in fact, is what the Folio's lines imply— only through catastrophe.[30] Nevertheless, through his suffering Edgar can be said to have earned it; the way down has been the way up. The wonder is he hath endured so long.

[29]The word "charity" is used only in the subplot, where it refracts the failure of love so evident in the main plot: Tom bids us, "Do poor Tom some charity" (3.4.60), Gloucester wishes that "my charity be not of him perceiv'd" (3.3.16–17), and Edgar, after he has mortally wounded Edmund and in response to Edmund's forgiveness, says "Let's exchange charity" (5.3.166). To "enforce" charity seems to be a continuing concern in the subplot.

[30]Clearly, I accept the Folio's attribution of the final four lines to Edgar rather than the Quarto's attribution of them to Albany.

Chronology of Important Dates

	Shakespeare's Life	*Other Events*
1564	Baptized April 26, at Stratford-upon-Avon (born April 23?).	Sixth year of Elizabeth's reign. She is 31 years old.
1576		James Burbage builds The Theater, first permanent playhouse in England, on the outskirts of London.
1582	Marriage to Anne Hathaway.	
1583	Daughter Susanna born.	
1585	Twins (Hamnet and Judith) born.	
1587		Death of Mary Stuart. Rose Playhouse built on the Bankside.
1588		Defeat of Spanish Armada.
1590–92	Active as actor and playwright in London. Known for success of his history plays (*Henry VI* trilogy). Early tragedy: *Titus Andronicus*. First efforts at comedy. Attacked as "upstart crow" (i.e., actor presuming to be a playwright) and defended as "upright" and "civil."	Rival playwrights Kyd (*The Spanish Tragedy*, probably an early *Hamlet*) and Marlowe (*Tamburlaine, Jew of Malta, Dr. Faustus*) active. John Lyly's plays published. Major literary works by Spenser (*The Faery Queene, I–III*) and Sidney (*Arcadia, Astrophel and Stella*) published.
1593–94	Publishes two narrative poems, *Venus and Adonis* and *The Rape of Lucrece*, dedicated to the Earl of Southampton. Becomes a principal member (shareholder, actor, playwright) of leading company of actors, the Lord Chamberlain's Men. Writes *The Taming of the Shrew, Richard III, Two Gentlemen of Verona, Love's Labour's Lost.*	Theaters flourish in London, despite periodic closings (at which time the companies tour) during outbreaks of the plague.
1595–96	*Romeo and Juliet, A Midsummer Night's Dream, Richard II, King John, Merchant of Venice.* Death of Hamnet.	Raleigh's voyages to Guiana. Rise of Essex.

1597–98	*Henry IV, 1* and *2*. Buys New Place, second largest house in Stratford. Mentioned as leading literary figure, for both his plays and poems. Lord Chamberlain's Men playing at The Curtain, at Holywell, Shoreditch.	Bacon's *Essays*. Chapman's *Homer*.
1599–1600	*Much Ado about Nothing, Henry V, As You Like It, Julius Caesar, Twelfth Night*. The company builds The Globe Playhouse, on the Bankside.	Essex fighting in Ireland.
1601–02	*Hamlet, Troilus and Cressida, All's Well That Ends Well*. Death of Shakespeare's father. The company very nearly gets prosecuted for playing *Richard II* to Essex and his friends just before the attempted coup.	Unsuccessful coup by Essex against Elizabeth. Ben Jonson emerges as friendly rival playwright (*Every Man in His Humor*).
1603–04	*Measure for Measure, Othello*. The company become The King's Men.	Death of Elizabeth. James I succeeds her.
1605–06	*King Lear, Macbeth*.	Jonson's *Volpone*.
1607–08	*Antony and Cleopatra, Coriolanus, Timon of Athens*. Marriage of Susanna, death of Shakespeare's mother.	Midlands riots.
1609–10	*Pericles, Cymbeline*. Unauthorized publication of *Sonnets*. Company adds indoor theater at Blackfriars to its regular playing venues.	Elaborate masques become the fashion at James's court. Jonson's *The Alchemist*.
1611–12	*The Winter's Tale, The Tempest*. Retirement to Stratford.	Publication of the authorized version of the Bible.
1613	*Henry VIII*. Globe Theater burns and is promptly rebuilt.	
1616	Death of Shakespeare, April 23.	
1623	Shakespeare's fellow actors, Hemings and Condell, publish the First Folio edition of his plays. Death of Anne Hathaway.	

Notes on Contributors

JANET ADELMAN is a Professor of English at the University of California, Berkeley. She is the author of *The Common Liar: An Essay on "Antony and Cleopatra"* and of the book from which the selection in this volume is taken, *Suffocating Mothers: Fantasies of Maternal Origin in Shakespeare, "Hamlet" to "The Tempest."*

W. H. AUDEN, the English poet who emigrated to the United States in 1939, had a lifelong interest in Shakespeare, manifested in many poems and essays, including *The Sea and the Mirror*, his complicated response to *The Tempest*, and the important essay on Iago included here, from his collection *The Dyer's Hand* (1962).

LYNDA E. BOOSE is Associate Professor of English at Dartmouth College. She is the co-editor of *Daughters and Fathers* (1988) and of important essays on *The Merchant of Venice* and *The Taming of the Shrew*.

JAMES L. CALDERWOOD is Professor of English and Comparative Literature and Associate Dean of the Humanities at the University of California, Irvine. He has written several books on Shakespeare, including *If It Were Done: Tragic Action in Macbeth* and *Shakespeare and the Denial of Death* and a forthcoming book on *A Midsummer Night's Dream*.

WILLIAM C. CARROLL is Professor of English at Boston University. He is the author of *The Great Feast of Languages in "Love's Labour's Lost"* and *The Metamorphoses of Shakespearean Comedy*, and the editor of Thomas Middleton's *Women Beware Women* in the New Mermaid Series. The essay on Edgar is part of a forthcoming book, *The Fat King and the Lean Beggar: Vagrancy and Marginality in Renaissance England*.

STANLEY CAVELL is Walter M. Cabot Professor of Aesthetics at Harvard University. His books include *Must We Mean What We Say? Pursuits of Happiness: The Hollywood Comedy of Remarriage, The Claim of Reason*, and *Disowning Knowledge: In Six Plays of Shakespeare*.

RICHARD FLY is Associate Professor of English at SUNY Buffalo and author of *Shakespeare's Mediated World*.

RENÉ GIRARD is University Professor of the Humanities at Stanford University. His books include *Deceit, Desire and the Novel* and *Violence and the Sacred* as well as *A Theater of Envy*.

STEPHEN GREENBLATT is Class of 1932 Professor of English at the University of California, Berkeley. His books include *Sir Walter Raleigh: The Renaissance Man and His Roles, Renaissance Self-Fashioning: From More to Shakespeare*, and *Shakespearean Negotiations: The Circulation of Social Energy in Renaissance England*.

RICHARD LANHAM is Professor of English at the University of California, Los Angeles. He is the author of *The Motives of Eloquence, Literacy and the Survival of Humanism*, and *A Handlist of Rhetorical Terms*. He is currently at work on a book about electronic text.

MAYNARD MACK, who taught at Yale for many years, is the author of many books, including *Alexander Pope: A Life* and the newly published *Everybody's Shakespeare*.

CAROL THOMAS NEELY is a Professor of English and Women's Studies at the University of Illinois at Urbana-Champaign. She is the author of *Broken Nuptials in Shakespeare's Plays* and co-editor of *The Woman's Part: Feminist Criticism of Shakespeare*. She is currently working on a study of madness, gender, and subjectivity in the literature and culture of early modern England.

MICHAEL NEILL, Associate Professor of English at the University of Auckland, New Zealand, is the author of numerous articles on sixteenth and seventeenth century drama. He co-edited *The Selected Plays of John Marston* and has recently completed an edition of *Antony and Cleopatra*.

MARK ROSE is Director of the University of California Humanities Research Institute and Professor of English at the University of California, Santa Barbara, and University of California, Irvine. He is the author of *Shakespearean Design* as well as other books on Renaissance literature. He has also published on science fiction and on the history of copyright.

MARVIN ROSENBERG studies Shakespeare's dramas as theater art as well as poetic art. In his books, *The Masks of Othello, The Masks of King Lear, The Masks of Macbeth*, and the forthcoming *The Masks of Hamlet*, he juxtaposes historic and current critical insights into a play with the insights of actors who have performed it. Professor Rosenberg is a member of the Department of Dramatic Art, University of California, Berkeley.

DANIEL SELTZER taught for many years at Harvard, and subsequently at Princeton, where his directing of plays and teaching of drama gave him unique insights into Shakespeare's plays. The essay on *Hamlet* excerpted here was first given at a symposium on *Hamlet* at Bucknell University in 1972.

ELAINE SHOWALTER is Avalon Professor of the Humanities and Professor of English at Princeton University. She is the author of several books, including *A Literature of Their Own, The Female Malady, Sexual Anarchy*, and most recently *Sister's Choice: Tradition and Change in American Women's Writing*.

SUSAN SNYDER is Professor of English at Swarthmore College, editor of Sylvester's *DuBartas* and of *"Othello": Critical Essays*, and the author of *The Comic Matrix of Shakespeare's Tragedies*.

BERT O. STATES is Professor of English in the Department of Dramatic Arts at the University of California at Santa Barbara. He is the author of *Irony and Drama: A Poetics, The Shape of Paradox: An Essay on "Waiting for Godot," Great Reckonings in Little Rooms: On The Phenomenology of Theater*, and *The Rhetoric of Dreams*.

DAVID YOUNG teaches at Oberlin College. He is the author of three studies of Shakespeare: *Something of Great Constancy: The Art of "A Midsummer Night's Dream," The Heart's Forest: Shakespeare's Pastoral Plays,* and *The Action to the Word: Structure and Style in Shakespearean Tragedy.*

Bibliography

Books on the Tragedies

Booth, Stephen. *"King Lear," "Macbeth," Indefinition and Tragedy*. New Haven: Yale University Press, 1983.

Bradley, A.C. *Shakespearean Tragedy*. 1904, reprinted 1950.

Danson, Lawrence. *Tragic Alphabet: Shakespeare's Drama of Language*. New Haven: Yale University Press, 1974.

Everett, Barbara. *Young Hamlet: Essays on Shakespeare's Tragedies*. Oxford: Oxford University Press, 1989.

Felperin, Howard. *Shakespearean Representation*. Princeton University Press, 1977.

Frye, Northrop. *Fools of Time: Studies in Shakespearean Tragedy*. Toronto: University of Toronto Press, 1967.

Heilman, Robert B., ed. *Shakespeare: The Tragedies: New Perspectives*. Englewood Cliffs, N.J.: Prentice Hall, 1984.

Holloway, John. *The Story of the Night: Studies in Shakespeare's Major Tragedies*. Lincoln: University of Nebraska Press, 1961.

Kirsch, Arthur. *The Passions of Shakespeare's Tragic Heroes*. Charlottesville: University of Virginia Press, 1990.

Nevo, Ruth. *Tragic Form in Shakespeare*. Princeton: Princeton University Press, 1972.

Young, David. *The Action to the Word: Structure and Style in Shakespearean Tragedy*. New Haven: Yale University Press, 1990.

Books and Articles on Hamlet

Alexander, Nigel. *Poison, Play and Duel: A Study in "Hamlet"*. Lincoln: University of Nebraska Press, 1971.

Bevington, David, ed. *Twentieth Century Interpretations of "Hamlet."* Englewood Cliffs, N.J.: Prentice Hall, 1968.

Bohannan, Laura. "Shakespeare in the Bush." *Natural History*, 75 (1966), 28–33. Reprinted in *Every Man His Way: Readings in Cultural Anthropology*, ed. Alan Dundes. Englewood Cliffs, N.J.: Prentice Hall, 1968.

Brown, John Russell, and Bernard Harris, eds. *Hamlet*, Stratford-upon-Avon Studies 5, London: Edward Arnold, 1963.

Calderwood, James L. *To Be and Not to Be: Negation and Metadrama in "Hamlet."* New York: Columbia University Press, 1983.

Heilbrun, Carolyn. "The Character of Hamlet's Mother." In *Hamlet's Mother and Other Women*, 257–74. New York: Columbia University Press, 1990.

Kernan, Alvin B. "Shakespeare and the Rhetoric of Politics: 'This must be so,' Act I, Scene 2 of *Hamlet*." In *Politics, Power and Shakespeare*, ed. Frances McNeely Leonard, 47–62. Arlington: Texas Humanities Resource Center, 1981.

Lacan, Jacques. "Desire and the Interpretation of Desire in *Hamlet*." *Yale French Studies* 55–56 (1977), 11–52.

Levin, Harry. *The Question of Hamlet*. New York: Oxford University Press, 1959.

Mack, Maynard. "The World of Hamlet." *Yale Review* 41 (1952), 502–23.

Price, Joseph G. *Hamlet: Critical Essays*. New York: Garland Press, 1986.

Rose, Jacqueline. "Sexuality in the Reading of Shakespeare: *Hamlet* and *Measure for Measure*." In *Alternative Shakespeares*, ed. John Drakakis, 95–118, New York: Methuen, 1985.

Rothwell, Kenneth S. "Hamlet's 'Glass of Fashion': Power, Self, and the Reformation." In *Technologies of the Self*, ed. Luther H. Martin, Huck Gutman, and Patrick H. Hutton, 80–98. Amherst: University of Massachusetts Press, 1988.

Young, David. "Hamlet, Son of Hamlet." In *Perspectives on "Hamlet,"* ed. William G. Holzberger and Peter B. Waldeck. Lewisburg, Pa., Bucknell University Press, 1975.

Books and Articles on Othello

Adamson, Jane. *Othello as Tragedy: Some Problems of Judgment and Feeling*. Cambridge: Cambridge University Press, 1980.

Bartels, Emily C. "Making More of the Moor: Aaron, Othello, and Renaissance Refashionings of Race." *Shakespeare Quarterly* 41 (1990), 433–54.

Berry, Ralph. "Othello's Alienation." *Studies in English Literature, 1500–1900* 30:2 (1990), 315–33.

Boose, Lynda E. "Othello's Handkerchief: 'The Recognizance and Pledge of Love'." *English Literary Renaissance* 5 (1975), 360–74.

Gross, Kenneth. "Slander and Skepticism in *Othello*." *ELH* 56, no. 4 (1989), 819–52.

Hunter, G. K. "Othello and Colour Prejudice." In *Interpretations of Shakespeare: British Academy Shakespeare Lectures*, ed. Kenneth Muir, 180–207. Oxford: Clarendon Press, 1985.

Neill, Michael. "Changing Places in *Othello*." *Shakespeare Survey* 37 (1978), 115–31.

Orkin, Martin. "Othello and the 'Plain Face' of Racism." *Shakespeare Quarterly* 38 (1987), 166–88.

Rosenberg, Marvin. *The Masks of Othello*. Berkeley and Los Angeles: University of California Press, 1961.

Seltzer, Daniel. "Elizabethan Acting in *Othello*." *Shakespeare Quarterly* 10 (1959), 201–10.

Snyder, Susan, ed. *"Othello": Critical Essays*. New York: Garland Press, 1988.

Snow, Edward A. "Sexual Anxiety and the Male Order of Things in *Othello*." *English Literary Renaissance* 10 (1980), 384–413.

Vaughan, Virginia Mason, and Kent Cartwright, eds. *Othello: New Perspectives*. Rutherford, N.J.: Fairleigh Dickinson Press, 1991.

Books and Articles on King Lear

Adelman, Janet, ed. *Twentieth Century Interpretations of "King Lear."* Englewood Cliffs, N.J.: Prentice Hall, 1978.

Calderwood, James L. *Shakespeare and the Denial of Death*, 136–66. Amherst: University of Massachusetts Press, 1987.

Colie, Rosalie L. and F. T. Flahiff, eds. *Some Facets of "King Lear."* Toronto: University of Toronto Press, 1974.

Danson, Lawrence, ed. *On "King Lear."* Princeton: Princeton University Press, 1981.

Dollimore, Jonathan. *Radical Tragedy: Religion, Ideology and Power in the Drama of Shakespeare and His Contemporaries*, 189–203. New York: Harvester Wheatsheaf, 1989.

Elton, William R. *"King Lear" and the Gods.* San Marino: The Huntington Library, 1966. Reprinted, Lexington, Kentucky: Kentucky University Press, 1988.

Kahn, Coppélia. "The Absent Mother in *King Lear.*" In *Rewriting the Renaissance: The Discourses of Sexual Difference in Early Modern Europe*, ed. Margaret Ferguson et al., 33–49. Chicago: Chicago University Press, 1986.

Kernan, Alvin. "Formalism and Realism in Elizabethan Drama: The Miracles in *King Lear.*" *Renaissance Drama* 9 (1966), 59–66.

Muir, Kenneth. *King Lear: Critical Essays.* New York: Garland Press, 1984.

Urkowitz, Steven. *Shakespeare's Revision of "King Lear."* Princeton: Princeton University Press, 1980.

Young, David. *The Heart's Forest: Shakespeare's Pastoral Plays*, 73–103. New Haven: Yale University Press, 1972.